Revisiting Psychology

Revisiting Psychology

A student's guide to critical thought

Jared M. Bartels and William E. Herman

First published 2019 by
RED GLOBE PRESS

Red Globe Press in the UK is an imprint of Springer Nature Limited, registered in England, company number 785998, of 4 Crinan Street, London, N1 9XW.

Red Globe Press® is a registered trademark in the United States, the United Kingdom, Europe and other countries.

ISBN 978–1–137–60429–3 paperback

This book is printed on paper suitable for recycling and made from fully managed and sustained forest sources. Logging, pulping and manufacturing processes are expected to conform to the environmental regulations of the country of origin.

A catalogue record for this book is available from the British Library.

A catalog record for this book is available from the Library of Congress.

Contents

Preface

The purpose, rationale, and structure of the book

We wrote this book with the goal of helping undergraduate students develop critical thinking and scientific literacy skills through the analysis of prominent studies and ideas in psychology. From our perspective as educators concerned about the teaching and learning of psychology, it is vital that students are presented with accurate, complete, and detailed information about the topics, studies, and theories in psychology. Our decades of teaching psychology have left us disappointed at times with the treatment of certain content including classic studies within psychology textbooks. As Jarrett (2008), notes, psychology's history is "built not of theory [like other scientific disciplines] but with the rock of classic experiments" (p. 756). Circumnavigating concerns over the scientific merits of such studies allows textbook authors to offer readers a coherent, engaging history of the field, yet leaves such studies with a veneer of sacrosanctity. Students learn that the ideas garnered from such classic studies do not need replication and lack critics.

We undertook the writing of this book, in part, to explore the approaches of such studies and, in part, to use these studies as a means to teach critical thinking skills. Such cognitive skills are often neglected or undervalued in psychological curricula. Though we critically explore the scientific merits of some classic studies, we are not, in our estimation, undermining the foundation and importance of such research. In fact, we will direct readers to studies that have addressed the shortcomings of classic studies and offer a more methodologically, theoretically, and in some cases ethically robust examination of the topic. In this sense, the classic studies in question might be better viewed as scaffolding that could lead to new knowledge, rather than simply add to the foundation of psychology.

The contested studies and theories included in this book cover a range of psychological points of view/topics including consciousness, developmental psychology, learning, memory, social psychology, motivation and emotion, and psychopathology. Evaluating controversial cases impartially is a challenge as our attitudinal tendencies often conflict with objective analyses. We often are disposed to hold on to our beliefs in the face of evidence that contradicts well-ensconced ideas, even distorting or denying what we see, hear, or read. Studies frequently covered in textbooks have a tendency to receive less critical attention, leading us to overlook the limitations and flaws when contradictions or confusions appear. Additional roadblocks to the development of critical thinking and scientific literacy include pervasive and seductive pseudoscience that effectively utilizes anecdotes, scientific language, and methods that appear at first glance to be scientific. We tend to be overconfident in our personal intuition and life experience, yet largely unaware of the many biases and errors in our own decision-making, including confirmation bias, heuristics or mental shortcuts, logical fallacies, and poor statistical reasoning.

Metacognition, the premise that human beings can think, reason, and correct their own personal thought process, is a major contribution from the cognitive view in psychology. The notion of self-regulation is a related construct that helps us become more adaptive by learning from our errors, making mental adjustments, and offering practical hope for improvement in human learning and life in general. Imagine that you arrive on the collegiate campus landscape with a set of thinking tools in your tool belt ready to examine what you have previously learned and build new knowledge and skills. You will then strive to add new intellectual tools to your repertoire as well as take stock of the selective usefulness of those cognitive skills already honed for further refinement, modification, and elaboration.

Smolin (2006) suggested that: "Science was not invented. It evolved over time, as people discovered tools and habits that worked to bring the physical world within the sphere of our understanding" (p. 298). We have consciously chosen to focus upon critical thinking "tools and habits."

As psychologists such as Albert Ellis have proposed, human beings have the biological potential to think both logically and rationally, leading to growth and actualization, and also illogically and irrationally. In light of these potential illogically oriented barriers and the importance of critical thinking, each chapter will highlight critical thinking tools (critical thinking toolkit sections) along with guiding questions aimed at developing metacognitive skills. These skills are essential to critical thinking and the key readings will direct the reader to sources that inform the debate. Each chapter provides an overview of the studies or theory (study background) and includes a section (current thinking) which considers how the study has aged and how contemporary research has confirmed or failed to confirm the findings. Each study or theory addressed will offer a critical thinking section related to methodological and theoretical questions, the aforementioned cognitive biases, and logical fallacies. Lastly, we will consider where research may be heading and how the research/ideas covered have furthered our understanding of psychology as a science.

Irving Kirsch, whose controversial studies on the placebo effect and antidepressants are featured in Chapter 12, provided the following advice for students: "My experience having been a teacher for many, many years is the best students are critical thinkers ... think critically, keep an open mind, look for alternative viewpoints and look at the data." We concur with Kirsch and hope this book contributes to the development of such a mindset among readers.

Acknowledgments

We are grateful to colleagues and friends who have provided critical and helpful comments on previous drafts of the manuscript. Our thanks are extended to Kelli Gardner, Jim Nevitt, Alden Klovdahl, Bryan Herman, Claire Starrs, Michael Tissaw, Arlene Stillwell, Heather Beauchamp, and Jamie Dojka. We also wish to thank Susan Abrahams for assistance in obtaining numerous research articles.

We would like to thank the original commissioning editor, Paul Stevens, for his confidence in the project and vital efforts in helping it take shape. We are also indebted to the current commissioning editor, Luke Block, for his patience, support, and guidance. His assistance has been indispensable in finishing this project. We also wish to thank Stephanie Farano for her support and assistance with the book.

Jared would like to acknowledge the love and support of his family – his wife, Flannery; his children, August and Jude; his parents, Marvin and Jackie; his brother and his family, Jordan, Shannon, Brian, and Brayden. This book would not have been possible without them.

About the Authors

Jared M. Bartels received his Ph.D. in Educational Psychology from the University of Memphis in 2008 and did postdoctoral work at the Center for Learning Innovation at the University of Minnesota Rochester. He is currently Assistant Professor of Psychology at William Jewell College in Liberty, Missouri. His research interests include achievement motivation and self-regulated learning, history of psychology, and clinical neuropsychological assessment. His scholarly work includes a social psychology textbook, chapters, book reviews, and research published in numerous academic journals including *Learning and Individual Differences; Aging, Neuropsychology and Cognition; the Journal of Psychoeducational Assessment; Personality and Individual Differences;* and *Teaching of Psychology.* He resides in Blue Springs, Missouri with his wife and two sons.

William E. Herman is Professor Emeritus of Psychology at the State University of New York College at Potsdam and earned his doctorate in educational psychology at the University of Michigan in 1987. His research and scholarly interests lie in the areas of test and performance anxiety, achievement motivation theory, values development, moral development, human memory, learning theory, excellence in teaching, and translating the teacher education knowledge base into professional practice. He has received several teaching honors and has accumulated nearly 50 published scholarly works including research studies, book chapters, book reviews, and conference presentations found in searchable databases such as PsycINFO, ERIC, Education Index, Historical Abstracts, to name a few. During his 40 years of full-time college teaching, he has accumulated considerable international education experience. He has earned two Fulbright Scholar Awards (Russia in 1993 and Thailand in 2011), taught graduate courses for five summers in Taiwan (1989–1993), taught education and psychology courses at the University of Potsdam in Germany, and lectured/presented papers on several other international campuses in the UK, Poland, and Romania.

Introduction to Critical Thinking

What is critical thinking?   Why is it important?   How do we learn it?

The ability to carefully dissect and critically evaluate thoughts, ideas, theories, and claims has never been more crucial to improving our individual and collective lot in life. Attacks upon science and scientists, political debate in public policy domains such as global warming, and ubiquitous "fake news" media reports besiege our current existence. How to make sense out of the scientific field of psychology, the scientific method itself, and everyday life has become a priority in the midst of confusion brought on by clashes between politicians, scientists, soothsayers, media representatives, and many other stakeholders. Distortion, delusion, and manipulation are direct threats to our democracy, our ability to make thoughtful personal and collective decisions, and our healthy way of life.

Critical thinking incorporates a modern-day paradigm to uncover useful versions of truth. This tradition has a long and storied history. Well over a century ago, John Dewey argued against recitation learning and described the antithesis of rote memorization as reflective thought: "Active, persistent, and careful consideration of any belief or supposed form of knowledge" (Dewey, 1910/1998, p. 6). America's foremost educational philosopher further outlined in his famous book *How We Think* (Dewey, 1910/1998) that reflection as "mental vision" included inductive and deductive reasoning, postponing judgment rather than making snap judgments, a healthy imagination, active learning, applying knowledge, and well-informed judgments.

While many operational definitions of critical thinking exist today, we employed the vision of John Dewey in our search for a more modern and unifying theoretical paradigm. A potential truth for a thoughtful person demands the careful and critical scrutiny of ideas. New and existing ideas require public debate, scientific testing, and constant revision. This process cannot allow for the interference of subtle and more obvious forces wishing to maintain the status quo and traditions of unexamined time-honored truths.

Howard Gardner (2006) just over a decade ago in his influential book *Five Minds for the Future* suggested that disciplinary thinking, synthesizing knowledge, creativity, respecting human differences, and ethical concerns in decision making are at the core of responsible decision-making for future professionals, teachers, parents, political and business leaders, trainers, and those who value cutting-edge cognitive skills. With increasingly accessible knowledge accumulating at a rapid pace, being able to think like a professional within a discipline and synthesize information across disciplines is at a premium. Those best positioned to meet the demands of the future will develop a scientific mindset allowing them to distinguish the relevant from the irrelevant, high from poor quality evidence and science from pseudoscience.

In our estimation, the following characteristics apply to critical thinking:

Critical thinkers...	Critical thinkers do not...
have the audacity to challenge existing truths	trust the unexamined judgments of others
fact-check the logic and personal judgments regarding the appropriateness and existence of evidence	remain rigid in their positions in the face of evidence that they deem powerful
are able to make decisions for themselves	cave in and conform to the beliefs of others
are able to withstand challenges from others who have opposing views, but willing to change one's thinking, if evidence supports such a stance	take a defensive stance in which "saving face" is more important than "seeking truth"

The learning conditions that would support such behaviors remind us very much of what counselors and therapists attempt to create in a therapeutic relationship with their clients: rational thinking, evidence-based decision-making, independence, healthy self-esteem, self-assessment, and awareness of one's strengths as well as one's imperfections.

A few authors have explored issues related to why critical thinking is so hard to teach. Willingham (2007) does an exemplary job in tackling this learning dilemma by highlighting the following pitfalls: (1) thinking often fails to transfer from one domain (subject area) to another, (2) learning often focuses upon surface structure rather than deep knowledge, and (3) critical thinking in a domain often requires considerable knowledge within that domain. The advancement of critical thinking skills therefore is not a "skill" to be learned, metacognitive strategies increase the chances of critical thinking, and such metacognitive strategies need to be situated within domain knowledge with considerable praxis.

Willingham (2007) specifically addresses scientific thinking when he stated: "Recognizing *when* to engage in scientific reasoning is so important because the evidence shows that being able to reason is not enough; children and adults use *and* fail to use the proper reasoning processes on problems that seem similar" (p. 14). This suggests that we need to teach not only metacognitive skills, and offer considerable practice of such skills and deep knowledge structures within a specific domain of learning, but also "when," "where," and "why" we need to employ certain strategies to solve scientific problems.

Since teachers introduce the scientific method so early in formal schooling, some assume that college students already enter higher education with a substantial amount of knowledge of science, think like scientists, and value science. Unfortunately, we have not found this to be the case. Psychology, like other sciences, relies upon the scientific method, an experimental research paradigm designed to explore problems and the use of statistics in order to support or not support hypotheses. Any student of psychology must begin with his/her views regarding how scientists think and operate.

How do you view science?

Think about your agreement or disagreement with the following statements. Why do you agree or disagree with such statements?

1. Scientists do not criticize other scientists' work.
2. People do not need to understand science because it does not affect their lives.
3. Only thinking is important to scientists, not how they feel about something.
4. Science helps solve the problems of everyday life.

The National Science Foundation (NSF) helped fund the development of these four sample items taken from the more extensive *My Attitudes Toward Science (MATS)* 40-item K-12 survey instrument (Hillman et al., 2016). Such items offer a golden opportunity to explore your personal thinking related to science. In the real world of science, scientists **do** critique the work of other scientists before and after the publication of research findings on the grounds of methodology, sampling, theoretical operational definition, statistical approach employed, generalization of the results, and so on. A "true" scientist should try to avoid criticism based upon a dislike for a certain pompous author they have met or the fact that such an author might hold an appointment at a rival school of thought or university. Petty jealousy and competition are part of the scientific world, as well as other life situations, so disagreements and contentious arguments are inevitable. Item #3 certainly highlights the importance of cognitive reasoning that is a hallmark of any scientist, but it is crucial to remember that every scientist is a human being that also possesses emotions, values, and belief systems that may or may not offer a bias in one's work. Item #4 offers the hope that science could solve everyday problems and make this a better world.

Psychological science has made a substantial positive impact on our lives (Zimbardo, 2004); however, misunderstandings about such research and the field in general can diminish our appreciation for this contribution and applications in practice. Unfortunately, the reality is that science can also make this a more confusing and dangerous world and allow new unforeseen challenging problems to emerge that were never initially detectable.

Scientists learn how to ask questions that result in testable experiments or studies that may or may not eventually support stated hypotheses. Asking a question in a unique or different manner can sometimes advance thinking. One of the authors of this book recently overheard a student ask his clinical psychology professor friend, "Do you believe in Carl G. Jung's collective unconscious?" This is a common way for introductory students to frame such a question.

However, psychological theory should not be like a religious belief that demonstrates an unthinking and slavish faith to a theory, methodology, or an expected outcome. A better question would be, "Does Jung's notion of the collective unconscious best fit the clinical data available and help to better understand a client's behavior?"

As a critical thinker, you must be able to sort out fact from fiction and good science from bad science, while being able to offer a logical explanation that supports your decision. Sometimes we have a purposeful need to "agree to disagree," if the arena of disagreement rests upon an understood, but unaligned philosophy or other form of fundamental assumption. As you read in later chapters about misunderstandings and points of confusion and controversy within the field of psychology, we draw in liberal arts fashion from the Nobel and Pulitzer prize-winning literary author Ernest Hemingway. We believe that it is time for both readers, writers, and rational thinkers to take Hemingway's advice of sorting out the wheat from the chaff and truth from untruth (Plimpton, 1958).

The most essential gift for a good writer is a built-in, shock-proof, shit detector.
— Ernest M. Hemingway

As you read the chapters that follow, we urge you to implement the critical thinking tools in each chapter with the aim of detecting what Hemingway might have called "bullshit." Our hope is that each chapter will challenge what you have already learned and implore you to ask yourself the following question: "And why do I believe that to be true?" The quality of evidence for a particular research finding, theoretical idea, or claim regarding public policy is exactly what we hope you will seriously question. A careful examination of the controversies and points of debate within the field of psychology means that you are well on your way to thinking more like a psychologist. If we have accomplished our goals in this chapter, you will have already critically considered our invitation and should be anxious to read about contentious issues in psychology within the pages that follow.

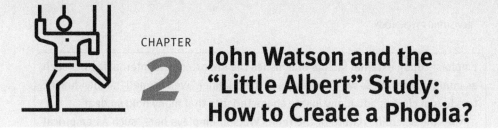

2 John Watson and the "Little Albert" Study: How to Create a Phobia?

Primary source: Watson, J. B., & Rayner, R. (1920). Conditioned emotional reactions. *Journal of Experimental Psychology, 3,* 1–14 (Reprinted in *American Psychologist, 55,* 313–317, 2000).

Chapter objectives

This chapter will help you become a better critical thinker by:

- Understanding crucial details regarding the classic study conducted by John B. Watson
- Comparing the behaviorist viewpoint to other contemporary perspectives on the etiology of phobias
- Grasping the historical lack of protection during experiments for human subjects
- Considering how the findings from behavioristic theory have been merged with newer cognitive theories
- Evaluating the characteristics of a sample in terms of generalizability

Introduction

Consider the following claim by John B. Watson in 1930:

> *Give me a dozen healthy infants, well-formed, and my own specified world to bring them up in and I'll guarantee to take any one at random and train him to become any type of specialist I might select – doctor, lawyer, artist, merchant-chief and, yes, even beggar-man and thief, regardless of his talents, penchants, tendencies, abilities, vocations, and race of his ancestors.* (p. 104)

This quotation is a classic representation of behaviorism and its claim that environmental forces shape human development. It is easy even for those outside the field of psychology to see the "truth" to this statement. The home in which you are raised, the schools you attend, the quality of teachers in those schools, the friends in your midst, and the opportunities available to you in life in summation have a powerful influence upon who you might become in this world. However, this emphasis upon external factors diminishes the importance of internal factors such as intelligence (unless we include this in the qualifier "well-formed"), individuality, freedom of choice, and many innate characteristics that many hold so dear.

Note the scientific nature of the terms Watson employs here, such as **empirical** (a dozen healthy infants) and randomness (take any one at random). How is training different from educating and learning? Most would suggest that you can train people, animals, and perhaps robots to do certain mundane tasks, but professional training in medicine and law demand uniquely human cognitive skills such as moral/ethical judgments, creativity, decision-making, and perspective-taking. Do we "train" an artist or do we help an artist discover his/her own unique method of seeing and understanding this world? If Watson was correct in his belief that the environment controls who we become (even a beggar-man and thief), how can we hold human beings accountable for their condition in life or the choices they make? As suggested by a song lyric in the musical *West Side Story,* perhaps juvenile delinquents just have a "social disease."

Study background

Take a look in your introductory psychology textbook and you will be sure to find the fascinating story of little Albert conducted by John Watson and his graduate assistant Rosalie Rayner. After reading about the little Albert study, assuming that the textbook author doesn't address this, it is only natural to wonder what happened to Albert. Did he grow up to be an adult afraid of animals? A closer look at the study raises additional questions such as: Did Albert actually develop a phobia? Was the study ethical? And is the study still relevant? Psychologists have learned a lot about phobias and have developed methods for accurately measuring them in the lab and treating them in the clinic. So, in addition to addressing the question of what happened to little Albert and questions about the methods used, this chapter will attempt to address the question of what the little Albert study might look like if it were conducted today.

Before the little Albert study, Watson (1913) had written of his desire to make psychology a more objective science, in line with the natural sciences, which required the field to move away from a focus on consciousness and reliance on the imprecise method of **introspection** to a focus on behavior and a reliance on methods limited to observing and recording detectable behavior. With respect to emotions, Watson sought to challenge the prevailing view that the emotions were instinctive, arguing instead that they are acquired in the first years of life. Emotional responses were the result of learning and, thus, could be changed or modified. Watson and Rayner (1920) sought to address three questions in their work with little Albert (Harris, 1979): Can you condition an infant to fear an animal? Would the fear transfer or generalize to other animals and objects? And would this fear persist? Watson and Rayner began working with little Albert when he was 9 months old. Initially, Albert was presented with a white rat, a rabbit, a dog, a monkey, masks, cotton wool, and burning newspapers. As expected, but importantly, Watson and Rayner noted that none of the objects produced fear in Albert. The next step was to condition Albert to fear the white rat. **Classical conditioning** involves the pairing of a neutral stimulus (NS) with an unconditioned stimulus (UCS) as illustrated in Figure 2.1. Through repeated pairings, an association between the NS and UCS develops and, because of this association, the NS is able to elicit a response from the organism that was previously produced from the UCS.

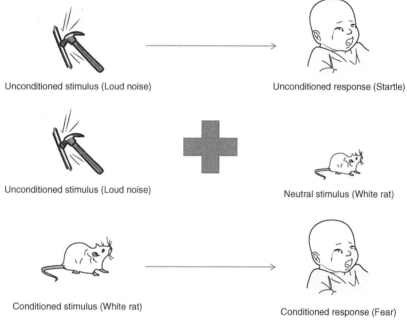

Unconditioned stimulus (Loud noise)   Unconditioned response (Startle)

Unconditioned stimulus (Loud noise)   Neutral stimulus (White rat)

Conditioned stimulus (White rat)   Conditioned response (Fear)

Figure 2.1   Process of conditioning fear of white rat in little Albert

When Albert was 11 months old, a metal bar was struck with a hammer at the same time the baby was reaching for a white rat. This was repeated and Albert seemed to be startled both times, though he did not cry. A week later he was presented with the rat by itself and seemed to be tentative, suggesting that although a phobia was not present, the conditioning was "not without effect" (p. 314). Watson and Rayner then presented the rat and the noise three more times before again presenting the rat by itself, which this time produced whimpering and avoidance from Albert. They then presented the rat and the noise together twice more and then the rat alone, and this time, after a total of seven presentations of the rat with the noise, Albert's reaction was pronounced. Watson and Rayner (1920) note:

The instant the rat was shown the baby began to cry. Almost instantly he turned sharply to the left, fell over on left side, raised himself on all fours and began to crawl away so rapidly that he was caught with difficulty before reaching the edge of the table. (p. 314)

With the emotional reaction conditioned, Watson and Rayner turned to the second and third questions of generalization and whether or not the fear persists. This was addressed five days later when Albert was presented with a rat, and while he did not cry, he did whimper and attempt to avoid the rat. Watson and Rayner then presented a rabbit and a fur coat which brought Albert to tears. Cotton wool, a dog, and the hair of the two observers were presented. Interestingly, Watson's hair and a Santa Claus mask he put on produced a negative response from Albert. Five days later, when presented with the rat, Albert was not particularly distressed. Presentation of the rabbit was also met with a less intense negative reaction as the first time after conditioning.

Watson and Rayner (1920) then took Albert to a different room (a room other than that in which conditioning took place) to see if the fear would transfer. The dog seemed to produce the strongest reaction in this new environment, though Watson and Rayner generally concluded that the fear did transfer. Persistence of the fear was examined as Watson and Rayner's final tests were conducted when Albert was nearly 13 months old (roughly one month later). Watson and Rayner concluded that Albert's responses indicated that the fear persisted and speculated that the fear would persist indefinitely as Albert was no longer available for testing. Moreover, this was not only the end of the little Albert experiment, but marked the end of Watson's academic career (Samelson, 1980). Watson had an affair with Rayner (his graduate assistant), went through a highly publicized divorce and was forced to resign his position at Johns Hopkins University (Hunt, 1993).

Current thinking

Despite its storied history and prominence in introductory psychology texts, several critics (e.g., Paul & Blumenthal, 1989; Samelson, 1980), after careful evaluation of the literature on the little Albert study, concluded that it was essentially an interesting but uninterpretable **pilot study** – a preliminary study often conducted before the comprehensive research project (Smith and Davis, 2013). In fact, Watson and Rayner acknowledged as much in their "work at Hopkins was left in such an incomplete state that verified conclusions are not possible; hence this summary, like so many other bits of psychological work must be looked upon merely as a preliminary exposition of possibilities rather than a catalogue of concrete usable results" (p. 493).

Moreover, while it is the case that some people with phobias will recall a distressing experience that suggests the fear was learned, studies of various phobias have failed to find evidence that their development can reliably be traced to such conditioning experiences (e.g., Poulton et al., 1998). If not conditioning, then what explains the development of phobias? Such fears may develop vicariously through modeling from parents or the influence of media (Doogan & Thomas, 1992). If evolutionarily relevant (e.g., fear of spiders as opposed to the dentist), such fears may be evident when we first encounter the stimulus or environment and then dissipate with repeated exposure (Menzies & Clarke, 1995; Poulton et al., 1998). The phobia or irrational fear may eventually develop in genetically vulnerable individuals experiencing general psychological stress rather than a specific experience with the fear-relevant stimulus or environment (Menzies & Clarke, 1995). Recent research suggests that predispositions for phobias can transmitted from parents to children through alterations of structure and function of the offspring's nervous system (Dias & Ressler, 2013).

Contemporary perspectives in abnormal psychology attempt to account for the interaction between genetic vulnerabilities and environmental stressors via the **diathesis–stress model** and **biopsychosocial model**. Within the diathesis–stress model, the diathesis is a vulnerability (e.g., a personality trait such as neuroticism) that, by itself, does not produce the disorder (Zuckerman, 1999). However, it does lower the threshold for significant psychological stress to potentiate a disorder. In sum, many contemporary clinicians favor accounts of mental illness that include genetic, psychological, and social influences and take an eclectic approach to treatment rather than operating from the perspective of a single model or treatment (Comer, 2015). It is important to note that classical conditioning and the behavioral approach are a part of these contemporary treatments and, in fact, treatments grounded in behavioral principles are among the most effective (Chambless et al., 1998).

Applying critical thinking

Logical fallacies

Let us return to the oft-cited quote from Watson at the beginning of this chapter. In *Behaviorism*, Watson (1930) makes a case for his brand of psychology in the face of a strong bias toward the inheritance of traits. The doctor, lawyer, artist, merchant-chief, and beggar-man and thief were who they were because of genetic inheritance. Watson points out that whether criminals come from "good" homes (i.e., "we raised him the best we could, but look at his grandfather") or a long line of criminals, inheritance gets the credit and the environment gets ignored. Hence, the following quote:

> Give me a dozen healthy infants, well-formed, and my own specified world to bring them up in and I'll guarantee to take any one at random and train him to become any type of specialist I might select – doctor, lawyer, artist, merchant-chief and, yes, even beggar-man and thief, regardless of his talents, penchants, tendencies, abilities, vocations, and race of his ancestors. *I am going beyond my facts and I admit it, but so have the advocates of the contrary and they have been doing it for many thousands of years.* (p. 104)

Note the highlighted sentence that was missing from the quote at the beginning of the chapter. A quick Internet search for Watson's claim about a dozen healthy infants will produce all but this last sentence. Yet this one little sentence is incredibly important, providing context for his claim. **Contextomy** (fallacy of quoting out of context) occurs when a quote is misrepresented by being taken out of context (Bennett, 2015). As Abramson (2013) has pointed out, the inclusion of Watson's "I am going beyond my facts…" changes the meaning of the statement. Out of context, the quote has been used to discredit behaviorism as an extreme form of environmentalism (e.g., Hunt, 1993). With further context in the pages preceding Watson's quote, it becomes clear that Watson believed that claims about inheritance lacked empirical support. The claim about the dozen healthy infants was purposefully as bold and as empty as claims about inheritance.

KEY READING – Hunt, M. (1993). *The story of psychology*. New York: Anchor Books.

Critical thinking toolkit
Illusory correlations

Guiding question: Have I considered all instances that do not fit the expected pattern?

As noted earlier, some people with dog phobias (like presumably little Albert) can tell you about a traumatic encounter they had with a dog in childhood. One of the author's brothers, for example, has such a phobia and can trace the roots of this back to a dog attack that occurred in childhood. Based on his brother's experience and the experience of other similar cases that he witnessed, it would be reasonable for the author to conclude that such phobias develop because of these frightening and often traumatic encounters with dogs. As we will discuss at numerous points in this book, such **anecdotal evidence** is subject to biases. Fortunately, there is research suggesting that people with dog phobias often report that the fear sprang from an early negative experience with dogs. Before we definitively conclude that behaviorism explains the development of phobias as was suggested by the little Albert study, we have to give a bit more thought to the **correlation** we believe we have found:

A positive correlation between dog phobias and frightening experiences with dogs: People who have dog phobias recall traumatic experiences with dogs

What else do we need to consider, you ask...?

People who have dog phobias yet recall no traumatic experiences with dogs

In this case, considering only the former (people who have phobias and recall negative experiences) would have led us to an erroneous conclusion or an **illusory correlation**. Research suggests no difference between those with dog fears and those without in terms of reported attacks. In other words, people without dog fears recall just as many attack experiences as those with fears (Doogan & Thomas, 1992).
   We must also consider instances in which...

People have a phobia, but no attack experiences

As noted earlier, there is research that traces the development of various phobias to causes other than learning or conditioning. Various models emphasize the evolutionary basis for fears, the influence of genes and personality traits as well as social factors.

Convenience samples

Guiding question: What characteristics of the sample might impact the results of the study?

Though the little Albert study involved a single participant, imagine that there were a number of Alberts in Watson's study. If in fact Albert's mother was a nurse at the hospital on the campus of Watson's university, such a sample would be considered a **convenience sample**. Within the context of psychological research, the term "convenience" often carries with it a negative connotation. It is certainly an oversimplification to evaluate samples as good or bad based on the difficulty or ease with which participants were obtained. Dismissing a convenience sample offhand is not characteristic of a critical thinker. The question we should ask is:
Is there a reason to believe that the results are unique to this sample and would not generalize?

In other words, it requires a consideration of what was studied, the context, and which variables might influence the results. Is there reason to believe that the findings might be biased by use of a college student sample (Henry, 2008; Sears, 1986)? How are college students different from the general population on variable x?

Review the following two studies and consider which one you would be most concerned about in terms of the exclusive use of college student participants:

Study 1	Study 2
A laboratory experiment examining the influence of movies on political attitudes. Participants were randomly assigned to watch a movie with no political messages (control condition) or to a movie with subtle political messages (experimental condition). Results indicated that those in the experimental condition were more likely to indicate a change in political beliefs. Thus, people are susceptible to political attitude influence through movies.	A laboratory study examining the influence of the style and appearance of the print in a magazine on the reader's mood and ability to recall what was read. Participants were given 20 minutes to read an issue of a magazine with proper typesetting (control condition) or poor typesetting (experimental condition). Results revealed significantly poorer mood and recall among those in the experimental condition. Thus, poor typesetting may reduce mood and recall among readers.

If you said study 1, you have identified the study that would be more susceptible to bias for the following reasons:

Adolescents have less crystallized attitudes and thus would be more likely to change attitudes. (Sears, 1986)

Adolescents have spent years in a school environment in which compliance and conformity are reinforced. (Sears, 1986)

Research examining basic universal processes like memory and perception [i.e. study 2 above] are less susceptible to sample bias. (Rubenstein, 1982)

There are studies in which the characteristics and representativeness of the sample are crucial (e.g., public opinion) and those in which it is less important (e.g., attempts to falsify a theory; Landers & Behrend, 2015). Nonetheless, researchers need to consider the characteristics of a college student sample such as a fully undeveloped sense of self and identity and how this condition may relate to the variables under examination (Sears, 1986). If a researcher desired a more diverse sample, an equally convenient option has emerged in the last several years. Crowdsourcing options like Amazon's Mechanical Turk (MTurk) give workers an opportunity to complete tasks including psychological studies. The workers come from 100 different countries and studies with more traditional samples have been replicated with MTurk samples (Berinsky, Quek, & Sances, 2012). Yet there is an ethical concern that connects the convenient college student, MTurk samples, and little Albert. Critics have voiced concerns over the vulnerable status of all three. MTurk workers are paid little money for their participation, leading some to refer to it as a "digital sweatshop" (Cushing, 2013). Similar concerns have been raised with college student samples who are seldom paid and are often participating to receive course credit (Rubenstein, 1982). Lastly, Albert's mom was vulnerable considering her position as a wet nurse and the fact that she was employed at the hospital on Watson's campus and was poorly compensated for her son's participation (DeAngelis, 2010).

In summary, "used a convenient sample" and "need a more diverse sample" are often reflexive and not reflective critiques of a study. We need to understand that biased sampling is ubiquitous in science and good data/bad data is not synonymous with hard to collect/easy to collect. As critical thinkers, we want to consider the characteristics of the sample and the variables under investigation.

A closer look at the methods

Was the little Albert study a **case study**? On the surface, it may appear so as the study involved the evaluation of a single subject. However, while a case study is descriptive, the little Albert study did involve the systematic investigation of the effects of a treatment (in this case the fear conditioning) and thus, represents a **single-case design** (Christensen, Johnson, & Turner, 2014). While experiments with multiple participants involve comparisons between an **experimental group** and a **control group** to assess the effects of a treatment, in a single-case design the comparison is between the behavior of the participant before and after the treatment. In an **ABA single-case design**, the behavior is assessed prior to treatment (A) in this case Albert's responses to various objects like the white rat and rabbit. The point here is to establish a **baseline** or recording of behavior prior to an intervention or treatment essentially serving as a control group. Then, the treatment (B) is introduced, in this case the loud noise paired with the presentation of the rat; and finally, the treatment, loud noise, is removed and the behavior or response (A) to the white rat, rabbit, etc. is once again assessed. The importance of the ABA design can be observed if we imagine that Watson and Rayner might have simply conditioned Albert to fear the rat and then assessed his response to the fur coat, rabbit, and mask (without documenting baseline conditions). Assuming he responded with fear to these objects, would we be able to conclude that Watson's treatment was responsible? While this might be the case, it might also be that Albert feared those objects prior to the treatment (maybe he had encountered them before or maybe the novelty of them would have produced fear). Thus, even without the treatment, Albert would have responded with fear.

Though appearing methodologically sound, the implementation of this design in the little Albert study was inconsistent and disordered. Let's take the example of the hair of the two observers and Watson himself. There was no baseline observation of Albert's reaction to the hair of the observers and Watson. Additionally, Albert only responded negatively to Watson's hair and not to that of the other two observers (whose identity remains unknown). The problem with such details is that **confounds** are introduced. Could the sex or gender characteristics of the adults present have explained this? In other words, if the two observers were females, it could be that Albert's response was, in part, explained by differences in his responses to males and females. Another possibility is that Albert feared Watson because he was often aggressive in presenting items, most notably the Santa Claus (Harris, 2011).

This brings up another potential problem: Watson was the one conducting the test and observing and recording the behavior. There are many reasons why this is problematic. In order to enhance the internal validity of a study, contemporary researchers often utilize two research assistants blind to the hypothesis and assigned conditions of participants who observe and record behavior. The researcher can then look at the agreement or lack of agreement of the two observations to determine if fear is being measured reliably. However, as we will discuss in the section "What might the little Albert study look like if it was conducted today?," contemporary researchers would not likely rely solely on these observations. Lastly, in terms of the design of the study, time is of the essence. A researcher wants to eliminate any other possible explanations for the results other than the treatment, in this case conditioning. The baseline condition in which Albert's response to various stimuli was being assessed occurred when Albert was 9 months of age, yet the conditioning took place two months later when he was approximately 11 months old. Why does this matter? The longer the chronological age gap (especially at this point in the lifespan), the more likely it is that Albert had life experiences that affected his responses to the stimuli or that developmental changes might account for changes in his reactions. Such threats to internal validity are referred to as **history** and **maturation** respectively (Smith & Davis, 2013). Fridlund and colleagues (2012) speculate that the two-month delay in testing may have been due to the timing of the study, as the Christmas holiday may have accounted for the interruption. A hypothetical example of history, or an experience other than the conditioning that could influence Albert's reaction to the mask, could be a scary encounter with a Santa at a department store. There is no evidence of this, but the longer the gap, the less confidence one has that it is the treatment and not an **extraneous variable** accounting for the results.

Did Watson actually produce a phobia?

It may seem obvious when first encountering the representation of the little Albert study in a standard introductory textbook that Watson and Rayner had successfully conditioned a phobia in Albert. Many critics, however, found the results unconvincing (Beck, Levinson, & Irons, 2009; Harris, 1979; Jarrett, 2008; Paul & Blumenthal, 1989; Samelson, 1980). Part of the skepticism is due to the methodological weaknesses of the study, but also the ambiguity in Watson's notes on his observations.

That objective assessment was lacking is evident in Beck and colleagues' (2009) description of Albert's initial response to the rat after conditioning as "what Watson interpreted as fear" (p. 606). Albert's behavior was clearly inconsistent: he wasn't always avoiding the animals or stimuli; he wasn't always crying or upset. While Albert showed a strong negative response to the rat after repeated pairings of the rat and loud noise, and a strong nega-tive reaction to a rabbit, Watson's hair, and the Santa Claus mask five days later, many of the other responses were much less clear. For example, five days after the initial conditioning in which after seven presentations of the rat and loud noise Albert cried, he whimpered and turned away from the rat. Five days after this, Albert's response was so mild that Watson decided to once again introduce the loud noise with the rat. After eight joint presentations of the rat and the loud noise, Albert was taken to a different room and pre-sented with the rat. Watson and Rayner (1920) described Albert's reaction as: "No sudden fear reaction appeared at first. The hands, however, were held up and away from the animal. No positive manipulatory reactions appeared" (p. 315). Likewise, the dog did not produce much of a reaction from Albert until barking 6 inches from his face. Yet Watson and Rayner claimed success in the transfer of the fear. Thirty-one days later Albert was again presented with the Santa Claus mask and only became upset when he was forced to touch it.

Presumably, Albert had developed a phobia of the rat that transferred to fuzzy objects (Watson & Watson, 1921). Yet the overall strength of the responses from Albert do not suggest the development of a phobia (Hobbs, 2010). The evidence for generalizability is also tenuous – Albert's most neg-ative response to the dog came after the dog barked in his face and Albert did not consistently respond with fear to hair. The responses to the dog and rabbit from Albert can also not be said to be a pure test of generalizability as both were also paired with the loud noise (Harris, 1979). There is one other notable aspect of Watson and Rayner's interactions with Albert that casts doubt on the conclusion that Watson and Rayner had conditioned a phobia or even that the study was a powerful demonstration of the power of condi-tioning. Watson and Rayner (1920) noted that Albert would frequently suck his thumb and this seemed to prevent the conditioned response. Thus, they frequently "had to remove the thumb from his mouth before the conditioned response could be obtained" (p. 316). Watson and Rayner, of course, assumed that Albert's negative behavior was a conditioned response, but what if the conditioning did not work? Is it possible that Albert would still display a negative response when being prevented from sucking his thumb? The removal of the thumb from Albert's mouth may be the source of some of the negative behavior (Cornwell, Hobbs, & Prytula, 1980; Paul & Blumenthal, 1989; Samelson, 1980). Watson's study did motivate **replication** attempts, but these were unsuccessful (Bregman, 1934; English, 1929; Valentine, 1930), though these studies also suffered from significant methodological flaws (Field & Nightingale, 2009).

Was the little Albert study ethical?

Answering the question of whether or not the little Albert study was ethical is not as easy as it may initially appear. Textbook authors have a tendency to state that studies like little Albert "could never be conducted today." It is easy to look back at classic studies and declare the researchers conducting them were unethical, but let's consider the context. We might want to consider:

What were the ethical standards or guidelines at the time of the study?
What were the prevailing societal attitudes toward science and child-rearing?
What potential risks were involved?

Even critics of Watson acknowledge that evaluating the research by today's standards or **presentism** is unfair (Fridund et al., 2012). For example, a quick search of the Internet will provide you with numerous examples of condemnation of Watson and the study as unethical. Watson, however, was not aware of and cannot be fairly evaluated in terms of today's ethical standards for research. The American Psychological Association (APA) did not adopt a formal code of ethics until the 1950s. Digdon, Powell, and Harris (2014) note that when the Watson and Rayner study was conducted there was a desire on the part of the public for science and government to inform child-rearing; parents were eager to abandon old-fashioned ideas and adopt innovative, scientifically grounded parenting practices (Bigelow & Morris, 2001). Digdon, Powell and Harris (2014) note that:

> In Watson and Rayner's time, ideas about the proper treatment of children were different than ones favored today … Moreover, to Watson and Rayner's contemporaries, exposing infants to loud noises would likely have seemed no more dangerous than many events that occur in everyday life (i.e., what we now call "minimal risk" research). (p. 321)

Viewed in this light, we might be less ethically offended by the little Albert study and less outraged by the child-rearing advice offered by Watson and Rayner.

This advice to parents included discouraging too much overt displays of love and affection. Here too we have to avoid presentism. Watson's advice was aimed at helping parents develop an emotionally stable and independent adult. It is the suggestion to avoid hugging and kissing that can be easily regarded as inconsistent with current knowledge. Yet these ideas were consistent with some child-rearing advice during the 1920s and some of Watson and Rayner's advice (e.g., establishing daily routines, not relying on punishment) was consistent not only with the ethos of this era but also with contemporary ideas on parenting. However, what is troubling is that Watson and Rayner knew in advance that Albert was leaving the hospital yet did not decondition him (Harris, 1979; Paul & Blumenthal, 1989). This is particularly troubling because Watson and Rayner (1920) seemed to believe that the fear would likely continue for some time without any intentional efforts to reduce it.

More serious ethical questions were raised by Beck and colleagues (Fridlund et al., 2012; Beck, Levinson, & Irons, 2009). Because little Albert's mother was a wet nurse, a position of low stature at the time, and poor financial standing, this might have led to her being subtly or not so subtly coerced into consenting to her son's participation in the study. More serious yet was the charge that the identity of little Albert had possibly been established (Douglas Merritte) and evidence suggested that Douglas, who died at the age of six due to complications from hydrocephalus, had actually been neurologically impaired at the time of the study. Watson and Raynor, however, reported Albert B. to be a healthy child. The idea that Watson conditioned a neurologically impaired child and then misrepresented his health status is a serious charge and one that has been challenged by a separate group of researchers (Powell et al., 2014). Powell and colleagues (2014) identified Albert Barger as the more likely candidate. Not only was his name fitting, but Albert's mother was also a wet nurse at the hospital from which Albert B. stayed and gave birth to her son the same day that Douglas Merritte was born. Psychologists were not required to conceal the identity of participants as, again, there was no formal ethics code to guide researchers at the time of the little Albert study (Beck et al., 2009; Powell et al., 2014).

There is no doubt that we would judge the little Albert study unethical when applying today's ethical standards. Watson was most concerned with helping solve practical problems and believed that what was learned from the little Albert study had the potential to help eliminate unnecessary fears in children and, for that reason, the minimal harm caused to Albert was justified (Fridlund et al., 2012).

Impact of the little Albert study

Determining the appropriateness of the study should also involve a consideration of its potential value. In other words, we want to ponder what good came from such research. In the case of little Albert, we want to ask what impact the study had on **psychotherapy** or psychological treatments of mental disorders. Not surprisingly, there is disagreement on the answer. Some argue that many fears and phobias are not produced through the means by which little Albert's were created (i.e., classical conditioning; Paul & Blumenthal, 1989) and that some of Watson and Rayner's suggestions for deconditioning were not in line with contemporary therapies (Digdon, Powell, & Harris, 2014). Others argue that not only was the study the first to demonstrate that classical conditioning could account for phobias, but several of Watson and Rayner's (1920) suggestions were consistent with yet-to-be developed therapies, including exposure therapy, counter-conditioning, systematic desensitization, and modeling (Field & Nightingale, 2009). Joseph Wolpe developed systematic desensitization as a means of treatment for what were believed to be classically conditioned fears by having clients, either directly or through visualization, encounter fear-evoking stimuli while in a relaxed state (Corsini & Wedding, 2005). If years after the study Albert sought treatment for his phobia, it is likely that he would encounter exposure therapy or systematic desensitization as exposure-based treatments are particularly effective treatments for phobias in children and adults alike (Chambless et al., 1998; Silverman & Ollendick, 2005; Wolitzky-Taylor et al., 2008).

Thus, Watson and Rayner, as well as Watson's student Mary Cover Jones (1924), are properly credited as pioneers of this treatment (Field & Nightingale, 2009). However, Watson viewed conditioned fears as reflexive. Watson's rigid view of this process did not account for factors like how the individual interprets the UCS, the temperament of the child, and previous neutral experiences the person has had with the conditioned stimulus. These factors are important to contemporary learning theory which suggest that fears don't operate like reflexes but are conditional and influenced by subjective perceptions (Ollendick & Muris, 2015). Under what conditions does Albert feel the animals will be accompanied by the UCS? Was Albert prone to fear new situations and objects (all accounts by Watson and Rayner suggest he was not)? Did Albert have any experiences with the animals and objects that he would later be exposed to during the study? These are all important questions from a contemporary perspective (Muris et al., 2002; Ollendick & Muris, 2015). In addition to these factors, we also know that the development of phobias is influenced by parents and maintained by cognitive biases (Muris et al., 2002). A child's fear can develop from information provided by parent's about animals (e.g., rats have sharp claws and will scratch you) and indirectly through anxious parenting (e.g., parents being overly cautious and worrisome; Muris et al., 2010). Numerous studies have also documented the transmission of fear among animals through observational learning (e.g., Cook, Wolkenstein, & Laitsch, 1985; Mineka et al., 1984).

With our current understanding of the multiple factors that contribute to phobias, it is easier to understand the inconsistent findings in the early conditioning research. An evolutionary perspective, for example, accounts for important differences among the conditioning stimuli with animals (i.e., Watson & Rayner, 1920) being easier to condition with than, say, toys (English, 1929) or household items (Valentine, 1930). Important individual differences in temperament may also help us make sense of the reported success of conditioning with Albert yet failure of a replication attempt by Horace English. English (1929) used a similar UCS (i.e., loud noise) as Watson and Rayner did, yet he was unable to condition a child to fear a wooden toy duck. That the UCS was unable to consistently evoke a startle in the 14-month-old child shocked English: "The writer must confess his surprise – and admiration – at the child's iron nerves" (p. 222). Lastly, we further know that cognitive biases mean a tendency to devote more attention to the fear-provoking stimulus and to overestimate the tendency for the fear stimuli to be associated with negative outcomes (Muris et al., 2002). Contemporary behavioral therapies often blend principles of learning like classical conditioning with efforts to change maladaptive thought patterns that often maintain the disorder (Corsini & Wedding, 2005) and develop coping skills patients can utilize when encountering the fear-inducing stimuli (Sanderson & Rego, 2002).

What might the little Albert study look like if it was conducted today?

In thinking about what the little Albert study might look like today, let's first consider, due to the difficulty of assessing fear in infants and the ethical constraints, that Albert is a 6-year-old rather than a 9-month-old. Technologies not available during Watson's time would likely be utilized to provide a more objective assessment of fear, relying on a number of methods and sources of information which would remove the uncertainty about the presence of a phobia (Ollendick & Muris, 2015). Ironically, many of the cognitive tools available to researchers today would be rejected by Watson as too subjective. Today, researchers interested in studying phobias could use a Stroop-like task to assess the aforementioned attentional bias. In a **Stroop task** a participant is presented with the word of a color (e.g., GREEN) written in a different color (e.g., written in red) and asked to name the color of the ink rather than the printed word. If the colors matched, of course, this would be much easier, so the slower naming times with non-matching colors is referred to as the Stroop effect. Watts and colleagues (1986) presented participants with a spider phobia with a modified Stroop task in which they had to name the color of spider-related words like hairy, legs, crawl, and fangs. Compared to a control group, individuals with a spider phobia were slower to name the colors. However, in a second study, the authors found desensitization therapy reduced the interference caused by the spider-related words. There are several other tests that researchers can use to document the cognitive distortions that accompany phobias (see Muris & Field, 2008). Phobias and anxiety in general can also be documented with physiological measures like skin conductance, an indicator of sympathetic nervous system activity (e.g., Gao et al., 2010). There are also less technologically impressive but creative means of assessing the behavior of those with a phobia. Clinicians and researchers might utilize a Behavioral Assessment Test (BAT) in which a client or participant is presented with increasingly fear-arousing situations and how far they get can be recorded along with their subjective ratings of fear as well as physiological indicators (Antony, Orsillo, & Roemer, 2001). Cochrane, Barnes-Holmes, and Barnes-Holmes (2008), for example, presented college students with a version of the BAT in which they were asked to put their hand in jars that increasingly (or so they thought) involved the risk of coming into contact with a spider (see Figure 2.2).

Figure 2.2   Jars presented to participants in the Cochrane et al. (2008) study. The risk of coming into contact with a spider increases with each successive jar

Cochrane and colleagues (2008) found significant differences among participants varying in their level of spider anxiety with many of those in the high fear group unwilling to go further than jar 3. The authors also provided support for the **validity** of this BAT as the number of steps taken correlated with scores among participants on a questionnaire of spider fear. Perhaps a similar produce could be used with participants conditioned to fear small animals in a contemporary little Albert study.

Though Watson's interest in the contemporary measures of fear would have been limited to the behavioral and physiological, there is an obvious benefit to being able to document a phobia at a behavioral, cognitive, and physiological level. It is also beneficial to have multiple sources of measurement regarding variables of interest including parents and teachers (Ollendick & Muris, 2015). The use of such measures and multiple informants in a hypothetical contemporary little Albert study helps to ensure that one is accurately and reliably measuring fear and avoiding the ambiguity of the notes of Watson and Rayner (e.g., "negative response").

Correcting the record on little Albert

Drawing conclusions about this famous study is made more difficult by the misreporting of the study. Numerous authors have reported inaccuracies in coverage of the study in textbooks (Cornwell & Hobbs, 1976; Griggs, 2014; Harris, 2011; Hobbs, 2010; Jarrett, 2008; Paul & Blumenthal, 1989; Samelson, 1980). How is it possible that textbooks can get it wrong? Some have speculated that a study's status as a classic breeds overconfidence in one's memory of the details (Cornwell & Hobbs, 1976). Others argue it may be a conscious effort on the part of authors to leave out details that take away from the story (i.e., Watson's triumph of conditioning little Albert which ushered in behaviorism as psychology's dominant paradigm; Griggs, 2014). Regardless, it is important to correct the record on the Watson and Rayner study. If you have read an account of the little Albert study in a textbook or elsewhere, you can check for the following inaccuracies:

– Little Albert did not display a generalized fear of white objects or animals; most of the stimuli, including the rabbit, were not white
– Albert was not deconditioned; Watson and Rayner did not make an attempt to decondition Albert before he and his mother left the hospital
– Albert was 9 months old at the beginning of the study, not 11 months old (the age at which conditioning began)
– There were several failed replication attempts as the nature of the study did not incite an ethical outrage at the time
– Albert was the only participant in the study
– A conditioned response did not occur after a single pairing of the rat and the noise

> **KEY READING** – Harris, B. (1979). Whatever happened to Little Albert? *American Psychologist*, *34*, 151–160.

Chapter summary

Watson and Rayner purported to document the etiology of phobias with their conditioning study of little Albert. The study has been challenged on ethical grounds for, among other concerns, Watson and Rayner's failure to decondition Albert and methodologically for the subjective assessment of fear and the introduction of several confounds. Theoretically, we know that classical conditioning by itself cannot account for all phobias as contemporary research has documented the important role of a child's temperament, cognitive vulnerabilities, and the social transmission of fear. Phobias are not classically conditioned reflexes, but are influenced by our perceptions and interpretations of the events and biological predispositions (note these explanations draw more upon cognitive explanations of behavior). There are now numerous objective, valid ways to assess phobias that were unavailable during Watson's time. If we hold our present "cognitive frame of reference" in check, we have to marvel at the ingenuity of the little Albert study and appreciate that, at least compared to some researchers at this time, Watson was well ahead of his time as the seeds of later successful behavioral therapies, with a strong empirical track record, were planted in this 1920 publication; a testament to the continued relevance of the landmark study.

Future directions

Much of therapy today might include some use of the behavioral therapeutic techniques such as stimulus flooding, aversive conditioning, and desensitization, but with a healthy dose of cognitive retraining. The Cognitive Revolution in psychology has contributed to clinical applications of cognitive constructs such as perception, self-regulation, and reframing. Albert Ellis (1913–2007) has been called the grandfather of cognitive behavioral therapy and the founder of Rational Emotive Behavior Therapy (REBT) (see Capuzzi & Stauffer, 2016). A careful examination of REBT clearly shows the integration of behavioral techniques with cognitive processes ("We think what we feel"). Irrational beliefs, for example, are replaced by rational (healthy) alternative behaviors in life. Critical thinkers will be able to spot the influence of behaviorism in such therapeutic approaches. Furthermore, it is likely that the contemporary models of psychopathology will continue to identify crucial environmental experiences that interact with biological, psychological, and social vulnerabilities.

Discussion questions

1. How would you design a study using the methods of Cochrane et al. (study of spider phobia) to assess a fear of heights? Hint: Think of systematic desensitization.
2. What if we were able to rid humans of the pain or fear associated with seeing snakes in a zoo? What new problems might emerge here?

3 The Nurture Assumption: Does Parental Influence during Childhood Offer the Greatest Impact on Personality Development?

Primary source: Harris, J. R. (1995). Where is the child's environment? A group socialization theory of development. *Psychological Review, 102,* 458–489.

Chapter objectives

This chapter will help you become a better critical thinker by:

- Evaluating the role "nature and nurturance" play in child development
- Examining the group socialization theory of Judith Rich Harris
- Understanding socialization research in developmental psychology
- Grasping the criticism of Harris's group socialization theory
- Discerning the role media misrepresentation plays in Harris's theory

---

Introduction

Task: Consider each of the factors below in terms of causative origins of child development and circle either "nature" or "nurture" for each option. Answers are on the next page.

#1 Genetic endowment	nature	or	nurture
#2 Poor parenting skills	nature	or	nurture
#3 Social relationships outside the family	nature	or	nurture
#4 Effective parenting skills	nature	or	nurture
#5 Pre-wired skills for language development	nature	or	nurture
#6 Influence of our culture or subculture	nature	or	nurture

#1 (nature), #2 (nurture), #3 (nurture), #4 (nurture), #5 (nature), and #6 (nurture)

The answers to all of these may initially appear straightforward. Nature is genetic endowment (#1) and when we think about an environmental influence far removed from genetic impact, culture (#6) may come to mind. To suggest that something is "pre-wired" (#5) is to suggest that it owes to nature rather than nurture. Factors 2, 3, and 4 are where we encounter the most difficulty in separating nature and nurture. Though you may have identified each as belonging to "nurture," be prepared to have this position challenged in the pages that follow. We will revisit these factors at the end of the chapter.

Study background

Imagine your psychology professor asks you to write a paper on the role parents play in shaping a child's personality. Intuitively, you believe that parents influence children in important ways, but as a student of psychology you also know you cannot rely on your intuition and need to examine relevant research. A quick database search reveals a wealth of studies on the effect parents have on children, such as the following (e.g., Hair et al., 2008):

> Researchers assessed the relationship between the quality of the parent-child relationship (e.g. how supportive the parents are) and the well-being of the child and engagement in delinquent behavior. Participants in the study completed measures assessing their relationship with their parents, their well-being and engagement in delinquent behavior. Results revealed that the quality of the parent-child relationship was, as predicted, positively correlated with well-being and negatively correlated with delinquency.

You, of course, are not at all surprised by results such as this as it seems a very safe assumption that parents play a significant positive role in determining the extent to which their children are well-adjusted. With dozens of studies producing similar results, you are quite confident in concluding that the way a parent raises a child has a major impact on how that child turns out. But, not so fast. Psychologist Judith Rich Harris (2009), in her controversial book *The Nurture Assumption*, concluded that the way a parent raises a child has almost no lasting impact on the child's personality! Harris, instead, pointed to the peer group as the major force shaping personality. But Harris looked at the same research you did, so how did she conclude that parents have such little influence? The answer, as we will discuss in this chapter, in part, lies in the way these studies were designed as well as how they are interpreted.

> **KEY READING** – Harris, J. R. (2009). *The nurture assumption: Why children turn out the way they do, revised and updated*. New York: Free Press.

The nurture assumption – the idea that how a parent raises a child will determine how that child turns out – is deeply ingrained in US culture, argues Harris. Think about high-profile cases of child actors who experience problems as adults. Aren't parents usually the first to be blamed by the media and, often, by the actor? What about the highly publicized cases involving school shootings? So often parents are at the top of the media blame list in these cases as well.

Ever heard of the Tiger Mom? Amy Chua (2011), in *Battle Hymn of the Tiger Mom*, wrote about her experiences raising her two daughters utilizing a traditional, no-nonsense Chinese parenting style (what psychologists would call an authoritarian style). Chua was criticized harshly and even accused of child abuse. This critique is itself a testament to the nurture assumption and controversy surrounding the complex relationship between parenting and childhood outcomes. But, despite the parenting described as "harsh" (or because of it?), it has been argued her kids turned out fine as described in this headline from a website in the UK (Stern, 2016): *Tiger Mom's tough love worked! Five years after Amy Chua published her "Battle Hymn", her Ivy League-educated kids are proof the strict upbringing pays off (and both say they plan to raise their children the same way).*

The credit and the blame that parents receive for the successes and failures of their children, beyond uncontrollably providing good or bad genes, is undeserved according to Judith Rich Harris, and is a result of the nurture assumption. Beyond high-profile cases, think about your own personality and what or who shaped it. Do your parents come to mind? Most likely you could point to numerous experiences involving your parents that were influential in making you the person you are today. But as critical thinkers we have to challenge the everyday assumptions deeply embedded in our culture, assumptions such as venting anger is healthy, labels stigmatize, and, as Harris suggests, how parenting practices (barring extreme forms of abuse) have a lasting impact on a child's personality.

Socialization is the process by which we all learn the rules, customs, norms, and language of our culture. Though we may intuitively credit the home environment – parents in particular – for this process, Harris focuses instead on forces outside of the home, primarily peer groups. As the term group socialization implies, the theory suggests that socialization is a group process. But isn't the family the most important group, you might wonder? Harris argues this is not the case because a home doesn't create a strong group identity. As children get older they are increasingly influenced by environments outside the home and, for example, schools become fertile ground for creating strong group identities. When we identify with a group there is pressure on us to conform to group norms which results in **within-group assimilation** and a tendency for groups to emphasize and even exaggerate differences between our group and others, referred to as **between-group contrasts**. Contrasts within a group, or **within-group differentiation**, also occur and allow a member of the group to establish a unique identity or niche while still holding to group norms. Group socialization theory suggests that these three forces operating within and between peer groups, not the home environment, have lasting impacts on our personality. Harris relies on **evolutionary psychology** to make the case for the importance of the peer environment.

Therefore, to return to the earlier question of why the family is **not** the most important group, Harris (2009) suggested the family unit, in evolutionary terms, is a "modern invention" (p. 336). For millions of years we needed to survive in groups larger than the nuclear family. As Harris (1995) suggested:

> In order to survive and reproduce, children must be able to function successfully in the world outside their home. They must form alliances that go beyond the nuclear family. (p. 477)

Within these larger groups, one of the important differences among members is that between children and adults. Because children need to learn how to be successful in the world outside their home it would not make good evolutionary sense for learning to take place predominantly within an isolated home environment. Children, Harris (2009) notes, "don't identify with their parents because parents are not people like themselves – parents are grownups. Children think of themselves as kids, or … as girls and boys, and these are the groups in which they are socialized" (p. 337). Additionally, Harris argues, genes have already created similarities between parents and children, so for the sake of greater variability it would make sense for us to be more sensitive to socialization outside the home. Harris does acknowledge that parents shape the attitudes and values of children, but argues that this happens at the group level. The norms of the parents' peer group have the potential to be adopted by the peer group(s) of the children. So, the transmission of culture is from group to group rather than from parent to child or from individual to individual. What we learn in the home, group socialization theory suggests, is not lasting and it is not generalizable outside the home.

Lastly, one of the key assumptions of Harris's group socialization theory is that behavior is context-specific. In other words, people learn how to behave in various environments such as the home environment and this behavior seldom transfers to different contexts such as school and work. The way you learn to behave at home around your parents tells us little about how you will behave in school around your peers. Nearly 50 years ago psychologist

Walter Mischel (1968) made a similar argument in a critique of the field of personality. For example, Mischel, as does Harris, pointed to a classic study conducted in the 1920s that found that the moral behavior and moral attitudes of children vary across settings such as home and athletic competitions. The correlations were in the range of 0.3 to 0.4. Studies such as this provide support for the idea that behavior is context-dependent and highly variable within people.

Current thinking

So, is personality context-dependent and variable? While it may be the case that personality traits will not perfectly predict behavior in any one situation at a given time, research suggests that a person's behavior is quite consistent when you look at it over the course of several weeks. For example, if I am an extravert, I may display a range of behavior across situations that at times reflect a high level of extraversion, yet at other times exhibit a low or moderate level of extraversion. However, if you look at the *average* level of extraversion across a number of weeks, it would be high (Fleeson, 2004).

To her credit, Harris's work highlighted the methodological flaws in some developmental psychology research, particularly socialization studies. She rightly questioned the conclusions that could be drawn from studies correlating an aspect of parenting with developmental outcomes and brought attention to the failure to control for the influence of genes. Genes account for roughly 40–50% of the variability in most traits. However, even among personality traits (e.g., impulsivity) that are highly heritable, there is still room for the environment to wield influence. Though there is little doubt that peers are an important development influence, we need to be aware of research suggesting that even above and beyond the influence of peers, parental behaviors still have an impact on child development (Galambos, Barker, & Almeida, 2003; Sroufe et al., 2005). Additionally, much contemporary research is more sophisticated in design than that targeted and critiqued by Harris (Vandell, 2000).

> **KEY READING** – Vandell, D. L. (2000). Parents, peer groups, and other socializing influences. *Developmental Psychology, 36,* 699–710.

For example, studies looking at the relationship between parents' use of behavioral and psychological control and the psychological adjustment of children have employed a longitudinal method in which they assessed parental behaviors, the influence of deviant peers, and the adjustment of children across multiple time periods (Aunola & Nurmi, 2005; Galambos et al., 2003). Likewise, even if researchers do not control for the influence of genes in a study, they will often acknowledge that there is potential for genes to explain the correlation they are finding between an environmental variable and a developmental outcome.

Though Harris's theory appears consistent with other psychological theories – an important criterion for evaluating a theory – few studies represent a direct test of group socialization theory (e.g., Loehlin, 1997). Behavior genetics offers the greatest potential for insights into the relative influence of nature and nurture. The results from behavior genetics research would call into question the binary choices (nature or nurture) provided for you in the task at the beginning of the chapter. A point made by Harris and supported with behavior genetics research is that the line we draw between nature and nurture is more blurred and obscured than we appreciate. Genes influence the environment and environments influence genes in complex and seemingly inextricable ways.

Evaluating the socialization research

One of the challenges Harris faced in making her case was the mountain of research showing a relationship between parenting practices and various outcomes in children. Research that seeks to find a correlation between an aspect of parenting such as parenting style and an outcome like academic achievement, what Harris refers to as socialization research, has been a popular product in **developmental psychology**.

Use of an authoritative parenting style has been associated with greater competence, maturity, self-esteem, and academic achievement and lower substance abuse, depression, and delinquent behavior than the other two styles (i.e., permissive and authoritarian) in numerous studies (e.g., Milevsky et al., 2007). So abundant is the research showing a relationship between authoritative parenting and positive developmental outcomes that most psychologists consider authoritative parenting to be the best style (recall that the Tiger Mom used a style characterized by harsh discipline – authoritarian). This research is grounded in the nurture assumption according to Harris, because it is assumed that parenting styles produce these outcomes. Harris rejects this deterministic parenting assumption and suggests that the conclusions that can be drawn from parental socialization studies are quite limited. Let's consider an example. Researchers gather a group of students who have ADHD (Attention Deficit Hyperactivity Disorder) and a control group consisting of an equal number of children without ADHD (e.g., see Moghaddam et al., 2013). Parenting styles were assessed and the hypothetical results revealed no significant difference between the two groups in authoritative parenting (see Table 3.1).

Table 3.1   *Differences between ADHD and controls across the three parenting styles*

A p value of .05 or lower is considered statistically significant

Parenting style variables	ADHD	Normal	p value
Permissive	9.5	11.5	0.05
Authoritarian	13.2	10.1	0.01
Authoritative	11.2	11.1	0.70

Let's assume the scale measuring parenting styles produced scores ranging from 0 indicating no use of this parenting style to 15 indicating a high level of use of the parenting style.

Disappointing, right. But wait! There were significant differences between the two groups in the other two styles, permissive and authoritarian. Those with ADHD had parents who were less permissive and more authoritarian. We might interpret this study as suggesting that parents with a tendency to be more authoritarian and less permissive are more likely to have kids with ADHD or at least to make symptoms of ADHD worse in kids that already had it. This is not an unreasonable conclusion, but it is not necessarily the correct one. There are a number of problems in drawing any conclusion from a study such as this. First of all, it is equally reasonable to expect that in dealing with a child with ADHD (a child who is impulsive, easily excitable, possibly aggressive and hyperactive) a parent is likely to be more authoritarian and less permissive in *response* to this behavior (see Figure 3.1). Correlational studies do not allow us to determine which causes the other, parental behavior or ADHD symptomology. Another possibility is that the parenting styles have nothing to do with ADHD after we account for the influence of genetic transmission. In other words, if parents contribute – are deserving of any blame – it is through the genes they have passed on to their children. Socialization studies fail to control for genetic influence and, thus, it is impossible to conclude that parenting styles and not genes are accounting for outcomes. Parents who have a tendency to be inconsistent may genetically pass on this tendency to their children. All the traits that make someone a poor parent in adulthood might have their origins in behavioral problems during childhood. This also applies to the delinquency and well-being study described earlier. The researchers may assume that the way the parent treats the child impacts his/her behavior and well-being, but it is also possible that this relationship is accounted for by genetic transmission. Parents with genetically inherited tendencies toward delinquency themselves are less likely to foster a positive relationship with their child and more likely to pass on a predisposition toward delinquency. Likewise, parents who are well-adjusted have kids who are well-adjusted. It's in the genes. So, both the parent–child relationship quality study and parenting styles study and those with similar designs are limited by a failure to control for the influence of genes and are limited in terms of drawing cause–effect conclusions.

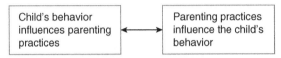

Figure 3.1   Indicates the bidirectional influence between parents and children. The temperament/personality of the child evokes responses from parents.

Let's go back to the delinquency study for a moment to address an additional limitation of some socialization studies. Harris, of course, might criticize the results for the reasons just discussed, but additionally, she would criticize the study on the grounds that the relationship that the researchers found might be, at least partially, due to something psychologists called **common method variance**.

Critical thinking toolkit
Common method variance

Guiding question: Did the researchers use a variety of methods to measure variables in the study?

Participants in the well-being study were given numerous self-report measures on the quality of their relationship with their parents, their well-being, and their delinquent behavior. What's wrong with this, you might ask? There may be nothing wrong with it, but how the questions are asked is important and has the potential to affect the correlation that we observe between variables such as the quality of the parent–child relationship and well-being. Imagine the scales that participants completed in the study were as follows:

Please respond to the items below using the following scale:

1	2	3	4	5
Strongly disagree	Disagree	Neutral	Agree	Strongly agree

1. I enjoy spending time with my parents. _____
2. I want to be like my parents. _____
3. I admire my parents. _____
4. My parents are supportive of my interests. _____
5. My parents praise me when I succeed. _____

In the past month...

1. I have often felt happy. _____
2. I have often felt calm. _____
3. I have often felt at peace. _____
4. I have often felt depressed. _____
5. I have often felt downhearted. _____

Now let us suppose that the researchers examine the **correlation** between scores on the first five items (quality of the parent–child relationship) and the last five (child well-being). Let us assume they find the correlation to be $r = 0.6, p = 0.001$, a statistically significant positive correlation. Though a correlation may exist, it is also possible that the correlation is a bit higher than it would be if the variables were treated in a different way. Notice that the measures are both self-report, requiring the participant to supply the responses. Using the same type of instrument (e.g., self-report) and the same scale (1 = strongly disagree, 2 = disagree, etc.) across multiple measures can produce similar responses which artificially inflate the correlation between the variables (Podsakoff et al., 2003). In order to help address this problem, researchers could have the parents report on the quality of the parent–child relationship or the well-being of the child. For example, in a study assessing the relationship between positive (e.g., providing support) and negative (e.g., using psychological control) parental behaviors and adjustment in adolescence, researchers had parents report on their parental behaviors and adolescents report on their own adjustment problems (e.g., depression or drug use; Galambos et al., 2003).

Another problem related to the interpretation of responses to this 5-point Likert-like response scale (strongly agree–strongly disagree) involves the meaning of a neutral (#3) response. All we really know when a respondent selects this "neutral" option is that they do not agree or disagree with the statements provided. We do not know "why" they selected the "neutral" option. Perhaps this is a defensive reaction of the respondent to the statement. Perhaps the respondent is confused by the wording of the statement or wishes to add qualifiers to his/her response.

Correlations within the socialization research

Another of Harris's (2009) criticisms of the socialization research is that correlations are low. She specifically notes that "a correlation of .19, even if it is significant in a statistical sense, is all but useless" (p. 17). The same criticism was leveled at Brad Bushman (Chapter 7) and other researchers who argued that exposure to violent media is a public health concern. When you consider the range of a positive correlation from 0 to 1.0, a correlation of 0.19 does seem small and, in fact, is according to generally agreed upon guidelines: 0.1 is small, 0.3 is medium, and 0.5 or greater is large (Cohen, 1988). But a small correlation does not necessarily indicate that an effect is meaningless. It may be helpful to compare correlations produced by developmental psychologists with those obtained in research in other fields such as medicine (Bushman & Huesmann, 2001). Consider the following small to medium effects that are hardly meaningless: cigarette smoking and lung cancer, $r = 0.35$; Vietnam service and alcohol problems, $r = 0.07$; and aspirin use and heart attacks, $r = 0.04$ (Bushman & Huesmann, 2014; Rosenthal, 1994). Additionally, the correlations between condom use and sexually transmitted HIV, nicotine patch use and smoking cessation, and calcium intake and bone mass are all below 0.2 and are unlikely to be considered useless by public health officials.

Researchers would, of course, like to discover perfect correlations ($+1.0$ or -1.0) or near perfect correlations ($+0.96$ or -0.96), but most psychological researchers are genuinely excited about correlations in the vicinity of $+0.75$ and -0.75 (Bushman & Huesmann, 2001). There are several reasons for this, but most relevant to the socialization research that Harris criticizes is the fact that there are so many variables that impact a child's behavior, the parents being just one of them. The psychologist Deborah Lowe Vandell (2000) explains it as follows:

> The size of the reported parenting effects also reflects the fact that parenting is part of a complex developmental system that includes children's own capacities and proclivities, multiple social relationships (with parents, siblings, friends, peer cliques, teachers, and neighbors) and multiple developmental contexts (homes, schools and neighborhoods). Within complex developmental systems, it is very unlikely that any single factor will account for a huge, or even substantial amount of variation. (p. 701)

While Harris takes issue with much of the socialization research due to weak correlations, a failure to control for genetic influence, problems with interpreting the causal nature of the relationship, and common method variance, her group socialization theory draws heavily on a different type of research referred to as behavior genetics.

Behavior genetics research

Twin studies, a staple of **behavior genetics** research, involve comparisons between nature's clones (identical, monozygotic (MZ) twins and fraternal, dizygotic (DZ) twins).

Identical twins should be more similar to one another than fraternal twins, if genes are a prominent factor. Adoption studies also allow for the estimation of the relative influence of genes and environment. We, for example, can compare intact families that share genes and the environment with adopted children who have separate biological parents (genetic relatives) and adoptive parents (environmental relatives). These comparisons allow for a test of nature and nurture. If the behaviors of adopted children are more like their adoptive parents, environment is assumed to have more influence. If the behaviors of adopted children resemble their biological parents, genes are assumed to have more influence. Behavior geneticists further divide the environmental factors into what are called shared and non-shared factors. **Shared environment** factors are non-genetic influences that make family members similar to one another (Plomin, 2013). These might include parent education and parenting behaviors. **Non-shared environment** includes influences that make family members different from one another and may include aspects of the home environment like differential treatment from parents and influences outside the home environment like peer influences.

What behavioral genetics research indicates is that shared environments, relative to genes and non-shared environments, play a small role in developmental outcomes such as personality. Thus, the research to date suggests that if we focus on the similarities between parents and offspring, we would attribute this mostly to genes, although differences would be attributed to non-shared environmental factors.

Imagine you have a couple of siblings that are both highly conscientious – reliable, always on time, well-organized, etc. You might credit the parents who provided consistent rules and high standards for their kids. This would be the explanation favored by socialization researchers who endorse the nurture assumption. Harris's argument, based on behavior genetics research, is that this can just as easily be attributed to the genetic transmission of conscientiousness rather than parenting practices, and whatever is not accounted for by genes is likely due to non-shared environmental factors such as the influence of peers. But, let's assume that though these two siblings are similar in their levels of conscientiousness, they are quite different in terms of their anxiety levels or neuroticism, with one being highly anxious and the other not. It could be the case that the parents were rather anxious in their treatment of one child (perhaps their first child), but not their other child. This aspect of the home environment created differences in the siblings and is, thus, a non-shared environmental factor.

The issue is not whether non-shared factors are more important than shared factors (behavior genetics research clearly indicates that non-shared factors are more important), but rather what qualifies as a non-shared factor. Harris argues that non-shared factors are exclusively outside of the home influences, while inside the home factors make up the shared environment. But behavior geneticists, unlike Harris, do not limit parents to the shared environment. Although behavior geneticist Robert Plomin notes that different experiences outside of the family (e.g., different friends) can be a non-shared factor, "differences in their family experience" and "different treatment by parents" (p. 96) can be non-shared environmental factors as well (Plomin et al., 2013; Turkheimer & Waldron, 2000). In other words, parents matter, but maybe they matter in an unexpected way, providing differential treatment and experiences among siblings that leads to differences between them (Vandell, 2000). Only if parents treat siblings exactly the same and this treatment produces similarities among them would parents be confined to the shared environment. Behavior genetics research, however, suggests quite different experiences in the home environment among siblings including differences in maternal affection and family interactions and negative parental behaviors directed at one sibling, making these non-shared factors (Plomin et al., 2013).

Although Harris has dismissed these non-shared factors attributed to parenting in general, she does point out – rightly – that genes account for some differences attributed to the environment. Behavior geneticists call these **gene–environment correlations** and, applied to the example above, it might be the case that the child high in anxiety brought about anxious parenting because of a difficult temperament (a highly heritable factor). This is a special type of gene–environment correlation referred to as an **evocative gene–environment** correlation. It is labeled evocative because the genetic trait the child possesses evokes or brings about certain behavior from the parents. So, to return to the example of the ADHD study, it could be that the genetically influenced cluster of traits referred to as ADHD brought about or evoked an authoritarian and permissive style on the part of parents and is therefore accounted for, in part, by this evocative gene–environment correlation.

Genetically influenced traits such as height and temperament influence the environments to which people are exposed, influence how people respond to and treat a particular person, and help to shape those environments to which people are exposed. It is important to keep in mind that genes often exert their influence in ways that are subtle and not as obvious as more salient factors such as the behavior of parents.

Critical thinking toolkit

Evaluating a psychological theory

Guiding question: Did I properly evaluate the value and validity of the theory?

In evaluating a psychological theory, Cramer (2013) recommends that we consider the comprehensiveness, heuristic value, empirical validity, applied value, and precision (and testability). With respect to comprehensiveness, we want to consider to how many psychological phenomena it can be applied (i.e., is it sufficiently broad or too narrow), while heuristic value refers to the theory's ability to inspire work or ideas beyond psychology. Empirical validity and precision refer to the ability of the theory to stand up to scrutiny which requires clearly defined constructs and reliable and valid measures. Applying these to group socialization theory, we might ask whether Harris has clearly defined what she means by personality and how reliably behavior genetics can measure genetic and environmental influences.

In evaluating a psychological theory, we also want to consider how consistent it is with other well-established theories (Cramer, 2013). Harris's theory, for example, appears consistent with a conceptual, modular approach to the mind proffered by evolutionary psychologists who suggest that the mind is composed of domain-specific modules. Two of these modules are key to Harris's theory. She suggested that we have a relationship module which is involved in developing an emotional connection with our parents – an important task from an evolutionary perspective. But equally important, or more important from Harris's perspective, is the task of affiliating with a group and achieving status within that group, which is why we also have a group module for such outside-the-home experiences (Harris, 1995) – experiences that have a lasting impact on personality. Harris's views on peer socialization are also consistent with a theory of moral judgment referred to as the social intuitionist model (Haidt, 2001). Moral decision-making, according to the model, is driven by emotions and intuition rather than moral reasoning. Drawing on Harris's theory, psychologist Jonathan Haidt suggests that late childhood and adolescence are particularly important life junctures in which peers shape these moral intuitions.

While group socialization theory seems consistent with social intuition theory, it appears to conflict with the notion that attachment is stable and strongly influenced by parents (Bowlby, 1982). Early attachment experiences influence later relationships because of our tendency to generalize, and perhaps overgeneralize, these experiences. Harris (1995) argued that these experiences are person-specific; the relationship you have with your mother will not influence your expectations in other relationships. Numerous longitudinal studies, however, attest to the impact of parental care on attachment and how attachment patterns change depending on parental care and how early parental relationships shape later peer relationships through the expectations children bring to them (Sroufe et al., 2005).

Another criterion for evaluating a theory is its applied value (Cramer, 2013). In 1996 the parents of Alex Provenzino, a 16-year-old convicted of multiple criminal acts including burglary and drug related offenses, were themselves convicted of a misdemeanor for failing to properly control their son (Meredith, 1996). Though parent responsibility laws hold parents responsible for failing to control or adequately supervise their child rather than holding the parents responsible for something the parent did wrong in raising the child, the underpinnings of the nurture assumption are still evident. Even if the parents are not held legally responsible for the "sins" of their children, they are often tried and convicted of these in the court of public opinion. Taking Harris's argument at face value means changing the way we explain delinquent behavior. The only blame parents would receive in Harris's world is blame for passing on bad genes (as if they had knowledge of these) or for putting the child in a bad neighborhood where delinquency was common (as if they had complete control over their economic circumstances).

An adoption study conducted by Beaver and colleagues (2015) examined the relationship between a host of parenting variables such as parental involvement and attachment as related to engagement of their child/children in criminal behavior. Although many of the parenting variables significantly predicted the criminal outcomes among non-adopted participants, none were significant among adoptees. Using adoptees allowed the researcher to control for genetic influence and the results support Harris's criticism of the nurture assumption. Results such as these support Harris's claim that studies which fail to control for genetic influence may produce findings that mistakenly lead us to blame the environment and parenting practices. We might, for example, find a strong correlation between the number of criminal acts the parent engages in and the number of delinquent acts of a child. It is certainly reasonable to attribute this transmission of criminal behavior to learning (i.e., the parents modeled the behavior). However, it is also likely that if we controlled for genetically transmitted traits such as impulsivity, the link between parent behaviors and child behaviors becomes one that we can better understand on a biological level. The fact that Harris's theory and the research it has inspired may cause lawmakers, prosecutors, and the courts to rethink attempts to hold parents legally responsible for their child's behavior speaks to the applied value of group socialization theory.

Misrepresenting psychological science in the media

Guiding question: Did the media report include appropriate interpretations of the study and cautious generalizations and conclusions drawn?

While there are some legitimate criticisms of Harris's theory, some are unwarranted, based on a misrepresentation of Harris's argument. Unfortunately, there is also a long history of the media misreporting the findings of psychological research. Although psychologists usually are cautious about the conclusions that can be drawn from their studies in terms of generalization and implications, the media, motivated to grab a reader's/viewer's attention, is not as restrained. Even ten years after the publication of Harris's book *The Nurture Assumption*, in which there was sufficient time to read the book and digest the arguments, a Question and Answer article on an interview with Judith Rich Harris on the state of her theory is titled, "Why parents still don't matter." As psychologist Samuel Mehr (2015) has noted, selling psychological science to the general public with catchy titles is not, by itself, bad. It's the gross misrepresentation of the science that's a problem and this Mehr has personally experienced.

> **KEY READING** – Mehr, S. A. (2015). Miscommunication of science: Music cognition research in the popular press. *Frontiers in Psychology*, *6*, 1–3.

Mehr and colleagues (2013) examined the effects of a brief musical enrichment program (compared to an art enrichment program and a control group) on the cognitive skills of preschoolers. They did not find significant differences among the groups. The title of their published article was "Two randomized trials provide no consistent evidence for nonmusical cognitive benefits of brief preschool music enrichment." The media reported the results of this study with the following headlines by suggesting that the researchers had found evidence that music does not provide any cognitive benefits (e.g., "Academic benefits 'a myth'"; "Music doesn't make you smarter, Harvard study finds"). The cleverest headline, unfortunately, was also the most inaccurate: "Do, Re, Mi, Fa-get the piano lessons: Music may not make you smarter." The problem, noted Mehr (2015), was that "we studied neither piano lessons nor general intelligence" (p. 2). Another issue in the reporting of the research was that the authors found evidence in support of the **null hypothesis** rather than failing to reject it.

There were many cautionary statements about the study and results (as there often are in the discussion section of articles). For example in the Mehr and colleagues (2013) article, the authors noted the following:

> We might have observed cognitive benefits of music classes had the classes continued for a longer time [the program lasted for six weeks]. (pp. 9–10)

> We might have observed transfer effects had our music curriculum involved more intense music instruction. (p. 10)

> The lack of consistent positive effects in our studies might be due to our choice to use tests of specific cognitive abilities instead of a general IQ measure. (p. 10)

> We note the possibility of "sleeper effects": there may be effects of brief musical experiences that do not emerge immediately following music training. (p. 10)

Often these cautionary notes do not make their way into the eye-gripping media headlines, but are nonetheless important because they reinforce the notion that the researchers "failed to reject the null hypothesis." In other words, the researchers did not find evidence that music does not improve cognitive functioning, rather they failed to provide evidence that it does improve cognitive skills. The results of their study does not mean that *there is no effect* or that there is no effect to be found, but that they did not find an effect in this study. That there is *no effect* is among the possibilities, but the other possibilities remain (see Table 3.2). For example, as they noted, it may be that a longer intervention may produce a benefit in cognitive abilities. A statement that they found evidence of no effect would mean that they have been able to rule out all of these possible differences that may produce an effect (Dallal, 2002).

Table 3.2   *Possible explanations for the finding of an effect or failure to find an effect*

There is no effect	Did not find an effect
~~A longer intervention~~	A longer intervention might be needed in order to see the impact
~~More intense musical instruction~~	More intense musical instruction could possibly lead to the expected outcome
~~Different tests~~	Different tests might produce different results
~~Sleeper effect~~	Sleeper effect (more time might be needed to see the impact of the intervention)
No effect	No effect

Mehr (2015) notes a couple of typical errors that the media make in reporting findings. The first is reporting the results of correlations studies in a way that suggests one variable was found to cause the other. For example, imagine that you were reading a study in which researchers reported a correlation between watching television and obesity. Adolescents in the study were asked about how much television they watched per week and were asked to report their weight. It would not be surprising to see a report of this study in a popular magazine with the headline "Study finds watching television leads to obesity." The study, however, did not find that watching television caused obesity. It may be the case that obesity leads to more television watching or that there is a third variable related to both (e.g., a personality trait such as conscientiousness or a tendency to eat more junk food while watching television) that explains the actual cause of obesity. Sound familiar? Imagine how the media might report the socialization studies discussed earlier.

The second consistent problem in media reports of psychological research is inaccuracy in reporting the measures used. For example, Mehr points to a study on the effects of music on memory in which memory was assessed using word recall. The study was reported as finding an effect of music on vocabulary. The previously mentioned study by Mehr and colleagues involved cognitive skills assessment, but the media reported on assessing IQ. Obviously, there are many types of IQ tests that measure different facets or components of intelligence. In fact, psychologists often disagree on even the definition of intelligence (e.g., Does intelligence include creativity?). There are also many cognitive skills not depicted in traditional IQ tests such as the Wechsler and Binet versions. What about measures of social and emotional intelligence? The problem with such media inaccuracies is that they are not so easily corrected; they tend to stick in the minds of recipients.

Now let's return to Harris's theory; media reports tended to exaggerate her claims about the role parents play in their children's lives. Harris (2009) explains the media misrepresentation in the introduction to the second edition of *The Nurture Assumption*:

> This proposition [that parents have no lasting influence on their children's personalities or on the way they behave outside the home] doesn't mean that parents are unimportant – they have other roles to play in their children's lives. But the subtleties were lost when the media compressed my argument into three little words. "Do parents matter?" asked the cover of *Newsweek* (p. xvii).

Readers need to be alert for extreme positions taken by authors that might evoke a passionate one-sided, simplistic, and an overly emotional response to produce "shock and awe." For example, Harris writes in her 1995 Psychological Review article:

> *Do parents have any important long-term effects on the development of their child's personality? This article examines the evidence and concludes that the answer is no.*

Such a strongly worded position encourages the media and readers to oversimplify the topic rather than logically examine what parents **and** peer groups bring to the table in the complex topic of parenting and child development. However, Harris is not without blame for the media exaggeration.

Chapter summary

Let us return to the Tiger Mom example referenced earlier in order to summarize Harris's group socialization theory. Harris would argue that the Chua children turned out the way they did not because of the parenting practices, but because they were raised in a neighborhood and school environment consisting of individuals who valued hard work, learning, education, etc. Harris would also argue that the Chua children are smart, successful, and conscientious because they inherited these tendencies from their smart, successful, conscientious parents. If the Chua family had moved when the children were young to a neighborhood with different values (e.g., where education was not valued) the children would likely have turned out differently. Likewise, if the Chuas stayed put and a family with two kids from this neighborhood in which education is not valued moved next door to the Chuas, you could see a different outcome among these children. The school environment and the neighborhood are the most powerful forces of socialization according to Harris. Chua gets undue credit, or blame, in some cases, for her parenting. Let us also return to items #2 and #4 in the nature/nurture task at the beginning of the chapter. Are poor and effective parenting practices rightly classified as nature or nurture? The answer from Harris and behavior genetics is "both." In fact, modern genetics would suggest that it is inappropriate to represent all of the influences at the beginning of the chapter as dichotomous. Lastly, Harris would suggest that #3, if referring to peer influences, is the prevailing environmental influence.

Group socialization theory proposes that the primary agents of socialization, agents that play a prominent role in the formation of adult personality, are peer groups rather than parents. Harris brings attention to the limitations of much socialization research and uses behavior genetics research which points to the importance of genes and the non-shared environment to support her theory. Critics, however, point to contemporary developmental research that better addresses the relative influence of parents and peers and attachment research that highlights the importance of parents. However, most contemporary developmental studies still leave open the question of the influence of parenting practices beyond what is accounted for by genes and, thus, Harris's group socialization theory remains an important caution to developmental researchers and critical readers of the literature.

Future directions

The nature versus nurture debates began with scholars taking extreme positions such as the musical genius of Mozart and the intellectual giftedness of Einstein were due to natural endowment (nature). Then the environmentalists argued persuasively that the external environment (nurture) was crucial for developing whatever we inherited through our genetic backgrounds. Next, the arguments shifted to the position that both are important and it is the relative importance of nature or nurture in a given contextual example that should be considered. The Harris group socialization theory approach argues for determining what is most crucial within the nurture domain. Obviously, both parents *and* the peer group play a crucial role in child development. Contemporary developmental psychology utilizes more complex methodology than the studies Harris targeted in her critique of the field (Collins, Maccoby, Steinberg, Hetherington, & Bornstein, 2000). Yet, as we have seen, even methods attempting to account for additive genetic and environmental inputs are limited by significant gene-environment interactions. Thus, future research that accounts for how genetic influences are shaped through interactions with environments will be particularly valuable. Look for future studies to emphasize the role of various forms of nurture in specific contextual circumstances.

Finally, critical thinkers will need to be alert to the social and political implications for public policy that emerge from any and all research findings.

Discussion questions

1. At the same time as we might be critical of the media for exaggeration, in this age, when there is so much research, do even competent scientists have to state their arguments in very strong terms if they are to get anyone to pay attention to them?
2. Especially when we are younger, we are often with our parents outside the home and observe how they behave with others. We might observe how they interact with other adults they may invite home for dinners, parties, etc. To the extent that these observations affected our behavior long into the future, do they raise questions about Harris' theory?

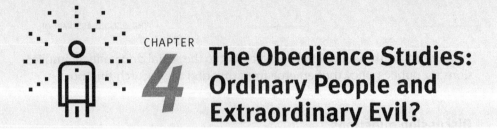

4 The Obedience Studies: Ordinary People and Extraordinary Evil?

Primary source: Milgram, S. (1974). Obedience to authority: An experimental view. New York: HarperCollins.

Chapter objectives

This chapter will help you become a better critical thinker by:

- Evaluating the experimental realism of Milgram's methods
- Considering how generalizable the results on obedience are outside of the laboratory
- Examining the importance of consistency across conditions in a study
- Contemplating the value of theories to guide psychological research
- Evaluating the ethical challenges of studying obedience in the laboratory

Introduction

How authority oriented are you?

Consider your personal response to the following questions:

1. Did you do things as a child/adult that were expected, even though you did not agree with such actions?
2. Might you have felt guilty for disappointing authority figures such as your parents, teachers, bosses, etc.?
3. If you make a deal (promise or contract), how likely are you to follow through on your commitment?
4. Would you do something that conflicted with your personal values that an authority figure asked of you if you had a trusted friend at your side who openly challenged the authority figure?

Do you think your answers to the questions above reveal how you might respond in a situation in which you are instructed by an authority figure to engage in a harmful act?

Notice that the initial question posed was how "authority oriented" are you? Whether your answers to the above questions suggested a high or low orientation to authority, it is important to ask what such an orientation represents. Is it a component of personality in which there are vast individual differences or is it a product of one's culture in which individual differences may be constrained? Answers to these questions should come from studies that attempt to predict obedience to authority figures from personality measures and compare levels of obedience across cultures and generations. If these answers fail to support either contention, then we have to carefully consider the situational factors and how those situational factors are experienced. If the answer lies in situational forces, we may have to conclude that the above question reveals little about how one might respond when presented with destructive instructions from an authority figure. Let us consider the possibilities.

Study background

In the early 1960s psychologist Stanley Milgram conducted a series of experiments on obedience that are among the most famous and controversial in psychology. Milgram wanted to understand the obedience to authority evident in the atrocities committed against Jews and others during the Second World War. As a situationist, he focused his investigations on the situational forces that act on an individual (Blass, 2004). In order to examine these forces, Milgram put his research participants in a situation in which they were asked to comply with requests to harm another person. Initially, participants believed that they were participating in a study on the effects of punishment on learning. They had responded to an ad in the paper and were given the following details about the study when they arrived at the lab:

> Psychologists have developed several theories to explain how people learn various types of material ... One theory is that people learn things correctly whenever they get punished for making a mistake ... But actually we know very little about the effect of punishment on learning, because almost no truly scientific studies have been made of it in human beings ... So in this study we are bringing together a number of adults of different occupations and ages. And we're asking some of them to be teachers and some of them to be learners. We want to find out just what effect different people have on each other as teachers and learners, and also what effect punishment will have on learning in this situation. (Milgram, 1974, p. 18)

The experimenter drew names for the role of teacher and learner; however, this drawing was rigged so that the participant was always assigned the role of teacher. The teacher and learner were then taken to another room where the learner would be hooked up to a shock generator with 30 switches ranging from 15 volts (slight shock) to 450 volts (danger: severe shock). Milgram went to great lengths to make sure the situation was believable. Not only did he have the shock generator custom-built for the study by a Yale employee

(Blass, 2004), but also had the teacher receive a real "test" shock (45 volts). After the shock, the teacher returned to the previous room, was situated in front of the shock machine and read a list of word pairs to the learner (e.g., tree–dog, old–sun etc.). The learner was then given one of the words (e.g., tree) and choices for the correct paired word (e.g., sun, old, and dog) where by the learner would select his/her option. If he/she got the word wrong, the teacher would have to administer a 15-volt shock and increase the shocks in 15-volt increments with each additional wrong answer. The learner, by design, purposefully did a poor job on the task getting three incorrect for every correct answer. The study would end when either the teacher delivered the maximum 450-volt shock three times or the teacher decided to stop. Teachers often expressed hesitation about continuing because in the most often cited version of the experiment, participants were told that the learner had a history of heart problems and responded to the shocks at various points in the experiment in ways that indicated he was in pain and refused to continue (see Figure 4.1). Upon hesitation from the teacher, the experimenter put pressure on him through the use of four scripted "prods," the first of which politely provided by the teacher to "please continue" to the final one which was more forceful: "You have no other choice, you must go on" (Milgram, 1974, p. 21). Though teachers often hesitated, 65% obeyed the experimenter and delivered the 450-volt shocks!

During the 1960s Institutional Review Boards (IRBs) and Human Subject Review procedures were not in place as they are today. A case can be made for the fact that this famous study was a key factor in reminding educational institutions that they could be sued and researchers that greater safeguards were needed to protect human subjects involved when conducting experiments. Today we believe that no research study that involves the use of human subjects can guarantee that no harm will come to research participants. In other words, some risk is always involved among research participants. For example, consider responding to an innocuous appearing survey item such as: "I am so tense that my stomach is upset." This could for some respondents trigger increased anxiety both in the research setting and later after participation in the study has long been completed. The pressure placed upon some research subjects, like "You must continue the experiment," could yield stress reactions. Proper treatment of human subjects today includes the fact that any subject can decide to discontinue his/her participation in the study at any time.

If you have ever served in the military, you know the importance of the "chain of command" and "following direct orders." Milgram reminded us that obedience is more than a crucial and desirable behavioral action for military personnel. All human beings must submit to some sort of authority in life. Therefore, the significant importance of such research is easy to establish. History continues to document that humans can be kind, caring, and

120 volts	150 volts	180 volts	195 volts	210 volts	270 volts	300 volts	315 volts	330 volts
Subject indicates that the shock hurts.	Subject expresses pain and indicates that his heart is starting to bother him. Asks to be let out of experiment.	Subject indicates that he can't tolerate the pain and again asks to be let out.	Subject insists that his heart is bothering him and that no one has the right to keep him here. He demands to be let out.	Subject refuses to continue and demands that the experimenter let him out.	Subject screams in agony and demands to be released.	Subject screams in agony and refuses to answer any more questions. Demands to be released.	Subject screams in extreme agony and refuses to continue.	Subject releases prolonged scream of intense agony. Subject indicates that his heart is bothering him and demands to be released.

Figure 4.1 Learner responses (Milgram, 1974)

helpful to others, but also that humans can be cruel to others if they do not relate to them, see them as a threat or enemy, or can transfer the responsibility for mistreatment to others in higher levels of authority.

Current thinking

Did Milgram uncover an uncomfortable truth about human nature? Are we all capable of committing horrible and painful atrocities? Are we blindly obedient? The question assumes that Milgram found evidence of obedience. In one study, he did. Sixty-five percent, in fact. However, Milgram found fluctuating levels of obedience and disobedience across dozens of studies in which factors like the distance between the experimenter and the teacher were varied. In *Obedience to Authority*, Milgram (1974) reports the results of 18 variations of the study. Obedience levels in several of these were below 50%.

Why have the results of these variations been overshadowed by one producing a high level of obedience? Replications of the study have likely contributed as they have aimed at a variation (study 2) that produced high level of obedience (Burger, 2009; Doliński et al., 2017). In 2009, psychologist Jerry Burger replicated the study, but for ethical reasons did not allow participants to administer shocks beyond 150 volts. Burger found similar levels of obedience as did researchers conducting a replication in Poland (Doliński et al., 2017). How do Milgram, Burger, and Doliński and colleagues explain participants' willingness to obey? Milgram himself offered numerous explanations including the "agentic state" (Reicher, Haslam, & Smith, 2012). Milgram (1974) suggested that when one enters an agentic state, he is blindly obedient and focuses narrowly on the execution of the task itself:

> The subject typically wishes to perform competently and to make a good appearance before this central figure [the experimenter]. He directs his attention to those features of the situation required for such competent performance. He attends to the instructions, concentrates on the technical requirements of administering shocks, and finds himself absorbed in the narrow technical tasks at hand. (p. 143)

While popular, this account has been challenged and a new understanding of obedience has emerged. What appears to snap some individuals out of an agentic state in Milgram's studies is hearing cries of pain and protest from the learner. The cries, for some, had the effect of awakening teachers to their moral obligation to the learner (Packer, 2008). Up to that point, the teacher may have felt as if he/she was on the same page with the experimenter – "we are contributing to science."

Consider that in one of the variations of the study there was no vocal protest from the learner regardless of the shock level. In another variation, two experimenters seem to be at odds as they give opposing commands to the learner. These two studies produced dramatically different levels of obedience. In the "no vocal protest" condition, as you might have guessed, obedience was much higher (65%). In fact, the "two experimenters that challenged each other" condition produced no obedience (Milgram, 1974). Why such dramatically different results? In looking across all the variations, obedience was highest when the importance of the experiment and experimenter was foremost in the mind of the teacher while not enough was done to bring the well-being of the learner to the teacher's attention. Rather than mindlessly obey, Reicher and colleagues (2012) argue that people obey when they identify with the leader and the mission (e.g., "This is an important study and we are contributing to science"). Disobedience occurs when one does not "buy in" or when one identifies with another group or individual. It is as if we start such an experiment with the default mindset that this is a legitimate scientific exercise and the experimenter or learner has to do something to challenge the scientific integrity of the study. Two experimenters arguing with one another undermines their scientific credibility and has the potential to produce disobedience as does the cries of the learner (Reicher & Haslam, 2011).

Psychologist Gina Perry (2012) raised serious concerns about the Milgram studies. She uncovered evidence in Milgram's notes on the experiment that many participants suspected the shocks were fake and were more likely to disobey when they believed the shocks were real.

> **KEY READING** – Perry, G. (2012). *Behind the shock machine: The untold story of the notorious Milgram psychology experiments*. New York: The New Press.

Her investigation also raised concerns with the way the studies were executed. Though the actors that Milgram hired to play the part of the experimenter and learner had a script, it appears that John Williams, the experimenter, got creative in some conditions giving more prods than the script instructed, talking to the learner (not in the script), and arguing with participants in a coercive manner (Perry, 2012). Such inconsistency in "going off script" introduced a new variable in the study. Ethical concerns were raised as well, as it appeared that some participants were not properly **debriefed** or informed about the details after completion of the study. Some, in fact, may have left the lab believing that they had actually hurt the learner with genuine life-threatening electric voltage.

Despite the questions regarding how to explain Milgram's results, the execution of the studies, and the ethics of the study, the findings have held

up remarkably well over the decades. There have been numerous replications producing consistent rates of obedience and disobedience (Burger,
2009; Doliński et al., 2017; Haslam, Reicher, & Millard, 2015). Recall
from Chapter 3 ("Critical thinking toolkit: Evaluating a psychological theory") that empirical validity and applied value are among the criteria for
evaluating a theory. Pratkanis (2017) notes that Milgram (and his con-
temporaries) succeeded in establishing both. Milgram "provided a set of
reliable experimental operations (that have been effectively used by others)
... and research showing which factors increase and decrease the effect."
Additionally, notes Pratkanis, "His research gives insight into how simply
unbelievable events – the Holocaust of the Jews and genocides in general –
can happen" (p. 158).

Reluctance to criticize

Since many psychological scientists have challenged the methods and conclusions of Milgram it is worth exploring the study with a critical eye. Before
we begin, however, it is also worth considering why we may be reluctant to
critically examine such a study. Wilson and colleagues (1993) found that
even among seasoned academics there was a tendency to be so persuaded
by the importance of a study that they overlooked some key flaws in its
design and conclusions. The reasoning goes like this: If you have read the
textbook account of the Milgram studies, then you know the significance. By
most accounts, Milgram's obedience studies were a forceful demonstration
of the power of the situation to create obedience among normal, average,
ordinary individuals. Milgram identified an inherent "obedience" weakness
in all of us. As uncomfortable as it is to admit, most of us are all capable
of hurting others and being a cog in a genocidal machine, if certain conditions were present to encourage this behavior. Setting aside the importance
of the study and looking at it more closely is our continual challenge in this
chapter.

Did the participants believe they were delivering shocks?

Social psychology research commonly relies on the use of deception in experiments. In other words, researchers disguise the true purpose of the study by
creating a false purpose or **cover story** because knowing the true nature of
the experiment would likely affect the results (see **experimenter effects and
demand characteristics** in Chapter 6). The cover story needs to be plausible and delivered in a convincing and believable manner. Additionally, the
experimenter needs to be consistent across the conditions in terms of how
he/she interacts with participants, as even slight variations – for example,
the clothing worn or smiles provided to only some respondents by the experimenter – might have the potential to influence the behavior of participants
(Harmon-Jones, Amodio, & Zinner, 2007). In fact, clothing was important in

the obedience studies, as Milgram wanted the experimenter to wear a gray rather than a white lab coat so that participants would not confuse him for a medical doctor (Blass, 2004).

Before we discuss the Milgram results in more detail, let us return to the cover story for a moment. The attention to detail in trying to sell the cover story is extraordinary as evidenced by the thought put into the label of the shock generator that included a fictitious company based in Waltham, Massachusetts (Milgram, 1974). Milgram hired a high school biology teacher and an accountant to play the role of experimenter and learner (the participant would assume the role of teacher). In spite of such attention to detail, there is evidence, as discussed in the remainder of this section, that some participants had suspicions.

Milgram did attempt to assess the extent to which participants believed they were administering shocks by having them complete a follow-up questionnaire using a **Likert scale**. A Likert scale provides participants with an opportunity to indicate their level of agreement or disagreement with a collection of statements. Psychologists often use such scales to assess attitudes.

In the scales designed by Milgram, the responses ranged from (1) I fully believed the learner was getting painful shocks to (5) I was certain the learner was not getting the shocks. Though more than half of the participants indicated that they fully believed the learner was getting shocks and very few participants indicated that they were *certain* the learner was not receiving shocks, nearly one-fourth endorsed the following item: "Although I had some doubts, I believed the learner was probably getting shocks." Interpretation of this item seems to depend on your overall assessment of the research. In other words, Milgram lumped those who endorsed this item with those who endorsed the first item and suggested that roughly 75% of participants believed they were administering painful shocks. Critics, however, interpreted the results as suggesting that roughly 50% bought the cover story (those who endorsed item (1) and roughly 50% did not (all those who endorsed all the other items including number (2)). A replication attempt reported by Orne and Holland (1968) reported even higher levels of uncertainty with three-fourths of participants reporting suspicion.

Orne and Holland (1968) believed that participants in the Milgram studies could figure out the purpose of the study. Psychologist Gina Perry (2012), looking through Milgram's notes on the experiment, not only found evidence of suspicions raised by participants (see Table 4.1), but one of Milgram's research assistants made the following observation that raised doubts about Milgram's conclusions when he found that participants were more likely to disobey and to give lower level shocks when they believed the shocks were real. These concerns about how well the cover story worked and whether or not the participants realized the shocks were not real led to questions about the ecological validity of the study which we will address next.

Table 4.1 Suspicions raised by some participants (from Perry, 2012)

Surprised at how the experimenter did not react to the learner noting that he had a heart condition.	Thought psychologists knew that punishment was ineffective.
Why was the learner not given the check for participation at the same time that the teacher was paid?	Why wasn't the learner given a sample shock?
How was it possible that the learner would mention a history of heart trouble and this would not raise concerns from the experimenter?	Cries of learner did not seem real (sounds like a recording).
The learner did so poorly on the memory test that it was not believable.	Why is the experimenter watching me and not the learner who is potentially being hurt?
Suspicious that Yale would allow a learner to be subjected to such harsh shocks.	Descriptions on the shock generator seemed inauthentic (e.g., strong shock).
Why is there a loudspeaker in the corner of the room?	Why am I in a separate room from that of the learner?

Critical thinking toolkit
Ecological validity

Guiding question: How generalizable are the results outside of the laboratory?

Imagine you won a contest to visit the set of your favorite zombie program (e.g., *The Walking Dead*) and the director, while showing you around, orders you to pick up one of the guns on the set and shoot a zombie. "No problem," you say as you pick up the gun and fire away. Does this tell us anything about the likelihood of you obeying a similar order outside the context of a zombie television show studio set? You would likely say "no" because you made a very important assumption about the reality of this situation based on your knowledge of fantasy television shows. Psychologists Martin Orne and Charles Holland (1968) suggested that some important assumptions uniquely apply to the psychological experiment as well which can limit their **ecological validity**. As a participant, I assume that I am playing an important role in contributing to the advancement of science and will therefore do what the experimenter asks and expects. We also assume that the experimenter will not harm participants.

If participants obey the scientist in the laboratory because of these assumptions, what do the results tell us about obedience outside the confines of the lab? When we have concerns about whether the results generalize outside of the laboratory we are raising doubts about the study's ecological validity. Erich Fromm, who questioned the ecological validity of the Stanford Prison study (Chapter 6), raised similar concerns about Milgram's study. He, like Orne and Holland (1968), suggested that the influence of someone representing science is uniquely influential and carries the assumption that what is being done is for the good of people and could not be immoral (Fromm, 1973).

In response to the ecological validity criticism, Sheridan and King (1972) sought to demonstrate that participants in the Milgram studies were not "playing along" or simply electing to shock learners knowing that the shocks were fake. The solution: administer actual shocks! Though this procedure might provide little comfort for pet owners and animal rights advocates, the real shocks were delivered to a puppy and not a human subject. Obedience rates for male participants were similar to those produced by Milgram; however, all 13 female participants administered the maximum level of shocks!

Lastly, an interesting result emerged in the Sheridan and King study. Some subjects tried to "coax" the puppies to avoid the shock, tried to minimize the shock by quickly flipping the switch, and lied to the experimenter telling him that the puppies had solved the problem (which was actually unsolvable). Did such efforts reflect disobedience among the participants?

Disobedience in the Milgram studies

In which of the following Milgram variations would you expect participants to call into question the legitimacy of the experiment or experimenter? Which would cause participants to think about the needs of and identify with the learner? Consider the following variations and which ones produced more obedience and which ones more disobedience:

Experiment 7: *After giving initial instructions, the experimenter leaves the lab and gives further instructions by telephone.*

Experiment 10: *The lab is moved to an office building in an industrial city and the study has no ties to a prestigious university.*

Experiment 13: *The experimenter is called away and an ordinary man who appears to be a participant takes over the experimenter's role and comes up with the idea of increasing shocks each time the learner makes a mistake.*

Experiment 4: *The learner rather than being in another room is in the same room as the teacher. The teacher has to place the learner's hand on a shock plate for him to receive a shock. At 350 volts the learner refuses to place his hand on the shock plate. The experimenter orders the teacher to force the learner's hand onto the plate.*

Experiment 9: *The teacher and learner sign a release stating, "In participating in this experimental research of my own free will, I release Yale University and its employees from any legal claims arising from my participation." When signing this, the learner says he has a heart condition and that "I'll agree to be in it, but only on the condition that you let me out when I say."*

If you said all these variations produced more disobedience than obedience, you are correct. One factor that reduced obedience was decreasing the physical distance between the teacher and the learner. With the teacher and the learner in the same room, obedience dropped to 40% and when the experimenter had to touch the learner to administer shocks (Experiment #4), obedience dropped to 30%. Obedience also dropped below 50% when the experimenter left the laboratory and gave the orders from the phone (Experiment #7), when the experiment was conducted in a building away from Yale University (Experiment #10), when the experimental authority is the victim, and when two authorities give conflicting commands. Another manipulation that was successful in producing disobedience was having two other teachers (confederates) go ahead of the actual participant. Teacher 1 refused to administer shocks beyond 150 volts and teacher 2 stopped at 210 volts. Both Burger's replication and an earlier one (Rosenhan, 1968) attempted to replicate this modeling of obedience finding (Experiment #17) in which 30% of participants (teacher 3) stopped at 210 volts and only 10% of participants delivered the maximum voltage. Both replication attempts, however, found that the majority of participants in modeled disobedience conditions still obeyed. Perhaps the key difference between the two studies and Milgram's study was that only one participant modeled disobedience whereas in Milgram's two actors had modeled disobedience.

Disobedience in the Milgram studies did not necessarily involve the participant refusing to continue; more subtle forms of disobedience were evident as well. In Milgram's studies, the teacher was administering a memory test which required the learner to select the correct match from word pairs. In a replication study by Bégue and colleagues (2017), the authors found that nearly a quarter of participants engaged in non-compliance by trying to "cheat" and help the learner avoid shocks by vocally accentuating the correct answer. Such results are similar to what we saw in the Sheridan and King (1972) study.

Lastly, recall that Milgram had the experimenter use four prods when participants were hesitant to continue. Look at the prods below and consider which would be the most inappropriate for an experimenter to use in a study. Which would a participant in a study be least likely to hear from an experimenter?

Prod #1: "Please continue"
Prod #2: "The experiment requires that you continue"
Prod #3: "It is absolutely essential that you continue"
Prod #4: "You have no other choice, you must go on"

If you said the last one, "You have no other choice, you must go on," you are correct. What is different about this prod? Prod #4 is clearly a direct order and not something that you would expect to hear from an experimenter. Replications have found near zero obedience when this prod is given (Burger, Girgis, & Manning, 2011; Haslam et al., 2015). Recall that as long as the experimenter does not do anything to disrupt our assumption about the integrity of the scientific study and our tendency to identify with the experimenter, we might expect considerable obedience. Also, recall that the Milgram studies are often taken as evidence of blind obedience to authority, our tendency to follow orders. These results turn this idea on its head. It seems clear that the levels of disobedience produced in Milgram variations along with the non-compliance and resistance to Prod #4 in Milgram's studies and replications suggest that blind obedience is far too simple a conclusion.

Internal validity

There are, of course, planned differences between the experimental and the control groups as researchers are manipulating the independent variable in a study. Researchers want to eliminate or reduce any other differences between the groups so they can say with confidence that this independent treatment variable produced the differences in the dependent variable. In Burger's (2009) replication of Milgram's study, the experimenter, the same person throughout the experiment, used the same prods, in the same order, that Milgram employed. Keeping to the script is extremely important to the internal validity of the study and was likely much easier to do so in the much less extensive study that Burger conducted. Burger noted that only slight variations in the wording of the prods would occur to avoid sounding repetitious. In order to appreciate the importance of "staying on script," imagine the experimenter joking with participants in one study and not in the next, wearing the gray lab coat in one, but not the other, being polite in one condition and rude in the next. These all introduce potential **confounds** or confounding variables. Though the actors that Milgram hired to play the part of the experimenter and learner had a script, it appears that John Williams, the man hired to play the experimenter, strayed from the script in some conditions by giving more prods than the script instructed, talking to the learner (not in the script), and arguing with participants in a coercive manner (Perry, 2012).

A theoretical account

Though not all variations of the study produced obedience, it is still surprising that many participants across the variations were willing to administer all the shocks. One factor appears to have been the gradual increase in shocks (15-volt increments). Do you think participants would have administered a 450-volt shock after the first wrong answer if instructed? Psychologist Steven Gilbert (1981) did not think so. He argued that the gradual shock allowed the commitment of the participant to gain "momentum" and allowed the participant an opportunity to justify quitting. In other words, if the participants are willing to administer a 135-volt shock, then why not a minimally stronger 150-volt shock? A look back at Milgram's results seems to support the momentum hypothesis, but Milgram did not directly test this hypothesis.

One of the weaknesses of Milgram's research was that there was no theory guiding the studies. **Theories** help organize and explain observations or results from research and help us formulate testable predictions or **hypotheses**. These educated guesses allow us to add support to existing evidence or further question the effectiveness of the theory. With respect to momentum, Milgram might have hypothesized that obedience rates would be lower in an all-or-nothing condition in which participants have to administer a 450-volt shock than in a condition in which participants start low and administer increasingly severe shocks.

Though Milgram did not have an a priori theory to account for the results, he did speculate that they could be understood in terms of participants entering an "agentic state" during the experiment. Milgram (1974) described this state as one in which the individual, overwhelmed by situational forces, feels less like he is autonomous or acting according to his own desires and more like an "agent" carrying out the experimenter's wishes. Milgram's findings have, however, been interpreted through contemporary theories including **moral disengagement theory** (Bandura et al., 1996). Bandura (1999) argued people are more likely to engage in morally reprehensible behavior when they do not feel personally responsible for their actions. He proposed that Milgram's results are consistent with the theory because obedience was higher when the experimenter was likely perceived as legitimate and when the experimenter was closer to the learner.

Reicher and colleagues (2012) argue that identification with the group is the key to explaining a participant's behavior in the Milgram studies. They argue, through **social identity theory**, that the participant is most likely to identify with the experimenter at the start of the study, but this identification is challenged at several points in the study. As noted, one example is the fourth prod in which the teacher is given a direct command (you must go on) and the other when the learner objects to continuing in the experiment. These points lead to an alternative identification, that with the learner.

These researchers had participants read a brief description of Milgram's variations and then estimate the level of identification with the experimenter and learner. Obedience was positively correlated with their perceptions of identification with the experimenter and negatively correlated with identification with the learner. The idea that identification with the experimenter or learner was the determining factor in whether or not someone obeyed is further supported by one of Milgram's experiments that was never published (Rochat & Blass, 2014). In this condition participants brought a friend with them (e.g., a neighbor) and one of them would be the teacher and one the learner. Not only is identification with the friend stronger from the outset, but during the memory test the learner is talking directly to the teacher and not the experimenter (and the teacher is speaking to the learner). Among the 20 participants in this condition, only three were obedient and nearly half stopped by or before the 150-volt shock level.

Power of the situation

Milgram, like fellow social psychologist Zimbardo (Stanford Prison study; Chapter 6), was a situationist who believed that contextual forces can overpower a person's character, values, morals, or personality traits. Both studies support a narrative that destructive acts are not committed by evil people but by ordinary people that are overwhelmed by the situation. Zimbardo's prison guards were ordinary college students, Milgram's teachers were ordinary adults, but their behavior was anything but ordinary or at least expected. Yet, it is easy to lose sight of the fact that not all of Zimbardo's prison guards were abusive and not all of Milgram's participants obeyed. In fact, half or less than half of participants were obedient in 13 of Milgram's conditions. This raises an interesting but often ignored question of what the difference is between those who obey and those who do not in such situations. In Burger's (2009) replication of Milgram's study, he did assess personality attributes. Though empathy did not predict disobedience, it was associated with earlier reluctance to continue the experiment.

KEY READING – Burger, J. M. (2009). Replicating Milgram: Would people still obey today? *American Psychologist*, *64*, 1–11.

Logical fallacies

Zimbardo (2007) also reported high empathy scores among two of the "good guards" in the Stanford Prison study. Personality traits may, at best, be moderately predictive of how someone acts in a situation like those created by Zimbardo and Milgram. Traits have the potential to be strong predictors of how someone acts across time and situations rather than how a person will act at any one point in time in a specific situation (Fleeson, 2004). The Milgram experiments may not suggest that we are all blindly obedient (Haslam & Reicher, 2012), but Milgram's results do suggest that we would be wise to promote both situational awareness and empathy to combat blind obedience. Another takeaway from the Milgram studies is that we do need to be aware of the **argument from authority fallacy** or arguments/claims that rest solely on the authority of the person advancing the position, whether that is an eminent scientist in a gray lab coat or a high-ranking government official wearing an Armani suit (Kida, 2006).

Ethical challenges

Though there were certainly numerous researchers who challenged Milgram's findings and conclusions over the years, ethical concerns have perhaps been the most prominent reactions. As with the Stanford Prison study, we want to avoid justifying such research by employing a **two wrongs make a right fallacy**: the suffering of participants in Milgram's studies is justified because, for example, other psychologists (e.g., Zimbardo) have put participants through worse. Similarly, those who have conducted ethically questionable studies would be in the position to argue that those criticizing them have themselves engaged in ethically questionable practices. This **tu quoque**, or "you too," **fallacy** detracts from rather than helps us logically evaluate arguments about the ethics of research (Van Vleet, 2011).

Psychologist Diana Baumrind was concerned about the potential long-term harm caused to participants in the Milgram studies and the potential harm caused to the field of psychology by using deception in research (Baumrind, 1964, 1985). Milgram described a **debriefing** procedure in which every participant was told that the learner had not received shocks and obedient subjects were reassured that their behavior was not out of the ordinary (Milgram, 1974). Critics were unconvinced that such strong emotional conflict displayed by participants was effectively dealt with during this debriefing (Baumrind, 1964; Perry, 2012). Even more serious a concern was that not all of the participants in the studies were told before they left the laboratory that the shocks were not real. In fact, for some it may not have been until a year after their participation (Perry, 2012). It is important, however, when examining the ethics of the Milgram studies, to keep it in historical context. In doing so, we might come to the conclusion that Milgram was ahead of his time in terms of his post-experimental treatment of participants as there were no specific IRB guidelines at the time (Blass, 2004). As mentioned earlier in the chapter, Human Subjects Reviews that are part of IRB policies are now commonplace in many, though not all, research settings around the world.

There are many subjects in psychology that present ethical challenges as they are associated with creating psychological distress. In an attempt to strike the right balance, researchers often times recreate distress that is thought to be *qualitatively* similar, and thus ecologically valid, yet *quantitatively* less intense. For example, in order to better understand post-traumatic stress disorder (PTSD) it would certainly be unethical to expose participants to harsh trauma in order to generate PTSD. However, researchers might expose participants to film scenes that depict trauma and produce emotional responses that are similar to those seen in PTSD, but are less intense and only temporary (Weidmann et al., 2009). However, we might still question if the legitimate PTSD symptoms would emerge while sitting in a comfortable seat watching a film clip. Perhaps the anxiety created while watching a film scene is qualitatively different than an actual PTSD response. Such a study, considered an **analogue study**, may provide a more ethical avenue for studying obedience in the laboratory. In the next section, we will consider how such methodological advances allow us to continue to study obedience.

Logical fallacies

Lastly, in terms of the ethical implications of the Milgram studies, a quick perusal of online headlines of the Milgram studies will reveal references to "obedience is in our nature." If we accepted the "we are obedient by nature" interpretation of the Milgram studies, we would have a convenient justification for our own and others' obedient, destructive behavior. Aside from the contested results of Milgram's work, vague appeals to "human nature" or an individual's "nature" does not make for sound reasoning. The fact that something is natural is not, by itself, a basis for evaluating its goodness (**appeal to nature fallacy**) or determining that it is morally right (**naturalistic fallacy**; Bennett, 2015). Equally faulty is the reasoning on the other side of the coin, the **subjectivist fallacy**: "That may be true for others, but it's not for me" (Van Vleet, 2011).

Chapter summary

Stanley Milgram conducted a series of studies on obedience in the 1960s. In the most cited of Milgram's variations, 65% of participants were willing to deliver a potentially lethal 450-volt shock to, as far as they knew, a fellow participant in a learning study. In the decades since the study, the results have been interpreted as a demonstration of our tendency to blindly follow orders which Milgram referred to as an agentic state. Critics have raised concerns about the extent to which participants were aware of the deception employed in the study and have argued that the results do not generalize outside of the laboratory. More problematic for the blind obedience interpretation of results is the fact that several variations within Milgram's studies failed to produce obedience among many participants. How the participant responded seems to depend on the extent to which he identified with the experimenter or learner. Also concerning was the inconsistency of the actor playing the role of experimenter and the failure of Milgram to fully debrief all participants in a timely fashion. Consideration of these shortcomings and the strength of alternative explanations should cause us to critically evaluate the conclusion of widespread blind obedience. Nonetheless, the Milgram studies stand as an important corrective benchmark shift away from our tendency to explain behavior in terms of the characteristics of the person and ignore situational factors.

Future directions

Milgram's obedience studies created a paradox. He opened Pandora's Box and an incredibly important area of study emerged. Unfortunately, Milgram utilized procedures that were so ethically troubling that researchers were unable to engage in further study. A common response to such ethically concerning studies like Milgram's is that "it could never be conducted today." Yet, as is the case with other controversial studies, there have been replications that rectify or appease the ethical concerns. Burger's (2009) replication utilized a number of ethical safeguards including stopping at 150 volts rather than 450 volts. Slater and colleagues (2006) took the Milgram paradigm into the virtual reality lab and presented participants with a task similar in most ways to that of Milgram's studies. Slater and colleagues were able to produce a high level of realism, yet less distress among participants in replicating Milgram's results. Haslam, Reicher, and Millard (2015) were able to study obedience in the lab by using actors to play the role of participants in the study (referred to as Immersive Digital Realism). The creativity and resourcefulness of these researchers have sparked renewed interest in the study of obedience and have led to important developments in the understanding of conformity and compliance.

Discussion questions

1. What parallels might you see between Zimbardo's and Milgram's study? Consider the domains of social versus individual (personal) control;

personal choice versus the diffusion of responsibility for actions; pain and punishment as a tool for social control; and moral and ethical considerations.

2. Other than empathy, what personality traits do you think may be influential in terms of how someone responds as a participant in Milgram's study?

5 On Being Sane in Insane Places: Pseudopatients or Pseudoscience?

Primary source: Rosenhan, D. L. (1973). On being sane in insane places. *Science, 179,* 250–258.

Chapter objectives

This chapter will help you become a better critical thinker by:

- Considering the strengths and limitations of a naturalistic observation
- Examining the impact of confirmation bias on research and scientific progress
- Assessing the researcher's attempts to avoid confirmation bias
- Evaluating the evidence used to support Rosenhan's conclusions
- Appraising the evidence used to support labeling theory

Introduction

Imagine the individual pictured here sitting in the hallway of the psychology department at your school during finals week talking to himself. He has not been diagnosed with any form of mental illness, as far as you know. In this situation, you might infer that he is nervous about an upcoming Psychology exam. Now, imagine he is sitting in the hallway of a psychiatric institution talking to himself. Days earlier, he was admitted and diagnosed with schizophrenia. How do you interpret his behavior? What about that rather blank stare? What do you make of his left hand gesture? Are these non-verbal expressions further evidence that he is mentally ill? Which of the following would influence the way in which you interpret the behavior:

A) The setting or the psychiatric institution?
B) Your personal experiences?
C) Your knowledge base?
D) The diagnostic label of schizophrenia?

The study that is the focus of this chapter suggested that each of these options (A, B, C, & D) has the potential to color the interpretations of clinicians and nurses in psychiatric facilities to the degree that they cannot recognize normal behavior when they see it. That student in the hallway of the psychology department exhibiting behaviors suggestive of test anxiety is, behind the walls of the psychiatric institution, exhibiting pathological behavior. However, such bold claims demand a closer look at the study from which such conclusions are drawn. Let's take a look.

Study background

David Rosenhan's view of psychiatry was evident in the title of his celebrated study "On being sane in insane places." In other words, the psychiatric institution was to blame for mental illness, not the person. In an attempt to investigate life within a mental institution, Rosenhan and seven colleagues gained admission to 12 psychiatric hospitals in the USA. Rosenhan and company (as pseudopatients, but actually researchers) entered the hospitals complaining of voices in their head saying "empty," "hollow," and "thud." The voices or auditory hallucinations were the only symptom they reported. Other than this fictitious symptom and the use of a pseudonym or phony name, the pseudopatients presented their life histories as they actually were – relatively normal. All received a diagnosis of mental illness, and in all but one case the diagnosis was schizophrenia (note the strong interrater reliability in diagnosis here). Once admitted to the institutional setting, the pseudopatients stopped faking the hallucinations and were compliant with staff orders, spent a lot of their time taking notes, and documented their observations at the hospital. Rosenhan (1973) provided several **anecdotes** about how the pseudopatients were mistreated in the hospitals and how their behavior, even perfectly normal behavior, was now interpreted by staff through the lens of mental illness or psychopathology.

We now invite you to go back in history to better understand the social/cultural context of Rosenhan's research. The early 1970s might be seen as an outgrowth of the powerful events of the 1960s in the USA. The war in Vietnam had intensified and led more and more people to questions such as: Why are we fighting this war? It was not only this war in Southeast Asia that was questioned. The radical nature of this time soon caused people to select other domains that might ameliorate the ills of society. The Civil Rights Movement, Women's Liberation, prison reform (after the Attica Prison riot/rebellion in 1971), and the Mental Health Movement were just some of the arenas where protests occurred and change was demanded. Within such a milieu and related to the Rosenhan study, we acknowledge the influence of a radical book (banned by some high school libraries) as a key benchmark for this era. This landmark book, *One Flew Over the Cuckoo's Nest* (first published in 1962) by Ken Kesey, was adapted as a stage play and later became a well-known 1975 movie that won a total of five Academy Awards. The moving plotline of this story became an anthem in the quest to rebuild society and offered a critique of mental institutions. This story, play, and film prompted readers and viewers alike to question the effectiveness of mental hospitals, the behaviors of those who worked there, and the influential power of the medications, psychiatric treatments, and labels used on those individuals held behind bars.

As noted, once admitted, the pseudopatients made no further efforts to feign symptoms, yet Rosenhan contended that the patient's innocuous behavior was seen as further evidence of insanity by the staff. This is why, according to Rosenhan, several psychiatric nurses in Rosenhan's study made special note that patients engaged in "writing behavior." This rather ordinary behavior outside the institutional walls was seen as unusual and further evidence of illness within the institutional setting. Therefore, despite the fact that all pseudopatients stopped reporting the symptom of auditory hallucinations after being admitted, they were neither recognized as fakers nor immediately discharged by the professional staff. In fact, Rosenhan (1973) even claimed that "it was quite common for the patients to 'detect' the pseudopatient's sanity" (p. 252).

The pseudopatients were held in the institution for an average of 19 days before being released with the diagnosis: "schizophrenia in remission." Rosenhan explained that this new diagnosis meant that even though the patient's symptoms had subsided, they still had the disorder; they would always carry with them the label of schizophrenia. Outside the institution, these labels tend to lead to discrimination, which itself reinforces psychopathology (Link & Phelan, 2013). Rosenhan was troubled by the swift diagnoses based on only a single symptom. The ease with which the pseudopatients were admitted with the diagnosis of schizophrenia and kept in the hospital despite normal behavior led Rosenhan (1973) to conclude: "It is clear that we cannot distinguish the sane from the insane in psychiatric hospitals" (p. 257). Rosenhan saw psychiatric institutions as sterile and depersonalized. Physicians were physically far removed from their patients and interactions with them involved little more than a search for pathology. Interactions with staff were infrequent and hostile. Staff and patients were clearly segregated creating a sense of division, powerlessness, and depersonalization, concluded Rosenhan. According to Philip Zimbardo, the architect of the Stanford Prison study, these same institutional forces were responsible for the pathological behavior among guards and prisoners in his study (see Chapter 6). For Rosenhan, these forces were the source of pathology and dehumanization. Zimbardo, like Rosenhan, suggested that evil doesn't reside in the individual, but reveals itself when normal people are put in evil situations. It is important to note that Rosenhan's study was not the first to demonstrate the powerful effects of labels.

Nearly a decade earlier, Rosenthal and Jacobson (1966) demonstrated this in the context of schools rather than psychiatric institutions. The authors gave teachers false feedback about student potential based on an IQ test. The grade school students in the experimental condition were presented to teachers as those capable of significant intellectual gains, yet no such information about students was provided to teachers in the control condition. Eight months later, students were retested and those in the experimental condition showed greater gains than those in the control condition. The study demonstrated the power of the **self-fulfilling prophecy**, and the conclusion was that expectations on the part of the teachers led them to treat the students in such a way (e.g., providing greater attention and anticipating quality academic work) that led them to fulfill that expectation.

Current thinking

The way forward for psychiatry, suggested Rosenhan, was to eliminate the use of diagnoses and focus instead on specific behaviors like crying often or having trouble sleeping. In his critique of psychiatry, Rosenhan pointed out that mental illnesses are **constructs** or abstract ideas; they often do not exist in a physical sense. Psychiatrists agree that there are certain observable behaviors or symptoms like crying and sleeplessness that are characteristic of depression. However, depression is not directly observable; it is a construct. As Kutchins and Kirk (1997) explain, it is important for us to be aware that "constructs such as Generalized Anxiety Disorder are held together by agreements and that agreements change over time" (p. 23). Increases in the number of diagnoses of any particular disorder are influenced by the lowering of diagnostic thresholds as well as increased societal awareness (Lilienfeld et al., 2015). This does not mean that the constructs are not useful; we want to consider whether they help us understand, predict, and treat a person with such a diagnosis (Levy, 2010).

Since Rosenhan's publication in 1973, numerous critics have raised concerns about the design of the study, the interpretation of the results, and his conclusions regarding stigmatization and diagnostic labels (Ruscio, 2015; Spitzer, 1975). As displayed in Table 5.1, all of Rosenhan's interpretations of the results have been challenged. Rosenhan believed that the *schizophrenia in remission* diagnosis he and his fellow pseudopatients were given suggested that clinicians were unable to recognize them as normal. Spitzer (1975), on the other hand, argued that schizophrenia in remission was a rare diagnosis, suggesting that the clinicians recognized the patient's behavior as normal.

> **KEY READING** – Ruscio, J. (2015). Rosenhan pseudopatient study. In R. L. Cautin & S. O. Lilienfeld (Eds.), *The encyclopedia of clinical psychology* (pp. 2496–2499). Hoboken, NJ: Wiley.

Controversy over the study was reignited in 2004 when Lauren Slater, in her book *Opening Skinner's Box*, claimed to have conducted a replication of Rosenhan's study. Slater, like Rosenhan and the other pseudopatients, presented herself at psychiatric institutions for an evaluation with the chief complaint of an auditory hallucination. She did so nine times and though she was not admitted to any of the institutions, she reported being given the diagnosis of *depression with psychotic features* "most times." Additionally, she reported that she was prescribed over 80 medications. Skeptical of the diagnoses reported by Slater, Spitzer and his colleagues (Spitzer, Lilienfeld, & Miller, 2005) presented psychiatrists with a case in which a woman who looked depressed came to a psychiatric emergency room with the single complaint of an auditory hallucination. The psychiatrists in the study were asked what diagnosis, if any, they would give the patient. Contrary to Slater's results, most of the clinicians avoided any specific diagnosis. However, 34% were willing to prescribe an antipsychotic medication.

Lastly, psychology textbooks continue to cite Rosenhan's study as evidence of the stigma attached to diagnostic labels (Bartels & Peters, 2017). Aside from the flaws of the Rosenhan study, there is no evidence that stripping away the label applied to a cluster of behaviors would result in less stigma. While people might respond in a similar fashion whether labels or behaviors are used, the label has the benefit of providing an explanation for the behavior and reducing personal blame. The benefits of labels, the flaws with the Rosenhan study and other studies used to support the idea that labels produce stigma, and the fact that stigma existed long before the diagnostic system used by psychiatrists, led Scott Lilienfeld and colleagues (2010) to conclude that the idea that psychiatric labels produce stigma is a myth.

> **KEY READING** – Lilienfeld, S. O., Lynn, S. J., Ruscio, J., & Beyerstein, B. L. (2010). *Great myths of popular psychology: Shattering widespread misconceptions about human behavior.* West Sussex, England: Wiley-Blackwell.

Table 5.1 *Rosenhan's interpretation of the study results and response from critics*

Rosenhan's results	Rosenhan's interpretation	Critic's response
Diagnoses were made based on pseudopatient reports of a single symptom	Clinicians were too eager to diagnose illness; diagnosis should not have been made with only one symptom present	Some pseudopatients were also nervous and anxious and were voluntarily seeking admission suggesting they were upset enough to seek help
Nurses noted writing behavior of pseudopatients	Using the notation "writing behavior" suggested that the nurses saw this as abnormal because of their diagnosis	There was no attempt to verify that nurses interpreted the behavior as psychopathological
Pseudopatients were held in the institutions for an average of 19 days	This is further evidence of staff and clinicians' inability to recognize the patients as normal	The symptom reported by the pseudopatient (auditory hallucination) was serious enough to warrant caution on the part of hospital personnel

| Pseudopatients were released with a diagnosis of schizophrenia in remission | This common diagnosis for patients with schizophrenia suggested clinicians did not recognize the normal behavior of the pseudopatients | This was a rare diagnosis upon discharge and suggested that clinicians did recognize the normal behavior of pseudopatients |

Considering the strengths and limitations of Rosenhan's methods

While Rosenhan, like Rosenthal and Jacobson, examined the power of labels, he did not employ the same rigorous experimental methodology. If Rosenhan and his fellow pseudopatients had set up cameras in the institutions and examined the recordings of staff and patient interactions, we would classify the study as a **naturalistic observation**. In naturalistic observations, researchers want to observe, but not influence, the behavior in the environment in which it occurs (as opposed to in a controlled laboratory). Because the pseudopatients in the Rosenhan study were insiders (knowledgeable regarding mental health) in the institution, their study would be considered a special type of naturalistic observation referred to as a **participant observer study** (Elmes, Kantowitz, & Roediger, 1999). One of the advantages of this type of research is the high **external validity** or generalizability. Because the behavior was studied in the natural environment, we have less reason to be concerned about its authenticity as opposed to behavior studied in artificial settings like a laboratory. However, one of the disadvantages is that it is susceptible to the biases of the experimenter as he/she is directly observing and recording the behavior of interest (Christensen, Johnson, & Turner, 2014). In such situations, **confirmatory bias** could become a problem. For this reason, it is important to have additional information that corroborates the researcher's observations.

It is often the case that when external validity is high, **internal validity** suffers and vice versa. Rosenhan was concerned about the interactions between the doctors and the patients and the staff and the patients across the institutions in the study. One takeaway from the Rosenhan study may be that the impersonal and infrequent interactions with staff and doctors created an environment that actually made patients worse. However, if we want to draw this conclusion we need to make sure that we have ruled out other factors that might account for the worsening symptoms among patients. Can you think of some other factors that might account for this? You might consider the institutions themselves. In what ways were they different? Were there an equal number of staff members and doctors? Were these mental health workers all trained in the same professional manner? Was the quality of interactions the same across the institutions? Were some institutions private and some public? What were the individual differences among the pseudopatients? How "normal" were these pseudopatients and how well did they stay within their assigned roles? For example, Rosenhan (1973) reported that one "pseudopatient attempted a romance with a nurse" (p. 256). Could gender have impacted the results in that staff responded differently to the male and female patients? Because these factors were not controlled for, we do not know whether such variables played a role or not. We also do not know how consistent the presentations of the pseudopatients were across institutions. Might it be reasonable to assume that there were some differences in how pseudopatients presented themselves to the staff? For example, were some more nervous than others and did they all respond to questions in the same way? In order to shore up the internal validity of such a study, researchers would have to control for these factors.

Lastly, a significant problem with interpreting the results of the Rosenhan study is that it was not a test of whether or not clinicians could distinguish the sane from the insane. In order to address this question and avoid some of the problems with the design of Rosenhan's participant observer study, Millon (1975) proposed the following: Have sane and insane individuals present themselves as they are for psychiatric admission. If the sane were admitted and the insane turned away, Rosenhan's hypothesis would be supported. Psychologist Bernard Weiner (1975) had a similar idea: have 20 individuals diagnosed with schizophrenia and 20 matched healthy individuals placed in a mental hospital and then have these participants classified as sane or insane based on the observations of hospital staff. A matched control group is an alternative to random assignment that allows a researcher to control for at least some individual differences. If clinicians were unable to classify the individuals correctly, Rosenhan's hypothesis would be supported.

Critical thinking toolkit
Confirmation bias

Guiding question: What can researchers do to avoid prejudicially confirming their hypotheses?

Let us consider how both the psychiatric staff and the pseudopatients themselves may have been susceptible to biases. Growing up, one of the authors of this book used to occasionally fight over toys with his older brother. Our parents, however, would later insist that this fighting was constant rather than occasional. They could certainly find numerous examples of us arguing over toys, but seemed to miss the many times we were playing together and sharing toys. If they fell victim to confirmation bias, they let this notion about continual fighting influence the way they processed information and perceived outcomes. Specifically, they noticed the instances of fighting and tended to ignore the instances of sharing. Psychologists refer to this tendency to selectively attend to information confirming one's hypothesis as confirmatory or confirmation bias.

Under the influence of confirmation bias we: (1) selectively recall information that confirms our hypotheses, (2) place more importance on information that is congruent with our hypothesis, and (3) reinterpret information that contradicts our hypotheses (e.g., it's the exception that proves the rule). This is most likely to occur when the hypothesis is already established and we are motivated to confirm such a finding (Oswald & Grosjean, 2004). It is not hard to imagine a researcher motivated to confirm a hypothesis, yet we would like to believe scientists are immune to this sort of bias. Unfortunately, research suggests that psychologists positively evaluate research that confirms a hypothesis and, in particular, confirms well-established findings or something that we "know" to be true. Studies get more scrutiny and less credibility when they confirm theories psychologists disagree with and when they disconfirm established theories. We will explore the consequences of this in more detail a bit, but in light of these findings, let us consider how we can counter this bias.

One way to combat confirmation bias is to make sure that those observing the behavior under scrutiny are unaware of the purpose of the study. In many studies, the observers are unaware of the condition the participant is in and unaware of the hypothesis of the researcher. If a researcher, for example, was studying aggression among schoolchildren in a naturalistic setting, she should train research assistants to ensure they are unaware of the research hypothesis as they observe and record behavior.

How comfortable should we be that Rosenhan designed the study, was a participant observer (pseudopatient), analyzed the quantitative and qualitative data set, and published the article outlining the findings of the study? We cannot know whether confirmation bias played a role in the Rosenhan study, but it is likely that he and possible that the other pseudopatients were aware of the hypothesis and were motivated to confirm it. If this were the case, it would also seem a reasonable concern that confirmation bias may have played a role in the observations of the pseudopatients and the subsequent recall of their experiences in the institutions. Though not intentional (confirmation bias usually is not premeditated), it could be the case that the pseudopatients in Rosenhan's study paid more attention to the behavior of staff that confirmed their hypothesis and ignored their behavior that disconfirmed it. Likewise, the pseudopatients may have been caught up in their own self-fulfilling prophecy – expecting cold, insensitive behavior on the part of the mental health staff and behaving in such a way that elicited just such behavior from the staff. Though entirely speculative, this contextual framework would be consistent with what we know about confirmation bias. Of course, the clinicians and nursing staff in the Rosenhan study were not immune to confirmation bias either.

The impact of confirmation bias

Treating new hypotheses with undue skepticism and preventing the publication of findings that contradict an established theory can impede scientific progress (Oswald & Grosjean, 2004). A provocative article appeared in a 2014 issue of *Time* magazine titled "Don't blame fat." One of the themes of the article was that the connection between saturated fat and cardiovascular disease had been overstated, if it existed at all. Some of the research that challenged this connection was conducted in the 1990s, so why were we just hearing about this in 2014? The "war on fat" was being waged in the 1990s and the idea that people needed to eat a low-fat diet was accepted as an undeniable fact. Unfortunately, confirmation bias created a significant obstacle to the publication of research that contradicted this fact.

A related issue is the **file drawer problem** (Rosenthal, 1979). This refers to the tendency for researchers to "file away" rather than attempt to publish studies that fail to produce positive results (technically results that fail to reject the null hypothesis; Meehl, 1990). The potential impact of the file drawer problem is illustrated in Figure 5.1, which shows that for one of the Food and Drug Administration (FDA) approved drugs, there were numerous unpublished studies suggesting it was ineffective. Turner and colleagues (2008), a study we will return to in Chapter 12, examined publication bias in antidepressant drug trials and found that while 74 studies had been conducted, 23 had not been published (these results went into the file drawer). Roughly, 70% of the studies not published failed to produce positive results, while over 90% of the studies that were published produced positive results. The problem that this creates is an inaccurate estimate of the effect the drugs have in medical practice. This problem may contribute to both confirmation bias and the file drawer problem as journal editors apply heavy scrutiny to studies contradicting an established finding and reject research findings that fail to support established hypotheses.

In 2002, the American Psychological Association (APA) launched a new professional journal, the *Journal of Articles in Support of the Null Hypothesis*, whose goal is to offer the "missing link" in the psychological literature by reducing bias in the published literature and combating the file drawer problem. This publication is still in operation and open to all areas of psychological research where the research findings did not reach the traditional statistical significance levels ($p < 0.05$).

Negative or questionable results	Positive results
NP NP NP NP NP NP P P P	P P P P P P P

Figure 5.1   Published and unpublished trials for an FDA approved drug
Note: NP = Not Published; P = Published

The evidence for Rosenhan's conclusions

Once admitted, the eight Rosenhan pseudopatients were in institutions for an average of 19 days. This may seem like an excessive amount of time for patients who are acting normal. However, it is worth considering that the symptom (auditory hallucinations) reported by the pseudopatients was severe. If the situation was genuine (i.e., these were real patients and not pseudopatients), it would be expected that the patient's status would improve upon hospitalization and that clinicians would want to continue to monitor patients before releasing them. Moreover, there is no reason to expect that clinicians and nurses should have recognized the pseudopatients as fakers, as there would have been no clear motivation for doing so (Spitzer, 1975).

The 19 days is significant for a different reason. With eight pseudopatients in the hospitals for that length of time, there was potentially a wealth of observational data available. Rosenhan notes that the daytime nursing staff and afternoon and evening staff came out of their stations a combined 20.9 times per shift. That would amount to over 3,000 opportunities for potential observation. Of course, not all of these were intended to be observations, but even if we assume that only 5% involved a documented observation of patients by staff that would result in roughly 158 total observations. To support his claim that staff interpreted normal behavior as pathological, Rosenhan points to three instances when nursing staff documented patients' note-taking as "writing behavior." Recall that Rosenhan interprets the term "writing behavior" as an indication that the nurses perceived the behavior as pathological or suggestive of their illness. According to Rosenhan, this was evidence that "once a person is designated abnormal, all of his other behaviors and characteristics are colored by that label" (p. 253). Beyond the instances of writing behavior, however, Rosenhan presented no data to support this claim (Ruscio, 2015). Nevertheless, even if Rosenhan had provided dozens of examples of the nursing staff documenting writing behavior, would that have supported his pathological oriented claim? Critics of Rosenhan's study might argue that the number of times it was documented would not matter because there was no direct notation of pathology (Ruscio, 2004, 2015). In other words, it was an unsubstantiated stretch on Rosenhan's part to assume that the staff were viewing the behavior as pathological when noting that they engaged in "writing behavior."

More generally, anecdotes, though compelling, are not sufficient as evidence. As skeptic Michael Shermer (1997) notes, "Without corroborative evidence … ten anecdotes are no better than one, and a hundred anecdotes are no better than ten" (p. 48). The fact that a few anecdotes were used as support for the hypothesis does nothing to lessen concerns about confirmation bias. Considering the quality and quantity of the evidence, it would be advisable as a researcher to be cautious in interpreting the results and important to note the limitations. Rosenhan, some critics have claimed, not only ignored evidence that would disprove his hypothesis, but also misinterpreted evidence that seemed to contradict his hypothesis, as we will discuss shortly.

Rosenhan, however, did present some compelling data collected after the pseudopatients were released. Staff at one of the hospitals that had admitted a pseudopatient was told that over the next several months one or more pseudopatients would try to gain admission to the hospital (no such pseudopatients presented themselves). Each hospital staff member (attendants, nurses, psychiatrists, physicians, and psychologists) was asked to rate each of the 193 patients presenting for admission on the probability that they were a pseudopatient. A 10-point scale was used, and according to Rosenhan, a 1 and 2 reflected "high confidence that a patient was a pseudopatient" (p. 252). The results are displayed in Figure 5.2.

Number of patients	Suspected with high confidence by one staff member	Considered suspect by at least one psychiatrist	Considered suspect by a psychiatrist and staff member
193	41 (21.24%)	23 (11.92%)	19 (9.84%)

Figure 5.2   Hospital staff member ratings of pseudopatient status

Based on these results, Rosenhan concluded, "any diagnostic process that lends itself so readily to massive errors of this sort cannot be a very reliable one" (p. 252). However, there are several problems with Rosenhan's conclusion, beginning with the problem that he provides no information on what "considered suspect" meant. Was this any number higher than a 2? Without this detail, it is hard to interpret the results. Does "suspect" mean that the staff member was suspicious? If suspicious, should that be taken as an error? What also complicates the interpretation is a failure on the part of Rosenhan to distinguish which staff members indicated high confidence. In other words, some of the staff members do not have the training and experience in diagnosing disorders (Wolitzky, 1973). If you look closely at the above results, it could be the case that not a single psychiatrist, the individuals responsible for diagnosis, made an error (by indicting high confidence in a patient being a pseudopatient). However, even if we took "suspect" to be the equivalent of an error, only 12% of the true patients were suspected of being a pseudopatient by a psychiatrist. These results might actually be something psychiatry could boast about! What would you make of the following headline: "Study finds that psychiatrists able to correctly identify 88% of patients as real among fakers!"

The diagnosis of schizophrenia

Were the clinicians in the Rosenhan study wrong to diagnose patients with schizophrenia? The seemingly obvious answer to this question is "yes." The pseudopatients were faking the symptom and were by all accounts psychological healthy. Before concluding that the doctors got this wrong, let us give this some additional thought. Auditory hallucinations are a hallmark symptom of schizophrenia with 60–70% of patients experiencing them (Slade & Bentall, 1988). Considering that auditory hallucinations are prominent symptoms of schizophrenia, Spitzer (1975) concluded that, though the diagnosis was premature, schizophrenia was the only appropriate diagnosis. It is much easier to find fault with the diagnosis using contemporary diagnostic criteria (DSM-5, APA, 2013) than the version employed at the time of the 1973 Rosenhan study (DSM-II). Psychiatrists and clinical psychologists use the *Diagnostic and Statistical Manual of Mental Disorders* (DSM) to diagnose patients and though the DSM-II described many symptoms in addition to auditory hallucinations that characterize schizophrenia, there were no guidelines as to a specific number of symptoms needed in order to diagnose. If the Rosenhan study had been conducted today, the diagnosis of schizophrenia would be much more difficult to justify. In fact, one would not get beyond the first criteria, which requires the presence of at least two of a variety of symptoms including hallucinations, delusions, and disorganized speech (American Psychiatric Association, 2013).

Just as important as the diagnosis upon admission was the diagnosis upon release. Rosenhan argued that the "in remission" addition was a technicality that would usually be applied when a patient with schizophrenia was discharged. One of Rosenhan's most vocal critics, Robert Spitzer (1975), on the other hand, believed that the clinicians in Rosenhan's study recognized the patients' behavior as normal and thus gave them the rarely used diagnosis of *schizophrenia in remission* upon discharge. Spitzer examined the records of hundreds of patients and surveyed several hospitals on the use of the diagnosis. Results suggested, as Spitzer predicted, that the diagnosis rarely occurred (with some hospitals suggesting it was never used). The fact that all of the psychiatrists released the pseudopatients with the *in remission* diagnosis seems to argue against their inability to see past the label. Rather, the diagnosis seemed to suggest that the psychiatrists recognized that the individual was no longer symptomatic or was in fact "*normal*" upon discharge.

If nothing else, the diagnoses upon admission and release were consistent. The fact that 11 of the 12 pseudopatients were given the same diagnosis after reporting the same symptom speaks to the **reliability** of the diagnosis or consistency of results. If, on the other hand, pseudopatients had received a variety of diagnoses, this would have indicated that the diagnostic system was unreliable. The consistency of the results, however, does not tell us whether the diagnostic system is accurate or valid. To demonstrate **validity**, researchers would need to show that people who meet the criteria for a disorder are significantly different than those who do not. For example, research indicating poorer educational outcomes and social functioning (e.g., fewer friends) among those meeting the criteria for Attention Deficit Hyperactivity Disorder (ADHD) compared to those who do not would speak to the validity of the ADHD diagnosis.

Stigma and mental disorders

One of the studies often cited as evidence of labeling theory or the stigma of labels was conducted by psychologists Ellen Langer and Robert Abelson (1974). In their study, Langer and Abelson had psychiatrists whose training aligned with the diagnostic system at the time (psychoanalysts) and those who were skeptical of the system (behaviorists) evaluate an individual in a videotaped interview. Half of the psychiatrists were told that the interviewee was a patient and half were told that the person was a job applicant. The psychoanalysts rated the patients as more poorly adjusted than the job applicants.

However, before we put this in the win column for labeling theory, let us consider the role of **demand characteristics** (see Chapter 6 for a detailed discussion of demand characteristics). If you tell a therapist who uses the DSM to diagnose (to evaluate a *patient*), then that therapist will make an underlying assumption that there is some validity to this person already being labeled a patient (Davis, 1979). In other words, if this person is a patient, then professionals have already evaluated him/her and assumptions of pathology already exist. This is different than asking someone to determine if an interviewee *should be* a patient.

Should labels tell us something about the probability of behavior of those with the diagnostic label? Should the psychiatrists in a study like Langer and Abelson's not consider this? In other words, it is perfectly reasonable that the psychodynamic practitioners suggested more maladjustment among patients than job applicants because they assumed that there is typically more maladjustment among patients than job applicants (Davis, 1979; Ruscio, 2004). Imagine we were talking about a label with perhaps less stigma attached. What if we had two groups of physicians watching an interview of a heart patient or non-patient describe their diet and lifestyle. Would we fault the physicians for evaluating the heart patient less favorably in terms of their diet and lifestyle, including behaviors that may potentially impact this condition?

Finally, let us consider another issue in labeling, that of the potential difference between a general label and a specific illness. Martinez and colleagues (2011) found evidence of greater negative evaluations, including dangerousness, of patients labeled mentally ill than those labeled with a bipolar disorder. In the first study, separate groups of participants were asked "to imagine meeting someone diagnosed with a chronic mental illness" and "someone with a chronic physical illness" (p. 7). Perceptions of dangerousness were higher among those who imagined the person with a mental illness than those imagining a person with a physical illness. However, let us return to the issue raised by Davis (1979) in response to the Langer and Abelson study. It would be wise to consider the actual likelihood of certain behaviors that the labels would predict. We do not know what the participants imagined in this scenario, but if many imagined an individual with schizophrenia then perceptions of dangerousness would not necessarily be unwarranted. Research has shown that some symptoms of schizophrenia, such as command hallucinations and persecutory delusions, may increase the risk of violence, though these symptoms are rare (Scott & Resnick, 2013). Whether this was what participants imagined cannot be determined, but it is likely that some, possibly a small percentage of participants, imagined such an encounter.

The results of the second study by Martinez and colleagues (2011) seem to contradict labeling theory. In this study, participants were given information about a person who was diagnosed with bipolar disorder, but was currently in remission. Participants read a brief story about a day in the life of that person and answered questions about their perceived humanity, their dangerousness, and their willingness to interact with the person. Despite the mental illness label (bipolar disorder) and a description of the patient in which his behavior was not pathological, just "ambiguously hostile," there were no greater perceptions of dangerousness for this person compared to a control group given the same information but a different label (melanoma). Additionally, participants rated the individual with a mental illness as more human. The authors interpreted this as a sort of overreaction to the fact that the behavioral description and in-remission status suggested the person was not dangerous. Interestingly, study 1, in which participants rated the person with a mental illness as less human, and study 2, in which participants rated the person with a mental illness as more human, were both interpreted as supportive of labeling theory! The problem with this is that a theory needs to be falsifiable (Cramer, 2013). If less humanity and more humanity were interpreted as supportive of the theory, then how would one falsify it?

Lastly, much of the labeling theory research relies on the use of hypothetical vignettes (short imagined patient descriptions) that participants respond to, as with the Martinez study. It is much easier to find evidence of discrimination in the responses people give to hypothetical persons in vignettes, but does this really tell us how a person will actually interact with a real individual with a form of mental illness? Consider the discrepancy between attitudes and behavior in the following:

> in 1930 Richard LaPiere studied racial prejudice by traveling around the United States with a Chinese couple. Over the course of two years, they visited a total of 251 hotels, restaurants, and other business establishments, encountering racial discrimination just once. Six months after visiting, LaPiere sent a questionnaire asking each hotel proprietor whether Chinese individuals would be allowed as guests. Of the 128 responses he received, 118 said they would not, 9 gave conditional responses and 1 said yes. (Ruscio, 2004, pp. 12–13)

Let's consider how we could design the Martinez and colleagues (2011) study to eliminate the confounds. An important question is whether we would select a between-subjects or a within-subjects design. In a within-subjects design, each participant in the study is exposed to all of the conditions, while in a between-subjects study we randomly assign participants to one of the possible conditions. For reasons we will further address in Chapter 11 ("Benjamin Libet: Do Human Beings Really Have Free Will?"), a between-subjects design is most appropriate. Next, we need to consider how many variables we have and how many levels there are of each variable. In a factorial design the number of independent variables is indicated by how many numbers are separated by the "×." Therefore, a 2 × 2 design involves two independent variables and a 2 × 2 × 2 design involves three. The value of each number indicates the number of levels for each independent variable. Therefore, for a 2 × 2 study, there are two independent variables each with two levels and for the 2 × 2 × 2 study, there are three independent variables with two levels each. As you can see in Table 5.2, we must consider the general versus the specific manipulation, the disorder status, and the background information. Thus, we have three variables and two levels of each variable. So, we would have a 2 × 2 × 2 between-subjects design.

Table 5.2 2 × 2 × 2 between-subjects design of Martinez et al. (2011) study

General versus specific	Disorder status	Background information
"mental illness"	in remission	background information present
specific mental illness (e.g., "bipolar disorder")	chronic	background information not present

The difficulty of implicating the label by itself is that the way individuals respond to the mentally ill is likely to be influenced by the behavior or symptoms of the patient and not just (if at all) by the label. Additionally, certain patient behaviors – for example, social withdrawal – that we may attribute to the stigmatizing effects of labels, are in some cases symptoms of the disorder (e.g., PTSD) and in some cases may reflect the self-stigmatization of mental illness (a sort of self-fulfilling prophecy where the patient is expecting rejection from others and thus withdraws to avoid the rejecting experience) (Martinez et al., 2011; Ruscio, 2004).

Chapter summary

David Rosenhan's (1973) study raised important questions about the diagnoses of mental illness, the stigma of labels, the conditions in mental institutions, and psychiatric practices in general. The mental health profession continues to face criticism regarding the ongoing refinement of disorders, overdiagnoses of certain disorders, and overreliance on medication for treatment, despite considerable current evidence supporting the efficacy of psychotherapy for many disorders (evidence-based psychotherapies). The Rosenhan study continues to be cited as evidence of labeling theory and/or the power of diagnostic labels to produce stigmatization. However, Rosenhan's methods and conclusions have been heavily scrutinized and critics have raised their own compelling questions about the selective use of observational data and the lack of direct evidence for the notion that staff and clinicians failed to recognize normal behavior. Confirmation bias is a concern and researchers, like the rest of us, need to be aware of the tendency to selectively interpret information. Confirmation bias, along with the underreporting of studies that do not support our hypothesis or the file drawer problem, gives us a distorted and false picture of the evidence. Beyond Rosenhan's study, much of the labeling theory research has failed to produce strong evidence. So weak is the evidence, in fact, that stigmatization of diagnostic labels is considered a myth (Lilienfeld et al., 2010).

Future directions

The stigma that Rosenhan drew attention to with his study in the 1970s is still very much in the public consciousness. Recent campaigns to ban words like "crazy" have been initiated by several universities in the USA. These efforts are aimed at combating the stigma of mental illness. Though we discussed the limitations of both Rosenhan's study and others cited in support of labeling theory, researchers continue to examine the relationship between diagnostic labels and stigma. Early proponents of labeling theory argued that the labels, by themselves, were responsible for stigma and even for producing the illness itself. Contemporary researchers, on the other hand, acknowledge the contributions of the illness itself, but argue that the diagnostic label adds to the stigma. Although a small effect, researchers have found greater negative perceptions of individuals with mental illness among research participants given the label of schizophrenia and symptoms compared to those with the symptoms alone (Imhoff, 2016). However, diagnostic labels can also have positive effects by providing individuals with an explanation of their symptoms and distress, and a better general understanding of abnormal behavior, and facilitating access to services and treatment (Lilienfeld et al., 2010; Spitzer, 1975). Future research will likely examine the extent to which public campaigns effectively combat stigma and inaccurate perceptions of mental illness.

Discussion questions

1. Where do you see parallels between Rosenhan's study and Milgram's study? Think about issues of social expectations, personal perceptions, physical environment, and reward and punishment issues.
2. Why would it have been helpful in a study like Rosenhan's to provide data on the clinical interview and examine the notes of the psychiatrist at intake and discharge?

6 The Stanford Prison Study: Are Ordinary People Capable of Extraordinary Cruelty?

Primary source: Haney, C., Banks, C., & Zimbardo, P. (1973). Interpersonal dynamics in a simulated prison. *International Journal of Criminology and Penology, 1*, 69–97.

Chapter objectives

This chapter will help you become a better critical thinker by:

- Questioning whether the study design or selection of the sample may have impacted the results
- Considering whether conclusions drawn from the study are appropriate for the methods utilized
- Questioning the role of the experimenter and critically evaluating information given to participants about the study
- Evaluating the level of realism in a psychological experiment
- Questioning whether the researcher took appropriate steps to protect study participants and reduce personal biases

---

Introduction

In the early 1970s Palo Alto, California, was home to one of the most controversial prisons in the USA, whose prison guards were infamous. Guard Dave Eshleman described his own demeanor as follows: "[I was as] intimidating, cold and cruel as possible." Eshleman had earned a reputation in the prison as a sadistic guard by waking prisoners at random times in the middle of the night, having them do push-ups, sing songs, recite rules, and perform other menial tasks. His attempts to humiliate and intimidate prisoners was evident in an exchange with prisoner #2093. Eshleman called the prisoner a "stinkin' liar" and posed the following question in a tone suggesting that he had absolute power over the prisoners: "What if I told you to get down on that floor and fuck the floor, what would you do then?" After refusing this bizarre and unrealistic request, the prisoner was forced to lie on the floor and do push-ups... with two other prisoners on his back. Eshleman and a

---

fellow prison guard broke out in laughter as the exhausted prisoner collapsed on the floor after a failed push-up attempt.

Consider the following question:

Which of the following terms would you use to describe Guard Eshleman?

☐ Ordinary
☐ Sadistic
☐ Psychopathic
☐ Evil
☐ Crazy
☐ Deranged
☐ Mentally ill
☐ Aggressive

Based on the information you were given, it is unlikely that you selected "ordinary" as a fitting attribute. However, as you learn more about Eshleman and the prison where he served as a guard, you may become a bit more comfortable with this option. We say this because there was no evidence of psychopathy or mental illness in Eshleman's earlier background. However, there were powerful situational forces in the prison acting upon him. What those forces are have been a source of debate since the prison was shut down.

If you selected the last option, "aggressive," you will find in the following pages that such personality traits play an important role in drawing people to and shaping behavioral situations like the prison in Palo Alto.

It should become clear in the pages that follow that the use of vague terms like "crazy," "deranged," and "evil" (the latter imbued with theological overtones) used to describe Eshleman's behavior are imprecise and not helpful from the perspective of psychological science.

Study background

In the USA the early 1970s were characterized by public debate about the efficacy of the prison system, campus protests, and clashes between police and protesters (Haney & Zimbardo, 2009). The above events actually took place in the early 1970s, but the prison was not real and Eshleman was not an actual prison guard. He was a college student taking part in the Stanford prisoner study (commonly referred to as the Stanford Prison Experiment, or SPE) in which he was assigned the role of prison guard. In the summer of 1971 psychologist Philip Zimbardo placed an advertisement in local papers seeking college student participants for a study of prison life that would run for two weeks. Seventy-five individuals responded to the ad and out of those, 24 of those considered the most "normal" individuals were selected as participants. As displayed in Figure 6.1, 21 were then randomly assigned to play the role of either guard or prisoner in a simulated prison in the basement of the Stanford University Psychology Department. Prisoners were publicly arrested at their homes, taken to the mock prison, booked, stripped, and deloused before being taken to their cells. Zimbardo described the first 24 hours as uneventful, but on the second day friction between the prisoners and guards developed. Some of the guards, having had their authority challenged by prisoners refusing orders and eventually barricading themselves in their cells, began to wield their power over them, engaging in increasingly abusive behavior; the above example of guard Dave Eshleman was not an isolated incident. The two-week study was discontinued after six days, as a number of prisoners had to be released due to severe psychological stress.

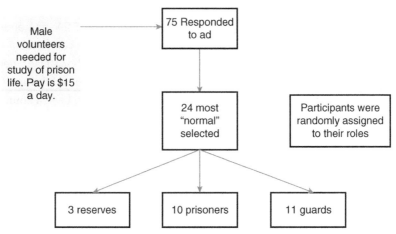

Figure 6.1   Zimbardo placed an ad in to two local newspapers in California. One of the authors of the study, Craig Haney, interviewed the 75 who responded to the advertisement. Twenty-four were selected from the 75 and randomly assigned to the role of either prisoner or guard. Three served as reserves and functioned as replacements when a participant was released

Zimbardo created a powerful situation capable of producing evil behavior in seemingly good people. The mock prison had some of the same features of a real prison, such as bars on the cell doors and uniforms for prisoners and guards. Prisoners participated in parole board hearings and had visitations from family members and there was even a prison Chaplin. The researchers were trying to recreate the "feel" of a prison – a sense of powerlessness, emasculation, and a loss of individuality. There were a number of factors that contributed to the abusive nature of the mock prison system according to the study's authors, including taking away a sense of individuality among the prisoners by making them wear uniforms, covering their heads with stockings, and referring to them by their prisoner numbers. Thus, like real prisoners, Stanford study prisoners were stripped of their humanity and individual uniqueness, they became "just a number." Guards were referred to as "Mr. Correctional Officer" and wore dark reflective sunglasses so that prisoners could not see their eyes. All of this contributed to a loss of personal identity or what Zimbardo considers deindividuation. In this sense, the surrogate prison that Zimbardo created was very real to the prisoners.

The purpose of the Stanford study was to demonstrate that situations could be a more powerful and influential behavioral factor than dispositions or personality characteristics in determining behavior. Powerful situations can override such personal dispositions. The prison guards in the study were normal human beings, but the extraordinary situation they encountered was capable of producing abnormal behavior.

Current thinking

Would you describe Dave Eshleman as evil or sadistic? Consider a real-life case of abuse. In early 2004 pictures were released by news agencies depicting the abuse of Iraqi prisoners at Abu Ghraib prison in Iraq. Some of the American soldiers who operated the prison tormented and tortured prisoners and documented the abuse. When the horrific images of prisoner abuse surfaced, many wondered what kind of sadistic person would engage in such brutality. Many people asked: "Who were these bad apples?" According to Zimbardo, while Eshleman stood out among the guards in terms of abusive behavior, he was indistinguishable in terms of his personality. Likewise, Guard Chip Fredrick, one of the prison guards at the Abu Ghraib prison, was implicated as a ringleader. However, after spending time with Fredrick as part of his defense team, psychologist Philip Zimbardo was struck by how ordinary he appeared (Zimbardo, 2007).

> **KEY READING** – Zimbardo, P. G. (2007). *The Lucifer effect: Understanding how good people turn evil*. New York: Random House.

Fredrick seemed to be a fairly by-the-book officer and dedicated family man. By all accounts the then college student of the 1970s, now real estate broker and part-time actor Dave Eshleman, was normal as well. To Zimbardo, Eshleman and Fredrick were not bad guys but ordinary people working in bad prison systems (one fake and one real).

Image 6.1   U.S. soldier involved in abuse of detainees in Abu Ghraib prison

The atrocities committed at Abu Ghraib prison in Iraq in 2004 were familiar to Zimbardo and renewed his interest in the Stanford Prison study (Zimbardo, 2007). Zimbardo interpreted the Abu Ghraib case as another example of normal individuals overwhelmed by situational forces. The lesson of the Stanford study is that we have to be cautious about condemning the prison guards as bad people. We should give careful consideration to the contextual environment and the extent to which they are criminally liable. Zimbardo, this time in the role of expert witness for Chip Fredrick, pointed to the prison environment as a major determinant of the abusive behavior. The prison was lacking in proper resources, training for soldiers, and supervision. There was a constant threat of attacks from outside the Iraqi compound. Like the Stanford Prison, the Abu Ghraib prison was ideal for producing the kind of sadistic behavior displayed by some prison guards observed decades earlier.

While the Stanford and Abu Ghraib guards may not have been evil, recent research suggests that prison environments may attract individuals with characteristics that make abuse more likely. This increases the likelihood of violence and degrading guard behavior within prison walls.

KEY READING – Carnahan, T., & McFarland, S. (2007). Revisiting the Stanford Prison Experiment: Could participant self-selection have led to the cruelty? *Personality and Social Psychology Bulletin, 33,* 603–614.

Carnahan and McFarland (2007) found a crucial difference between individuals willing to volunteer for a psychological study and those interested in volunteering for a psychological study of prison life. The latter possessed personality traits that would make them susceptible to administering abuse. This study highlights an issue in psychological research, participant **selection bias**, that we will return to in the "Applying critical thinking" section. It also forces us to consider the possibility that some participants in the Stanford study and the abusive guards at Abu Ghraib may have been predisposed to such behavior. While Zimbardo's impression of Chip Fredrick was that he was ordinary, psychiatrist Henry Nelson had a different impression after evaluating him. Nelson (2005) noted the presence of "psychological factors of negativity, anger, hatred, and desire to dominate and humiliate" (p. 449).

Another more recent study of prison life, the BBC prison study (Reicher & Haslam, 2006), also gives us a better understanding of how both personality and situational forces influence behavior.

> **KEY READING** – Reicher, S., & Haslam, S. A. (2006). Rethinking the psychology of tyranny: The BBC prison study. *British Journal of Social Psychology, 45,* 1–40.

If the Stanford study is the only prison study you have heard about, prepare to be shocked. There are some important differences between the Stanford study and the BBC study in terms of the design, but the results were drastically different; guards were not abusive and prisoners were not passive. What was key to producing the seemingly surprising results? Once settled into the prison, guards and prisoners were told that there was the opportunity for a prisoner to be promoted to the station of guard if he had the right characteristics. While the guards were initially led to believe they were assigned their role because of suitable characteristics, several days after the promotion of the selected prisoner, they were told such differences never existed. As the study progressed, the prisoners cohesively came together as a group, yet the guards did not. Prisoners became increasingly confident in their ability to change their condition while guards became less confident in their ability to maintain order. When the prisoners challenged guard authority, the prison system collapsed and an egalitarian commune formed. While the prisoners in the Stanford study did not operate as a group, the BBC prisoners came to increasingly identify as members of a group fighting for better accommodations and power. The study's authors concluded that people do not mindlessly adopt roles. The key is the extent to which we identify with the group and adopt shared norms and values. When group identity fails to coalesce and systems fail, we are susceptible to authoritarian systems that offer control and order.

If you have watched a video on the Stanford study or read about it in a textbook, you may be aware that Zimbardo served as both the principal

investigator in charge of conducting the study and as the prison superintendent. While this is an oft-noted criticism, even by Zimbardo himself, another
concern seldom addressed in textbooks is how aware participants were as to
the purpose of the study. Research suggests that individuals given the information that the Stanford participants were presented with are quite aware
of the purpose of the study (Banuazizi & Movahedi, 1975). Thus, though the
Stanford study serves as a cautionary tale about the power of the situation,
it also serves as a lesson about research methods, to which we will turn our
attention in the following section.

> **KEY READING** – Banuazizi, A., & Movahedi, S. (1975). Interpersonal dynamics in a
> simulated prison. *American Psychologist, 30*, 152–160.

Given the lack of criticism of the Stanford study in introductory psychology
textbooks and courses (Bartels, 2015; Bartels, Milovich, & Moussier, 2016;
Griggs & Whitehead, 2014), you might be wondering what to make of the
study at this point. According to psychologist Erich Fromm, the results of
the Stanford Prison study actually contradict Zimbardo's claims about the
power of the situation. Fromm (1973) notes that only one-third of the guards
were labeled by Zimbardo as sadistic. So, despite the efforts of Zimbardo and
colleagues to create an environment conducive to abuse, two-thirds of the
guards failed to engage in such behavior (see Table 6.1).

Table 6.1   Range of responses from guards (Zimbardo, 2007)

Abusive guards	Some guards were observed pushing prisoners back in their cells; screaming obscenities at prisoners; making prisoners do jumping jacks, push-ups, and sit-ups; threatening prisoners
By-the-book/good guards	Some guards had to be encouraged to be tougher as they were too quiet and passive; some were tough on prisoners in terms of enforcing rules but were not aggressive; some wanted to be liked by prisoners and did favors for them

Fromm concluded: "The experiment seems rather to prove that one can
not transform people so easily into sadists by providing them with the proper
situation" (p. 81). Yet the study has weathered such scrutiny and criticism.
Our aim is not to resolve the debate, but to examine the Stanford study and
the subsequent research inspired by it. By doing so, we may have a better
understanding of the inconsistent results among prison studies and a greater
appreciation for the importance of both personality traits and situational
forces.

Critical thinking toolkit
Selection bias

Guiding question: Is it possible that the study and how it is presented may attract individuals who possess characteristics (unaccounted for by the researcher) that influence the results?

Imagine coming across an ad for a psychological study regarding human sexuality. Whether this would be an appealing study to you would likely depend on a number of factors including your religious beliefs and attitudes toward and experiences with sex. Research suggests that those who would choose to volunteer for such a study are likely to have less traditional or conservative attitudes toward sex, to be more sexually experienced, and to be higher in sexual sensation-seeking (Wiederman, 1999). Selection bias occurs when different characteristics of people, such as their sexual attitudes and experiences, influence the types of environments they select and tasks they prefer. Convenience samples (Chapter 2) are susceptible to this bias, which can lead to inaccurate conclusions about populations. For example, if the study about sex was asking participants how often they engage in various sexual acts, the researchers might erroneously conclude that certain acts are common among all college students. Similarly, if participants were asked to view sexually explicit films, the researchers may get an inaccurate sense of college students' emotional and physiological responses to such films.

If we consider selection bias in the Stanford study we want to ask ourselves whether or not there may be differences between those who would volunteer for a study about prison life and those who would not, a question addressed by Carnahan and McFarland (2007). These authors created the following advertisements that were published in the campus newspapers of several universities in the USA.

Male college students needed for a psychological study **of prison life**. $70 per day for 1–2 weeks beginning May 17th. For further information and applications, email: [e-mail address].

Male college students needed for a psychological study. $70 per day for 1–2 weeks beginning May 17th. For further information and applications, email: [e-mail address].

The first ad, like the ad used in the Stanford study, sought volunteers for a study of prison life and the second solicited volunteers for a psychological study with no indication of the study's focus. Those who responded to the ads completed measures designed to assess various personality traits. When comparing scores with those who responded to the generic study, Carnahan and McFarland found aggression, authoritarianism, Machiavellianism (characterized by lying, manipulation, and a tendency to use people), narcissism, and social dominance to be higher and empathy and altruism to be lower among those responding to the prison life ad. If aggressive individuals are more likely to volunteer for a study of prison life, then (1) the generalizability of the results are more limited, and (2) it cannot be argued that the situation was the sole or major determinant of behavior.

Consideration of restriction of range

Guiding question: Is it possible that there is a narrow range in scores because of the design of the study or the selectivity of the sample?

As we saw with the Carnahan and McFarland (2007) study, it is possible that the Stanford study attracted participants high in aggression and other personality traits that would predispose them to abusive behavior in the "prison laboratory." When such scores are not representative of the population, **restriction of range** becomes a concern. The elimination of high and low scores can also create this problem. Recall that the selection process involved evaluating the 75 individuals who responded to the ad and selecting the 24 most normal of those for participation in the actual study. The process of selecting the most normal individuals should result in less variability in personality. In a sense, if we take out those scoring high and those scoring low we have only those in the middle remaining. When scores on a personality measure lack variability, it reduces the potential correlation or association between personality and behavior. The problem of restriction in range is illustrated in Figure 6.2.

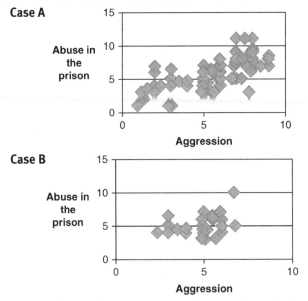

Figure 6.2 Correlations between aggression and abuse in the prison in two hypothetical prison studies. Case B illustrates restriction in range

Let us assume that we have participants completing a personality measure of aggression. Scores on the measure range from 1 to 10 with 1 being a low level of aggression and 10 being high. With this data, the researchers can look at whether aggressive personality correlates with or predicts abusive behavior in the prison. In Case A the range of aggression scores among those in the sample ranged from 1 to 9 and in Case B they are more restricted, varying from 3 to 7.

In Case B let's assume that the researchers eliminated those subjects scoring low in aggression as they were assumed to be dishonest about their true aggression and those with scores too high as they were assumed to be too aggressive. As a result of the restriction in range, the correlation drops from $r = 0.70$ in Case A to $r = 0.30$ in Case B and is no longer statistically significant. The problem is that the correlation in Case B may underestimate the relationship between the two variables. The design of the Stanford study likely reduced variance in some traits that the authors were interested in and could explain why personality accounted for an "extremely small part of the variation in reactions to this mock prison experience" (Haney et al., 1973, p. 81).

Considering whether the conclusions are justified

As noted earlier, the Stanford study is famously known as the Stanford Prison Experiment (SPE). The term **experiment** is often used interchangeably with study or research, but in psychological science an experiment has some characteristics that distinguish it from other types of studies. Recall that one of the variables that Zimbardo thought influential was a loss of personal prisoner identity. Imagine that to test this a researcher randomly assigned participants to one of two conditions. In the first condition, participants would be treated in the same manner as Stanford participants. That is, they would wear stockings over their head, a prison uniform, and be referred to by number rather than name. This would be the **experimental group** or the group receiving the manipulation under investigation. In the second condition, participants in the **control group** would not have to wear the stockings or uniform and would be referred to by name. The control group or comparison group does not receive the manipulation. During the 24-hour period, participants' level of psychological stress, the **dependent variable** or outcome variable, will be assessed.

All of the elements of an experiment are here. First, a control group provides the basis for comparison. In order to appreciate the importance of the control group it may help to imagine a study in which there was no comparison group. Let us say, in this study, all participants wore the stockings and uniform and were referred to by number and a high level of psychological stress was reported. It would be tempting to conclude that this loss of individuality resulted in a high level of stress. However, it might be the case that in the study with the control group, participants who did not wear the stockings and uniform and were referred to by name reported a similarly high level of stress.

Now, the conclusion does not seem to be as warranted and it may be that other situational factors produced the stress. The second requirement for an experiment is manipulation of the **independent variable**, which in this case was the deindividuation variable. In the experimental condition, participants experienced deindividuation and in the control condition they did not. Lastly, other variables that may influence the results, variables other than the independent variables, need to be held constant (Elmes, Kantowitz, & Roediger, 1999). This is where random assignment comes into play. **Random assignment** helps ensure that the independent variable is the only variable that the groups differ on (Christensen, Johnson, & Turner, 2014). If we randomly assign participants to the groups, we help ensure that any variable that might impact the results (e.g., IQ of participants) is equally distributed across the groups. Random assignment, however, does not ensure that other variables did not influence the results. For example, imagine that prisoners in the control condition were housed together in a single cell, but those in the experimental condition were in individual cells and were isolated from one another. This could have been an intervening variable in producing psychological stress.

Study	Presence of independent variable	Effect on dependent variable	Absence of independent variable	Effect on dependent variable
Stanford Prison study	High authoritarianism	Aggressive behavior	?	?
Lovibond study	High authoritarianism	Aggressive behavior	Low authoritarianism	Absence of aggression

Figure 6.3 Comparison of the Stanford Prison Experiment and the Lovibond experiment

Now let us return to the Stanford study. In order to determine whether it was an experiment, we have to ask if the participants were randomly assigned to groups. In this case, they were and, thus, one of the conditions is met. Next, we might consider whether there was a control group and manipulation of the independent variables. The answer here is no. The independent variables that Zimbardo and colleagues thought were important were deindividuation and the far-reaching power possessed by guards. While these variables were not manipulated in the Stanford study, a similar study conducted in Australia meets the requirements of an experiment. Lovibond, Mithiran, and Adams (1979) randomly assigned participants to one of three prisons that varied in terms of authoritarianism or the extent to which obedience to authority was emphasized. As illustrated in Figure 6.3, the Lovibond experiment showed what the Stanford Prison study could not: that the absence of authoritarianism resulted in an absence of aggression.

Another study on prison life gives us a better understanding of how both personality and situational forces influence behavior. Recall that experiments involve the manipulation of the independent variables and with an experimental and control group, like in the Lovibond study, we can examine the effect that the presence and absence of the independent variable has on the dependent variable. But there is another option to having separate groups exposed to different conditions and it's called a **time-series design**. In such a design the dependent variable is measured before *and* after an intervention. So rather than have three separate prisoners like Lovibond, the aggressive encounters among participants could be recorded in a prison in which authoritarianism is low. Researchers would then change the character of the prison, increasing authoritarianism (e.g., changing prison rules), and then, again, record the number of aggressive encounters. This was the approach taken by the authors of the BBC prison study. They selected participants in much the same way as was done in the Stanford study by placing ads and screening participants. Fifteen male participants were selected and five were assigned the role of guard and 10 the role of prisoner. This random assignment, however, occurred in conjunction with matching the participants on key personality variables. Matching allows for the improved control of individual differences like authoritarianism over random assignment by itself when the sample is small (Haslam & McGarty, 2014). Figure 6.4 depicts the process of matching and assignment in the study.

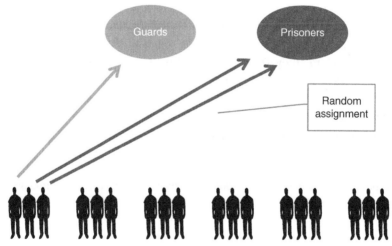

Figure 6.4 Five groups of three matched participants were formed. Participants were matched on racism, authoritarianism, and social dominance. Participants from these matched groups were then randomly assigned to prisoner or guard groups. One was assigned to be a guard and two were assigned to be prisoners

Critical thinking toolkit
Demand characteristics

Guiding question: Might some aspect of a study serve as a cue to participants, inadvertently producing hypothesis-confirming behavior?

Imagine you have signed up to participate in a study as part of a research require-ment in your Psychology 101 course. When you arrive at the laboratory, the exper-imenter greets you and asks you to wait for a minute while she finishes up with a participant. Moments later, this other participant comes out of the laboratory and the experimenter asks you to wait while she gets the experiment set up for you. While the experimenter is away, the other participant lets you in on a little secret: the study involves selecting pictures projected on the left and right sides of a screen and the experimenter's hypothesis is that people will pick those of the left more often. The experimenter, a friendly and affable woman, now enters the waiting room and calls you into the lab. She tells you about the study, has you sign a consent form, and flashes the pictures up on the screen asking you to select one from either the left or the right. What do you do? Do you help the experimenter out by selecting those on the left? Do you sabotage her by picking those on the right? Does this insider information affect you at all? Do you choose not to participate?

According to psychologist Martin Orne we all want to be good subjects and help the experimenter confirm his/her hypothesis. Because of this **good-subject effect**, researchers have to be careful not to provide too many clues as to the purpose of the study. These cues can include information that is in the informed consent and communication between experimenter and participant during the experiment. As critical thinkers, we want to consider whether demand characteristics were influ-ential in the Stanford study. Did the results of the Carnahan and McFarland study suggest demand characteristics? You may have correctly identified the ad itself as a source of demand characteristics in that the nature of the study (i.e., study of prison life) attracted certain personalities. Those who volunteered for the Stanford Prison study were given the following information about the problems the research-ers were studying:

> How powerful are labels (such as 'prisoner,' 'guard') in exercising a controlling influ-ence on behavior? Will our simulating 'prisoners' and 'guards' come to behave in a relatively short time in a manner similar to prisoners and guards in real life prisons?

Did cues about the purpose of the study and the experimenter's expectations or demand characteristics influence the participants' behavior? So convinced that demand characteristics were a problem in the Stanford study, researchers Ali Banuazizi and Siamak Movahedi (1975) decided to examine the likelihood that peo-ple could guess the purpose. The researchers gave Boston area college students information that the Stanford study participants had prior to entering the prison. When asked to identify the hypothesis, as shown in Table 6.2, over 80% were able to guess correctly. Additionally, when asked what they expected from the guards, nearly 90% expected hostile, oppressive behavior.

Table 6.2 *Parentage of different predictions by respondents regarding self and others' behavior in the roles of guard or prisoner*

Referent of prediction	Respondents' sex	Predicted behaviors								
		When assigned to guard role				When assigned to prisoner role				
		Oppressive, hostile, etc.	Lenient, fair, etc.	Other	Total	Rebellious, defiant, etc.	Passive, docile, etc.	Fluctuating	Other	Total
Others	Male	85.1	10.4	4.5	100.0	23.5	38.2	32.4	5.9	100.0
		(57)	(7)	(3)	(67)	(16)	(26)	(22)	(4)	(68)
	Female	93.8	1.2	4.9	100.0	39.0	25.6	29.3	6.1	100.0
		(76)	(1)	(4)	(81)	(32)	(21)	(24)	(5)	(82)
	Both sexes	89.9	5.4	4.7	100.0	32.0	31.3	30.7	6.0	100.0
		(133)	(8)	(7)	(148)	(48)	(47)	(46)	(9)	(150)
Self	Male	48.4	33.9	17.7	100.0	15.6	18.8	32.8	32.8	100.0
		(30)	(21)	(11)	(62)	(10)	(12)	(21)	(21)	(64)
	Female	46.3	38.8	15.0	100.0	12.7	40.5	17.7	29.1	100.0
		(37)	(31)	(12)	(80)	(10)	(32)	(14)	(23)	(79)
	Both sexes	47.1	36.6	16.2	100.0	14.0	30.8	24.5	30.8	100.0
		(67)	(52)	(23)	(142)	(20)	(44)	(35)	(44)	(143)

Source: Reproduced with permission from the American Psychological Association (APA)

Note: Numbers in parentheses indicate frequencies of the different predictions by the respondents; frequency totals that are less than 150, the total number of respondents, resulted from unscorable responses to items in a particular category

We might also consider the following comments by guards in the Stanford study reflecting on their experiences:

> Guard Eshleman: "I arrived independently at the conclusion that this experiment must have been put together to prove a point about prisons being a cruel and inhumane place." In a later interview he explained: "I was going to make something happen in this experiment ... That would be a good thing because it would help show the evils inherent in a prison-type environment."
>
> Guard Arnett: "I felt that the experiment was important and my being 'guard-like' was part of finding out how people react to real oppression ... The main influence on my behavior was the feeling, even though vague, that real prison is brutal in that it is dehumanizing." (Zimbardo, 2007, p. 188)

Eshleman's and Arnett's words seem a close match with Orne's (1962) description of the typical participant's response nearly a decade before the Stanford study: "The subject's performance in an experiment might almost be conceptualized as problem-solving behavior; that is, at some level he sees it as his task to ascertain the true purpose of the experiment and respond in a manner which will support the hypotheses being tested" (p. 779).

Why does knowing the purpose and expected outcome of the study (potentially) matter? Let us return to the hypothetical study asking you to select pictures on the left or the right. What do you do with the tip given to you by a fellow participant? Nichols and Maner (2008) actually ran such a study to examine the good-subject effect and the results indicated a tendency among participants to bend to the experimenter's expectation and select the pictures on the left.

Logical fallacies

While the comments by Eshleman and Arnett appear to be a powerful indictment of the Stanford study, we have to consider that both were in a position of having to justify abusive behavior that numerous introductory psychology students have not only read about but also seen in videos and movies. If they consider themselves good, peace-loving persons, then this mismatch between their behavior in the study and their attitudes creates what psychologists refer to as cognitive dissonance. This dissonance could motivate **rationalization**, a defense mechanism in which one offers an explanation that puts the person in a better light. The dilemma faced by Eshleman and Arnett was to either acknowledge they might not be the good guys they think they are or suggest that the behavior was all in the name of helping Zimbardo and advancing science.

Let us consider one last aspect of the Stanford study that may have contributed to demand characteristics: the guard orientation. Before the prisoners had arrived, Superintendent Zimbardo held an orientation session in which the guards, while discouraged from engaging in physical abuse, were not discouraged from engaging in psychological abuse.

Zimbardo speaking to the guards during the orientation stated: "You can create in the prisoners feelings of boredom, a sense of fear to some degree, you can create a notion of arbitrariness that their life is totally controlled by us, by the system, you, me..." (Haslam & Reicher, 2007, p. 618). Later in the orientation session, Zimbardo (1971) notes:

> The important thing obviously is that the prisoners think this is all going to be fun and games, they're signing up for fifteen dollars a day to sit around and not do anything for 2 weeks. We don't know how long it's going to run; it can run as much as 2 weeks' time. Every prison study has 2 weeks' time and we do. If it looks like it's too heavy, we might have to end earlier ... If something else happens ... we will run up to 2 weeks. We have the space and freedom to do that ... We'd like it [the study] to have a real impact from the beginning and not just be some silly ass study.

Bartels and colleagues (2018) examined demand characteristics in the guard orientation by asking participants how they would respond in such a prison study. During the orientation session, participants were assigned to either an experimental condition in which they were exposed to the above language used in the guard orientation (e.g., you can create fear and boredom in prisoners) or a control condition in which they were given basic study information. Across two studies, participants in the experimental group responded more aggressively.

In a subsequent account of the Stanford study, Zimbardo (2007) himself notes that one of the guards, John Markus, was encouraged by the "Warden" to take a tougher approach in dealing with the prisoners. Warden Jaffe explains to Guard Markus:

> The guards have to know that every guard has to be what we call a 'tough guard' ... we need you to act a certain way. For the time being, we need you to play the role of 'tough guard.' We need you to react as you imagine the pigs would. We're trying to set up the stereotype guard – your individual style has been a little too soft." (p. 65)

The problem with the guard orientation and the exchange between the guard and Warden is that the purpose of the study becomes clear to participants (Haslam & Reicher, 2007). If participants know the purpose of the study and have a positive attitude toward the experiment and the experimenter, the possibility of this influencing the behavior of participants increases and poses a risk to the validity and integrity of the study. Whether guard abuse is explicitly sanctioned as in the above exchange or implicitly so as in the guard orientation, the problem of strong demand characteristics surfaces.

Assessing realism in the laboratory

Guiding question: Was the laboratory environment sufficiently realistic?

You may have heard the common criticism that psychological research in the laboratory is too artificial. Participants are often given tasks or challenges that most people would never expect to encounter in the real world. When people challenge whether or not the results of a study will translate to the real world they are challenging the study's **ecological validity**. If the task seems too artificial, it is lacking in **mundane realism**. Is this a fair standard by which to judge a psychological study? While this everyday realism may appear to be important, it is not critically important if the task is engaging to participants and experienced as real or possesses **experimental realism** (Wilson, Aronson, & Carlsmith, 2010).

Let us consider another well-known study as an example before returning to the Stanford study. Bandura, Ross, and Ross (1963) had preschool children watch models engage in aggressive behavior toward an inflatable doll. The children were later taken to a separate room that contained the doll. After being frustrated by being denied access to toys, observers recorded the aggressive acts of the children. Do you think this study possesses mundane realism? Experimental realism? If you answered no to one or both, you are not alone. This study is a common target for attacks on the artificiality of laboratory research. Before we dismiss the study, however, there is one additional type of realism, **psychological realism**, we should ponder. This type of realism refers to the extent to which there is consistency between the psychological processes in the experiment and the real world (Wilson et al., 2010). While we might immediately recognize the presence or absence of mundane realism, psychological realism is difficult to detect. Beating an inflatable toy doll, as was done in the famed Bobo doll study (Bandura et al., 1963) discussed further in Chapter 11, seems artificial. However, Bandura and colleagues (1963) argued that children learn behavior from models, internalize these responses, and then use them in "real" situations that elicit frustration. In other words, the *psychological mechanisms* in the experiment were realistic.

The purpose of the Stanford study and other prison studies including the Lovibond and BBC studies was not to try to recreate a real prison environment, but to examine psychological factors that were characteristic of prison environments. The BBC prison study authors reflected upon this issue as follows:

> The aim of the study was not to simulate a prison (which, as in the Stanford study, would have been impossible on ethical and practical grounds) but rather to create an institution that in many ways resembled a prison ... as a site to investigate the behavior of groups that were unequal in terms of power, status, and resources. What is critical, then, is not that the study environment replicated a real prison (which no such environment ever could), but that it created inequalities between groups that were real to the participants. (Reicher & Haslam, 2006, p. 7)

Guiding question: Did the researcher ensure that the manipulation had the intended effect?

A related question becomes crucial: How effective was the manipulation used in the study? Researchers use **manipulation checks** to determine whether they were successful in producing the desired effect. Let us assume that researchers, inspired by the Stanford study, wanted to determine whether the sense of power among guards and powerlessness among prisoners is responsible for hostile encounters in a simulated prison. Like Lovibond, Mithiran, and Adams (1979), they set up several simulated prisons that varied in the amount of control possessed by guards. We may accept that they have, in fact, created environments varying in the perceived guard power. Most researchers, however, are not comfortable with the assumption and will attempt to measure guard power as a manipulation check. The BBC study authors were interested in determining whether manipulations presumed to give participants the sense that they could change the prison environment would have the intended effect. As a tool to assess the impact of the manipulations, the authors asked participants whether they perceived the relationship between prisoners and guards as changeable.

Let us consider another example. In this study described below (Chao, Cheng, & Chiou, 2011), the authors attempted to elicit shame in participants by having them fail at an easy task. In order to ensure the manipulation had the intended effect, they asked participants about their emotional state after receiving the failure feedback.

... Method

We induced shame in participants by informing them that they failed a competitive reaction time task. In the shame condition, the participants were told that their opponent was one of the slowest contestants tested so far. After they clicked the "Completion" icon, which was hyperlinked to the contestant rankings posted on the Web page of the laboratory, they saw their own name at the bottom of a ranking list (below their opponent's name) ...

Following the affect manipulation, participants were asked to choose an affective state from six affective states that best described their current feelings (i.e.,
shamed, pleasurable, embarrassed, proud, humiliated, or neutral) ... Those
participants whose chosen affects were not congruent with the affect manipulation were excluded from subsequent analyses. (p. 204)

Notice that the authors asked participants about their affective state and participants that were not experiencing the anticipated shame response "were
excluded from subsequent analyses."

Considering whether the study was ethical

The Stanford Prison study was reviewed by an **Institutional Review Board** (IRB)
that is responsible for ensuring the rights and safety of research participants.
Though the study was approved and the American Psychological Association
(APA) later determined the existing guidelines were followed, Zimbardo (2007)
acknowledged several ethical problems. These problems include the unreasonable amount of distress to participants, failure to disclose the actual arrests
of prisoners at their homes in the instructions, and deceiving parents when
visiting the prison. Lastly, Zimbardo acknowledged, as illustrated in the quote
below, that he should have ended the study sooner, but he lost objectivity by
occupying the dual roles of prison superintendent and research investigator:

> In retrospect, I believe that the main reason I did not end the study sooner, when it
> began to get out of hand, resulted from the conflict created in me by my dual roles as
> principal investigator, and thus guardian of the research ethics of the experiment, and
> as prison superintendent, eager to maintain the integrity and stability of my prison at
> all costs. (Zimbardo, 2007, pp. 234–235)

The question of whether the Stanford Prison study was ethical is more complex than it may initially appear. When we look back at the abuse that took
place, with the benefit of hindsight, it may seem obvious that it should never
have been approved and would not be approved today. Though humiliation
was anticipated, the extent of the abusive behavior was not anticipated by
the IRB members or the researchers. Zimbardo did provide informed consent and an extensive debriefing and has made a strong argument for the
numerous benefits of the study (Zimbardo, 2007). However, using the current
ethical IRB guidelines, the study would likely not be approved today. As we
have seen, however, there have been modified **replications** of classic studies
and the Stanford Prison study is no exception.

In many countries, such as the UK and the USA, there are clear ethical guidelines in place regarding the use of human subjects employed in
research. For example, a set of guidelines were published in 1979 by the USA

National Commission for the Protection of Human Subjects of Biomedical and Behavioral Research. Referred to as the Belmont Report, this emphasizes the principles of respect for persons, beneficence, and justice (Fischer, 2006). The **informed consent**, according to the report, needs to include such information as the purpose of the study, anticipated risk and harm, benefits of participation, and should include a statement that participants can withdraw at any time. This is where the Stanford study would run into trouble if submitted to an IRB today. In the research proposal, Zimbardo notes that subjects will be "discouraged from quitting" and the language in the informed consent did not suggest that the participants could withdraw at any time. The Belmont Report is also clear that any inhumane treatment of participants will not be allowed. As mentioned, the inhumane treatment of participants in the Stanford study may not have been anticipated at the outset, but when the abusive guard behavior and prisoner breakdowns escalated, the study should have been discontinued.

Logical fallacies

It might be tempting, but inappropriate, to apply a **two wrongs make a right fallacy** to an evaluation of the ethics of studies like the Stanford Prison study. In other words, "the bad things that happened to the Stanford study participants are justifiable because bad things happen to people in prisons every day."

Considering the objectivity of the researcher

As you will recall from Chapter 2, adopting a questioning attitude is an essential element of critical thinking. Much of this attitude is aimed at addressing methodological and theoretical issues. However, there may be circumstances in which we need to question the objectivity of researchers particularly when the research is surrounded by heated debate, as is the case for much of the research in this book.

There is little doubt that Zimbardo was seeking results that could be used to support arguments for prison reform, an endeavor to which he has devoted much of his career. Zimbardo has described himself as anti-corrections and anti-prison (Sommers, 2009) and, assuming he held these attitudes at the time of the study, this would certainly raise concerns about his objectivity in light of his role as both prisoner superintendent and principal investigator.

Did this anti-prison attitude affect Zimbardo's interpretation of the results? There is likely no definitive answer, but there are some questions we can ask ourselves in this situation. First, we want to consider whether the results have been replicated or are consistent with other similar studies. We might also consider the transparency of the research or the extent to which the researcher described how data was collected and analyzed and his/her will-ingness to share data.

Lastly, other troubling revelations about the objectivity of Zimbardo have surfaced (Blum, 2018; Le Texier, 2018).

KEY READING – Blum, B. (2018). The lifespan of a lie. *Medium* (June). Retrieved from https://medium.com/s/trustissues/the-lifespan-of-a-lie-d869212b1f62.

As any student of introductory psychology classes will attest, the behavior of the guards is presented as spontaneous and sadistic. Guards became increasingly abusive as situational forces overwhelmed them. Contrary to this portrayal, Thibault Le Texier (in press) at the University of Nice has, through an extensive review of the study's records and interviews with participants, uncovered evidence that guard behavior was hardly spontaneous. Guards were given rules; they did not create them as Zimbardo has maintained. Waking the prisoners in the middle of the night for "counts," one of the iconic images of sadistic guard tendencies, was scripted by Zimbardo and the prison warden, David Jaffe. The scripting did not end there as Le Texier explains:

> And it was Zimbardo and Jaffe who suggested to the guards to tyrannize the prisoners by being sarcastic or ironic, humiliating them, depriving them of their privileges, lengthening the counting sessions, opening their mail, having them clean their cells or inflicting meaningless punishments on them like removing burr and straw from their blankets. (p. 14)

Considering the drastically different results obtained by the BBC prison study authors, it is not surprising that they and Zimbardo debated the studies in the literature (Haslam & Reicher, 2006; Zimbardo, 2006). While the results of the BBC study, as is the case with any study, can be contested on methodological, theoretical, and ethical grounds, Zimbardo engaged in **ad hominem** attacks on the BBC authors, questioning their scientific integrity (Zimbardo, 2006). Such attacks take the focus off the argument (i.e., an alternative to Zimbardo's assertion about situational influences) and shift it to the person. By discrediting the person, we indirectly discredit the argument they are making (Van Vleet, 2011).

Chapter summary

Let us return to the questions raised at the beginning of this chapter. How do we understand the perpetrators of evil acts? Does the explanation lie in the person and his/her characteristics or in the situation or the system? The

Stanford study highlighted the importance of often-overlooked situational forces. Yet, as critical thinkers, we now know there is much to learn from looking closely at the sample and asking how participants were recruited, whether those interested in the study may differ from those who would pass, and how the information given to participants may influence their behavior. In the Stanford study, the problem of selection bias forces us to consider the personality characteristics that lead people to a study of prison life and those who work in prison environments. A consideration of demand characteristics suggests we exercise caution when interpreting some of the extreme behavior displayed in the study. We also know that we need to be aware of the language used to describe the results of a study. Causal conclusions are appropriate for more scientifically controlled experiments like the Lovibond and BBC prison studies, but not the Stanford study.

The job of the researcher is not an easy one. Researchers attempt to create a psychologically compelling and realistic task for participants, while ensuring that subjects are not unnecessarily stressed, all the while keeping potential biases in check. While Zimbardo and colleagues may have failed in some respects, as critics point out, we want to be careful about dismissing studies that may appear to present participants with unrealistic situations. Creating a "real" prison environment for the Stanford study participants would have been impossible to achieve, unethical, and overly costly. As it was, the study generated significant debate, particularly between the Stanford and BBC study authors. This makes drawing conclusions about the study difficult. Rather than picking a side, we will likely form a more nuanced opinion if we attempt to understand the motivations among those embroiled in the debate, consider the consistency of results across studies, and closely evaluate the strengths and weaknesses of each viewpoint.

Future directions

If you have come across second-hand accounts of the Stanford study, you have likely seen the following remark: "Studies like this could never be done today." As we have seen with the Lovibond and the BBC study, this is not the case, though notably these studies were not conducted in the USA. There is no reason to believe that future research will not tackle the questions that remain unanswered by the Lovibond, BBC, and Stanford studies. While Zimbardo has argued passionately for the power of the situation, others have countered by highlighting the role of personality characteristics. As critical thinkers, we want to be wary of definitive statements about the power of either influential factor in isolation. Think about your own personality and how you would describe yourself. Are you outgoing or an extrovert? If so, think about all the situations you encounter over the course of a week that involve extroversion. If you think about each, you will realize that your personal extroversion varies across situations. You were a little more hesitant to talk the first day of classes at university than you were when you went out with friends on the weekend. However, if we were to measure your extroversion in each situation and calculate an average level for each week, it would be remarkably consistent (Fleeson, 2004).

While we can be certain there will be other prison studies and, unfortunately other Abu Ghraib situations, the debate about the relative importance of personality and situational forces is unlikely to be resolved. Recall that one of the Abu Ghraib guards, Chip Fredrick, was described by Zimbardo as an ordinary guy. Yet, while the psychiatrist (Nelson) who evaluated him noted concerns about his character, he also cautioned that Fredrick's traits by themselves could not account for the abuse. An environment in which there was no oversight and no threat of punishment was also a key factor. Neither dispositions nor situational forces by themselves were sufficient to explain the abuses that occurred in Palo Alto, California, in 1971 or Baghdad, Iraq, more than 30 years later.

When we consider future research addressing the questions raised by the Stanford study, it is important to consider the evolution of research ethics. We must interpret the Stanford study and other studies into the historical, social, and cultural milieu of its times. It is unfair, misleading, and deceptive to interpret research results out of context. A study like the Stanford study that was designed, carried out, and reported nearly 50 years ago cannot be judicially and critically interpreted through the lens of today's established standards of ethical treatment of human subjects and the social/cultural setting in which we now live. However, it is important that we learn from the aforementioned shortcomings of the Stanford study. This is how research ethics evolve.

Discussion questions

1. How would you design an experiment to determine whether the orientation of the guards affected their behavior? Consider that you might offer different instructions to guards randomly assigned to two groups.
2. How are prisons and prison guards typically depicted in movies and on television? Do you think this could influence how someone would act in a study like the Stanford Prison study? What is the most important goal in creating television or movie depictions of prison guards.
3. Why do you think the Stanford Prison study has attracted so much attention over the years and evoked such passion among citizens?

CHAPTER

7 Media Research: Is Violent Media Making Us More Aggressive?

Primary source: Bushman, B. J., & Anderson, C. A. (2009). Comfortably numb: Desensitizing effects of violent media on helping others. *Psychological Science, 20*, 273–277.

Chapter objectives

This chapter will help you become a better critical thinker by:

- Evaluating arguments over the influence of violent video games on aggression
- Comparing and contrasting the strengths and limitations of laboratory studies and field studies
- Assessing the strengths and limitations of laboratory measures of aggression
- Weighing the merits of the General Aggression and Catalyst models
- Recognizing the logical errors that surface in politically charged debates

---

Introduction

Imagine that you just finished playing a violent video game where you seek out a target and by moving the controller and pressing a button your selected target for extermination falls by the wayside on the screen and you move on and up to the next level of play. Everything looks very realistic in high definition on screen and you take pride in eliminating your adversary with quick thinking and lightning quick reflexes.

Questions:

#1 How likely are you the next day to "live out" this fantasy game and commit an actual violent act in the "real world"?

#2 Would this be a better world if we could somehow suddenly outlaw violent video games through federal legislation?

Our guess is that most of you would claim to have a crystal clear grasp of the difference between "fantasy" and the "real world" and not commit such an act of violence in response to Question #1. However, hopefully you recognize that the

---

question presents you with the most extreme and unlikely outcome of exposure to video game violence. Even critics of research demonstrating the harmful effects of violent media would not suggest that an individual will mindlessly act out the video game script. We might be better served by asking how long these effects might last and do the games provoke more subtle forms of aggression?

Question #2 also demands some deeper thinking. What if it was true that 99% of those in society who enjoy playing violent video games on screen failed to commit violent aggressive acts? How do we protect people in our world from such violence of the 1% without infringing upon the rights of the majority who seem to be able to handle this "fantasy versus reality" dilemma? Even a ban on the creation, selling, and use of such violent video games would not prevent those who had a high desire to play such games from finding these games on the "black market."

Think about the Prohibition days in the 1920s and 1930s when drinking alcoholic beverages was made illegal in the USA under the Volstead Act. Were the individual rights of many sacrificed for the sins of the few? How might we differentiate those in society who safely use firearms for hunting and other socially acceptable purposes from those who employ such firearms to commit crimes and kill other human beings? Can we learn something from past history here?

As we employ our normal human tendency to seek causal explanations for violence in society, we must also consider how strong the link is between the assumed antecedent of such violence and media sensationalism of violence. For example, in the tabloids we rarely see issues presented such as how individuals can be held responsible for actions; how individual freedoms are highly revered in society; and how social control mechanisms deemed to be for the public good might be best administered.

Study background

In the early hours of April 9, 2013, 60-year-old Ljubisa Bogdanovic went on a shooting spree in a village outside the Serbian capital of Belgrade. Before taking his own life, Bogdanovic killed more than a dozen people, mostly neighbors and family members, including his wife and son. His background revealed potentially traumatic experiences including his father's suicide when Ljubisa was a child. It is what his background did not reveal that is the focus of this chapter, namely a history of playing violent video games.

Such games were, however, implicated in a mass shooting that took place only months earlier in Newtown, Connecticut, USA. If this chapter is about violent video game research, why discuss a case in which such games appeared to play no role rather than the Newtown massacre in the USA?

The fact that the media *did not* mention that violent games played no role in the mass killing in Serbia is revealing. A selective use of cases which fit the narrative of violent video games as a cause of violence may lead to inaccurate perceptions among the public and unnecessarily impact public policies (social, governmental, etc.) regarding video games or violent media in general (Ferguson, 2013). So, it is not just the media research itself that demands our critical analysis, but the dissemination of this research to the public. Let us look at an example of research on the effects of violent video games.

In Study 1 of their research, psychologists Brad Bushman and Craig Anderson (2009) randomly assigned participants to an experimental or control condition in which they would play either a violent or a non-violent video game for 20 minutes. Several minutes after playing, when the participant was in the process of completing a questionnaire, a staged (fake) fight began outside the laboratory. The fight, in which two females or two males were arguing over a significant other, was clearly audible to participants. Near the end of the "fight," one person injures an ankle, the aggressor leaves, and the victim groans in pain. The experimenter is timing how long it takes the participant, moments after playing the video game, to come to the aid of the fight victim. The violent/non-violent content of the video games served as the **independent variable** and the response time to helping the supposedly injured person was the **dependent variable** in this laboratory study. Results revealed that those who played violent video games took longer to help the victim and rated the fight as less severe compared to those who played a non-violent game. In Study 2, Bushman and Anderson staged an incident outside a movie theater in which a female **confederate** with a wrapped ankle dropped her crutches. The experimenter, out of the sight of participants, recorded how long it took moviegoers to come to the aid of the confederate who had purposefully dropped her crutches. As in Study 1, participants exposed to violent media took longer to help.

Helping behavior is one of several outcomes predicted by the **General Aggression Model (GAM)** (Anderson & Carnagey, 2004). According to this model, violent video games produce aggressive thoughts, feelings, and increased arousal. The GAM adopts a social cognitive view of aggression, suggesting that exposure to video game violence influences behavior and personality (decreased helping and increased aggression) over time by increasing the accessibility of violent scripts, or mental representations for how to act in a situation, and increasing insensitivity to violence.

The literature on video games specifically and media violence more generally is extensive. When such a large body of research exists, **meta-analyses**, which combine findings across studies, become useful tools to help draw general conclusions. In a meta-analysis by Anderson and colleagues (2010), the average **effect size** between violent video games and aggressive behavior was 0.189. Across studies, violent video game exposure was associated with aggressive behavior, cognition, and affect and less prosocial behavior and empathy.

Current thinking

Estimates for the correlation between violent video games and aggression have been as low as 0.04 and as high as 0.29 across meta-analyses. While the aforementioned meta-analysis by Anderson and colleagues (2010) suggested a causal relationship between violent video games and aggression, a meta-analysis by Ferguson (2007a) suggested no such relationship exists. Moreover, some researchers have argued that while most studies have focused on the violent features of video games, an overlooked feature, competitiveness, may better account for the resulting aggression.

Even if the overwhelming majority of studies suggest that exposure to violent video games causes aggression, critics note the importance of considering the effect sizes across studies. Guidelines for interpreting effect sizes suggest that correlations of 0.10, 0.30, and 0.50 are small, medium, and large effects, respectively (Cohen, 1994). The estimates for the effects of violent media vary, but are generally small. Put in the context of other contributing factors such as genetics, self-control, and childhood abuse (correlations ranging from 0.25 to 0.75) the video game contribution to violence pales in comparison (Ferguson & Kilburn, 2009).

Support for the GAM has been inconsistent, as some contemporary research (Ferguson et al., 2008) testing the model has indicated no greater aggression produced by short-term exposure to violent video games than that by non-violent video games. Likewise, long-term exposure does not seem to produce greater aggression in the laboratory. Ferguson and colleagues (2008) have proposed an alternative model, the **Catalyst Model**, which considers one's predisposition to aggression and violence. These authors suggest that individuals genetically predisposed to violence will be more likely to consume violent media and will be more easily provoked to violence when experiencing environmental stress. Though such individuals may model the violence they have seen (e.g., in video games), the violent media did not cause the act. Thus, the proponents of this model emphasize the predispositions to violence and the active role that the individual plays in seeking out violent media.

> **KEY READING** – Ferguson, C. J., & Konijn, E. A. (2015). She said/he said: A peaceful debate on video game violence. *Psychology of Popular Media Culture*, 4, 397–411.

Thus, the key differences between the GAM and the Catalyst Model has to do with causality. Fundamental to the GAM is that violent media causes an increase in aggressive responding, whereas in the Catalyst Model it influences the form that the aggressive act takes (i.e., acting out what they have seen in a game or movie), but plays no causal role. There has also been concern expressed with the measurement of aggression in the laboratory. Key among these concerns is whether aggression inside the lab generalizes outside of this highly controlled setting. As you will read about in this chapter, the debate has become quite contentious with one side accused of exaggerating the influence of the media and the other accused of denial. Such politically charged arguments have a tendency to distract from and negatively influence the science so critical to better informing public policy and the public at large.

> **KEY READING** – Ferguson, C. J. (2008). Violent video games: How hysteria and pseudoscience created a phantom public health crisis. *Paradigm*, *12*, 12–13, 22.

Field studies

Studies like Bushman and Anderson's (2009) Study 1 are often criticized for lacking **external validity** (Wood, Wong, & Chachere, 1991). Bushman and Anderson (2009) addressed this criticism in Study 2 by conducting a **field study**. Field studies involve the examination of the variables of interest (e.g., violent media and aggression) in a natural (more realistic) setting. Technically, Bushman and Anderson conducted a field *experiment* as they manipulated the type of movie (violent versus non-violent). An advantage of this type of study is that it is a closer approximation of behavior that would naturally unfold in everyday life. However, there are degrees of "naturalness" in such studies and, ideally, a researcher, in order to maximize external validity, would observe and record behavior in a setting in which the independent variable really does occur naturally without any manipulation from the experimenter (Tunnell, 1977).

In the Bushman and Anderson study, participants were helping who they thought to be an injured person (a natural behavior) at a movie theater (a natural setting), but this situation was staged by the researchers. Still, this experience is something that a person might encounter in the real world outside of the laboratory. Compare this to the typical lab study in which a person plays a video game in a college classroom for a specified amount of time and then responds to a hypothetical vignette. Which example sounds more like an everyday encounter?

If external validity is so much better in a field study, you may wonder why researchers would ever rely on anything else. Unfortunately, the enhanced external validity comes at the expense of internal validity. For one thing, it is challenging to control for **confounds** or variables other than the independent variable that might impact the results. However, there are some factors that you can control equally well in the field study as in the laboratory. For example, in a study by Wispe and Freshley (1971) involving a confederate dropping a grocery bag, the independent variable was the race of the person dropping the groceries. The researchers went to great lengths to make sure that other differences between the two women who served as "bag droppers" were controlled for (e.g., shirt color, height, weight, etc.). The thought given to internal validity and the consistency of the "drops" are evident in the following description:

> As the groceries hit the pavement, the dropper gave appropriate gestures of surprise and displeasure. In apparent dismay, she circled the groceries slowly for about 5–10 seconds, thereby giving the subject time to come to her aid. Each drop was timed so that the subject was approximately 10 feet from the dropper when the groceries hit. Since the dropper stood with her back to the approaching subject, and her gaze fixed on her spilled groceries, no eye contact was possible before the helping behavior began. (p. 60)

Let's return to the Bushman and Anderson (2009) study. Recall that the researchers staged an incident outside a movie theater involving a female confederate ostensibly in need of assistance.

There are likely several factors to consider in the scenario. Perhaps you wondered whether the number of individuals in the vicinity of the person in need of help might impact how long it would take a person to respond. Another factor that might be less apparent is that the variability in personality traits or individual differences among participants is greater in the field as opposed to a study conducted on a college campus using college student participants. The cultural context and country of the location might offer still other clues to research findings here. Bushman and Anderson (1998) also note, in comparing field and laboratory studies, that there is a greater ability to control the content and the timing of exposure in the lab and that laboratory studies generally involve more aggressive content and a shorter interval between exposure to the content and the measurement of aggression. Lastly, if the confederate is not blind to conditions or is aware of them, there is potential for this knowledge to affect the confederate's behavior in a manner that supports the hypothesis (Ramos et al., 2013).

Though there are many factors that could impact the results of field studies, it would be cynical to dismiss the research on the grounds that these uncontrolled factors could have had a non-trivial effect on the results. Bushman and Anderson (2009) did find that participants having viewed a violent film took significantly longer to help the "victim" than those having viewed a non-violent movie. Our confidence in these findings should be strengthened and doubts about the internal validity lessened considering these results were similar to those obtained in the laboratory (Study 1).

Inconsistent results across meta-analyses

As noted earlier, the meta-analytic results on the effects of video game violence on aggression have been inconsistent. The same groups of researchers who point to different single studies showing effects/no effects are conducting the meta-analyses that also produce very different results (Anderson & Bushman, 2001; Anderson et al., 2004; Anderson et al., 2010; Ferguson,

2007a; Ferguson, 2007b; Ferguson, 2015a; Ferguson & Kilburn, 2009). For example, as mentioned above, estimates for the correlation between violent video games and aggression have been as low as 0.04 and as high as 0.29 across meta-analyses. How could researchers produce such different results? In order to answer this question, we need to consider differences in the design. In meta-analyses, researchers have to make a decision as to what studies to include. For example, in a meta-analysis by Anderson and colleagues (2010) all studies up to 2008 including those published in peer-reviewed journals and those that went unpublished were included. Across studies, the average **effect size** between violent video games and aggressive behavior was 0.189.

Quite lower effect size estimates were produced in a meta-analysis by Ferguson (2007b). As displayed on the top portion of Figure 7.1, a key difference across studies is the degree to which researchers controlled for variables other than video game violence. The reduction in correlations suggests these variables were significant contributors to aggression. However, in the Ferguson (2007a) study in which effect sizes were lower, the author included only peer-reviewed journal publications from 1995 to 2007; a much more limited sample of studies. Estimated effect sizes ranged from 0.04 to 0.14. In a more recent meta-analysis, Ferguson (2015a) found similar estimates (0.17–0.6), while expanding the inclusion criteria. Therefore, these differences have essentially allowed both "sides" to argue that the other's meta-analysis is flawed. Including some of the older, poorly designed studies was a flaw and only including peer-reviewed publications leads to an inaccurate estimate of the effect, the other side would charge respectively. Aside from the meta-analysis, a closer look at the individual studies reveals some additional sources of contention between the two "sides."

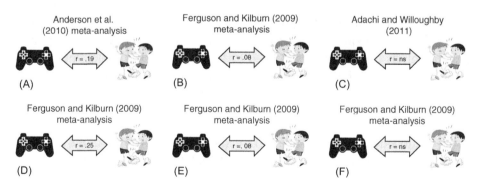

Figure 7.1

Note: Top portion of the figure: The Anderson et al. (2010) meta-analysis (A) indicates that violent video game exposure is significantly correlated with aggression (r = .19). The correlation is reduced (r = .08) when controlling for third variables like family violence and personality as in the Ferguson and Kilburn meta-analysis (B). The correlation is further reduced (r = ns) when controlling for video game features like competitiveness, as in the Adachi and Willoughby (2011) study (C).

Bottom portion of the figure: Ferguson and Kilburn (2009) demonstrate that across meta-analyses, the more direct the measure of aggression (from a proxy measure as in D, aggressive behavior towards another person as in E, and violent behavior as in F) the lower the correlation between it and violent video game exposure.

Video game dimensions

Video games differ on a number of dimensions. Some games are fast and some are slow, some are realistic and some are pure fantasy, some are competitive and some are not. Some of these features may have nothing to do with aggression, yet some may be related (see the top portion of Figure 7.1). The extent to which such features matter depends on their relationship with the dependent variable, in this case aggression. If related, the feature is a potential confound. For example, it is a well-established finding that frustration, whether induced by a video game or some other situation, produces aggression (Berkowitz, 1989). So, let us assume that a researcher had participants in an experimental group play a video game that was both violent and frustrating and concluded that the violent features of the game accounted for the increased aggression. Violence may be the key variable, but if the researcher had not controlled for or systematically varied frustration, it remains possible that the frustration element of the game could account for the increased aggression.

In the study discussed above (Bushman & Anderson, 2009) the researchers had participants play a variety of violent games (e.g., *Mortal Kombat*) and later rate the games on a number of dimensions including how action-packed, involving, arousing, and exciting they were. These game features by themselves, however, did not influence the relationship between violence and aggression. Adachi and Willoughby (2011), on the other hand, suggested that researchers had overlooked a key game dimension – competitiveness – and hypothesized that controlling for this feature would influence the relationship between game violence and aggression. As hypothesized, the researchers found no significant differences in aggressive behavior among participants playing a violent and non-violent game matched on competitiveness (as well as difficulty and pace of the game). In a second study, the researchers found that those playing a competitive non-violent game were more aggressive than those playing a less-competitive violent game. So, not only is competitiveness related to the dependent variable, but violent video games tend to be more competitive than non-violent games. The Adachi and Willoughby (2011) study raised doubts about conclusions on the role of video game violence in studies failing to control for competitiveness. There are other reasons why researchers fail to replicate previous findings including differences in the controlled variables which may be confounding, differences in the samples used, and different methods used such as different measures of aggression.

Critical thinking toolkit
Measuring constructs of validity in the laboratory

Guiding question: To what extent have the researchers evaluated and reported the validity of the measure(s) they employed in the study?

In addition to considering the important differences that may exist among games, media researchers have the equally difficult task of defining and measuring aggression. To make matters of interpreting the video game research even more of a challenge, scholars also disagree on how best to do this. Adachi and Willoughby (2011), as cited earlier, used a method referred to as the hot sauce paradigm, in which participants are told that as part of a food preference study they will be preparing a hot sauce tasting for a person who does not like spicy food. This, of course, is the **cover story** given to the participant and no one is actually consuming the infernal hot sauce. Thus, the *intensity* of the hot sauce the person selects and the *amount* of hot sauce served function as the measure of aggression. Another popular option involves participants competing against a fictitious opponent in an arranged reaction time task. When the participant responds more quickly than his/her opponent, he/she has the opportunity to administer a blast of noise to the loser through headphones. While the original version of this task involved the administration of shocks rather than noise blasts – raising ethical concerns – the modified version has been criticized because it has not been used in a standardized or uniform fashion and has questionable external validity (Ferguson & Rueda, 2009). Additionally, the competitive nature of the task has caused some to question whether participants may perceive the blasts as a way to gain a competitive advantage as the task progresses (Adachi & Willoughby, 2011).

So, how good are these measures? The most fundamental question is whether this measure is valid or is actually measuring what it is designed to measure (i.e., aggression). Researchers can establish **validity** by pointing to correlations between their measure and other established measures of aggression which have documented strong validity. Think about the process of joining a club. In order to gain membership you may need to have an established member to serve as a sponsor and vouch for you as a new member. Similarly, researchers could validate a measure of parental ratings of a child's aggression by showing that they correlate with aggressive ratings from teachers for the same research subjects. When researchers demonstrate correlations between measures of the same construct (i.e., aggression) in different formats (parenting ratings and teacher ratings) they are establishing **convergent validity**. Lastly, researchers can establish **predictive validity** if they can show that scores on a measure of parental ratings predict the likelihood of a future event like the child being expelled from school for fighting. Such support has been found for the hot sauce paradigm (Adachi & Willoughby, 2011; Lieberman et al., 1999).

In a peer-reviewed journal article, researchers will typically provide a brief review of the research supporting the reliability (consistency) and validity of a measure like the hot sauce paradigm or will direct the reader to the original publication of the measure which provides detailed reliability/validity information. For example, consider the development of a hypothetical measure of aggression (Hypothetical Aggression Measure (HAM)). The authors administered several measures of aggression (Hostility Inventory (HI); Physical Aggressiveness Scale (PAS); and Aggression

Inventory (AI)); a measure of social desirability (Social Desirability Scale (SDS)); and a measure of neuroticism (Neuroticism Inventory (NI)), a personality trait involving anxiety and moodiness. The results of the hypothetical correlational analysis are shown in Table 7.1. The significant positive correlations with the other measures of aggression and hostility suggest convergent validity. Researchers often look at the correlation between a measure like the HAM and social desirability to rule out the possibility that people are responding to the measure in a way that reflects how they want to be seen rather than how they truly are. The near zero correlation between the HAM and the SDS suggests that we can rule this out. Lastly, an important part of establishing validity is demonstrating that the measure is distinctive and is *not related* to certain other measures, referred to as divergent or **discriminant validity**. Discriminant validity is demonstrated in the non-significant correlation with the NI, suggesting that aggression and neuroticism are two distinct constructs.

Table 7.1 *Correlational results*

Measure	Hypothetical Aggression Measure (HAM)	
Hostility Inventory (HI)	0.52*	
Physical Aggressiveness Scale (PAS)	0.45*	Significantly correlated with the Physical Aggressiveness Scale (PAS)
Aggression Inventory (AI)	0.44*	
Social Desirability Scale (SDS)	0.08	
Neuroticism Scale	0.11	Not significantly correlated with the Neuroticism Scale (NS)
Note. $* p < 0.05$.		

The research that has relied on the noise blast method has generally found that exposure to video game violence leads to increased aggression (more intense or longer blasts relative to controls), though questions have been raised about the validity of this procedure (Ferguson & Rueda, 2009). As illustrated in the bottom portion of Figure 7.1, these indirect or proxy measures of aggression like the noise blast produce much higher correlations than those that directly measure aggression and violence.

Additionally, critics have pointed to the inconsistent use of aggression measures across studies (as illustrated in Table 7.2), lack of standardized procedures, the use of measures without well-established validity, and the lack of ecological validity (e.g., Ferguson & Kilburn, 2009). Figure 7.2 provides a summary of these criteria for evaluating laboratory studies and the measures used including the questions we want to ask to be able to determine their value.

Table 7.2   *Inconsistent use of the noise blast procedure*

Measure	Description	Studies	How measure was used	Results
Noise blast procedure	Participants compete against a fictitious partner in a competitive reaction time task. The winner of each trial is allowed to deliver a noise blast into the headphones of the loser. The **intensity and duration** of the blast serve as the measures of aggression. Participants can be told that if they select the highest levels this could cause hearing damage.	Anderson & Dill (2000)	Used duration and intensity. Participants were not told about potential hearing damage.	Results were significant for intensity, but not duration.
		Konijn, Nije Bijvank, & Bushman (2007)	Used intensity, but not duration. Participants were told about potential hearing damage.	Results were significant for intensity.
		Ferguson et al. (2008)	Used intensity, but not duration. Did not tell participants about potential hearing damage.	Results were not significant for intensity.
		Hasan, et al. (2013)	Used intensity and duration. Did not tell participants about potential hearing damage.	Results were significant for intensity and duration.

Are results consistent with a theory?

Results using the competitive reaction time task have been consistent with the General Aggression Model which is based on social-cognitive theory.

Are the results externally valid?

Attempts to correlate the competitive reaction time task and "real world" aggression have been unsuccessful. Likewise, video game consumption and violent crime rates are *negatively correlated.*

Is the behavior ecologically valid?

Some aggression paradigms involve behaviors like shooting someone with a (pellet) gun or giving someone a potentially painful dose of hot sauce to drink, which are forms of aggression that appear outside of the laboratory and, thus, are ecologically valid. Administering electric shocks or noise blasts are not.

Is the participant in the lab actually acting aggressively?

Participants in some studies using the competitive reaction time task have been told that levels 8, 9, and 10 could cause permanent hearing damage. However, critics have suggested that participants may be blasting to gain a competitive advantage in the task (a competitive rather than aggressive response) and that they may be responding to *demand characteristics.*

Is the measure valid?

Some aggression paradigms (e.g., the hot sauce paradigm) have been shown to correlate with other valid measures of aggression. Such results attest to their convergent validity. Research suggests that this type of validity is lacking in the competitive reaction time task. A related issue is wheather or not there are agreed upon rules or standards for the use of the measure (the measure is standardized).

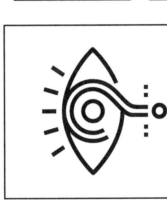

Figure 7.2 Criteria for evaluating laboratory studies

Generalizability of results

It might be tempting to dismiss laboratory research in psychology, if you focus on the superficial aspects of aggressive behavior in the lab and look for similarities between it and "real world" behavior. What does hitting an inflatable doll, such as in the classic Bobo doll study conducted by Albert Bandura, or giving people too much hot sauce, or blasting noise in people's ears, have to do with real aggression? This is a fair question and is a signpost of critical thinking. Some psychologists suggest that the form of aggression has little to do with the basic concept of aggression (Tedeschi & Quigley, 1996); yet it can also be misleading to focus only on the superficial aspects of behavior. Anderson and Bushman have found an impressive level of correspondence between laboratory studies and field studies of aggression (Anderson, Lindsay, & Bushman, 1999). For example, personality trait aggressiveness predicts real world aggression and aggressive behavior in the laboratory (Bushman & Anderson, 1998). Recall the consistent results obtained by Anderson and Bushman (2009) in both a laboratory and a field study on the effects of violent media on helping behavior. It is the "theory" that is generalized or the "conceptual relations among variables" that are generalized (Bushman & Anderson, 1998, p. 44). Consider a study by Bushman and Anderson (2002) in which participants were given hypothetical scenarios to respond to after playing either violent or non-violent video games. One of the scenarios is as follows:

> Todd was on his way home from work one evening when he had to brake quickly for a yellow light. The person in the car behind him must have thought Todd was going to run the light because he crashed into the back of Todd's car, causing a lot of damage to both vehicles. Fortunately, there were no injuries. Todd got out of his car and surveyed the damage. He then walked over to the car.

Participants were then asked to write down what they thought Todd would "do or say, think, and feel as the story continues" (p. 1684). Participants in the violent game condition produced significantly more aggressive responses in these scenarios than those in the control condition. You could dismiss the results of this study as being "artificial," after all participants are simply responding to a hypothetical situation in a psychology lab. But rather than dismiss the findings, consider the results in terms of the theory which suggests that exposure to violent media increases the aggressive expectations that people have in such ambiguous but potentially frustrating situations and, again, the correspondence between these findings and those in field studies which is high.

Evaluating theoretical accounts of video game violence and aggression

As noted earlier in the chapter, the dominant model of video game violence is the GAM. A good theory is comprehensive and benefits from consistency with other theories. In some ways, the GAM appears inconsistent with other theories. Critics, for example, have argued that it does not adequately account for biological and personality inputs (accounted for by an alternative model, the Catalyst Model, Ferguson et al., 2008), does not make a distinction between real violence and fictional violence (a distinction the human brain obviously makes), and presents a view of aggression that is inconsistent with evolutionary theory (Ferguson & Dyck, 2012), all of which diminish the credibility of a model (Haig, 2009).

Precision and falsifiability, two other important criteria for evaluating a theory, go hand in hand. The less precise the theory the more difficult it is to falsify. Unfortunately, for the GAM the operational definition of video game violence and aggression is surprisingly imprecise. There are important differences among the violent video games (shooting, fighting) and between violent and non-violent video games (e.g., competitiveness). Imprecision has also been an issue with the defining of and measurement of aggression and violent video games (Ferguson & Dyck, 2012). Ferguson and Dyck (2012) explain the problem with the latter: "compiling primitive old-school games such as Pac-Man with multi-player games such as World of Warcraft with shooter games like Call of Duty under the concept of violent video game is likely about as meaningful as compiling the Christian Bible, the Red Badge of Courage, and Cujo together as 'violent literature' in a single conceptual space because all happen to contain violence" (p. 657). Employing valid and reliable instruments is crucial to the success of a theory, and without it the constructs remain vague and the theory cannot be put to the test and potentially falsified (Cramer, 2013).

Another criterion on which to evaluate a theory is its practical application. Ideally, the GAM would be capable of predicting youth violence and, therefore, be used to inform public policy. Though proponents of the model have argued for its applied value, critics have noted that trends in crime rates do not coincide with trends in violent media exposure (Ferguson & Dyck, 2012). Likewise, these critics argue that the GAM's application to criminology and criminal justice is limited at best.

Most important for the survival of a theory is supportive data. While a single study with results that contradict the theory may not be enough to invalidate it, it is important to keep a few things in mind about the weight of evidence. First, psychologists suggest that it is inappropriate to take a "box score" approach (Ruscio, 2004) in which you add up the number of studies for and against and whichever side has more prevails. Studies producing results that are inconsistent with the theory should be given more weight than those that support it (Cramer, 2013). Scientists are not supposed to "prove" their theory "true," but to attempt to falsify it. Second, direct replications that produce data inconsistent with the theory should be given more weight than conceptual replications that use different instructions and instruments (Ferguson, 2015b).

Logical fallacies

Failings in a politically charged debate

At the beginning of some articles demonstrating the negative effects of violent video games, researchers discuss some sensational cases of mass violence in which the perpetrator consumed violent media. At the same time, these researchers note how difficult it is to predict extreme violence and certainly media researchers should not be expected to produce such results or be held to such a standard. This selective and convenient use of sensational cases represents **confirmation bias** as those in which violent media plays no role, like the mass shooting in Belgrade in our "Study background" at the beginning of the chapter, are conveniently ignored (Ferguson, 2013). Highlighting only those cases which fit the narrative leads to inflated estimates of risk on the part of the public. We have a tendency to overestimate the likelihood of lethal events like mass shootings because of the sensational coverage in the media. Because of this media exposure, these instances are more accessible or readily available in our memory and their frequency overestimated (referred to as the **availability heuristic**; Tversky & Kahneman, 1973). In the aftermath of a recent school shooting in the USA, one of the authors of this text listened to callers on a radio program suggest that schools are out of control and parents should consider pulling their children from school and have them complete their studies online. Yet statistics suggest that school shootings in the USA are not on the rise and that more children are killed each year in bicycle accidents and pool drownings (Nicodemo & Petronio, 2018).

Additionally, research suggests it is the vividness of the event that further inflates estimates. Compare, for example, the vividness (e.g., a bloody crime scene) and frequency with which the media covers homicides and stomach cancer (Reber & Unkelbach, 2010). It may not surprise you that according to media coverage, the greater risk to our survival is homicide rather than stomach cancer. Vivid cases and headlines can serve as a very useful, but often deceptive tool. In other words, we are more likely to die from stomach cancer than be involved in a homicide. The murder of another human being is more dramatic, sudden, shocking, regrettable, and sensational than watching a person slowly die from stomach cancer (unless you are a family member or friend of the ill person).

'Ad hominem' attacks

Bushman and others have been accused of promoting a "social engineering agenda" and creating a moral panic. Those on the other side have been accused of simply denying the undeniable proof. Both represent **ad hominem** attacks, the likes of which we have seen in other contentious politicized science debates including between the authors of the Stanford and BBC prison studies. Ad hominem attacks involve personal attacks which if successfully employed lead us to disregard the person's argument without adequately evaluating it. In other words, the flaws of the person making the argument have led us to the conclusion that the argument itself is not valid (Risen & Gilovich, 2007). One roadblock to escaping the mire of defensiveness that characterizes such debates is the linkage between one's identity and scientific findings (Pratkanis, 2017). In such cases, scientific criticism threatens their identity and can provoke attacks on researchers who produced contradictory finding. A humble attitude and self-criticism is essential to scientific progress.

Bushman (2016) points to several well-established findings in psychology to suggest why people might have a hard time accepting research findings that demonstrate a harmful effect from violent media exposure. First, it might be the case that people are concerned about such findings leading to government restrictions on such games. When we feel like our freedom of choice might be restricted or infringed upon, we experience **psychological reactance** which influences our attitude toward the games and motivates us to regain our freedom (Brehm et al., 1966). Second, Bushman suggests, **cognitive dissonance** may be at play here. For the same reason that smokers might deny the harmful effects of cigarette smoking, those who love to play violent video games might be motivated to deny the effects in order to avoid the discomfort of this behavior-attitude inconsistency. Lastly, research suggests people have a tendency to expect that video game effects have an effect on other people but not themselves – what researchers refer to as the **third-person effect** (Scharrer & Leone, 2008).

Problem of the 'straw man'

It is also important to consider how different sides of an argument get distorted. When arguments are purposefully distorted in order to make them easier to refute, this tactic is referred to as the **straw man** (Pope & Vasquez, 2005). This may take one of the following forms: "It's not like playing a game in which you steal a car means I'm going to go out and steal a car" or "I play violent video games but it's not like I've gone out and shot up a school." These comments are misrepresentations of the argument which are easy to knock over (hence "straw man"). While media researchers have been guilty of using high-profile cases to frame the argument and justify the need for such research, none are claiming that the specific behavior one engages in during the video game is going to be mindlessly reenacted elsewhere. Likewise, not only are forms of extreme violence difficult to predict, but these complex actions are not going to be solely explained by video games or any other form of violent media. One might even consider the title of a recent meta-analysis to be such an example of the straw man: "Do angry birds make for angry children?" It has been argued by media scholars touting the harmful effects of violent media that "they are not suggesting that violent media is the only cause of aggression." Those skeptical of the harmful effects are, however, not arguing that media scholars think it is the only cause. One such skeptic, Christopher Ferguson, notes: "Such a rational sounding argument seems to imply that skeptics don't understand multivariate causality ... Just because we agree violence/aggression is multicausal doesn't mean that media violence has to be one of those causes" (Ferguson & Konijn, 2015, p. 399).

The golden mean fallacy

Some of these arguments may also take the form of **false dilemmas** or invalid disjunctions (Pope & Vasquez, 2005; Risen & Gilovich, 2007). For example, violent video games either lead you to shoot up a school or they have no effect. The **golden mean fallacy**, or fallacy of compromise, suggesting that the truth may be a compromise between two conflicting sides, is also at play in this debate (Pope & Vasquez, 2005). Compromise between two competing positions may take the form of "well if some research shows that video games have positive effects and some that they have negative effects then the truth must be somewhere in the middle" or "if there is a lack of consensus on this issue and some research demonstrates positive effects, then there must be negative effects as well." Similarly, Ferguson and Konijn (2015) note that some scholars may prefer to "view themselves as 'middle ground,' viewing the 'middle ground' as inherently more valuable than either pole" (p. 12).

Critical thinking toolkit
Recognizing bias

Guiding question: Have I considered how my own biases might impact my search for and interpretation of research?

The research on violent media we have discussed in this chapter has produced inconsistent results which prompt us to consider the larger question about the psychology of scientific research. How is it that researchers come to different conclusions about the amassed evidence when looking at the same ambiguous research? There are a couple of studies that help us understand this common circumstance. In addition to the confirmation bias, another cognitive bias that we fall prey to is referred to as **assimilation bias,** a tendency to interpret inconclusive research as providing support for our position. This tendency to process such information in a biased fashion was first demonstrated a number of years ago in a study by Stanford University researchers Charles Lord, Lee Ross, and Mark Lepper (1979). Opponents and proponents of capital punishment were given two studies that were similar except in one important way: one provided results supportive of the death penalty and one suggested it was ineffective. Rather than temper the views of each side, after reading the studies opponents were less in favor and proponents more in favor of capital punishment. Subjects evaluated studies supporting their position as more rigorous and more convincing than the opposing studies. The Lord and colleagues' (1979) study demonstrates how mixed results can produce a counterintuitive increase in the certainty of one's position and certainly helps us understand why the mixed results in video game violence research do not leave researchers on either side to be less convinced of their "correctness."

The importance of a study also has an effect on our evaluation of quality (Wilson et al., 1993). Participants in two studies conducted by Wilson and colleagues (1993) were research psychologists and medical school faculty many of whom had significant experience as editors of scientific journals. Yet the authors found evidence of what they called a leniency bias or a tendency to recommend publication of an important study (a study about heart disease) compared to an unimportant study (a study about heartburn). They also found evidence of an oversight bias as they perceived the heart disease study to be more rigorous or better designed than the unimportant study. As critical thinkers, we need to be aware of the potential for bias among researchers and those evaluating such research, including the journal editors, and our biases as consumers of such research. In addition to considering the aforementioned cognitive biases, we have to keep in mind the probabilistic nature of psychology and the multitude of variables at play in such research. This makes isolating one variable (e.g., game violence) difficult (Ramos et al., 2013) and can lead to inconsistent results and replication failures.

Considering the complexity of media research, we need to employ not only critical thinking but also a tolerance for ambiguity. This brings us to the last consideration. Critics of Bushman and other media violence researchers may claim: "researchers like Bushman have not proved that violent video games are harmful." If by "proof" one means that there is no uncertainty and no doubt, then it is true that Bushman and other researchers have not "proven" violent video games are harmful through the mechanisms proposed in the GAM. However, this is not an appropriate standard to hold for any researcher. Uncertainty is the rule not the exception in science. When scientific studies offer us conflicting findings, we must think more deeply about the topic in order to escape the conundrum. There are numerous studies that support the theory, but all theories are tentative and can be modified and even discarded with contradictory evidence (Lilienfeld et al., 2015).

Chapter summary

Numerous studies have demonstrated that exposure to violent media, including violent video games, is associated with aggressive responses. Though these findings have been replicated across various types of studies using different instruments, there is a growing body of research that fails to find such an effect, in part, because of the greater influence of video game features like competitiveness. While meta-analyses can often help us draw more definitive conclusions about such relationships between variables, quite different results have been obtained across these studies due to the varying quality and characteristics of the studies included. The relationship between video game violence and aggression has been examined in various types of studies including laboratory studies and field studies. These studies complement one another as the laboratory studies offer increased internal validity and field studies increased external validity. The perceived weaknesses of each can be addressed by an appreciation for the importance of testing conceptual relationships in a theory and being vigilant about potential confounds, respectively. Regardless of the type of study, we also want to consider the validity of measures of aggression. It is not hard to imagine that some children who play violent video games also engage in aggressive behavior. With a theory in place to account for such observations, additional research accumulates showing such a relationship. The theory with all its accumulated support has gained widespread acceptance among scholars. This acceptance might be warranted as the theory is comprehensive and precise; consistent with other theories; generates novel hypotheses; and has accumulated supportive cognitive, behavioral, and physiological data across laboratory studies, longitudinal studies, and field studies. Proponents of the GAM, the dominant model in the field for some time, have argued as such. Critics have argued that the effects are context-specific, that there are personality and/or biological factors which moderate the relationship between violent video games and aggression and also play a role in the preference for and consumption of such media (i.e., aggressive personality; Adachi & Willoughby, 2013; Cacioppo, Semin, & Bernston, 2004). An alternate model has emerged – the Catalyst Model – that addresses these concerns. This inconsistency in the results is also evident in meta-analyses that combine the results of these studies. The implications of the research for social policy, among other factors including the ambiguous results, have led to passionate debates among researchers as well as among the general public. It is important to evaluate the results of the research by considering the methodological issues we've discussed in this chapter and to also be aware of the cognitive biases and faulty logic that emerge in these debates.

Future directions

There are two media violence scholars at the center of the aforementioned debate who will likely continue conducting research motivated by their respective models, the GAM and the Catalyst models. In recent studies, Bushman and colleagues have examined the effects of 3D technology on gaming effects. Lull and Bushman (2016), for example, found that those playing violent games in 3D felt more immersed during play and angrier after play compared to those playing in 2D. Recall that the Catalyst Model accounts for genetic predispositions toward violence and the tendency for this to influence the consumption of violent media – both limitations of the GAM. Ferguson and Dyck (2012) suggested that future studies seeking to test the Catalyst Model should examine the interaction of genetic and environmental factors with violent media exposure as well as family violence. The key to unlocking the potential of the Catalyst Model lies in establishing that stressful environmental factors (e.g., family violence) serve to instigate or trigger aggression in the violence-prone individual. Thus, advances in gaming technology and genetic research may lead to exciting new avenues of research in search of support for the GAM and Catalyst models. If genetic factors could be established in the future as antecedents of aggression, we shall then confront delicate and complicated moral and ethical dilemmas regarding how to best implement such knowledge.

As noted at the beginning of this chapter, your interpretation of the research evidence that has been accumulated regarding how violent video games might influence aggressive behavior in society demands even more critical thinking. It seems clear that violent video games along with alcohol and firearms are not going to vanish as in some sort of science fiction totalitarian state. The thoughtful people concerned with promoting the welfare of human beings in society need to reject simplistic solutions to complex social issues and explore more thoughtful and creative solutions designed to curb violence without infringing upon individual human rights of citizens. Since violence in its many forms is a worldwide problem, we would be wise to learn from the experiences of others in the world arena as we strive for maintaining greater human safety and dignity within the context of individual freedoms.

Discussion questions

1. Why do you think violent video games are so often implicated in mass shootings in the USA?
2. How do you think you would respond as a participant in a study using the hot sauce or noise blast paradigms? Which seems more authentic? Which best produces aggression? Why?

8 Recovered Memories: Do We Dare Trust Them?

Primary source: Loftus, E. F., & Pickrell, J. E. (1995). The formation of false memories. *Psychiatric Annals, 25*, 720–725.

Chapter objectives

This chapter will help you become a better critical thinker by:

- Considering the factors which lead to inaccurate and false memories
- Examining what we know about trauma memory and how these memories may differ from other memories
- Evaluating the research techniques used in trauma memory and the evidence that supports these techniques
- Considering the role of confirmation bias in recovered memories
- Evaluating the self-help industry and the scientific evidence that supports such an entrepreneurial approach to offering mental health services

---

Introduction

Consider the following explanations regarding how human memory operates and choose the description that you feel best describes such complex mental abilities.

Option A: The mind is like a video recorder in that it stores precise images of all of our life experiences. When we try to remember something from the past, we just need to hit the rewind switch and suddenly all the details of the actual experience are accurately recalled.

Option B: Memory is most like a jigsaw puzzle where we recall pieces of information and use other information that might be provided in order to see if these items fit into the puzzle properly to get an accurate and detailed picture of the scene.

Answer: You are most "in tune" with the research on human memory if you chose Option B. In general, we believe that memory is selective and based on what we choose to focus on in a given situation. We also think that memory is reconstructed, so that we might add additional details not present that seem to logically fit the scene, have great assuredness that certain items were present when they were not, and have great confidence in the accuracy of our remembrances, even when our recall fails us.

The text that follows will build upon this notion of memory retrieval as a reconstructive mental process. Additionally, this chapter will challenge you to consider the malleability of memory and the relationship between one's confidence in and the accuracy of memory, and evaluate the consistency between the recovered memories literature and the science of memory.

Study background

Tracey, a 46-year-old woman, moved on to Donald Truluck's property in Alachua County, Florida with her husband. She had an uneasy feeling when she was around Truluck and years later began to have flashbacks. Through therapy, Tracey recovered memories of abuse that took place when she was 12 years old and the perpetrator of the sexual abuse was her aunt's boyfriend, Truluck. He later admitted to the abuse (Blakeley, 2015). Olivia McKillop, a successful child actor, was, by all accounts "well balanced" until high school, when she experienced some emotional difficulties including panic attacks. Through therapy, Olivia eventually recovered memories of incest and believed that she had been abused by her father, grandfather, and her brother. Cases like these have sparked a contentious debate within the scientific community, often referred to as the Memory Wars. The 1990s marked the zenith of the Memory Wars, the battle between those who believed that memories of childhood sexual abuse are often repressed and can be recovered in therapy and those who questioned repression as a typical response to trauma, questioned the techniques used by therapists to recover memories and noted the ease with which false memories can be implanted.

What is problematic about the therapeutic techniques used to recover memories? Psychologist Elizabeth Loftus explains that as the person begins to believe that an experience may have happened (which in the case of a false memory it did not), the addition of details added through imagination exercises fortifies this belief (Newby, 2010). In this chapter, we will explore this debate with particular attention given to the experimental research of Loftus that has significantly informed this field and challenged many of the assumptions that we have about memory.

Across several studies conducted in the 1970s, Loftus and her colleagues presented college students with a series of slides depicting an accident in which a car hits a pedestrian (Loftus, Miller, & Burns, 1978). In one of the slides, half of the participants see the car involved in the accident in front of a yield sign and half see the same car accident in front of a stop sign. After viewing the slides, participants are asked a series of questions, one of which includes misleading information about the sign. Specifically, half of the participants were asked "Did another car pass the red Datsun while it was stopped at the stop sign" and half were asked "Did another car pass the red

Datsun while it was stopped at the yield sign." When later asked to select the slide that they had seen, those given the misleading information (they saw a yield sign, but they were asked about the stop sign) were more likely to select the incorrect slide than those given consistent information. These studies and many since (Loftus, 2005) have documented this **misinformation effect** or change in memory after receiving misinformation. Other studies go a step further in that they involve implanting a false **autobiographical memory** or a detailed false memory referred to as **rich false memory**.

Loftus and Pickrell (1995) demonstrated the ease with which false memories can be implanted with a method commonly referred to as the "lost in the mall" technique. Based on information provided by a relative (e.g., mother), participants are mailed a booklet containing a brief description of four events that occurred during their childhood. Three of these are actual events and one is a fictitious event about getting lost at a mall at the age of five. Figure 8.1 is an example of a page for the false lost event from a participant's booklet. Participants are asked to write about what they remembered about the event or write "I don't remember this." In later interviews, they are asked to recall as much as they can about the event. Results indicated that 25% of participants remembered the false event in the booklet.

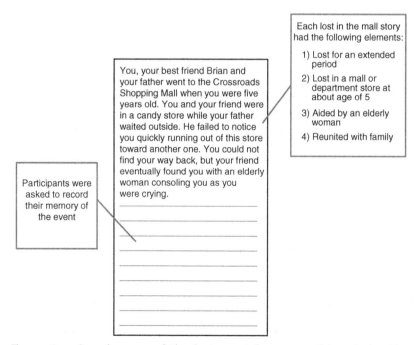

Figure 8.1 Sample page of the lost event from a participant's booklet. Participants are asked to write about what they remembered about the event

In another series of studies, Loftus and her colleagues (Braun, Ellis, & Loftus, 2002) removed any doubt that the memory was in fact false by introducing an impossible event – i.e., shaking hands with a Warner Brothers character (Bugs Bunny) while on vacation at Disney World or a character introduced years after the participants would have visited Disney as a child (Ariel from the Little Mermaid). Participants were shown two ads that contained false information about an encounter with a fictitious character at a Disney location. The information was presented in the form of an autobiographical advertisement:

> Go back to your childhood ... and remember the characters of your youth, Mickey, Goofy, and Daffy Duck ... Try to recall the day your parents finally brought you to their "home" at Walt Disney World®. (p. 6)

Before and after exposure to the ads, participants rated the likelihood of a number of events occurring before the age of ten, including shaking hands with Bugs Bunny/Ariel. Compared to those in the **control group** who received a non-biographical ad, those in the biographical ad conditions were more likely to report increased confidence in shaking hands with the character. Of those that received an ad about shaking hands with Bugs Bunny, 16% claimed that they had shook hands with the character after viewing the ad. The explanation for this increased confidence in false memories is what researchers refer to as **imagination inflation**. When told to imagine events that were reportedly unlikely to have occurred in childhood, participants report greater confidence in these events after imagination instructions. Garry and colleagues (1996), for example, found that nearly a quarter of subjects reported greater confidence in having tripped and broken a window with their hand when a child after imagining the event. This was double the increased confidence of the control participants. Similar results have been obtained across numerous studies, demonstrating the ease with which a false memory may be reported (Lynn et al., 2015).

Current thinking

Our intuition about memory tells us that memories of emotionally intense events, or **flashbulb memories**, are especially accurate, that the more confident we are in our memories the more accurate they are, that repression is a common coping mechanism in response to trauma, and that memory works like a tape or video recorder. Yet research suggests that flashbulb memories are not more accurate than any other type of memory (Talarico & Rubin, 2003), that confidence does not tell us about accuracy (Clark & Loftus, 1996), that repression is not a common response to trauma

(Fitzpatrick et al., 2010; Malmquist, 1986), and that our memories are reconstructions of events rather than recordings (Loftus & Ketcham, 1994). Survey research suggests that misconceptions among the public about memory persist (Loftus & Loftus, 1980; Lynn et al., 2015; Patihis et al., 2014; Simons & Chabris, 2011). Simons and Chabris, for example, found that 63% of individuals from a large representative sample in the USA agreed with the idea that memory works like a video camera and roughly 48% agreed that memories of events do not change over time. Such mistaken beliefs are held not just by the public, but by professional psychologists as well (Loftus & Loftus, 1980; Lynn et al., 2015).

> **KEY READING** – Lynn S. J., Evans J., Laurence J. R., & Lilienfeld, S. O. (2015). What do people believe about memory? Implications for the science and pseudoscience of clinical practice. *Canadian Journal of Psychiatry, 60*, 541–547.

The need to recover memories stems from the notion that trauma is associated with dissociation and repression. **Dissociation** is a sense of depersonalization that disrupts the retrieval of a memory, rendering it temporarily inaccessible. Likewise, **repression** or unconscious blocking of the memory, like dissociation, is believed by many (including clinicians) to be a common response to trauma (Patihis et al., 2014). McNally (2007) notes that some clinicians believe that sexually abused children learn to "disengage their attention during episodes of abuse" (p. 33). Research in which participants are exposed to trauma-related (e.g., rape) or neutral words (e.g., lamp) shows greater recall for trauma-related words than neutral words among childhood sexual abuse victims (McNally, Ristuccia, & Perlman, 2005). Some have argued that repression occurs in particular abusive situations. Terr (1991), for example, distinguished between memories that involve a single, isolated instance of trauma (Type I), which tend to be well remembered, and memories involving repeated trauma (Type II) more characteristic of childhood sexual abuse. With the latter, the victim is more likely to employ repression and dissociation and, as a result, remember less well.

Freyd (1994) has also proposed a theory to account for cases of memories recovered in therapy. According to **betrayal trauma theory**, the mechanisms by which normal memories are encoded, including memories involving trauma, are blocked when that trauma (childhood sexual trauma specifically) is perpetrated by a caregiver and thus involves the betrayal of an attachment figure. Forgetting or amnesia for the trauma is adaptive, Freyd argues, because the child is dependent on the caregiver and awareness of the trauma would lead to a fracturing of the relationship and would put the child in physical danger. Across numerous studies, Freyd and colleagues (Freyd, DePrince, & Gleaves, 2007) have found evidence of poorer recall among those reporting caregiver abuse relative to non-caregiver abuse, consistent with betrayal trauma theory. The distinction that Terr and Freyd make about the qualitative differences between these trauma memories and "regular" memories is crucial because experimental research would seem to contradict their theories.

Review of the research on trauma and repression has drawn somewhat different conclusions. Brewin (2007) notes that dissociation may be related to fragmented memory and that intense emotions experienced during trauma may disrupt explicit, autobiographical memory, while emotional or **implicit memory** may be enhanced. This would be consistent with Tracey's report at the beginning of this chapter of flashbacks as she had no memory of the abuse before her therapy began. On the other hand, Brewin's review did not produce strong evidence in support of the repression of childhood sexual abuse memories beyond case studies. Lindbolm and Gray (2010) have demonstrated that when factors or confounds like the age at which the trauma occurred are accounted for, results do not support betrayal trauma theory. While it remains an open question as to whether trauma can, in some cases, lead to repression and dissociation, the aforementioned suggestions about trauma memory are inconsistent with what we know about memory. Research suggests that among those who have been the victims of childhood sexual abuse, **post-traumatic stress disorder** (PTSD), a hallmark of which is intrusive symptoms (intrusive thoughts, dreams, flashbacks according to the DSM-5), is a common consequence (Fitzpatrick et al., 2010; Malmquist, 1986) and is not associated with dissociation (Roediger & Bergman, 1998). Additionally, intense emotions enhance the encoding and retrieval of memories (Lynn et al., 2015). Experimental research indicates that repetition improves memory (inconsistent with Terr's theory of Type II trauma memory). Additionally, Roediger and Bergman note that the notion of repression is inconsistent with thought suppression research demonstrating a paradoxical increased accessibility of the to-be-suppressed material. In sum, dissociation and repression in response to trauma are not consistent with our current understanding of how memory works (Lynn et al., 2014).

Confirmation bias: Do all roads lead to childhood sexual abuse?

The self-help books designed for victims of sexual abuse start with the premise that incest is common and that memories may be either partially or completely repressed only to surface years, possibly decades, later after the abuse occurred. E. Sue Blume, in the introduction to her book *Secret Survivors: Uncovering Incest and its Aftereffects in Women* (1990), notes that "Many, if not most, incest survivors do not know that the abuse has even occurred!" (p. xxi).

How is this possible? Through the two mechanisms we addressed earlier, repression and dissociation, as well as **denial**? Denial is, in some cases according to Blume, a coping mechanism invoked to avoid the emotional pain of being abused by a trusted family member. Bass and Davis (1994) describe dissociation or splitting as a common response to trauma in which the victim feels as though they have "left their body" and this "separation from the self," according to Blume, may lead to a temporarily inaccessible memory.

Denial and repression go hand in hand according to Blume. Denial results from repressing or burying the painful memories. Repression, Blume (1990) notes, "in some form is virtually universal among survivors" (p. 67). So most survivors employ denial, blocking, dissociation, and repression as a means of coping with the abuse and as a result have little if no memory of the abuse or, in Blume's words, a client "grows into adulthood relieved of the burden of her memories" (p. 95). This sounds perfectly logical and intuitively reasonable. A therapeutic recovery means that the patient has to break through the wall of denial and repression. So, how does one do this? The client is offered memory clues to assist in memory recall.

Bass and Davis (1994), authors of *The Courage to Heal*, tell clients that they are "engaged in a process of exploration and discovery which will ultimately help you know and understand more of your history" (p. 78). In the "Remembering" section of *The Courage to Heal Workbook*, readers are asked to "broaden their idea of what a memory is" and are asked to work through a number of exercises to help clarify and recover memories. Readers are given "pieces of memory" (e.g., "I remember hiding in the basement while my uncle beat my cousin with a belt") and asked to write as much as they can about these pieces of memory, sensory clues (e.g., "Whenever I see an ambulance or hear a siren, I get shaky all over"), body memories (e.g., "When I get aroused, I feel immediately disgusted"), creepy feelings (e.g., "When I see a father and his son walking down the street, I'm sure he's abusing that kid"), and gaps in memory (e.g., "I don't remember anything between the ages of eight and fifteen"). After "filling in the gaps" readers are asked to reflect on whether or not this was successful ("When put together, do the pieces of memory give me more of an idea about what happened to me?") Still unable to remember, readers are then asked to explore reasons for this in the "What am I afraid of?" section of the book.

There are several additional exercises that may help an individual remember, including a freewriting exercise in which the reader is asked to write whatever comes to mind and a collage-making exercise in which readers cut phrases or pictures out of magazines and are asked to let "your unconscious make choices" (p. 13). Later in the workbook, readers are offered opportunities to work through denial in the "Believing it happened" section. In therapy, clients may engage in similar imagery exercises to recover memories (Goff &

Roediger, 1998). While such techniques may help some of those who suffered childhood sexual abuse come to grips with the past and heal, concerns have been raised about the mindset or frame of reference of the therapist at the outset of therapy. Loftus (1993) suggests that some therapists are singularly focused on uncovering memories of childhood sexual abuse and helping the patient with no memories of abuse to construct such memories. Might some of these memories be false memories?

Loftus (1993) recounts the story of an investigator who went to see the therapist of a young women who had recently reported a recovered memory of childhood sexual abuse. The investigator claimed that she had nightmares and was having difficulty sleeping. After only a couple of visits, the therapist told the investigator that she was an incest survivor and had blocked the memory. Insisting that she had no memories of abuse, the therapist told her that "this was often the case" (p. 530). Thus, in addition to the concern about those who have experienced abuse not coming forward to seek help, there is a concern about those in therapy uncovering a history of abuse that never happened. This false history is, in part, recovered because of the **confirmatory bias** on the part of the therapist and the use of techniques that lead to the creation of false memories. The deck is stacked in favor of the sexual abuse explanation for psychological difficulties.

As Figure 8.2 illustrates, in addition to concerns about victims of childhood sexual abuse keeping the abuse a secret, there is the concern that patients with no such sexual abuse history may be led down the incest survivor "rabbit hole" by well-meaning therapists with a predisposed agenda. This predisposition toward discovering childhood sexual abuse can influence the questions that are asked and the way that the absence of memories is treated. For example, therapists may ask loaded and framed questions: "Your symptoms sound consistent with the profiles of other sexual abuse victims. How many times were you abused?" Clinicians may dismiss any hesitancy or resistance on the part of the client and the client's family members by viewing these reactions as denial. In general, research suggests we have a tendency to seek confirmatory rather than disconfirmatory evidence for our hypotheses (Nickerson, 1998). This general tendency also holds true for clinicians.

Mendel and colleagues (2011) gave psychiatrists and medical students a hypothetical vignette involving a 65-year-old patient who was being treated for a suspected overdose of sleeping pills. Participants were asked to select a preliminary diagnosis of severe depressive episode or Alzheimer's disease (which was the correct diagnosis), review brief summaries of additional information and then request more complete notes, and analyze detailed information based on the information in the patient summaries. Participants were supplied the requested information and then asked to make a final diagnosis. Thirteen percent of the psychiatrists and 25% of the medical students engaged in a confirmatory biased search or requested more information from summaries that

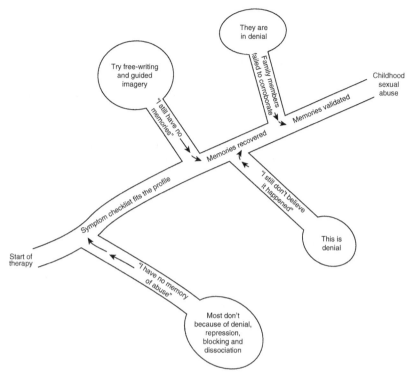

Figure 8.2   The road to memories of childhood sexual abuse. The figure illustrates how a therapist's mindset might influence the patient and produce false recovered memories over time

would confirm rather than disconfirm their original diagnosis. Those who engaged in confirmatory searches were also more likely to make an incorrect diagnosis. While the results do not suggest that the overwhelming majority of physicians engage in confirmatory searches, 13% is uncomfortably high when you consider the costs such as unnecessary tests, inappropriate treatments, and possible death due to improper medical treatment. In psychotherapy, the costs are also significant. Numerous books have been written about the legal battles and ruined families because of recovered false memories (e.g., Goldstein & Farmer, 1993, 1994; Loftus & Ketcham, 1994; Pendergrast, 1996). There is little doubt that confirmation bias is a concern among therapists utilizing techniques including the aforementioned self-help books aimed at recovering memories of childhood sexual abuse.

Starting with the presumption in therapy that an individual's current problems are due to childhood sexual abuse presents several disturbing problems. The importance of this is not only the potential for a biased search for confirmation on the part of the therapist, but also the potential impact the therapist's mindset has on what is recalled by the patient. In other words, if the patient is exploring the possibility of abuse, over time the ambiguous content of memories may be recalled in a manner which fits this goal (i.e., finding evidence of abuse; Marsh & Tversky, 2004; Tversky & Marsh, 2000). One does not have to suggest that the therapist is purposefully pressuring the client for such information. As Loftus and Davis (2006) explain:

> If the relationship develops as desired, the therapist will possess the primary attributes known to promote social influence: Likeability, credibility, and power ... The patient is likely to feel strong emotional attachment to, great respect for, and even dependence on the therapist, feelings which render her more susceptible to believing information and adopting behavioral suggestions such as joining survivor groups, reading survivor literature, or engaging in memory-recovery activities at home. (p. 489)

Another relevant factor in therapy is that patients are motivated to find an answer or explanation for their current problems. Tavris and Aronson (2015) explain that stories of victims overcoming traumas and tragedies are inspiring, so much so that it is not hard to imagine others seeking answers to life's problems finding this a desirable narrative. Additionally, this victim narrative allows one to reduce the **cognitive dissonance** one experiences when one believes they are much more capable than their current lot in life would suggest (Figure 8.2).

> **KEY READING** – Tavris, C., & Aronson, E. (2015). *Mistakes were made but not by me: Why we justify foolish beliefs, bad decisions, and hurtful acts.* New York: Houghton Mifflin.

Examining the techniques involved in recovering memories

Beyond concerns about confirmation bias, there are important questions to ask ourselves as mental health consumers when scrutinizing the therapeutic techniques for recovering memory:

Have the authors provided evidence that these techniques are effective?
What sources of evidence are the authors relying on?
What sources of evidence are questionable or dubious?
Do these techniques seem consistent with what current science suggests about memory?

Surveys suggest that the use of memory-recovery techniques such as **guided imagery** and **hypnosis** are not uncommon among psychotherapists who believe the use of which is capable of unearthing memories of childhood sexual abuse (Lynn et al., 2015). There are many reasons that this is cause for concern, including the lack of evidence that people commonly repress trauma. Additionally, the techniques used to recover memories are not only lacking in terms of research support for their effectiveness, but also may make the creation of a false memory more likely. Guided imagery, for example, involves the patient, in a relaxed state with eyes closed, imagining scenarios proposed by the therapist (Lynn et al., 2015). In addition to convincing the client that repression is common, as is denial, the sensory elaboration provided by guided imagery adds a realness to them or amounts to rich false memories (Bernstein & Loftus, 2009). Authors who promote the use of such techniques often rely on anecdotes or testimonial to support them. These along with those sources given in Table 8.1 are dubious sources of evidence.

Table 8.1 Poor sources of evidence

Testimonials
Anecdotes
Clinical expertise
Clinical experience/observation
Opinion of authority in field
Unvalidated instruments or checklists
News reports

While numerous studies have demonstrated the potential for guided imagery procedures to create false memories (Braun, Ellis, & Loftus, 2002; Garry et al., 1996; Loftus & Pickrell, 1995; Paddock et al., 1999), no studies have documented the effectiveness of guided imagery in recovering repressed memories of childhood sexual abuse or other trauma. Likewise, the reputation of hypnosis as an effective memory-recovery technique is inconsistent with the research suggesting that it unearths more memories, but not more accurate memories (Lynn et al., 2015). The potential for false memories is further enhanced by the use of other ineffective techniques such as past-life regression (explores problems in a previous life), the vulnerability of the patient and status of the therapist, the use of persistent and leading questions, and confirmation bias on the part of the therapist.

In their review of memory-recovery techniques, Lynn and colleagues (2015) include the use of bibliotherapy and abuse checklists. In such cases, therapists direct their clients to consult self-help books on childhood sexual abuse including Bass and Davis's (1994) *The Courage to Heal* or Blume's (1990) *Secret Survivors: Uncovering Incest and Its Aftereffects in Women*. Books like Blume's start with the premise that many women are victims of incest, that victims repress these traumas, and that there is a constellation of symptoms associated with childhood sexual abuse. Imagining scenes as guided by a therapist and exploring the checklist of symptoms in Blume's book appears to be a harmless exercise in the service of better understanding and relieving one's current pain. Yet, for some, this may be opening Pandora's Box.

Critical thinking toolkit
The Barnum Effect: Step Right Up...

Guiding question: Does the seemingly personalized information likely apply to most people?

Imagine you stumble upon a website that offers you a free personality profile. You answer a number of questions, submit your responses, and receive an e-mail with the following results:

You have a great need for other people to like and admire you.

You have a great deal of unused capacity, which you have not turned to your advantage.

Disciplined and self-controlled outside, you tend to be worrisome and insecure inside.

You prefer a certain amount of change and variety and become dissatisfied when hemmed in by restrictions and limitations.

At times you have serious doubts as to whether you have made the right decision or done the right thing.

At times you are extroverted, sociable, while at other times you are introverted, wary, reserved.

While you have some personality weaknesses, you are generally able to compensate for them.

"Wow! Spot on, right! That's me," you might say. If you believe that the majority of these statements are true of your personality, you are not alone. Given a similar profile, Forer (1949) found the majority of his students endorsed these universally valid and broad descriptions as accurate reflections of their personality. If we look closer at the descriptions, it becomes clearer that they would do a poor job of distinguishing among people. In other words, they do not tell you anything that is true of you, but not others. Would not most people feel that they at times have serious doubts as to whether they have made the right decision or done the right thing or feel that they have a great deal of unused capacity? The results by Forer demonstrate what psychologists refer to as the **Barnum effect** or the tendency to believe vague (e.g., you prefer a certain amount of change and variety in your life) or self-contradictory (e.g., at times you are extroverted, sociable, while at other times you are introverted, wary, reserved) statements applicable to most people are uniquely self-descriptive (Dickson & Kelly, 1985; Emery & Lilienfeld, 2004).

The demonstration by Forer in his classroom was harmless fun, but there are more serious implications for this Barnum effect. Self-help books for childhood sexual abuse, like Blume's *Secret Survivors: Uncovering Incest and Its Aftereffects in Women*, include checklists that can help readers determine if they are victims. Blume's book includes 37 items that are characteristics or symptoms shared by victims of childhood sexual abuse. These items include fear of being alone in the dark, nightmares, poor body image, headaches, arthritis, adult nervousness, fear of losing control, guilt, shame, low self-esteem, feeling crazy, and feeling different. Though those with a history of childhood sexual abuse may score higher on these checklists than those without, research suggests that those with a tendency to endorse these childhood sexual abuse checklist items also have a tendency to endorse Barnum items (Emery & Lilienfeld, 2004). Checklists like those in Blume's book, in other words, might be good at detecting those who are victims of childhood sexual abuse, what psychologists refer to as **sensitivity**. However, too many individuals who do not have such a sexual abuse history may be identified by the checklist as being abuse victims, in which case the checklist would have poor **specificity** and over-identify such histories.

The pseudoscientific playbook

It is important to make clear at this point, as Loftus and Ketcham (1994) have, that childhood sexual abuse is a serious reality and there are many talented and compassionate therapists working to help victims come to terms with such abuse. What the authors express concern over are memories of abuse that did not exist prior to therapy and repressed memories that were recovered through questionable therapeutic techniques. Further removed from a scientific grounding is a self-help incest industry possessing characteristics associated with **pseudoscience** (Pratkanis, 1995). A common tool of pseudoscience is the dramatic presentation of memorable cases or stories. Of course, there is nothing wrong with recounting the stories of abuse victims in self-help books. Books like *The Courage to Heal* and *Secret Survivors* are packed with vivid anecdotes of survivors who recovered memories. The problem, however, emerges when these cases are relied upon as the exclusive source of evidence.

The next concern is the necessity to establish a group with shared goals, beliefs, and feelings (e.g., survivor support groups) and shared enemies. Enter the Memory War and the battle over repression and recovered memories. Ellen Bass and Laura Davis (1994), in the third edition of their book *The Courage to Heal*, suggested that there have been attacks on survivors in response to the media coverage of recovered memories. The word "attack" is used numerous times in the 'Honoring the truth' section of the book. Hence, the enemies are those who doubt the authenticity of recovered memories and who doubt the pain and suffering of survivors. However, the authors speak broadly about survivors and, thus, fail to distinguish between those who are survivors with actual memories of childhood sexual abuse and those with questionable memories discovered in therapy. Character assassination and innuendo are also tactics employed by pseudoscience (Pratkanis, 1995). Bass and Davis (1994) suggest that those who challenge false memories are in denial and promote anti-survivor propaganda. Loftus herself has been personally disparaged by critics and accused of ethical breaches (Crook & Dean, 1999).

Critical thinking toolkit
Is the self-help approach actually helping?

Guiding question: Have I considered the quality of evidence used to support the program?

Consider the following fictitious self-help program advertisement:

A NEW BREAKTHROUGH PROGRAM TO CHANGE YOUR LIFE!

AS FEATURED ON "THIS MORNING IN BRITIAN" AND "MORNINGS WITH JACK AND JILL."

Bestselling author Dr. Jane Doe shows how her breakthrough program allows everyone to change his or her lifestyle in ways that will turn back the clock 20 years. We all have some undesirable predispositions in our family history, but Dr. Doe shows you how you can alter this history. You can change your genes by changing your lifestyle! This 5-week long program gives you the tools to rewrite your life history and will give you a new sense of health, confidence and ultimately a new lease on life.

I used Dr. Doe's program and loved it! It was so easy to do and the results were amazing!

—Joe Clark

I not only recommend this book to my clients, I use some of Dr. Doe's sugges-tions with my clients in therapy. In my 20 years of experience, this is the best program I've seen to promote physical and mental health.

—Dr. James Kirkpatrick

Director of the Kirkpatrick Counseling Institute

Let us start at the top with the headline for Dr. Doe's Program. Note that it is described as "new," as a "breakthrough," and seems to have received a lot of media attention. Successful psychological programs tend to progress slowly with rigorous clinical testing. Breakthrough clinical programs rushed to market are assuredly not properly tested. Scientists are cautious and skeptical about promising new treat-ments. They are quick to note caveats and precautions that warn against broad conclusions drawn with the preliminary results of a study or two. They do not speak of cures, miracles, and guarantees. The fact that this Program has received considerable media attention might give some of us assurance. However, consider which is going to garner more media attention – a breakthrough therapy that promises amazing benefits and a quick cure or a more accustomed longer-term treatment mode with modest benefits. You should be especially wary of any program that suggests that you "do not need any willpower" to accomplish clinical goals. Thus, critical thinkers have to adopt a healthy skepticism of programs we see in the media.

By early 2000, the self-help industry had created enormous wealth, with sales of £80 million in Great Britain and $600 million in the USA (Gunnell, 2004). While there is little doubt about their popularity, there are solid reasons to doubt their effectiveness. As with techniques for recovering memories, we need to think about the quality of the evidence, which varies considerably as detailed in Figure 8.3 (Rosen et al., 2015).

Quality

Low	Anecdotes, testimonials (it worked for me) and clinical judgment
	Book is based on techniques with documented effectiveness though effectiveness in self-help format has not been assessed
High	Effectiveness of program in self-help format has been demonstrated in randomized controlled trials

Figure 8.3   Quality of evidence used to support a self-help program

In order to demonstrate that the self-help book is effective (possesses high-quality evidence), researchers would need to compare the baseline scores of, for example, depression before and after treatment among those using the new treatment (treatment A) exclusively, those using the established treatment (treatment B), those on a waitlist (control condition), and a possible fourth condition which would be those using both treatments A and B. Replication studies would also be needed. Such research is scarce. Richardson, Richards, and Barkham (2008) reviewed self-help books on depression in the UK. The majority were not empirically tested and only a few books included references to research findings. While there are some studies that demonstrate the effectiveness of self-help books by themselves (i.e., self-administered programs), research suggests that as face-to-face therapeutic support diminishes so does the effectiveness of a program (Rosen et al., 2015). Rosen and colleagues (2015) expressed concerns about the insufficient application of sound psychological science in evaluating the effectiveness of self-help book programs marketed by psychologists. As consumers, we need to apply sound critical thinking in order to evaluate these products by considering the evidence for effectiveness, how consistent the evidence is with the claims that are made, and the credentials of those promoting such approaches (Rosen et al., 2015). Additionally, we need to be aware of the potential costs associated with such books and self-help programs. Monetarily the cost might be minimal, but the psychological costs and risks could be much greater. Arkowitz and Lilienfeld (2006) note that when a book promises great things and fails to deliver, the consumer might feel that this represents a personal failure and as a result lose hope in the possibility of change (referred to as false hope syndrome). Moreover, some self-help books include poor advice that runs counter to well-established psychological science findings (e.g., vent your anger; Bergsma, 2008).

If we apply the aforementioned criteria to the childhood sexual abuse self-help books, we are bound to be skeptical of such available print materials. *The Courage to Heal*, for example, as noted earlier, relies exclusively on anecdotes or testimonials to demonstrate effectiveness. Not only has the use of the techniques offered in the book not been documented in clinical practice as effective, but the strategies employed in the book have been shown to make the production of false memories more likely. Additionally, Rosen and colleagues (2015) note that some self-help books of the past have failed to help people toilet-train their children or treat a phobia. Yet toilet training, and to a lesser extent phobias, has a demonstrable and measurable end goal. Such is not the case with books like *The Courage to Heal* where one simply has to feel that a variety of symptoms and/or memory fragments are indicative of abuse and provide insight into one's current emotional problems in order to "feel" better.

What we know about trauma memory

Psychologists have generated different accounts for cases of recovered memories like Tracey's, discussed at the beginning of this chapter. Psychologists Jennifer Freyd and Lenore Terr have argued forcefully for the legitimacy and authenticity of recovered memories. Critics of recovered memory not only point to the overreliance on case reports, but note that the theories of Terr and Freyd are inconsistent with what we know about memory and there are many alternative explanations and methodological limitations of the research which cast doubt on the usefulness of such theories.

Critics have raised several issues regarding the studies employed by proponents of recovered memories. Imagine you come across a study demonstrating that children who been abused by a caregiver at two years of age and a group of children who had been abused by a non-caregiver at 3 years of age. Results revealed poorer memory for the abuse among the caregiver abused group. Results appear consistent with betrayal trauma theory, but two potential confounding variables need to be considered here. Ask yourself the following: Would you expect memory for abuse to be better if it happened when a child is 3 years old rather than 2? At the same time, would you expect memory to be worse as more time elapses since the abuse (more time has elapsed for the 2-year-olds). If you answered yes to the questions, you have identified what researchers have identified, age at the time of the trauma and time since the trauma as two potential confounds (Roediger & Bergman, 1998).

Concerns have also been raised about the murkiness of repression interpretations. Some cases of recovered memory could involve normal forgetting. Repression is only one theory that has been proposed to explain forgetting. It could also be the case that the abuse was experienced as traumatic at the time it occurred or that the victim did not want to report the abuse due to embarrassment (conscious non-disclosure rather than repression). Additionally, it could be that in some cases of what appears to be a repressed memory, the individual forgot that they had previous recalled the abuse (i.e., they forgot they remembered; Lindblom & Gray, 2010; Loftus & Davis, 2006).

One of the problems with the sexual abuse trauma literature in general and betrayal trauma theory specifically is the lack of clarity in terms of how memories are blocked, repressed, or dissociated and how they are recovered years and even decades later. Betrayal trauma theory provides no details about the mechanisms of blocking memories. How does a memory that is not encoded well when the trauma occurs become recalled with clarity and accuracy in later decades (Roediger & Bergman, 1998)? Research has not suggested that trauma invariably leads to dissociation, but has indicated that dissociation is associated with fantasy proneness, imagination inflation, and false memories (Lynn et al., 2012). Imagine Angela, a victim of childhood sexual abuse by a relative, is asked to write a narrative about the trauma. She agrees to write about it, but there seems to be a surprising lack of detail in her story. She does not recall details about the setting or the abuse itself and managed only a paragraph. Repression or dissociation seem like plausible explanations for Angela's hazy narrative. It appears that how close one is to the perpetrator determines the quality of the memory for the trauma, consistent with betrayal trauma theory. However, the "story" is not that simple. Let us think about other reasons for Angela's lack of detail in the narrative. Could it be that she intentionally left out these details? Could the fact that she was only seven years old at the time of the trauma explain the vagueness? Lindblom and Gray (2010) put the assumptions of betrayal trauma theory to the test by examining the narratives of trauma victims. Those who were victims of sexual abuse at the hands of a relative, like Angela, wrote less detailed narratives than those who were victims of accidental traumas (e.g., car accident). Yet when the researchers controlled for the age at the time of trauma, the intentional omission of details (associated with PTSD avoidance symptoms), and other confounds, relationship closeness was no longer a significant predictor of the length and detail of the narratives. Thus, this study suggests that while many researchers have focused their attention on repression as an explanation for memory failure, there are other equally, if not more, compelling and simpler explanations (Lynn et al., 2012). As critical thinkers, we should remain open to the possibility of dissociation and repression, but also demand more than sensational and compelling cases of recovered memory as evidence.

Chapter summary

Loftus and her colleagues have documented how susceptible we are to false memory creations, and demonstrated how misinformation can be incorporated into memory storage and how false memories for a childhood event can be created. There are clear implications for the recovered memories of childhood sexual abuse. Merely imagining an event can lead to greater confidence it occurred through imagination inflation. In situations where abuse did not occur, yet the therapist operates from the position that it did, the techniques employed like guided imagery have the potential to create false memories. While people believe repression is a common response to trauma, research does not totally support this position (instead suggesting that PTSD and intrusive thoughts of the incident are more common).

According to betrayal trauma theory, memories of childhood sexual trauma perpetrated by a caregiver are blocked and not properly encoded which explains the difficult recovery of repressed memories. There are, however, limitations of this theory, including the lack of accounting for how such memories are repressed, and methodological limitations, including a failure to account for several confounds. The techniques used in therapy for the purpose of recovering memories should raise suspicion if validation rests solely on testimonials, anecdotes, and clinical reports. One such technique, a sexual abuse survival checklist, is broad and equivocal enough to raise concerns about the Barnum effect. When evaluating self-help books or programs we need to keep in mind how science works and consider whether the program is consistent with this scientific framework. We should maintain healthy skepticism in the face of enthusiastic endorsement by the popular media. We need to look closely at the evidence, giving preference (greater credibility) to randomized controlled trials.

Tracey and Olivia at the beginning of the chapter are cases used by both sides in the Memory War. With the case of Tracey you have a corroborated case of recovered memory and with the case of Olivia you have a retractor whose false memories of abuse were recovered during therapy. With cases like Tracey's we have to be careful not to disregard a report of recovered memory offhand. Certainly, we do not want to disregard or minimize the suffering of those who are victims of childhood sexual abuse. However, if we endorse therapeutic practices that are susceptible to producing false memories as the research of Loftus has demonstrated and then uncritically accept any reports of recovered memories, some of which may turn out to be false we have done a disservice to the victims of abuse, those accused of such crimes, and society as a whole. The research by Loftus and others has challenged our intuition about how memory works and has demonstrated how fallible it is.

Future directions

Though the Memory Wars will likely continue, neuroscience may become the new battleground for the fight. More recent studies have sought to identify the neural basis of repression (Schmeing et al., 2013) and individual differences in the brain that may account for the accuracy of memory (Zhu et al., 2016). The American Psychological Association (APA) outlines questions that future research in the field needs to address (2018). Among them are questions as to the nature of trauma memory, the techniques that are effective in clinical settings with trauma victims and those capable of producing false memories, and individual differences in susceptibility to false memories. Additionally, it will be important to examine the mechanisms of repression and dissociation and, more basically, document the incidence of the recalled childhood events after a significant period of failure to recall (Lynn et al., 2015). In summary, we still have much to learn about sexual abuse, recovered memories, and repression. Our hope is that the future will provide evidence-based research that can offer clearly marked clinical pathways for those clients who suffer from sexual abuse and other mental health problems.

Discussion questions

1. Are studies involving implanting false memories ethically appropriate? Where would you draw the line in terms of the appropriateness of particular memories (e.g., memory of being kidnapped or committing a crime)?
2. What are some of the ethical challenges facing researchers in trauma memory, specifically childhood sexual abuse, and false memories? Think about the following issues: powerful symbolic connections to sexuality, childhood misunderstandings/confusions regarding sexuality, and why a human subject might "need" to create a false memory of a life event.

CHAPTER

9

The psi Studies: Psychological Science versus Pseudoscience

Primary source: Bem, D. J. (2011). Feeling the future: Experimental evidence for anomalous retroactive influences on cognition and affect. *Journal of Personality and Social Psychology, 100*, 407–425.

Chapter objectives

This chapter will help you become a better critical thinker by:

- Exploring Daryl Bem's precognition studies
- Wrestling with the failure to replicate Bem's findings and seeking explanations
- Examining why human beings are powerfully drawn to believe in psi
- Considering the question: "What is pseudoscience?"
- Contemplating examples of pseudoscience in clinical psychology
- Envisioning parapsychology as a pseudoscience

Introduction

Imagine that you were asking a precocious six-year old child why the lights in a dark room suddenly glowed when you flipped the light switch.

The child might make the observation that the two events (flipping the light switch and the appearance of light) that occurred in close time proximity demonstrated a cause and effect relationship. Therefore, moving the light switch caused the light to glow. The child might proudly state, "Pressing the light switch on the wall caused the light to go on."

You are likely pleased with this childhood observation, but as an adult you want to explore deeper contextual knowledge here. You might ask the following questions:

- Would this cause and effect relationship still exist, if there was a major interruption of electrical service in the power grid?
- Would this cause and effect relationship still exist, if the bulb had blown in the light fixture?
- Would this cause and effect relationship still exist, if there was a faulty light switch?
- Would this cause and effect relationship still exist, if there was a short in the circuit wires?

The general point that we wish you to consider here is that what often seems like a simple cause and effect (antecedent and outcome) relationship is often far more complicated when you begin to consider depth of knowledge factors related to any topic. Understanding cause and effect in the above everyday life experience involves going well beyond surface knowledge and exploring depth of knowledge. In other words, there are more than just two variables in play here.

What if a person observed the light going "on" in a dark room many times in succession and then suddenly one of the conditions listed above or another intervention occurred such that the light no longer turns on with the switch? Would some claim that the light switch no longer turns on the room light due to (bad) karma, spiritual interference, astrological resistance, (bad) luck/chance, or medium meddling? Perhaps someone far away is able to use mental telepathy to halt the "flow of electrons" resulting in the switch no longer being able to turn on the light. Obviously, human beings of different ages, cultural backgrounds, philosophical positions, religious beliefs, and so on might explain such an event in very different ways.

We urge you to critically consider the complex nature of cause and the extent to which we try to apply meaning and coherence to happenstance in the chapter content that follows.

Hypothetical Situation for Analysis:

James Hathaway, a 22-year-old college senior, was driving home from school to spend the weekend with his parents. James had not been getting along with his father for the last few years, but was overwhelmed on the drive home with a sense that he needed to talk with his father, that he needed to make things right because his father would not be alive much longer. When James arrived home later that evening he talked with his father who was more than happy to forgive his son. James's father passed away that evening. Eerily, five years earlier, James had a dream about the passing of his aunt days before she died.

Study background

The question of whether or not James's experience was coincidence or premonition is the focus of this chapter. Consider the topics of premonition, precognition, and clairvoyance during your analysis of these events. What is this doing in a psychology textbook, you ask? **Parapsychology** actually has a long but controversial history in psychology, sparked by extrasensory perception research in the 1930s (Joyce & Baker, 2008). Then, in 2011, psychologist Daryl Bem drew considerable media attention for reporting results of several studies (detailed in the Table 9.1) providing evidence of **precognition**.

Reading through Bem's article is like reading through F. Scott Fitzgerald's The Curious Case of Benjamin Button, where time is moving backwards. Bem took well-established psychological phenomena like the mere exposure effect – repeated exposure to stimuli results in greater preferences for them – and reversed the order of events to test for precognition. For example, in one study (study 8) participants were shown 48 words, asked to visualize the words, and then, unexpectedly, were asked to recall as many of the 48 words as they could. Simple enough, right? And, if as a participant you were beforehand given 24 of those 48 words to practice, you would expect these 24 practiced items to be better recalled than those which were not rehearsed. Again, everything sounds perfectly unremarkable, right? Here's the catch. Bem gave participants the 24 practice words *after* the memory test! Despite the reverse order of events, Bem reports that more practice words were recalled by participants than control words on the *initial* memory test. Bem's results, in other words, were taken to show that "practicing a set of words after the recall test does, in fact, reach back in time to facilitate the recall of those words" (p. 419). "Reach back in time?" It is no wonder Bem notes in his article, without any need of assistance from precognition, that it will be a little hard for some to swallow such results.

Table 9.1 Summary of Bem (2011) studies.

The studies	Summary of the research design
Study 1	Tested participants' ability to detect the position of erotic stimuli before the position was determined. Participants were shown two curtains on the computer screen and asked to select the one that had the picture behind it. The position of the picture was determined after the participants made their selection.
Study 2	Tested participants' ability to avoid negative stimuli. Participants were asked to select one of two neutral pictures, one of which would be randomly designated as the target after selection. If participants selected the target, a positive stimulus was subliminally presented. If they selected the non-target, a negative stimulus was subliminally presented.
Study 3	A retroactive priming study in which participants were shown an image and were asked to indicate whether it was pleasant or unpleasant. Participants were then shown a pleasant or unpleasant word that, if shown before the picture (as is typical in priming studies), would have led to faster response times when the prime and the picture were congruent (e.g., pleasant–pleasant).

Study 4	A replication of retroactive priming Study 3.
Study 5	A habituation study in which participants were shown two pictures on a screen and asked to select the one they prefer. The participant is then subliminally presented with one of the two pictures several times. If these subliminally presented pictures had been shown before, participants would be more likely to select the one they had been presented subliminally.
Study 6	A replication of habituation Study 5 but included trials with erotic images.
Study 7	Similar to Study 5, but tested the hypothesis that participants would be less likely, due to boredom, to select a target picture when that picture was supraliminally presented ten times after the participant made their selection.
Study 8	Participants were presented with a list of words, asked to recall as many as possible, and then given a subset of those words to practice afterwards.
Study 9	A replication of Study 8 with additional practice.

Current thinking

An important question to ask, especially when considering provocative findings such as Bem's, is whether the results have been replicated. Unfortunately for Bem, there have been numerous failed replication attempts, adding to the skepticism of such seemingly impossible results. The majority of these attempted **replications** have focused on the last two studies reported by Bem (Studies 8 and 9). Ritchie, Wiseman, and French (2012) conducted several replication attempts of Study 9 using the same materials and procedure that Bem used, yet failed to find evidence supporting precognition. Galak and colleagues (2012) also attempted numerous replications of Studies 8 and 9 with over 3,000 participants, but they differed from Bem's studies in that some were conducted online and the authors created a list of words that differed from those used by Bem. Again, the results were not consistent with those obtained by Bem. Additionally, these authors did not find the personality trait of sensation-seeking to correlate with performance, something that Bem reported across numerous studies. Galak and colleagues also conducted a meta-analysis, combining all of the replication attempts of Bem's Studies 8 and 9. Again, the results failed to support precognition. Lastly, Wagenmakers and colleagues (2011) reanalyzed the data using alternative statistical tests and, again, failed to provide support for precognition.

KEY READING – Ritchie, S. J., Wiseman, R., & French, C. C. (2012). Failing the future: Three unsuccessful attempts to replicate Bem's "retroactive facilitation of recall" effect. *PLoS ONE, 7*, 1–4.

Why might others have failed to replicate Bem's results?

There are several possible reasons why other researchers were unable to replicate Bem's results. First, critics have suggested that Bem went on a "fishing expedition," conducting a number of exploratory analyses (with different images, etc.) and then reporting only those that were significant (Gauvrit, 2011; Wagenmakers et al., 2011). Researchers often conduct exploratory analyses or **pilot studies** when they have a hunch but no solid hypotheses about expected findings. The problem is not conducting exploratory analyses, but reporting them as if they are confirmatory – in other words, presenting them as if there was a clear **hypothesis** in place before hand (what is referred to as **a priori**). Researchers typically set the **significance level** or probability level at 0.05. Such numbers (0.05 and larger) would indicate the probability that the results were obtained by chance. If the probability level or p value of my statistical test is 0.05 then that means the likelihood that I obtained the results by chance is low, but it's not zero. It is possible that if I conducted 20 studies I might obtain one positive result by chance or a false positive (Gauvrit, 2011). The way to deal with this situation, a situation in which multiple tests are being conducted, is to lower the p value to reduce the risk of false positives or **Type I error**. Bem failed to do this.

Here is another reason why it matters whether or not Bem's study was exploratory. When researchers have a hypothesis about the direction of a relationship between variables (e.g., the more fat one consumes the more one will weigh) they may elect to employ a **one-tailed test**, as this would be more powerful or better able to detect differences. The reason for this is that the 0.05 level of significance is not split between the two halves of the distribution (0.25 on each) like it is with the two-tailed test as illustrated in Figure 9.1. While the one-tailed test is more powerful, it is unable to detect differences in the opposite direction and the test is less conservative (less likely to produce false positives or Type I errors) which is why most psychologists use **two-tailed tests** (Jaccard & Becker, 2002). Parapsychologists also typically employ them as they accept scoring above or below chance as evidence of precognition (Alcock, 2011; Elmes et al., 1999). Bem elected to use one-tailed tests.

Being statistically unconventional, though, is not as egregious as conducting the analysis and then, after the fact, applying a directional hypothesis
(Jaccard & Becker, 2002).

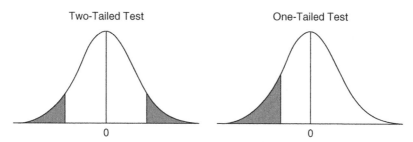

Figure 9.1   Two-tailed versus one-tailed hypothesis tests

Essentially what critics are arguing is that Bem conducted a number of
tests and reported those that were significant (among a number that were
not) and reported the one-tailed tests because these produced significant
results. Regardless of whether or not this was the case, researchers ideally
need to make a decision beforehand as far as directionality and the statistical
analysis and live with the decision. As Field (2005) notes: "if you don't make
a prediction of direction before you collect the data, you are too late to predict
the direction and claim the advantages of a one-tailed test" (pp. 30–31).

Can neuroscience resolve the psi debate?

Prior to the publication of Bem's precognition studies, Samuel Moulton and
Stephen Kosslyn (2008) at Harvard University attempted to resolve the psi
debate with neuroscience. In the study, a participant designated as the sender
is tasked with, by whatever means possible, "sending" the stimulus to the
receiver. The receiver's brain activity is being recorded as they try to identify
the sent psi image among two stimulus options. The receiver guessed the
correct psi response at chance (50% of the time) and **functional magnetic
resonance imaging (fMRI)** results (see Chapters 11 and 13 for extended dis-
cussions of fMRI) revealed no significant differences in brain responses to psi
and non-psi stimuli or differences in response times to the psi and non-psi
stimuli. Moulton and Kosslyn (2008) argue that their results should be seen
as a more powerful refutation of psi than negative results in behavioral studies because they are looking at this at a more fundamental or basic level
of analysis (brain activity). The brain has to be the source of psi in that all
behavior is correlated with neural events. In spite of the evidence against psi,
the search continues and the public's fascination with psi persists.

Extraordinary claims

When a researcher makes a claim as extraordinary as Bem's and bases it on (what appears to be supportive) data, the media takes note. Yet, argues Cohen (2002), a claim based on negative evidence (i.e., evidence not supportive of psi) is not likely to draw the same acclaim. This storyline appears to have played out in the psi debate initiated by Bem's findings. Failed replication attempts may not draw media attention, but critical thinkers take note. While some scholars argue over the legitimacy of the "extraordinary claims require extraordinary evidence" axiom made famous by astronomer Carl Sagan, psi research has failed to produce ordinary evidence much less extraordinary evidence.

When such extraordinary claims surface in the media, there is one brief yet important question we can pull from our toolkit – "So what?" Pratkanis (2017) notes that if we were to assume that Bem's claims were true, we would have some trouble reconciling this with the world as we know it:

> For example, if Bem's claims were true, then Las Vegas would not be possible; a slight skewing of the odds via paranormal processes would bankrupt the casinos, as well as the sponsors of state lotteries and other honest gambling games. If Bem's psi claim is true, there would be little need for spies and spy satellites; we should just be able to pick up on the thoughts of our adversaries. (p. 157)

Why people believe in psi

A belief in psi can be accounted for by a number of factors including, but not limited to, a skepticism of science, spiritual needs, and cognitive limitations. Carl Sagan (1995) noted that **pseudoscience** has the potential to fulfill emotional needs that science cannot satisfy. It also offers us a sense of control over seemingly uncontrollable life events. Things happen that are hard to explain and the idea that events are random and unpredictable – the product of (bad) luck or (bad) karma – is psychologically uncomfortable and problematic. Fortunately, there are a number of cognitive tricks we have at our disposal to lessen this discomfort. Consider some of the factors that are extremely important when we engage in tasks that involve skill rather than just chance, tasks that we can, to some extent, control. The more you practice, for example, the better you become and the more confident you are that you can master a task. Likewise, the less confident and less skilled your opponent, the more confident you are that you can outperform your opponent. These statements are not surprising to anyone, particularly athletes. However, research suggests that the amount of practice and the perceived competence of one's opponent influence people's perceptions of control even when they are engaged in games of chance (Langer, 1975). For example, imagine two individuals playing a card game in which both opponents are randomly drawing cards from a stack with the highest card winning (commonly referred to in the USA as "War"). Langer (1975) found that participants wagered less when their opponent appeared competent and confident. So, not only is there a general tendency for us to perceive control in uncontrollable situations, but individuals who believe in psi are more susceptible to this **illusion of control** (Blakemore & Troscianko, 1985).

Another factor that may make us more susceptible to psi is our poor judgment when it comes to randomness. Is the probability of heads greater after a run of four or five tails on coin flips? If you said "yes" you are wrong, but you are in good company. People commonly underestimate the runs that appear at random in such instances (e.g., seven heads in a row couldn't happen by chance) and also fail to appreciate that each flip of the coin is independent of the previous flips or the fact that there were four or five heads in a row has no bearing on the next flip (referred to as the **gambler's fallacy**; Tversky & Kahneman, 1974). The same logical or illogical error leads people to mistakenly believe that a basketball player with a "hot hand" has a great likelihood of making a shot after making several successive shots (Gilovich, Vallone, & Tversky, 1985). If you believe in psi, a few successive coincidences are less likely to be perceived as mere coincidences.

Still another explanation may come from research showing how the accessibility of information or how easily it comes to mind influences our estimation of the likeliness of an event. This is referred to as the **availability heuristic** (Tversky & Kahneman, 1973, 1974). A heuristic is just a mental shortcut or general rule that we can apply when making decisions and judgments, for instance if something is natural it is good for you or the longer a politician's speech the better the message. According to the availability heuristic we might, for example, after years of watching The Rising, In the Flesh, and The Walking Dead overestimate the likelihood of a zombie apocalypse. Individuals who believe in psi likely have had many experiences in the past in which they attributed a "cause" label to a coincidental event making these easily accessible. Likewise, the availability of a heuristic might explain a related bias, an **illusory correlation** or the erroneous perception that two events co-occur (Tversky & Kahneman, 1974). You may have had, for example, the experience of wishing that someone would text you, only to have that same person text you minutes later.

Most troubling of all though may not be the cognitive biases themselves, but how durable the beliefs are in life. The remedy to avoiding such biases should be as simple as becoming more aware of them. Unfortunately, we are much better at identifying these biases in others than in ourselves (Pronin, Lin, & Ross, 2002) which results in a defensive posture. One of the biases Pronin and colleagues investigated was the **better-than-average bias** or the tendency to rate oneself higher than the average person in terms of various personality dimensions like dependability and consideration for others. The participants rated themselves relative to other students of their university, were informed about the better-than-average bias, and then were asked to rate the accuracy

of their assessments. In other words, this was an opportunity for the participants to say, "Knowing what I now know about the better-than-average bias,
I probably overestimated how I rate compared to others." This is not what
happened. Over 75% of participants thought they were either right on or
had actually underestimated their ratings. Thus, awareness by itself is not
enough to neutralize these dogged biases.

The fact that we are not good at detecting bias in ourselves makes it understandable that we also tend to be unaware of our tendency to selectively seek
out or interpret evidence in a way that confirms our existing beliefs and ignore
information which disconfirms our hypotheses (Nickerson, 1998). This **confirmation bias** plays a role in fostering a belief in psi as illustrated in Figure 9.2
and can be exploited by pseudoscientists by providing ambiguous information
that allows one to see what one wants or needs to see. Imagine your horoscope
today says that you sometimes have trouble asking for help from others and
you should work on this deficiency. Who would not be able to personally identify with such a generic statement. Even when confronting information that is
not unequivocally supportive of our position, research suggests not only that
our position will not soften, but that our resolve for our initial position will actually harden or strengthen (Lord et al., 1979). A study by Russell and Jones (1980)
demonstrated that beliefs in psi can be as resistant to change, as those classified
as believers were less likely to remember studies that disconfirmed psi compared
to cases consistent with their beliefs. More troubling, in some cases, believers
falsely recalled disconfirming studies as being consistent with their beliefs.

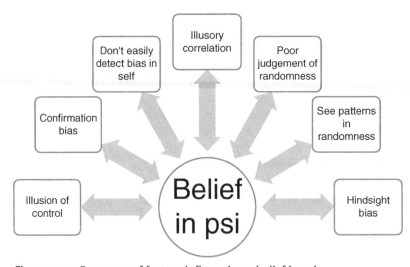

Figure 9.2   Summary of factors influencing a belief in psi

Lastly, research suggests that **hindsight bias** may also account for psi
beliefs (Rudski, 2003). Using a deck of 25 cards of various colors, Rudski
(2003) had participants guess the color the experimenter selected and he/she

attempted to transmit this selection telepathically. Subjects who were given the opportunity for hindsight bias by recalling whether or not they made the correct guess (as opposed to those in the control condition who were writing down their answer before given feedback) reported a higher success rate than those in the **control condition**.

It is important to note that the hindsight bias as with the other cognitive explanations for susceptibility in psi are normally adaptive for various reasons, including making sense of complex problems, reducing anxiety, and making fast and careful decisions (Hoffrage, Hertwig, & Gigerenzer, 2000; Rudski, 2003). These are limitations in some circumstances, but it may be more accurate to suggest that they are cognitive biases that are beneficial in many ways, but also come with a cost. For example, looking for patterns in our experiences is beneficial if we want to be able to understand how the world works, but not accepting coincidences is also costly. Baggini (2009) explains:

> It may seem amazing when I bump into an old friend I was thinking about only the day before, but, for every time that happens, I think of hundreds of people whom I don't fortuitously meet. What would be more amazing would be if I never meet anyone I had recently been thinking about. In a random world, the complete absence of coincidences would need explaining, not their occurrence. (pp. 173–174)

When one has such an experience like thinking about an old friend before bumping into him or her, some might chalk it up to coincidence and some might endorse paranormal or supernatural explanations. Research suggests that those more prone to rely on intuition or to be less reflective when encountering such experience are more likely to endorse such explanations than reflective thinkers. Bouvet and Bonnefon (2015), for example, "set up" participants to believe that they had a telepathic experience (i.e., were able to "send" randomly selected cards to a receiver). While most participants experienced this as unusual or extraordinary, intuitive thinkers were more likely to endorse supernatural explanations while reflective thinkers were more likely to see the occurrence as a statistical fluke. The Bouvet and Bonnefon study is another example of how individual differences in beliefs in psi lead to important differences in behavior.

Critical thinking toolkit
Pseudoscience

Guiding question: Have I carefully scrutinized the claim looking for the presence of pseudoscientific techniques and arguments?

Telepathy, the psi phenomena manipulated in the Bouvet and Bonnefon study may be considered a pseudoscientific enterprise, though, as we will discuss in the "What about parapsychology as a pseudoscience?" section, there is not a clear line drawn between science and pseudoscience.

Consider the characteristics of pseudoscience by evaluating the following fictitious advertisement from the website of a company offering training in telepathy:

Telepathy has been well documented throughout human history and there is evidence of its use by the ancient Greeks. In the late 1800s, the popular book Our Dreams *by German physician Herbert Wienbart documented his personal telepathic experiences in which he influenced his friends' dreams.*

We have all had the experience of transmitting thoughts. Just think about how many times you've had the experience of wanting a friend to call and then hearing the phone ring minutes later and finding your friend on the other end of the line. You may even have had a sense of what that friend was doing just prior to you making the call as confirmed when she called you.

Science has proven the existence of telepathy as well, but these studies have been kept out of public reach because numerous federal agencies do not want the general public to know about this communication device. Such deception is ironic, since the government has been conducting telepathy research in secrecy for decades.

Our training program couldn't be easier. In only 30–60 minutes a week you can significantly improve your own telepathic ability. You'll learn how to harness your internal channeling energy to promote telepathy and overcome common roadblocks and negative energy. *Just listen to Jan Huffington:* "I have been in the training program for only 30 days, and am already seeing results in my telepathic ability. I feel like I have a lot more power! This program changed my life!"

You too have the power to take control over your life!

Logical fallacies

Let's unpack this a bit and talk about how this website is using tricks employed by pseudoscience. First, though there might be a long history of the "use" of or belief in telepathy it does not logically follow that this is evidence of the phenomenon. This kind of faulty logic is referred to as the **fallacy of ancient wisdom** (Baggini, 2009). By this logic, I could argue that traditional Chinese medicine is good because it has been around for a couple of thousand years. The fact that something is old (e.g., hydrotherapy for mental illness) increases the likelihood that it has been replaced by a more effective treatment (e.g., cognitive behavioral therapy). This "useful today due to the long existence of an approach" is, however, a common appeal among pseudoscientists.

Also common among pseudoscientists is the use of **anecdotes** (Pratkanis, 1995; Shermer, 1997; Schmaltz & Lilienfeld, 2014). As discussed throughout this book, anecdotes are a seductive yet poor source of evidence. Regardless of the number of compelling anecdotes, they need to be supported by scientific research (Shermer, 1997). A striking anecdote about psychic abilities is likely to stand out in one's memory and be easily recalled, making one more susceptible to the biasing of the availability heuristic (Pratkanis, 1995). Curiously, if such extrasensory abilities exist, there should be a wealth of testimonials or reports regarding filthy rich statisticians who have beat the stock market and won the lottery (Kida, 2006).

> **KEY READING** – Pratkanis, A.R. (1995). How to sell a pseudoscience. *Skeptical Inquirer*, *19*, 19–25.

As discussed earlier, you may have had the experience of thinking of a friend only to have that friend text you shortly after. We could credit telepathy for this, but we may be more likely to describe this as a coincidence when we call to mind the instances in which we thought of a friend and they did not text (Shermer, 1997). We know from the previous discussion that we have a tendency to selectively focus on confirmatory evidence, or the hits, and ignore the misses. Also, it might be perfectly understandable that you had a sense of what your friend was doing because you know her tendencies.

One of the red flags for pseudoscience is, ironically, the vague, inappropriate, and gratuitous use of the word science and the use of "sciency" language, yet the absence of true scientific scrutiny (Sagan, 1995). The phrase "science has proven" is not a phrase you will hear from psychological scientists. Scientists often find evidence in support of a hypothesis, but this isn't equivalent to "proving" the existence of something. Not even in Bem's article does he state that he has proven the existence of psi. The use of language that sounds scientific is an effective pseudoscience strategy, since the public holds science in such high esteem (Shermer, 1997). Equally problematic is the argument that if the claim cannot be disproven, then it must be true. By this logic the burden is on the skeptic to prove that psi does not exist, and if he/she can't then psi must exist (Shermer, 1997). Lastly, terms like "channeling energy" have the flavor of scientific language without the substance.

Similarly, pseudoscientists may borrow terms from scientific disciplines in order to lend credibility to their message, yet apply them inappropriately. While there may be references to scientific credibility, there may also be suggestions that this information is top secret and there are individuals (often in government agencies) who want to keep this away from the public. This makes us feel like we are being given some special information that others may not know about with the possibility of such information being kept from us as part of a conspiracy (Pratkanis, 1995). Lastly, this program gives you "power" and the ability to "take control of your life." Skeptic Michael Shermer (1997) notes that the use of emotive words such as these are purposefully used to elicit strong passions. The benefit of this is that while in an enthusiastic, positive emotional state we are more likely to rely on mental shortcuts and less likely to critically analyze the argument (Lerner, Li, Valdesolo, & Kassam, 2015).

There are a couple of other important characteristics of pseudoscience to discuss, namely a lack of **falsifiability** and the panacea problem. The above advert on the fictitious website suggests that your life, in general, is going to improve as a result of your training in telepathy. This general benefit or broad applicability is also characteristic of pseudoscience (Olatunji, Parker, & Lohr, 2005). Pseudoscientists often offer solutions to a range of problems and unattainable goals (Herbert et al., 2000; Pratkanis, 1995). Olatunji, Parker, and Lohr (2005) provide an example of Thought Field Therapy (TFT) which in addition to some other characteristics of pseudoscience purports to offer a quick fix to many psychological disorders and offers almost no scientific evidence to support its efficacy.

Pseudoscience has the tendency to disregard negative findings or explain them away and in general sidestep the all-important scientific criteria of falsifiability. Falsifiability is essential in science and avoided in pseudoscience. Walach and Kirsch (2015) explain that Traditional Chinese Medicine avoids falsifiability by referring to an invisible energy in the body called Qi. Obviously, an invisible force like Qi would be a challenge to observe, measure, and verify through scientific means. With respect to psi, imagine that I conduct a study similar to Bem's and I suggest that higher than average hits (guessing where pictures are located) would indicate the presence of psi, but average or below average hits would indicate the suppression of one's psi capabilities. In other words, there is no way for the "psi argument" to lose here; no way to falsify the theory of psi. A critical thinker might ask: "How could we know if suppression of psi is even possible?"

Determining the scientific validity of psychological treatments

Unfortunately, the applied field of clinical psychology is no more immune to pseudoscientific practices than other subfields within psychology. One example of clinical pseudoscience, according to Herbert and colleagues (2000), is rapid eye movement desensitization and reprocessing (EMDR).

Patients in EMDR rapidly move their eyes by following the back and forth movements of the therapist's hand while recalling traumatic memories (www.emdr.com). Initially used to treat anxiety disorders, EMDR became more broadly applied to a variety of other disorders. Yet negative findings have been dismissed by proponents of the treatment making falsifiability impossible. Furthermore, proponents have made bold and unsubstantiated claims about the effectiveness of the treatment (e.g., 100% success). Lastly, vivid anecdotes have been used in lieu of empirical support as has obscure language that sounds scientific but is disconnected from other scientific fields (Herbert et al., 2000). Much like with Bem's precognition research, there is no explanation for the effectiveness of EMDR beyond speculation.

Thought Field Therapy (TFT) is another treatment with a track record of pseudoscientific practices, including suggesting the lack of peer-reviewed publications establishing the effectiveness of the treatment was due to editor and reviewer bias (special information targeted by "enemies"; Olatunji et al., 2005). Falsifiability is elusive as well because the therapy works on bioenergic channels in the body that have not been scientifically verified, like the aforementioned Qi in Traditional Chinese Medicine (TCM; Schaltz & Lilienfeld, 2014). The inaccessible and therefore unmeasurable phenomena are common in pseudoscience (Bunge, 1984). What EMDR and TFT have in common is that they were completely novel treatments that did not build on existing knowledge in the field, but rather seemed to "come from nowhere" (Olatunji et al., 2005). Such breakthrough treatments often capture media attention and immense public interest, but have received much less scholarly attention. Olatunji, Parker, and Lohr (2005) compared the popular and research attention of various treatments by looking at the number of Web hits compared to citations in a popular psychology research database (PsycINFO). While a well-established and research-based treatment like token economies had nearly 7,000 web hits, it also had nearly 1,000 PsycINFO citations.

A popular treatment like TFT had nearly 20,000 web hits and less than 30 PsycINFO citations. Similar ratios were found for popular but scientifically suspect treatments such as past-life regression and subliminal self-help audio/video tapes. As human beings, we are excited by the possibility of new treatments for those suffering from chronic, debilitating conditions. As critical thinkers we should investigate the research record and ask ourselves whether such documented findings suggest that the treatment works better than a placebo or better than other established treatments (Herbert et al., 2000).

The problem is not only that there are often relatively few studies in support of the above mentioned therapies, but that there are methodological limitations which make conclusions difficult to draw. Herbert and colleagues (2000) note that the EMDR literature is plagued by the follow-ing: **effort justification**, experimental demand or **demand character-istics**, expectation for improvement or **expectancy effects**, and possible **therapist allegiance** and **optimism bias**. Effort justification, experimen-tal demand, and the role of expectancy or expectations for improvement are closely related. Cooper (1980) provided a powerful demonstration of the role of effort justification in psychotherapy research by comparing the effects of an established therapy (Implosive Therapy) versus Sham Therapy on individuals with a snake phobia. Participants who were exposed to the Sham Therapy or assigned to the control condition were asked to engage in physical exercise, but were convinced that this would provide a therapeu-tic benefit. There was a significant improvement among those receiving Implosive Therapy as measured by their willingness to approach a "live" snake. Yet there was improvement among those in the Sham condition as well and no significant difference between the two groups in their level of improvement. The authors explain these results using **cognitive dis-sonance** theory suggesting that when individuals are engaged in a freely chosen activity like therapy and expend a lot of effort, they inflate the importance of that goal to justify the effort. This justification manifests itself as improvement from the therapy. In other words, it's as if the person is saying, "I've put all of this effort into this therapy, so I guess I must really want to get over this snake phobia. Oh, great! I can approach the snake! Well, I guess that was worth it." This is obviously a concern as is the pos-sibility that the patient is wanting to please the experimenter or therapist by demonstrating improvement. It may also be possible that the positive expectancies of the therapy held by the client or participant may account for change (Constantino et al., 2011).

In their critique of EMDR, Herbert and colleagues (2000) cite over a dozen publications from Francine Shapiro, a number of which are studies docu-menting the effectiveness of EMDR. Why does this (potentially) matter? Francine Shapiro created EMDR. This is not unethical and it doesn't neces-sarily suggest that there was any intentional or even unintentional bias at play in the research. However, studies conducted by those who created the treatment or trained those conducting the research tend to produce more pos-itive results than those which are not. This allegiance effect is attributed to the personal belief in the therapy as an a priori superior treatment (Dragioti et al., 2015). Similarly, Chalmers and Matthews (2006) warned of a more general unwarranted belief in effectiveness of new treatments. This optimism bias is associated with the mistaken belief that a "new" treatment is likely to be superior to an older and more established treatment. This can impact the behavior of both the clinician/researcher and the patients/participants in a number of ways. The experimenter may provide more attention to par-ticipants and may subtly convey this optimism to them, in turn inflating

their expectancies for successful treatment outcomes. In well-designed studies, these factors are controlled for, argue Herbert and colleagues (2000), and
in such instances EMDR looks much less like a breakthrough in psychotherapy. The effect of some of these biases can be reduced with the use of multiple experimenters or counselors, relying on individuals who are blind to the
experimental hypothesis to evaluate behavior and not relying exclusively on
client self-reports of improvement (Sheperis, Young, & Daniels, 2010). While
the aforementioned methodological errors in the research do not by themselves equate to pseudoscience, when the negative results are disregarded
and explained away and anecdotes become the primary source of evidence
for effectiveness pseudoscience has at least taken root.

What about parapsychology as a pseudoscience?

A Gallop Poll conducted in 2001 found that 50% of American believe in ESP
(extrasensory perception). An additional 20% indicated that they were not
sure. Yet the vast majority of scientists are skeptical (Joyce & Baker, 2008).
With this in mind, it would seem worthwhile to consider the scientific status
of parapsychology. Science moves forward, it progresses, it changes as theories are tested, refined, revised, and discarded. Pseudoscience, on the other
hand, is stagnant and resists abandonment – knowledge in the field does
not progress. Parapsychology according to Bunge (1984) is stagnant as it
simply retests the same hypotheses. For over 100 years, parapsychologists
have been searching for evidence of psi with little success, yet the search
continues (Robinson, 2009). A similar lack of self-correction or stagnation
exists in astrology (Schmaltz & Lilienfeld, 2014). When findings fail to be
replicated, the pseudosciences have a tendency to "explain away" negative
findings; in parapsychology, if negative results have not been dismissed or
ignored, proponents have suggested that negative findings were the result of
anything other than the absence of psi (Alcock, 2003). This is closely related
to a lack of falsifiability. Alcock (2003) explains how this can play out in psi
research:

> If subjects fail to obtain the above-chance scores predicted in a psi experiment,
> that is not taken as lending weight to the Null hypothesis. Instead – so long as
> they fail miserably enough that their data deviate statistically significantly in the
> non-predicted direction, then this is taken as support for the Psi hypothesis ...
> allowing the interpretation that the miserable failure was indeed a success. (p. 39)

Likewise, failures to replicate have often been explained as due to a
psi-experimenter effect or that certain researchers with psi abilities themselves are able to elicit psi in experiments and others are not (Alcock, 2003).
If a few researchers can occasionally produce positive findings (say 5% of
the time) and negative findings can be taken as evidence of psi or explained

away (psi-experimenter effect), then it becomes easier to understand why some are able to argue, in the face of numerous failed replications, that scientific support for psi exists.

Science, according to Bunge (1984), is "grounded in lawfully changing concrete things" (p. 38). Parapsychological phenomena like precognition observations conflict with basic physical laws such as an effect happening before a cause. Parapsychology does not build on existing knowledge, nor does it connect with other fields of inquiry. Critics have noted misguided attempts to connect parapsychology to physics. In fact, these defensive attempts seem inconsistent with established knowledge in biology, **neuroscience**, and physics. Some would argue parapsychology doesn't have a subject matter knowledge base, at least a subject matter that is clearly defined, accessible, and measurable (Alcock, 2003; Bunge, 1984). Bem (2011) himself attempted to connect psi to quantum physics. Though it was certainly not Bem's motive, we should be aware of those who attempt to attach any paranormal belief to quantum physics as a sort of diversionary tactic. As most people don't have a wealth of knowledge regarding quantum physics, it would be hard for us to challenge someone's argument on these grounds (Bennett, 2015). While Bem may struggle with finding an explanation for the results, the lack of an explanation by itself is not enough for us to conclude that psi, or any other phenomena that are currently unexplainable, is impossible (Baggini, 2009).

It seems reasonable to suggest that some ideas are resistant to empirical testing with our current measurement instruments and therefore might be unproveable at this point in time within the framework of scientific investigations. Science strives to not only know "that" something works (like the switch turning on a light as mentioned in the opening of this chapter), but "why" something works. The "why" knowledge will often guide us to explain phenomena when a known cause no longer has the effect we normally observe. This is why critical thinkers value depth of knowledge on a topic.

Logical fallacies

While some in parapsychology are content with anecdotes as evidence, others employ research methods that are subject to peer-review scrutiny. Yet, as we saw with Bem's research, methodological criticisms aside, the measures of these phenomena are indirect (scores above chance on precognition tasks), while more direct measures, brain activity, have failed to support precognition. When methodological errors are brought to light, some parapsychologists have argued that the critic bears the responsibility for showing how this might have affected the results. Pseudosciences put the burden of proof on the critic to demonstrate that the phenomena in question does not exist (critics should disprove psi). Shifting the burden of proof is a type of argumentum ad ignorantiam, or **argument from ignorance fallacy**, which incorrectly absolves the one making the argument from the burden proving its validity (Van Vleet, 2011). Even when results are positive as in Bem's case, there is no theoretical account for such results. Alcock (2003) humorously notes that such results could be due to a number of factors including "a non-random 'random generator', various methodological flaws, or … Zeus" (p. 43). Deflection of providing evidence onto the critic should be a red-flag of concern for critical thinkers.

One of the difficulties in distinguishing science from pseudoscience is the tremendous variability within a field like parapsychology in terms of how psi is addressed (i.e., rigorous science versus mainstream science can't answer the question; Alcock, 2003). Another difficulty is that there is often a legitimate scientific inquiry being pursued on the one hand and a commercialized version of the same phenomena on the other. Take essential oils as an example. There is legitimate essential oil research published in peer-reviewed scientific journals and there is the commercialized product that masquerades as possessing scientific evidence for its use. There are, for example, numerous peer-reviewed journal articles examining the effects of essential oils on cognition and mood (e.g., Moss et al., 2008), though there might be some legitimate criticisms of the theoretical accounts (i.e., how do essential oils enhance cognition?). Commercial claims, on the other hand, as illustrated in Figure 9.3, pardon the pun, smell pseudoscientific.

That being said, some have suggested that parapsychological topics like psi are not inappropriate topics for scientific investigation, but rather it is the refusal to accept the failure of empirical support that is pseudoscientific. It is possible that essential oil research might follow a similar path. Though there are studies that have demonstrated greater cognitive performance among those exposed to essential oils, there is the potential for future replication failures or a failure to provide a satisfactory theoretical explanation for enhancement (e.g., a clear pharmacological effect).

Scientific Orientation	Pseudoscience Orientation
Controlled studies with valid measures published in peer-reviewed journals	Vague claims about "scientific" evidence and reliance upon anecdotes
Claims limited to particular oil and effects examined in the study (e.g., cognition or mood)	General claims of health and wellness benefits
Conclusions drawn from accumulated research findings	Appeals to ancient wisdom (i.e., "these oils have been used for centuries")

Figure 9.3 Contrasting forms of evidence for essential oils

Chapter summary

The attention Daryl Bem's results drew reflected the public's fascination and perhaps obsession with paranormal experiences and the possibility of science being able to "prove" what many already believe to be true. However, replication is crucial to science and a number of studies failed to replicate Bem's results. Such has been the historical legacy of parapsychological research. Neither the public fascination nor the scientific pursuits of psi ended the public and scientific interest in exploring such phenomena. Pseudoscience benefits from our human cognitive limitations and biases, but also preys on our emotional and perhaps spiritual needs. Carl Sagan (1995) notes: "It [pseudoscience] caters to fantasies about personal powers we lack and long for like those attributed to comic book super heroes ... In some manifestations it offers satisfactions of spiritual hungers" (p. 18). Perhaps we have had experiences that are hard to explain and intuitively turn to supernatural explanations, but upon reflection we may realize that our experiences are also at odds with existing scientific evidence. We have to ask ourselves does our desire for control, our emotional and spiritual needs, our cognitive limitations and biases better account for James Hathaway's experience at the opening of this chapter or Bem's participants selecting the position of pictures slightly above chance. It is telling that Sam Moulton, the researcher who presented perhaps the most damning evidence against psi in the form of an fMRI study, set out to prove the existence of psi and has given up on the pursuit, concluding that he "didn't find a damn thing" (Bhattacharjee, 2012).

Future directions

It would seem that future research in the field of psychology could act as an "empirical testing" proving ground to either support observations, dispute observations and/or offer alternative explanations for parapsychological events. Psychology can be expected to offer ongoing theoretical and research evidence for why human beings might cling to paranormal explanations of phenomena, even in light of contradictory evidence. Psychology and other scientific fields hold an important position in society where learned people can obtain more objective information than parapsychology websites, personal blogs, and advertisements. One well-documented element of concern is that the Internet can easily encourage people with particular extreme views to overestimate how many others also hold such a viewpoint. Science and critical thinking can become the "great mediator" in offering a sense of balanced reasoning, scientific empirical evidence, and alternative explanations for these highly fascinating, unusual, and controversial human events. If precognition research has any hope of advancing, researchers need to demonstrate that something of significance can be predicted. Franklin, Baumgart, and Schooler (2014) explain:

> *What would provide the most compelling evidence for skeptics? Ultimately, we realize that the most convincing demonstration would be to show tangible effects applied in real-world settings. If a paradigm can make accurate predictions about events that people consider important and are incapable of predicting using standard means, then the significance of the paradigm becomes self-evident. Perhaps most compelling would be if an experiment could be devised to predict games of chance and/or whether it will be a good or bad day on the stock market.* (p. 2)

Discussion questions

1. Do you think the public's belief in psi will lessen with additional failed replications of Bem's results. Why or why not?
2. When you reflect on your own personal beliefs, is there any evidence that one could present which would convince you to change your position? If so, what kind of evidence would that be?

10 The Ethics of Caring about Human Beings

Primary source: Gilligan, C. (1982). *In a different voice: Psychological theory and women's development*. Cambridge, MA: Harvard University Press.

Chapter objectives

This chapter will help you become a better critical thinker by:

- Considering how Carol Gilligan's ethic of care differs from Lawrence Kohlberg's justice theme in moral development
- Examining the sample selection process (including sample size) and sample representativeness in research, especially as such issues might apply to gender differences
- Evaluating the stereotypical differences between men and women
- Pondering how meta-analysis and effect size can help us better interpret research findings
- Contemplating how public perceptions, politics, and intuitive thinking regarding gender differences have influenced research and the interpretations of findings
- Reflecting on the political, social, and personal implications of the nature versus nurture debate

Introduction

Consider the following hypothetical information regarding gender differences:

Robert claims that he found a recently published scientific research study on the Web that concluded that 100% of males were found to be more aggressive than all (100%) females.

What might we accurately infer from such results assuming that the study was conducted in a proper scientific manner?

1. **If we randomly selected males, they are likely to be more aggressive than females.** (True)
2. **Do we risk finding that some males are less aggressive than their male counterparts in our random sample?** (Uncertain)
3. **Do we risk finding that some females are more aggressive than their male counterparts?** (False)

Obviously, Question #1 is true based upon the initial results provided. The answer to Question #2 is uncertain because the results do not include an exclusive comparison of male aggression (males compared to other males). Question #3 is obviously false because all males were found to be more aggressive than all females. Please note that such a finding might lead us to expect that only males might serve in such work roles as police officers and military combat operations. But wait … what if our initial results were in error? Perhaps this was not a proper scientific study? What if we missed something here? Might this study have used an unrepresentative sample?

Most readers have observed that in industrialized societies men are on the average more aggressive than females, but what about the within-gender variation? We need to ask the question: Might some males and some females be more aggressive than their same gender counterparts? A second question worthy of a critical thinker is to ask the question: How accurately does the hypothetically extreme finding that 100% of males were found to be more aggressive than 100% of females match up to the real world as depicted by other studies?

Critical thinkers should still not be content with halting a probing analysis of this topic. For example, we might also ask the following questions:

1. Usually, research subjects "self-identify" as "male" or "female." How might this research **not** represent subjects who identify themselves as part of the LGBTQ community or those who do not identify with either "male" or "female" or those who identify themselves as "male" **and** "female."
2. Great caution is advised when oversimplifying and categorizing human behavior in terms of males always do *x* and females always do *y*. While this approach may help to explain the behavior of a large part of the human population and simplify our understanding, it does so at a price that marginalizes, demeans, and ostracizes all of humanity in different ways.

We conclude this section with the following caveat provided by Caplan and Caplan (1994) who reminded us that statisticians have developed a "file-drawer" formula statistic that claims that "for every one published study showing group difference, it is assumed (through the use of this formula) that a certain number of no-difference studies have been done that have not been published" (p. 63). This cautions us that even a meticulous examination of the published research literature on this topic may **not** lead to an accurate understanding of the "true" nature of such gender issues.

Study background

In the early 1990s relationship counselor John Gray described fundamental differences between men being from Mars and women being from Venus and how to navigate these differences to improve communication in human relationships. The book was enormously popular in the USA, but also drew criticism for exaggerating differences between men and women, for blaming women for communication problems between the sexes, and for reinforcing traditional gender stereotypes (Crawford, 2004).

A decade earlier, the same criticisms were leveled at psychologist Carol Gilligan after the publication of her popular book *In a Different Voice*, in which she challenged the dominant paradigm or model of moral development offered by Lawrence Kohlberg. Kohlberg suggested that regardless of culture or gender, we all progress through the same stages of moral development. Gilligan instead argued that women's reasoning was qualitatively different and mischaracterized in Kohlberg's model. In this chapter we will examine Gilligan's model and gender differences in moral reasoning, gender differences more generally, and the implications of ideas like those proposed by Gray and Gilligan.

In Kohlberg's developmental model of moral reasoning, justice takes center stage. Let us take the example of the infamous Heinz dilemma in which a pharmacist is dramatically overcharging for a drug desperately needed by a dying woman who can't afford it.

> *In Europe, a woman was near death from a special kind of cancer. There was one drug that the doctors thought might save her. It was a form of radium that a druggist in the same town has recently discovered. The drug was expensive to make. He paid $200 for the radium and charged $2,000 for a small dose of the drug. The sick woman's husband, Heinz, went to everyone he knew to borrow the money, but he could only get together about $1,000, which is half of what it cost. He told the druggist that his wife was dying and asked him to sell it cheaper or let him pay later. But the druggist said, "No, I discovered the drug and I'm going to make money from it." So Heinz gets desperate and considers breaking into the man's store to steal the drug for his wife.*
> (Colby et al., 1983, p. 77)

An individual at the lower stages of development frames the dilemma in terms of the personal needs of the involved parties. When asked whether or not her husband, who stole the drug, should have, such individuals might suggest "no" because Heinz will get in trouble or "yes" because Heinz's wife will appreciate it and it isn't fair that the pharmacist overcharged. At higher stages, reasoning reflects universal principles of justice (e.g., respect for the dignity of human life supersedes the rule of not stealing) rather than the rule-based reasoning of earlier stages (e.g., stealing is against the law; Kohlberg, 1975; Kohlberg & Hersh, 1977). According to Kohlberg (see Table 10.1), it is the cognitive explanation rather than exclusively the behavior that is employed to categorize moral reasoning. It is the middle stages, 3 and 4, however, that are most relevant to the issue of gender differences in moral reasoning. The concern for justice is embedded in relationships at stage 3 (e.g., a good husband would be right to steal the drug), whereas reasoning at stage 4 centers on the good of the community at large (e.g., for the good of society we can't allow Heinz or anyone else to steal property). Women's reasoning, some including Gilligan alleged, was more likely to be categorized as Stage 3, whereas men's reasoning was more likely to be classified as Stage 4 (Gilligan, 1982). Why? Gilligan believed that the hypothetical moral dilemmas typically used to assess moral reasoning didn't capture a type of reasoning more common among women. She contended that while men typically reason according to an ethic of justice, women typically reason according to an ethic of care (caring for and about others) (Gilligan, 1982).

Table 10.1   Stages of moral development (adapted from Kohlberg, 1976)

Level 1   Preconventional Level (Personal Needs and Personal Perceptions Focus)

Stage 1: Obey the established rules and avoid punishments or negative consequences

Stage 2: Personal interests drive behavior. "What I want is right."

Level 2 Conventional Level (Expectations of Society Focus)

Stage 3: Being nice to others drive behavior. Being good demands pleasing others in authority positions such as parents and teachers.

Stage 4: Law and order perspective. Judgements made based upon social conventions that must be preserved. Laws and authority figures need to be obeyed.

Level 3 Postconventional Level (Moral Principle Focus)

Stage 5: Social contract perspective. Judgements made based upon social contracts and the legal point of view such as due process and what is best for the majority.

Stage 6: Universal Ethical Principle perspective. Judgements now based upon a respect for individual human rights, human dignity, and social justice. Personal conscience formulated upon self-selected defensible standards is to be followed when dilemmas are confronted in life.

Gilligan's conclusions, detailed in her book *In a Different Voice*, were based on three studies: (1) the "college student study" involving 25 students (men and women) taking a course on moral and political choice, (2) the "abortion decision study" involving 29 women interviewed while considering abortion and then one year after their decision, and (3) the "rights and responsibilities" study involving 144 individuals (men and women) aged 6–60 interviewed about their conceptions of morality and given hypothetical moral dilemmas. The benefits of the inclusion of women in Gilligan's studies (Kohlberg relied on men) presumably resulted in greater **external validity** in that participants, at least in the abortion decision study, were interviewed about a real, personal moral dilemma rather than responding to a hypothetical dilemma.

Gilligan (1982) argued that the typical conception of development as a striving for individuation, autonomy, and independence, while an appropriate description of development for males, does not adequately capture female development which centers on relationships, attachment, and responsibilities to others or interdependence. The problem with this, according to Gilligan, was that in the history of development theories "different" always equated to "deficient" for women. This was believed to be true in theories accounting for various aspects of development – and moral reasoning was no exception. If women were reasoning based on relationships and care and concern for others, they were likely to be reasoning at a stage 3 level. Higher stages could be attained by a focus on rights and fairness reasoning (an ethic of justice) more commonly found among men. Men reasoning at a high level focus upon *individual* rights and freedom from infringement on those rights. Women more often reason based on an individual's obligations to help *others*. As long as one doesn't sacrifice one's obligations to oneself, Gilligan characterized this reasoning as a strength rather than a deficiency.

The "objective" of the previously described Heinz dilemma was to appreciate the intricate conflict between the values of property and life and the logic of life over property rights which might compel Heinz to steal the drug (Colby et al., 1983). Reasoning from an ethic of care, the concern is about the failure of the druggist to honor his obligation to others. Thus, the "different voice" of women is not heard in the traditional moral dilemma, according to Gilligan, because the key question from a care orientation is how a resolution could be achieved which would not require Heinz to steal the drug. Responses reflecting this ethic of care, according to Gilligan (1982), "fall through the sieve of Kohlberg's scoring system" (p. 31).

Like Kohlberg with justice reasoning, Gilligan suggested that care reasoning progressed in a stage-like fashion (Table 10.2), moving from rebelling against the authority of others to conforming and suppressing one's own needs to achieve a mature state in which one is acting in concert with others and there is no longer an imbalance between the needs of the self and others.

Table 10.2 Stages of care reasoning proposed by Gilligan (1982)

Stage 1	An initial focus on caring only for oneself
Stage 2	Care for the "dependent and unequal"; good is equated with caring for others
Stage 3	Care for others including self; care not equated with self-sacrifice but self is also beneficiary of care

In sum, Gilligan (1982), in *In a Different Voice*, was suggesting two things: women often differ from men in the level of reasoning within Kohlberg's dilemmas; and there is a type of reasoning, care reasoning, not accounted for by Kohlberg's theory which helps to explain this difference.

Current thinking

What if we examined what a moral person would be like without regard to gender stereotypes? Perhaps there would be a need for each of us to adopt the "justice" perspective at times and the "caring about others" perspective at other points in time. If so, then the crucial dilemma might be to determine exactly when and where contextually to employ one of these moral frames of reference. For example, Blakemore, Berenbaum, and Liben (2009) suggested that female moral orientations are "somewhat more likely to focus upon care for others than on abstract principles of justice, but they can use both moral orientations when needed (as can males...)" (p. 132).

Other critics have for decades challenged the direct link between what we say we would do in a moral dilemma and our actual moral behavioral outcome. For example, why do elected officials and religious leaders publicly state lofty moral beliefs and then fail to deliver behavior based upon their own stated standards? The inconsistencies of human behavior not matching our previously stated moral platform is a domain of moral psychology well worth exploring.

Reviews of the research on gender differences in moral reasoning have generally led to the conclusion that there is a small difference between men and women in the use of justice and care reasoning. However, Gilligan's claims that women utilize an ethic of care in moral reasoning deserve scrutiny in light of the characteristics of the sample she utilized in *In a Different Voice*. We must also be aware of those who, for political purposes, seek to promote or condemn the notion of significant psychological differences between men and women and how Gilligan's work and the work of others may be distorted and misused in either case.

The influence of Gilligan's book *In a Different Voice* was not limited to moral development research. Authors who have written about the movement for single-sex education, for example, have credited Gilligan's book as an inspiration (Rigdon, 2008; Salomone, 2013; Sommers, 2001). The idea that girls' voices were not being heard and were being drowned out by boys led to increased popularity of single-sex schooling in the 1990s in the USA (Rigdon, 2008). Kudos to Gilligan, right! Unfortunately for Gilligan, the differences between mixed-sex educational settings and single-sex educational settings were minimal. The same unfortunate yet familiar theme appears in explaining the popularity of single-sex schooling – powerful anecdotes, uncritical acceptance by the media, and a misinterpretation of neuroscience (Halpern et al., 2011).

> **KEY READING** – Rigdon, A. R. (2008). Dangerous data: How disputed research legalized public single-sex education. *Stetson Law Review, 37,* 527–578.

In conclusion, are all men oriented toward the justice viewpoint and all women oriented toward the caring viewpoint? Do we always act according to our publicly stated moral beliefs? When qualitative studies attempt to capture the rich and personalized nature of human responses, what is lost in the realm of controlling variables, measurement, and generalization?

Critical Thinking Toolkit
When and where do generalizations become problematic?

Guiding question: Have I fully considered the exceptions or cases that do not fit a stereotype or generalization?

"Men go to their caves and women talk," noted author John Gray in chapter 3 of his bestselling self-help book, *Men Are from Mars, Women Are from Venus.* Have you observed this in men and women? How many men are like this? How many women? Are there some men who do not seek cave life? Are there some women who do not love to talk? Might some men enjoy talking? Might some women seek cave life? Are there some men and women who even like to talk to each other in the cave? How many men and women do not fit the rigid stereotypical depiction of such gender-related behaviors?

These might be some of the many critical questions to consider when analyzing such a stereotypical overgeneralization regarding men and women. Of course, these generalizations are a result of inductive reasoning that create such a generalization and deductive reasoning that we use to apply such generalizations to specific situations. For example, if you ask a child to compare pictures of a train, plane, and ship to find what they have in common, they often might likely conclude that these are all modes of transportation (inductive method).

Obviously, inductive and deductive thinking modes are not good or bad in their own right. It is how these modes of thinking are employed that result in outcomes that either help us think critically or delude us into thinking that everyone sees the world in the same stereotypical way (a shared generalization) or every individual must fit the stereotypical generalization. As Figure 10.1 demonstrates, we often use the scientific method to examine how patterns of specific individuals can create generalizable theories (inductive mode) and how studies can explore how well a general theory can predict an outcome with a specific data set (deductive mode). The cycle depicted in Figure 10.1 shows how one mode of thinking leads to the next.

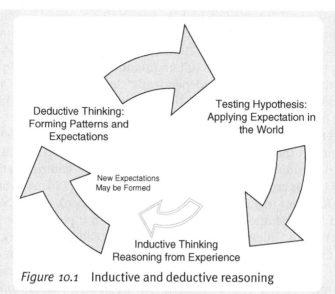

Figure 10.1   Inductive and deductive reasoning

Imagine that you asked adults who wear eyeglasses, "Where do you place your glasses while sleeping?" The majority of respondents would likely say on the night-stand or table near the bed. Of course, some people might place their glasses elsewhere and some might even sleep in their eyeglasses! The point is that this generalization or stereotype could be very useful in predicting the actual specific outcomes (deductive method) for many people. In some life situations, being accurate 80–90% of the time is very useful, such as when searching for lost eyeglasses or missing keys. As a patient needing crucial life-saving surgery, you might not be comfortable with a 10–20% sur-gical death rate. Stereotypical generalizations are therefore deeply embedded in how we think and reason, but also at times mislead and deceive us. Additional mental pro-cesses must be able to compensate for flaws or errors in such judgement.

Evaluating the evidence

Gilligan (1982) described the interviews with participants in her studies as follows:

> All of the studies relied on interviews and included the same set of ques-tions – about conceptions of self and morality, about experiences of conflict and choice. The method of interviewing was to follow the language and the logic of the person's thought, with the interviewer asking further questions in order to clarify the meaning of a particular response. (p. 2)

When a researcher has a standard set of open-ended questions and then allows for follow-up questions based on interviewee responses, the interview is considered semi-structured. A **semi-structured interview** stands between the rigid structured interview which is essentially a verbally administered questionnaire and the unstructured interview which is conversational (i.e., more open-ended and flexible; Gaultney & Peach, 2016). Typically, after conducting the interviews, raters (often graduate students working with and trained by the researcher) will independently classify the responses using an objective coding or scoring system. Then the level of agreement, **inter-rater reliability**, between the raters can be assessed.

For a peer-reviewed article in which the results are published, authors should report on the process of scoring or categorizing responses, inter-rater reliability, and provide detailed information on the characteristics of the sample. All of this crucial information is lacking in *In a Different Voice* (Luria, 1986). The fact that this information was not in the book would be less concerning if a more detailed account was provided in a peer-reviewed journal article which would allow other researchers to test Gilligan's theory. Not only did the results of the interviews not appear elsewhere, but concerns have also been raised about Gilligan's reluctance to make the data accessible upon request (Sommers, 2001). This reliance on **anecdotes** pulled from a select number of interviews, along with concerns about the generalizability of a dilemma (abortion decision) in which care about relationships and conflicting needs and responsibilities would obviously emerge, is a problem. Likewise, that there was no comparison with men to determine if there are differences in care between men and women raised doubts about Gilligan's conclusions among many social scientists and feminist scholars (Luria et al., 1986).

Are the gender differences real?

One of Gilligan's charges was that Kohlberg's model, developed from studies conducted exclusively with men, was biased against women. While there are individual studies that report gender differences, including a greater tendency for females to reason at stage 3 and males at stage 4, there are others that report no differences and others still that report an advantage for females. So questionable was the evidence of a male advantage, critics Greeno and Maccoby (1986) suggested that Gilligan was "attacking a straw man" (p. 312). When there are numerous studies with mixed results, researchers rely on **meta-analyses** (see Chapter 7) in which statistical procedures are used to combine the results of studies and help researchers draw more definitive conclusions (Cooper, 2017). You may wonder at this point, why not just add up the number of studies that support gender differences and the number of studies that don't support the hypothesis?

Recall from Chapter 7 that this "box score" approach is not as straightforward as it appears. The problems with the traditional literature review approach were dramatically illustrated in a study by Cooper and Rosenthal (1980). The researchers had a group of faculty and graduate students review research articles using either the traditional review method or the meta-analysis method. Ironically, the research participants were evaluating gender differences in persistence! Those using the traditional method perceived much less support for the hypothesis of gender differences in persistence than those using meta-analysis. Without statistically combining the results, reviewers of the research saw seven studies and only two of them found significant results supporting the hypothesis of gender differences. If one employed the box score approach, it would be easy to see how a conclusion of no significant differences could be drawn.

However, statistically combining the results produced a combined significance level of roughly 0.02. Considering the commonly regarded probability level of 0.05 for statistical significance, the results, though not overwhelming, supported the hypothesis. Nearly 60% of the participants using meta-analysis concluded that there was a small effect, yet only 27% using traditional methods did and they were also more likely to perceive that results did not support the sex differences hypothesis. These results highlight one of the limitations of traditional reviews, that is, a lack of standards for determining whether or not the studies were supportive of a hypothesis (Cooper, 2017). Additionally, traditional reviews cannot determine the overall magnitude of the relationship, for example between gender and persistence. Meta-analysis solves these problems by providing a standardized effect size or indicator of the strength of the relationship that can be used for comparisons across studies (Cohen, 1988; 0.2 small; 0.5 medium; 0.8 large) which also has the effect of reducing bias.

So, let us return to the question of gender differences in moral reasoning. What do the meta-analyses tell us? Three such studies have been conducted, two in the 1980s (Thoma, 1986; Walker, 1984) and one in 2000 (Jaffee & Hyde, 2000). The earlier meta-analyses found no evidence of men scoring higher on moral reasoning (in fact, one found an advantage for females; Thoma, 1986). The more recent meta-analysis by Jaffee and Hyde (2000) combined the results of over 100 studies with over 8,000 male and female participants. The effect sizes suggested a minimal advantage for men in justice reasoning ($d = 0.19$) and for women in care reasoning ($d = 0.28$).

KEY READING – Brabeck, M. M., & Shore, E. L. (2002). Gender differences in intellectual and moral development? The evidence that refutes the claim. In J. Demick, & C. Andreoletti (eds), *Handbook of Adult Development*, (pp. 351–368). New York: Plenum Press.

Now we can place these differences in context. The meta-analyses tell us that there is a small difference in justice and care reasoning, but what do we make of this? And, for that matter, how do we interpret potential differences found in a single study. Let's imagine for a moment that a media outlet reports the results of a single study that found significant gender differences. The headline reads: "Researchers find that men and women reason in different ways with women focused on relationships and men focused on abstract principles."

This might seem like a reasonable summation of the study as researchers found average care scores of 4.0 for women and 3.5 for men and an average 3.5 for women and 4.0 for men on a measure of justice reasoning. The problem with the interpretation "men and women reason in different ways" is that it takes small *quantitative* differences and interprets them as significant *qualitative* differences. In other words, as illustrated in Figure 10.2, we are taking mean differences in care and reasoning as categorical differences (women engage in care reasoning and men in justice reasoning), because, well, we like to categorize things (Pound & Price, 2013).

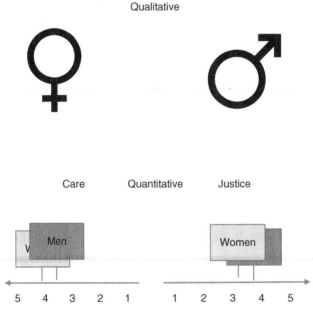

Figure 10.2   Minimal mean differences between men and women represented as categorical differences

Let's also assume that there is not one but several studies that have assessed gender differences and even a meta-analysis which found an effect size of 0.20 (*d* = 0.20), a nearly identical effect to the one reported by Jaffee and Hyde (2000). What do we make of a "small" effect? Let's look at this effect size a little closer. Hyde (2005) provides a visually striking example of what the distribution of scores – in this case scores for moral reasoning between men and women – would look like with an effect size of 0.2. Eighty-five percent of the area of the two distributions, as depicted in Figure 10.3, overlap.

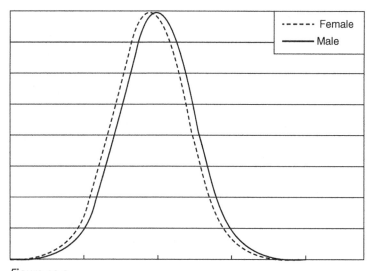

Figure 10.3

Source: reproduced with permission from the American Psychological Association (APA)

The similarities, it turns out, are more striking that the differences and this overlap is not limited to moral reasoning. Hyde (2005) reviewed meta-analyses across a number of domains including self-esteem, personality traits, job attitudes, and coping styles and found that nearly 80% of gender differences were either small or close to zero.

Recall that Gilligan also suggested that a care orientation progresses developmentally in the same way moral reasoning develops according to Kohlberg. Whether this is the case, however, is not entirely clear. To understand why, we need to examine the type of data suggesting a progression in care. Suppose we conducted a study in which we measure the care reasoning of a group of 20-year-olds, 40-year-olds, and 60-year-olds. We find that care, in fact, does seem to progress across development, with the 40-year-olds demonstrating greater care than the 20-year-olds and 60-years-olds greater care than both the 20-year-olds and the 40-year-olds. Thus, it seems that as one ages one develops greater care reasoning. However, the problem with this interpretation of **cross-sectional data** is that it could also be explained by **cohort differences**. It might be the case that differences in care reasoning result from generational differences. From the mid-1950s when the 60-year-old participants were born to the late 1990s, gender socialization in society has dramatically changed. Care researcher Eva Skoe (1998) explains: "Older people grew up in a more restrictive, gender-stereotyped society and they were raised by parents adhering to more conservative values and norms" (p. 152). Thus, we have to be careful about drawing conclusions about developmental progression from cross-sectional studies.

Where are the control variables?

In addition to the previously mentioned meta-analyses, Rest (1979) reviewed more than 20 moral reasoning studies finding only two reporting significant sex differences. Rest, however, noted that sex differences are more likely to be found when researchers fail to control for educational and occupational status. When these variables are controlled, sex differences are minimal or absent (Donenberg & Hoffman, 1988; Jaffee & Hyde, 2000; Walker, 1984). To better understand the importance of accounting for such variables, consider the following observation: People living in an upper-class neighborhood are more conservative than individuals who are not. Though this may be true, it may also be the case that people living in an upper-class neighborhood are older than those lower in SES (social economic status). This may help explain the relationship between upper-class neighborhood residence and conservatism. In such cases, researchers need to control for age by gathering such data and including it in statistical analyses. Specifically, researchers can conduct a **partial correlation** in which the effects of a third variable can be controlled (Field, 2005). As illustrated in Figure 10.4, without considering age, it appears that there is a correlation between upper-class neighborhood residence and conservatism.

Let's say that the correlation between upper-class status and conservatism is $r = 0.44$, $p = 0.01$. If researchers believe that a third variable like age is a potential **confound**, they might conduct a partial correlation in which age is controlled for. As you can see below, there is a great deal of overlap between age and conservatism. With age controlled for, the correlation between upper-class status and conservatism is a non-significant, $r = 0.12$, $p = 0.09$.

The same third variable problem was noted by those defending Kohlberg against charges of bias against women. Psychologist Lawrence Walker, for example, noted that education and occupational status were often confounded in studies reporting significant sex differences. In other words, the reason women were found to reason at a lower level than males in past studies was due, in part, to the higher educational and occupational status of males. In studies that better controlled for this, no sex differences emerged (Walker, 1984). Thus, even though differences were rarely found (only 8 of 108 studies reviewed by Walker found significant difference between men and women), they seemed to be better accounted for by educational and occupation status, in the same way that age better accounted for the differences in conservatism between those living in upper-class neighborhoods and those in less affluent ones.

Can we put gender differences to Rest?

Nowhere is the issue of group differences in scores more hotly debated than in the domain of intelligence. Research in the USA has consistently found significant IQ differences among Asian Americans, White Americans, and African Americans which often leads to charges of test bias. What is

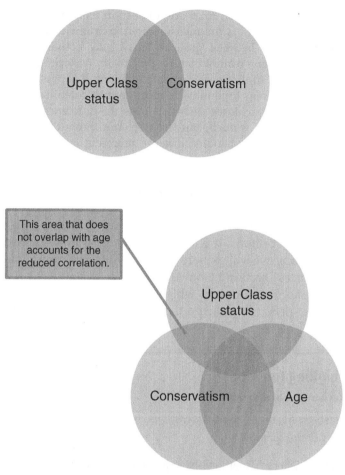

Figure 10.4   Illustration of a partial correlation

important (at least in terms of determining bias), however, is not the scores themselves, but how test scores are able to predict meaningful outcomes like academic and occupational success. The key issue, then, is whether or not the test predicts equally for all groups, what researchers call **predictive invariance** (Hunt & Carlson, 2007). For example, bias would be an appropriate charge if IQ scores were highly correlated with academic performance (e.g., $r = 0.70$) for Caucasians but not significantly correlated (e.g., $r = 0.10$) for African Americans. Likewise, if moral reasoning significantly predicts prosocial behavior for men, but not for women, bias could be the reason why. Yet psychologist James Rest (1979) notes a tendency on the part of Kohlberg's critics to "blame the test" for differences in scores between males and females. Rest challenged us to consider the logic of assuming that differences in scores could only be explained by bias and not reflect true differences.

If it is found that males as a group are taller than females, does this imply a sex bias in the foot ruler? Is the measurement instrument necessarily biased because of differences between groups? There may actually be differences between groups, and one cannot assume that the differences are due solely to measurement defects. In the case of moral judgment, it is possible that men in our society at the present time may be more sophisticated in moral thinking than women because the biases in society foster the difference. Currently, men earn more money than women, but this does not imply that the method of counting dollars is biased; it could, however, represent a bias elsewhere. (Rest, 1979, p. 122)

While gender differences have certainly been used inappropriately to argue for the genetic/biological inferiority of the lower scoring group, it does not have to be the case that there are only two alternatives: bad test or inferiority. Rest points to a third option – it is society or the environment that accounts for differences, a topic we will explore more fully in "The nature and nurture of gender differences" section below. If there were differences between men and women in moral reasoning, which Rest and many others concludes there were not, it does not indicate that Kohlberg's measure is necessarily biased.

Critical thinking toolkit
Representativeness of a sample

Guiding question: Beyond size considerations, have I given thought to the representativeness of the sample?

Several critics of Gilligan's methods have pointed specifically to the small size of the sample and the questionable representativeness of the selected sample. Recall that Gilligan's conclusions were based on the results of three studies: (1) a study with 25 college students at Harvard taking a course on moral and political choice, (2) abortion decision study involving 29 women from Boston considering an abortion, and (3) the rights and responsibilities study with 144 participants ranging in age from 6 to 60. Recall from Chapter 2 that the convenience of a sample is not, by itself, an indicator of representativeness. Moreover, while we may be tempted to dismiss Gilligan's findings because of the small sample size, this too is not *the* indicator of representativeness.

There are several sample size considerations that may initially seem contradictory. First, the size of the sample does matter in terms of variability (Kida, 2006). The smaller the sample, the more likely we will get an unusual result. Imagine I wanted to get a sense of the public's views on abortion in the UK. Assume I pick five people at random, what are the chances that I get an all pro-life or an all pro-choice sample? Safe to say a lot more likely than if I randomly selected 100 individuals. Therefore, it is tempting to suggest that the small size of the college student and abortion studies is the most glaring weakness of Gilligan's research, calling into question the generalizability of the results. However, the size and the representativeness are actually two separate issues and the fact that a sample is small does not *necessarily* reflect poorly on the quality and generalizability of the study (Morling, 2014). A small sample certainly raises concerns about representativeness, but is not a direct indicator of this. It is possible to have a small sample that is representative of the population and a large sample that is not. Imagine we have a sample of 60,000 individuals who responded to a survey on abortion in a politically conservative magazine in the UK. How representative is this sample? Though Gilligan's samples are small, the bigger issue is their questionable representativeness. Is a sample of Harvard University students taking a course on moral and political choice representative (Luria, 1986)? Some have also raised concerns about research with college students in general and how representative they are of the general population (Rubenstein, 1982). However, it is important to ask *what* is being generalized and to *whom*.

Figure 10.5   Consideration of generalization in Gilligan (1982)

To generalize from research with students at Harvard to either college students or the general population is not necessarily problematic (Figure 10.5). If we surveyed 100 people from the London, UK, borough of Islington (a distinctly liberal neighborhood) and sought to generalize to all Londoners, we might be rightly concerned about the representativeness of this sample if the survey was about political attitudes. However, if our survey is unrelated to political attitudes, representativeness may not be an issue. Likewise, while we may not be concerned about the generalizability of research with Harvard students if our research is on facial features associated with pain (why would we expect students at Harvard to be different than others in this respect), we may harbor concerns regarding a study on moral reasoning.

Selection bias could be an issue as well with this unique sample. Recall that students were enrolled in a presumably elective course on moral and political choice. Also recall the Carnahan and McFarland (2007) study from the Stanford Prison study (Chapter 6) in which participants volunteering for a study of prison life were higher on a number of personality variables compared to participants volunteering for a generic psychological study. Would we expect differences in moral reasoning among those who would volunteer for a course on moral and political choice than those who would not? If so, we might not only have concerns about generalizability to college students, but even concerns about how representative these students are of the larger Harvard student population.

Logical fallacies

The enduring popularity of Gilligan's ideas

The popularity of books like John Gray's *Men Are from Mars, Women Are from Venus* and Carol Gilligan's *In a Different Voice* in the public milieu is attributable to a number of factors, including the public's central belief in inherent differences between men and women (Carothers & Reis, 2013; Eagly & Wood, 2013) and the media's uncritical acceptance and dissemination of such ideas (Sommers, 2001). Ideas like Gray's and Gilligan's are appealing, critics suggest, because they reinforce beliefs that many individuals already hold about differences between men and women and they also benefit from our tendency to categorize and dichotomize (Fiske, 2010; Pound & Price, 2013) especially on the basis of sex (Stangor et al., 1992). In other words, we are attracted to ideas regarding human differences, however small. Our catergorization makes the world a simpler and less complex place to live. Yet we have to be careful to avoid and ready to spot arguments that appeal to our "natural" tendencies as men and women. The suggestion that women more naturally reason based on care and that because this *is* the way women reason, this is the way women *ought* to reason, is an example of a **naturalistic fallacy**, or is/ought fallacy (Bennett, 2015). The fact that something might appear natural and perhaps an evolved disposition, does not speak to whether or not it is desirable, morally right, or something that we should accept and promote.

Even when science fails to support these ideas, they persist for a number of reasons (Mednick, 1989). First, the science may not be consistent with our own observations ("I've seen greater care exhibited by my mother" or "My sister tells me that women are more caring"). In addition to the problem of mischaracterizing Gilligan's notion of care with "feelings" is the problem of our own observations and anecdotes from others being filtered through perceptual biases including confirmatory bias – we see what we want to see. That science is fighting an uphill battle against casual observation and anecdotes is illustrated in a humorous example by physician and skeptic Harriet Hall (2016): "If your neighbor had a bad experience with a Toyota, you're likely to remember his story and not buy a Toyota even if Consumer Reports says it's the most reliable brand." We "prefer stories to studies, anecdotes to analysis" concluded Hall. Could it also be the case that if a female friend or neighbor told you about a dilemma they faced in which their struggle reflected an ethic of care, we might more easily remember this than a study in a psychological science journal reporting that there are no significant sex differences in moral reasoning?

The politics of sex

The second obstacle is ideology. What one believes about fundamental differences between men and women and the role of men and women in society can lead one to disregard, misinterpret, or misuse research suggesting differences or similarities. These ideas are well ensconced in our society. Conservatives might embrace Gilligan's theory because they emphasize differences between men and women and favor biological explanations, whereas liberals could be more likely to reject Gilligan's theory as they seek to minimize differences and favor sociocultural explanations (in fairness to Gilligan she did not argue for or against biological or sociocultural explanations). But this is a problem for conservatives and liberals, science is not political, correct? While it may be cynical to suggest that all research on sex differences/similarities is biased, it is undeniable that the ideology of researchers influences what they study, how they study it, and how they interpret and seek to apply their findings (Eagly & Wood, 2013; Fiske, 2010). As consumers of research, we may be a bit naïve about the purity of scientific research (Neuroskeptic, 2012; Wagenmakers et al., 2012) and of the media reporting of such research. Brescoll and LaFrance (2004) examined the reporting of sex differences in newspapers and found a tendency for more conservative papers to attribute findings of gender differences to biological factors. Why does this matter? For one, some ambiguity in the research allows readers (conservatives/liberals) to read their conservative/liberal paper and find their ideologically satisfying biological/sociocultural explanation for the findings (Eagly & Wood, 2013). The Internet also functions in a similar manner to confirm or deny our existing beliefs.

Additionally, in a subsequent study with undergraduates by Brescoll and LaFrance (2004), the researchers found that reading articles in which biological explanations are presented increases the endorsement of gender stereotypes. This is where things got heated with respect to Gilligan's theory. It is the (mis)use of her research to reinforce gender stereotypes that drew the attention of social scientists, feminist scholars, and conservative scholars, as suggested by the responses in Table 10.3.

Table 10.3   Comments on how Gilligan's ideas have been misused

"(re)produce antiquated gender roles" (Crawford, 2004, p. 65)

"reifies the stereotype of women as caring and nurturant" (Hyde, 2005, p. 590)

"used to support a conservative political agenda" (Mednick, 1989)

"encourage the conclusion that women really are more nurturant than men" (Kerber et al., 1986, p. 307)

"permits her readers to conclude that women's alleged affinity for 'relationships of care' is both biologically natural and a good thing" (Kerber et al., 1986, p. 309)

"Campuses have become divided along race, class, and gender lines. Feminist scholars, many of them influenced by Gilligan's theories, have taken the lead in this politicization and polarization" (Kilpatrick, 1992, p. 148)

The nature and nurture of gender differences

Theoretical accounts for sex differences in moral reasoning are not political per se, though their explanations may be preferred by those with particular ideologies. Sociocultural explanations suggest that characteristics like care develop through gender roles (e.g., nurturing and care) that are associated with particular societal roles (e.g., home-maker; Eagly & Wood, 1999, 2013). The characteristics associated with a role are internalized and become part of one's self-concept. The assignment of these roles, however, largely depends on the characteristics of the culture and are subject to change. Psychological differences more appropriately exist in the roles and not in the men and women who occupy them. In other words, change the roles and the psychological characteristics in individuals can change.

From an evolutionary perspective (see **evolutionary psychology**), however, these psychological differences between men and women reflect adaptations to the different challenges faced by each in our historical evolutionary past. For example, psychologist Shelley Taylor and colleagues (2000) proposed that enhanced nurturing of offspring and reliance on social support (i.e., tend and befriend) was, as opposed to fight or flight, a response to stress that made evolutionary sense for women who, because of gestation and lactation, are higher in what evolutionary psychologists refer to as **parental investment**. Recall that Gilligan's critics often pointed to the implications of her findings as particularly troubling because they reinforced the idea of stark, biological differences between men and women. Sociocultural and evolutionary perspectives also carry with them implications about how "fixed" or stable differences are between the sexes and if changes are even possible.

Chapter summary

Carol Gilligan proposed two distinct forms of moral reasoning and suggested that women often approach moral dilemmas with relationships and the care and concern for others foremost in their minds. When we think about differences between men and women, we have a tendency to overgeneralize and, in the case of Gilligan's theory, we want to consider the quality of evidence upon which those generalizations are drawn. Critics have noted the limitations of Gilligan's methods and data, yet the results of several meta-analyses point to small differences between men and women in moral reasoning. Though this seems to support Gilligan's assertions, it is best to keep in mind that small differences across a population mean a great deal of overlap exists among its members. A closer look at the data also requires a consideration of control variables, two of which – educational and occupational status – play a significant role in accounting for gender differences in moral reasoning. When research does produce evidence of differences, another set of critical thinking concerns rise to the surface. We want to avoid a reflexive tendency to deny such differences by blaming the test, but at the same time be cautious of how such differences might be exaggerated for political purposes or distorted in either direction when filtered through our own biases.

Future directions

While research on care continues, a perusal of developmental and general psychology textbooks suggest that the issue has largely been settled – research has failed to support the idea that men and women are qualitatively different in their moral reasoning. Likewise, research on sex differences in communication styles do not suggest that men and women are from different planets (Hyde, 2005). Research on gender differences, however, continues to move forward including research in the moral development arena. Recent work suggests that women have greater sensitivity to harm than men (FeldmanHall et al., 2016) and show a greater tendency toward deontological responses – responses that evaluate an action based on its consistency with a moral norm (e.g., wrong to kill another person) as opposed to utilitarian responses in which killing could be justified if it saved others – to moral dilemmas than men (Friesdorf, Conway, & Gawronski, 2015). Given that the moderate effect size of $d = 0.57$ reported in the Friesdorf and colleagues study was larger than that produced in meta-analysis of care and justice reasoning (e.g., Hyde, 2005), the authors concluded that "previous work on moral reasoning underestimated gender differences in moral judgment" (p. 14). Regardless of whether or not significant differences in care and justice reasoning exist between men and women, Carol Gilligan has, even by her critics, been given credit for shedding light on exclusive use of males in the building of developmental theories and for challenging the universality of such theories.

Jonathan Haidt (2013) more recently argued that moral behavior is more reactive than deliberate, and the more thoughtful and cognitive explanations are an after-effect while trying to explain our behavior. There is a decidedly interdisciplinary framework in the field of moral psychology today that incorporates neuroscientists, evolutionists, social and developmental psychologists, primatologists, economists, philosophers, and historians. The trends are captured by the following three principles: (1) intuitions come first, strategic reasoning second, (2) there's more to morality than harm and fairness, and (3) morality binds and blinds. Haidt suggested that "moral reasoning" is currently seen "as being more interpersonal (done to prepare for social interaction), rather than intrapersonal (done to find truth or work out one's intrapsychic conflicts)" (p. 294). The interpersonal focus today speaks to the influence of Gilligan's caring framework while the intrapersonal framework speaks more to the justice framework offered by Kohlberg.

KEY READING – Haidt, J. (2013). Moral psychology for the twenty-first century. *Journal of Moral Education, 42,* 281–297.

Brescoll and LaFrance (2004) note that we may let our guard down when reading articles reporting on scientific research, assuming such reports are objective. Yet, whether reading media reports of research or the original reports, as wise consumers of research we need to be *particularly* vigilant when consuming research on sex differences (Fiske, 2010). We also have to be willing, in the face of convincing evidence, to set aside our own ideology and challenge our own observations and assumptions as well as the anecdotes that come our way. If successful, perhaps future researchers will not draw the conclusion that Eagly and Wood (2013) did that "science may not be winning" (p. 12) in the battle to better inform the public.

Discussion questions

1. Why have so many researchers devoted such a large extent of time, talent, and energy to exploring sex differences? Does the scientific method promote breaking down human behavior according to sex differences and sex roles?
2. In what morally relevant life situations do you think care reasoning would more likely be elicited? Justice reasoning? Think about the applied professions of medicine, law enforcement, social work, court system, and so on.
3. If we were to find substantial statistical sex differences rooted in biological factors, what should we do with this information? If we were to find substantial statistical sex differences based upon social factors, what should we do with this information? How prepared are we as a culture to alter biological and social factors?

11 Benjamin Libet: Do Human Beings Really Have Free Will?

Primary source: Libet, B. (1985). Unconscious cerebral initiative and the role of conscious will in voluntary action. *The Behavioral and Brain Sciences, 8,* 529–566.

Chapter objectives

This chapter will help you become a better critical thinker by:

- Reviewing the findings of the Libet studies and subsequent research on conscious free will
- Evaluating criticisms of the study including ecological validity and demand characteristics
- Considering the limitations of introspection in studies of conscious free will
- Contemplating the limitations of neuroscientific tools and the appeal of neuroscientific explanations
- Recognizing the importance of various levels of analysis and the pitfalls of reductionism

Introduction

Imagine you are interested in understanding human decision-making in the brain and set out to investigate the correct insertion of a jigsaw puzzle piece on the first try. Perhaps you might simply ask the participant why he/she chose to put this particular puzzle piece into the adjacent pieces so that it fits perfectly. This is a type of introspection where we ask research participants to go back in their minds and do two things: (1) recreate the memory of the experience, and (2) share this explanation with the experimenter. As you might expect, some participants will have difficulty reflecting on this experience while others will provide elaborate detail about the decision-making process.

Leap ahead perhaps 125 years from the early introspection studies and today neuroscience researchers might want to employ functional magnetic resonance imaging (fMRI) to better understand brain activity during the correct solution of inserting this individual piece of the jigsaw puzzle. In such a study, we might expect the results to indicate higher levels of activity in a particular region of the brain. Nevertheless, how much information regarding thinking and problem-solving in this particular condition is provided by the fMRI results? Though neuroscientific tools like fMRI appear to represent a technological leap forward over introspection, concerns over accuracy apply to both.

If we were to include a metaphorical analogy for fMRI and introspection studies within the context of everyday life, it might look like the following. Imagine that you positioned two highly trained researchers to interpret sounds at opposite sides outside a soccer (European football) stadium. The two researchers record their interpretation of the sounds in order to try and capture what is happening at a given moment in the match. How would this understanding of the soccer match compare to a well-trained commentator inside the stadium describing the play-by-play of the match? How would the commentator's description of the match differ from the players watching a video after the match and describing the strategic reasons for the decisions they made? The researchers outside the stadium had to put the "auditory" pieces of the stadium activity puzzle together without access inside the stadium. Similarly, the fMRI tries to put together the brain activity puzzle relying on "noise" from outside the brain. The commentator, relying on insight and experience with such games as well as observations, tries to provide a running narrative of the players' decisions, actions, and movements. Similarly, when relying on our insights and experience we may feel confident in our ability to provide an account of the inner workings of our own consciousness. However, the commentator and the participant in an introspection study have to divide their attention among many tasks and are likely vulnerable to inaccuracies despite their confidence in what they observed.

Read on to learn more about studying the brain and the freedom of personal choice.

Study background

In his provocative book *Hardwired Behavior: What Neuroscience Reveals About Morality* psychiatrist Laurence Tancredi (2010) describes how neuroscience is beginning to redefine our notion of free will and, in turn, individual responsibility. Neuroscientific findings, Tancredi contends, challenge notions that obesity may be the result of gluttony or a lack of self-control. How? Neuroimaging studies show the same area of the brain that "lights up" in the presence of drugs among those addicted also "lights up" in the presence of food (presumably among those "addicted" to food). Not only do these neuroscientific revelations change our understanding of addictive behavior and mental disorders, but they have the potential to influence the legal system, challenging traditional notions of criminal responsibility. How can we be responsible for our behavior if our brains really are in control? Such a question may seem odd unless we consider the results of a groundbreaking study by Benjamin Libet. Results suggested a diminished role for free will by demonstrating that some behaviors are initiated unconsciously by our brains before we are consciously aware of our intent to act. Considering the implications of Libet's research, it is not surprising that, like the other studies in this book, this publication drew considerable attention and closer scrutiny. In this chapter, we will meticulously examine the research and consider the potential pitfalls of trying to reduce psychological functioning to biological processes. We will also consider the appeal of neuroscientific explanations, and why, as appealing as they are, we should exercise great caution in generalizing such findings. At the end of *Hardwired Behavior*, Tancredi asks us to contemplate a future in which Libet's research and that of other neuroscientists has discredited free will. We will examine the status of free will and consider the implications of undermining one's belief in free will.

KEY READING – Tancredi, L. (2010). *Hardwired behavior: What neuroscience reveals about morality*. New York: Cambridge University Press.

Some psychological constructs would appear difficult to define and measure (e.g., happiness and aggression) and free will would seem to be among them. Benjamin Libet embraced the challenge in order to examine the timing of a freely willed act. More specifically, he examined the temporal sequence of the following: a simple motor action, awareness of the intention to initiate the action, and electrical activity in the motor cortex. In order to examine the coordination of a freely willed action, Libet had participants focus their eyes on the middle of a clock in which a spot of light (as opposed to a clock hand) rotated around the face (Libet, 1999). Participants were asked to note the position of the light when they first became aware of the urge to act. It was important for the purpose of the study that the act be spontaneous or freely willed and, thus, participants were instructed to press a key whenever they had the spontaneous "urge" to do so. At the same time, as illustrated in Figure 11.1, the participants were hooked up to an **electroencephalogram (EEG)** that was recording electrical activity in the motor cortex, an area responsible for initiating motor commands.

Figure 11.1   Benjamin Libet paradigm

Libet found evidence of brain activity in the motor cortex *before* the participant reported the conscious intention to act. Specifically, the electrical activity, what Libet termed a **readiness potential** (RP), occurred a few hundred milliseconds before the conscious awareness to act. The conscious awareness of the urge to act occurred 200 milliseconds before activation of the muscle, as illustrated in Figure 11.2 below.

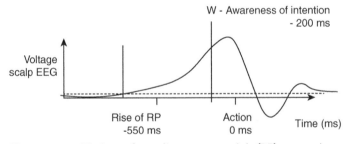

Figure 11.2   Timing of readiness potential (RP), conscious awareness, and motor act in Libet study

These results seem to conflict with our everyday or intuitive understanding of how free will works. We assume that when we have an intention to act we direct our brain to put this intention into motion. Some, including psychologist Daniel Wegner, have even taken the results as confirmation that we do not possess free will, that it is an illusion (Wegner, 2002). In the animated DreamWorks film *Trolls* (Shay, 2016), the one thing that makes the morose Bergens happy is eating trolls which they do annually on a holiday they call Trollstice. One holiday the trolls escape before becoming a meal for the Bergens and the chef is blamed and banished from Bergen Town. Years later, the former chef returns and convinces the King to bring back Trollstice. She also convinces him to bring her back as the chef. Yet the clever chef makes the King think that these were his ideas. This is going to be the best Trollstice ever, the King says, what a great idea I had. The King, like all of us, some argue, simply has the illusion of being in control.

Though the results, according to Libet, suggest that our intuitive under-standing may be a bit naïve, they do not suggest that we lack free will. Rather than initiate the act, our conscious free will has the ability to over-ride the unconsciously initiated act just before it occurs according to Libet. Just prior to the initiation of the motor act and after the RP, we can con-sciously veto the unconsciously initiated act. The window for this veto is brief as it is in the final 100 ms before the spinal motor nerve cells receive the signal that the veto is possible. To provide some perspective on how much time this is, the blink of an eye can take up to 400 ms (Schiffman, 2001). Once the motor nerve cells receive the signal it's too late for a veto (Libet, 1999).

> **KEY READING** – Libet, B. (1999). Do we have free will? *Journal of Consciousness Studies*, 6, 47–57.

It is as if our actions are rolling down the conveyer belt on an assembly line and conscious free will is the quality control inspector. Most of the actions seem well enough, though occasionally we spot one or two that clearly do not meet our quality standards and we discard them. Much like the quality con-trol inspector on the assembly line who does not have access to the numerous steps in the process before the product reaches his or her checkpoint, we do not have access to the unconscious processes that produce the act. Likewise, the inspector has only the option of discarding a product as it passes by, not the responsibility for the further processing or repairing of the product as it moves down the conveyer belt. Conscious free will, according to Libet, functions in a similar way; the action, if not stopped by the veto process, is moving down the line. Conscious free will is not necessary to initiate the act. Without the power to veto, conscious free will might be seen as nothing more than an illusion – a feeling that our thoughts cause our actions, yet both are created unconsciously (Wegner, 2002, 2003). While psychologist Daniel Wegner interpreted Libet's research as evidence of the illusory nature of free will, many questioned the design of the study and the interpretation of the results. The reactions to Libet's research were voluminous and passionate. Not surprising, after all, since free will was at stake here.

Current thinking

The following statement may be a fair summary of the current thinking about Libet's research and Libet-like studies:

> *Researchers have consistently identified neurological activity that <u>appears</u> to precede conscious awareness of what is <u>presumed</u> to be a decision to act or carry out a simple task.*

This is not exactly a statement supporting the supposition that free will is an illusion. There are far too many questions to draw such a conclusion. Let us start with the word precede. There is evidence that activity precedes but does not cause a freely willed act. However, there has been considerable variability in the timing of and location of the neurological activity (Papanicolaou, 2017). This is to say nothing of the act itself, which has drawn considerable questions. While the neurological activity might be associated with the decision to act, it might also be associated with other task-related cognitive operations (see Figure 11.3 below).

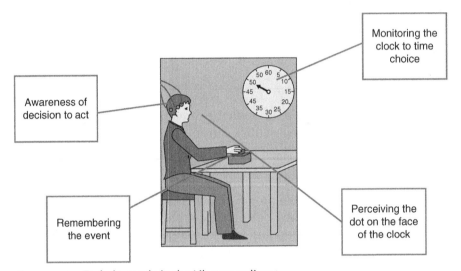

Figure 11.3   Task demands in the Libet paradigm

A second important question concerns the act itself. Is free will adequately captured in a study asking people to flex their wrist? Though participants were told to respond whenever they felt the urge, does this truly represent a freely willed action? The fact that the participants were given instructions and were responding to the instructions left some researchers with questions as to whether Libet's operational definition of conscious free will was precise and whether the task was ecologically valid (Bridgeman, 1985; Kuhl & Koole, 2004).

Another aspect of Libet's methods that has drawn criticism involves relying on an individual's retrospective reporting of when they experienced the will to move, a method that has serious drawbacks (Wolpe & Rowe, 2014). Some argued that it was not necessarily safe to assume that we have the ability to tell when we experienced the will (Papanicolaou, 2017; Rugg, 1985) or that the timing was off because Libet did not account for the time it takes, possibly several hundred ms, for the representation of the clock face to be processed by the brain (Rollman, 1985). In other words, I may recognize my intention to move and see the clock face at "3," but it took as much as 300 ms for this sensation to be processed by the brain and recognized as the "number 3." Additionally, some have suggested that Libet's findings may not hold if consciousness was viewed as gradual or graded rather than as an all-or-nothing phenomena (conscious or unconscious; Miller & Schwarz, 2014).

Even new methods for addressing the free will question have not allayed concerns. Neuroscientist John-Dylan Haynes (e.g., Soon et al., 2013) has taken a different approach to addressing Libet's fundamental questions about free will. Rather than look at increases in brain activity across tasks as is typical in fMRI studies, he and his colleagues have examined the patterns of activity across the brain. Haynes and others have demonstrated that patterns of activity precede freely willed acts, but the tasks are still circumscribed and numerous questions remain.

Let us return to Libet's methods for a moment to examine one additional question: What does the RP really represent? Did it represent, as Libet suggested, an intentional but unconscious plan for movement? One group of researchers had their doubts.

Consider the difference between the following two tasks: (a) You are instructed to press a button whenever you get the urge; (b) You are instructed to press a button as fast as you can whenever you hear a click. The first task (a) is essentially the task given to participants in the Libet study and, as we have discussed, the movement itself and the awareness of intent to move are both preceded by an RP. But if the RP represents what Libet suggested, you wouldn't expect it to be present in the second task (b). You certainly wouldn't expect it to be present when we are not even thinking about moving (we'll call this task (c)! However, this is exactly what Schurger, Sitt, and Dehaene (2012) found. Results indicated increased electrical potential before fast responses compared to slower responses. These results conflict with Libet's account of the RP because the participants could not be planning for a randomly occurring click. Accordingly, the authors contend, the RP is not an unconscious plan to act, but a randomly fluctuating brain event that influences the likelihood of acting as it builds in strength. The stronger it gets, the more likely we are to decide to act. However, because it represents a random process it is not exclusive to task (a), but would be present before task (b) and even task (c). Looking at the RP in this way suggests that free will was in no way diminished by Libet's results. The awareness of the urge to act (200 ms before the act) was not preceded by an unconscious "decision" to act, but by a randomly fluctuating RP that may have made that decision to act more likely. As you are reading this book right now, you may have a water bottle within reach. Whether or not you decide to reach for that water bottle would be influenced by random fluctuation in RPs. As the RP reaches the decision threshold, it is more likely that you reach for that water.

With Schurger and colleagues' (2012) model of the RP, even a thousand replications of Libet's findings only gives us confidence that we can reliably predict the presence of an RP before awareness of the conscious decision to act. These findings do not challenge free will. The substantial questions raised about Libet's research and others led Papanicolaou (2017) to conclude: "it is irresponsible for any scientist to declare or imply that there is credible scientific evidence supporting the hypothesis that the will is determined" (p. 334).

Considering demand characteristics

Were participants freely exercising their will or were situational factors impinging on their will? Recall that questions were raised about the influence of instructions given to guards in the Stanford Prison study (Chapter 6) guard orientation session. Could the same issue surface in the Libet study? Libet believed that participants were engaging in a freely willed act as participants were told to respond whenever they felt the urge. However, does this truly represent a freely willed action or does it involve highly constrained behavior in a heavily circumscribed task presented by the experimenter? One consideration when addressing such a question is the operational definition of key variables, in this case free will. **Operational definitions** specify how variables are manipulated and measured. For example, if you were conducting a study on the effect noxious odors have on behavior, you would need to operationalize or provide an operational definition of the noxious odors. One option, employed by (Tybur et al., 2011) involved covering the wall of a room with fart spray. As impressive as Tybur and colleagues' ingenuity was, Libet faced a significantly greater challenge in operationally defining free will. While Libet (1985) did report that participants "felt" that the acts were spontaneous, it may be the case that the participants were unaware of the influence of the experimenter or other stimuli in the environment including the clock (Dennett, 2003). Additionally, Schurger and colleagues (2012) explain the demand characteristic issues in Libet's studies as follows:

> Libet's instructions allow the subject to wait an indefinite amount of time to produce a single movement. However, it is implicit in the demand characteristics of the task that the subject should not wait too long: The task is to produce a movement on each trial, and the subject knows this. (p. 2905)

Questions over generalizability

A related issue is the **ecological validity** or generalizability of Libet's research. How representative is the behavior (clicking your wrist or finger or pushing a button) of the full range of willed volitional acts? There is a lot of planning that goes into most complex behavior and it is reasonable to argue that a task involving simple motor movements does not capture this complexity, nor are these practical examples of free will. However, it is important that we avoid being cynical about the generalizability of the findings. In another famous study, the Bobo doll study (Bandura, 1965; Bandura, Ross, & Ross, 1963), preschool children behaved more aggressively in interacting with an inflatable doll after watching an adult being rewarded for such behavior than those watching an adult being punished. It would be easy but inappropriate to disregard these findings based on poor ecological validity. We may fall victim to drawing this inappropriate conclusion about the findings because the victim, in this case, was an inflatable clown doll (a non-human object).

The results, therefore, have no bearing on how a child would act in the "real world," one might argue. However, the generalizable *principle* was that of vicarious learning or learning through the reinforcement or punishment of others' behavior. This represents a specific type of **external validity** called **construct validity** (Brewer, 2000). Effective critical thinking demands that we avoid disregarding the research based on the use of an inflatable doll and instead consider the extent to which the results have been replicated with various stimuli in various settings. The same can be applied to the Libet studies. Though it would be easy to criticize the simple motor act as compromising the external validity of the study, we need to consider subsequent replication studies. Libet (1999) reports that there is evidence that RPs precede other volitional acts such as writing, but these studies did not examine the timing of conscious intentions to act. Thus, we do not have evidence to suggest that acts that are more complex would reveal the same pattern.

In terms of assessing generalizability, it is also instructive to consider the research methods employed. While we might find a naturalistic study like David Rosenhan's (Chapter 5) to be more satisfying in terms of ecological validity, as discussed, this study left a lot to be desired in terms of internal validity. The opposite could be said for the internal–external trade-off in the Libet study with the **internal validity** being high and the external validity being more questionable.

Introspection

Introspection is a method that fell out of favor in psychology due to a number of factors including the unreliability of the method as practiced by some. This important event in the history of psychology also shifted the focus of the discipline from the mind to behavior, which required methods other than introspection (Locke, 2009). In the early history of introspection, the methods would have been confined to very basic elements of sensation and perception (Danziger, 1980; Hunt, 1993). Psychologist Wilhelm Wundt's use of introspection involved examining the perception of stimuli like colors and sounds. Participants were asked to reflect on and report on what they were experiencing in response to these stimuli and researchers were recording how long it took them to respond to these stimuli.

Regardless of the validity of introspection as a current research method, there are important questions about Libet's use of it in his free will studies. The ability to reliably identify the timing of events (RP, conscious awareness of intention to act) is hampered by a number of factors including the time it takes to perceive stimuli. The time it takes to perceive sounds is different than the time it takes to perceive sights and touch (Danquah, Farrell, & O'Boyle, 2008). While the participants in the Libet study engaged in what might be incontrovertibly characterized as a simple motor task (i.e., flicking wrist or finger), as noted earlier, critics of the study (Papanicolaou, 2017) have argued that the other task demands were taxing on the participant's attention (e.g., monitoring the clock). More fundamentally, asking people to report on their awareness of conscious decisions assumes that people are capable of accurately reporting on the vagaries of their own consciousness. Lastly, researchers have argued that an important division of conscious awareness is missing in the Libet research, that between full conscious awareness and unconscious processes. Miller and Schwarz (2014) have argued that the RP might precede full conscious awareness but, perhaps, not partial conscious awareness. These researchers suggest that conscious awareness should be viewed as a gradual process which builds over time, leaving open the possibility that partial awareness occurs before the report of full conscious awareness among Libet's participants.

Critical thinking toolkit
Brain mumbo jumbo

Guiding question: Have I considered the possibility that my interpretation of and confidence in the results of a study employing brain imaging technology (as opposed to a behavioral study) are unduly influenced by its neuroscientific character.

As noted, though full of inconsistencies, there have been several replications of Libet's findings (e.g., Soon et al., 2013). However, one recent replication attempt offered something different, at least technologically different. The researchers not only replicated Libet's findings in terms of the timing of events, but, using fMRI, found brain activity in the pre-supplementary motor area (pre-SMA) to be associated with the experience of intention (Lau et al., 2004). In this next section, we will consider the significance of this difference between the Libet study and the study by Lau and colleagues – the use of the fMRI. Perhaps at this point, you are feeling a bit frustrated by the inconsistency in the free will research, overwhelmed by the potential loss of a particular human construct (free will), and then reinvigorated at the possible restoration of free will. Perhaps you would feel better if you screamed, hit a pillow, or, better yet, an inflatable doll. Let us consider the potential benefits of **catharsis** to explore the power of the fMRI.

Catharsis or venting involves the discharge of aggressive impulses. You may have heard numerous anecdotal accounts of how effective catharsis can be or you yourself may have experienced the positive benefits of "getting it all out in the open." Despite the popularity of the belief, research fails to support the notion that catharsis is an effective way to deal with anger as it results in *increased* anger and aggression (Bushman, 2002; Denson, DeWall, & Finkel, 2012). Consider the following explanation provided by researchers:

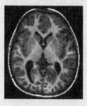

Brain scans indicate that this increase in anger happens because of the limbic system brain circuitry known to be involved in anger. Catharsis is ineffective because it does not lead to reductions in anger or aggressiveness. Anger and aggressiveness increase because catharsis is an ineffective strategy.

Finally, neuroscience researchers have discovered why catharsis is ineffective! Consider the explanation provided prior to the addition of the neuroscientific piece:

The researchers claim that catharsis is ineffective because it does not lead to reductions in anger or aggressiveness. Anger and aggressiveness increase because catharsis is an ineffective strategy.

Impressed by the neuroscientific "explanation"? Read the paragraph again and then ask yourself the following:

Guiding question: What did the neuroscientific information add to the explanation? Did it add to our understanding?

If we look closely at the differences in the table below (the difference between the two explanations is in bold), we will likely come to the conclusion that it added little.

Explanations "Using" Neuroscience	Explanations "Without Using" Neuroscience
Brain scans indicate that this increase in anger happens because of the limbic system brain circuitry known to be involved in anger. Catharsis is ineffective because it does not lead to reductions in anger or aggressiveness. Anger and aggressiveness increase because catharsis is an ineffective strategy.	The researchers claim that catharsis is ineffective because it does not lead to reductions in anger or aggressiveness. Anger and aggressiveness increase because catharsis is an ineffective strategy.

A brain scan showing the brain "lit up" when experiencing math anxiety is inherently interesting, but it does little to help us understand math anxiety (Tavris, 2012). We know that there are neurological correlates for emotional, cognitive, and behavior processes. Thus, these examples would qualify as what psychologist Carol Tavris refers to as pseudoneuroscience.

Neuroscience is seductive, and a study by Weisberg and colleagues (2008) clearly demonstrates its allure. The researchers gave participants descriptions of psychological phenomena such as catharsis and then explanations that were either good or bad and either contained neuroscientific information or did not.

KEY READING – Weisberg, D. S., Keil, F. C., Goodstein, J., Rawson, E., & Gray, J. R. (2008). The seductive allure of neuroscience explanations. *Journal of Cognitive Neuroscience*, 20, 470–477.

Recall from Chapter 5 that in a factorial design the value of each number (e.g., 2 x 2) indicates the number of levels for each independent variable. Technically, the researchers utilized a **2 x 2 factorial design** in that there were two independent variables with two values (good or bad explanations and neuroscientific information or no neuroscientific information). If Weisberg and colleagues would have compared neuroscientific information with images and neuroscientific information without images to a no neuroscientific information control, they would have been conducting a 2 x 3 factorial study as illustrated in Figure 11.4.

(1) Neuroscientific information with images	(2) Neuroscientific information without images	(3) No neuroscientific information (control group)

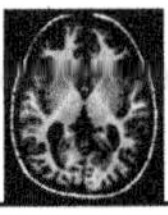

Figure 11.4   Hypothetical 2 x 3 factorial design of Weisberg et al. (2008) study

In general, explanations that included neuroscience information were rated by participants to be more satisfying than those that did not (see Figure 11.5).

–3	–2	–1	0	+1	+2	+3
Very unsatisfying			Neutral			Very satisfying

Figure 11.5   Rating scale for satisfaction with neuroscientific and non-neuroscientific explanations

However, the striking finding, as shown in Figure 11.6, was that while bad explanations without neuroscience were seen for what they were (i.e., bad), bad explanations *with* neuroscientific "window dressing" were rated as significantly more satisfying. Adding the words "brain scans" and "frontal lobe brain circuitry" or "limbic system brain circuity" was highly seductive and seemed to impress the raters. These results held even for experienced psychology students.

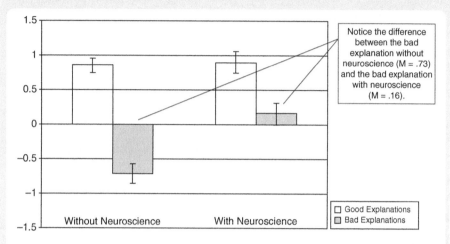

Figure 11.6   Novice group. Mean ratings of how satisfying subjects found scientific explanations. Error bars indicate standard error of the mean

Considering confounds in the neuroscientific studies

There is an additional variable to consider, in this case a potential confound. Recall that **confounds** are variables that are not controlled for or intentionally manipulated that might influence the results and thus compromise internal validity. In other words, the potential influence of these variables leaves the researcher uncertain as to whether it was the independent variable or the confounding variable that caused a change in the dependent variable. Did you recognize the confound? There is an image of a brain scan accompanying the neuroscience explanation. Could it be that an accompanying fMRI or Positron Emission Tomography (PET) scan picture adds to the seduction? While a study by McCabe and Castel (2008) suggested this might be the case, a more recent study demonstrated that the neuroscientific images do not add to the allure above and beyond neuroscientific information (Fernandez-Duque et al., 2015). Let us consider why these studies produced different results.

There is an important difference to note about the design of the Weisberg and colleagues (2008) study and both the McCabe and Castel (2008) and the Fernandez-Duque and colleagues (2015) studies. Weisberg employed a **between-subjects design** while Fernandez-Duque utilized a **within-subjects**

Within-subjects design

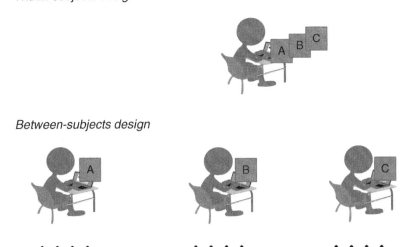

Between-subjects design

Figure 11.7   Within-subjects and between-subjects designs

design. As illustrated in Figure 11.7, in a within-subjects design each participant is exposed to all of the conditions. While this is more efficient and requires fewer subjects, it does introduce a potential confound referred to as **carryover effects** (Smith & Davis, 2013). Carryover effects occur when experiences in one condition influence those in a subsequent condition. For example, imagine you are in a study comparing the effects of beverage choice on the perceptions of psychological studies. We want to compare the effects of an alcoholic beverage (a depressant), coffee (a stimulant), and water (neutral) on how satisfying the explanations of psychological phenomena are (the dependent variable in the Weisberg study). If we ran participants through in this order, we might find that the second condition (coffee condition) produced the lowest satisfaction ratings. The explanation may lie in the carryover effect in that the effects of the alcoholic beverage interfered with the ability to understand the information in the second report. In order to deal with this potential confound, we can conduct a between-studies design in which we randomly assign participants to one of the three conditions or we could retain the within-subjects design and **counterbalance** the conditions. That is, we could balance the impact of this order across participants, some will get the alcohol first, some will get the coffee first, and some will get the water first, and so on. To return to the McCabe and Castel study, having a participant compare across the conditions allows one to observe that Report B has an image that Report A did not have and, therefore, is more powerful (Schweitzer et al., 2011). This contrast is not possible in a between-subjects design.

Functional Magnetic Resonance Imaging (fMRI)

If you've read media reports of fMRI studies you might be surprised that fMRI does not actually measure brain activity. It measures what we may infer is brain activity. What it detects is the increase in oxygenated blood in an area of the brain across conditions (Beck, 2010; Vul et al., 2009). In other words, it shows that oxygenated blood increases in brain area X when engaged in activity A compared to oxygenated blood in brain area X when engaged in activity B.

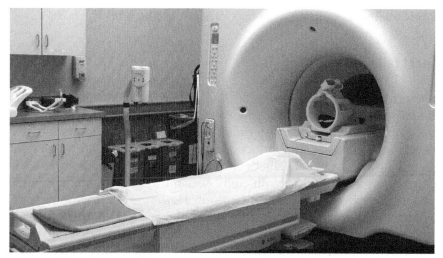

An example of an MRI machine

Therefore, it does not show brain activity itself; it shows a contrast. If I found no difference in these two conditions, I would not conclude that there was an *absence of brain activity* (Beck, 2010); rather, I would conclude that there was no difference in activity between the two conditions. To highlight the importance of the contrast and the potential for misunderstanding of what the fMRI shows, consider the following fictitious headline: "Researchers find that a love for chocolate has a biological basis, since eating chocolate is associated with activity in emotional centers of the brain." What the headline does not reveal is the comparison that was made. In this study, perhaps one group of participants ate chocolate and the comparison group ate Lutefisk, a gelatinous, aged fish dish. The results tell me about activity in the brain of those eating chocolate relative to activity in the brain of those eating Lutefisk. Additionally, the absence of a significant difference between the two conditions does not tell me that there is a lack of activity in the brain when eating chocolate. It may lead to the unsettling conclusion that people get as much pleasure from eating gelatinous fish as they do chocolate!

Perfectionistic fallacy

Concerns have also been raised more generally that complex thought, like that involved in a moral dilemma, can be entirely understood in terms of differences in oxygenated blood (Erickson, 2010). Specifically, Erickson (2010) suggests that neuroscientists are measuring something that they assume represents thought (brain activity). This is an assumption because we do not know how this activity becomes a thought. However, we do have to be careful to avoid the **perfectionistic fallacy** or the idea that we should abandon efforts to understand the relationship between the brain and the mind because we will never fully understand it. In other words, we should abandon this goal because there is such a low probability of attaining a "perfect" understanding (Van Vleet, 2011).

Logical fallacies

We have to ask ourselves whether the tools employed in contemporary efforts to address the free will question have offered greater insights or have simply dressed up the same results with brain mumbo jumbo. Unfortunately, there does not appear to be a straightforward answer to the question. Some studies have attempted to replicate Libet's findings with different methods, but some such research is qualitatively different, seeking to identify unique patterns of brain activity associated with decisions. However, we may be victims of the seductive allure if we uncritically accept the findings of the latter as evidence of mind reading and overlook the problems of accuracy that plague this research and the neuroscientific research more generally. Regardless, we do need to ask ourselves whether the use of fMRI technology has influenced the way that we interpret the findings. As one of the participants in Weisberg, Taylor, & Hopkins' (2015) study noted about the neuroscientific explanation: "Talking mumbo jumbo about the frontal lobes without explaining what is actually happening is bullshit" (p. 435).

Reductionism

In addition to narrowly focusing on the dazzling technology of neuroscience rather than the substance of a finding, psychologist and neuroskeptic Carol Tavris suggests that **reductionism** is another characteristic of pseudoneuroscience (Tavris, 2012). Reductionism comes in many forms, but, in general, we are concerned with the reductionistic assumption that psychological phenomena can be accounted for or understood in terms of more fundamental biological processes. Once we have identified the biological process we can dispense with the psychological explanation. It is tempting to assume that a brain-based or physical explanation is more fundamental than an explanation at a behavioral or cognitive level. For one thing, people may be more skeptical of the validity of more subjective self-reports. Additionally, if we fail to appreciate how behavior, thinking, and experiences affects the brain, then we are even more likely to find a biological explanation more satisfying because it must suggest that the phenomena is innate (Beck, 2010). Nowhere is the reductionism more apparent than in psychopathology. The fact that brain activity can be correlated with addiction, depression, or schizophrenia does not suffice to label the disorder a brain disease. As Miller (2010) notes, "by that reasoning, research documenting structural and functional brain changes after aerobic exercise would lead to the characterization of exercise as a brain phenomenon" (p. 719). Associating behavior with activity in a particular brain region is not by itself an explanation (Beck, 2010). As a critical thinker, it is important to be sensitive to explanations that seem to confuse correlation with causation and explanations that suggest such a correlation reveals a "biological basis." "Associated with" and "underlying" are not the same thing. Please recall that correlation does not prove that a cause and effect relationship exists.

Let us return to the Libet study for a moment. Does the reductionism that we discussed above apply to the Libet study? As noted earlier, some critics of the study argue in terms of generalizability, that the simple finger or wrist movement does not inform us about more complex behavior. According to **Self-Determination Theory (SDT)**, one of the basic human needs is the crucial component of autonomy and, regardless of the presence of RPs, if one's behavior is consistent with one's personal values, goals, and beliefs, then one maintains their personal autonomy (Ryan & Deci, 2004). The problem is when someone experiences their behavior as controlled, which was not the case in the Libet experiment; participants reported the experience of volition or of freely choosing their behavior. The point that Ryan and Deci are making is that while the Libet research is interesting, the question with practical importance is to what extent does the person *feel* in control of their behavior? A lack of autonomy is associated with psychological problems. The *Hardwired Behavior* book discussed at the beginning of the chapter (Tancredi, 2010) presented a hypothetical everyday moral dilemma in which a favorite uncle with a gambling problem has asked to borrow some money. He explains how your response to your uncle could be explained in strictly biological terms:

> Finally, you will experience his reaction to your "no." This will activate your sensory systems (auditory and visual), limbic structures – in particular the amygdala (emotional reaction to his affect), hippocampus (connecting memory to emotions), as well as anterior cingulate cortex (self-control), and hypothalamus (bodily response such as sweating, increased heartbeat) – and the frontal lobes.

Naturalistic fallacy

Tancredi then laments that we are more interested in the end results (what you did in this situation and why) rather than the examination of the underlying biological process. Tancredi's complaint reflects the appeal of neuroscience. References to the brain seemingly provide an essential answer to the question of why? Nevertheless, Ryan and Deci question what value this fine-grained biological analysis provides. This doesn't tell us "why" he decided not to give his uncle the money. We actually have a preference for the lowest level of analysis, yet psychology is aimed at understanding the control and prediction of behavior. This is why knowing that the nephew in Tancredi's example is worried that his uncle will gamble the money away and get himself further in debt is why he said no. Recall also that the title of Tancredi's book is *Hardwired Behavior*. Though a popular term, the notion that moral behavior is hardwired is misleading as psychological phenomena are modifiable (Lilienfeld et al., 2015). There is a thin line between "the behavior is hard-wired" and "it's in their nature" which brings us to the edge of committing the **naturalistic fallacy**, or reasoning that something is justifiable because it is natural (Levy, 2010). What comes naturally is not, ipso facto, moral.

It is important that people feel that they are in control or autonomous and, as a study by Baumeister, Masicampo, and DeWall (2009) shows, a *belief* in free will is important. These researchers had participants read sentences that induced either a belief in free will or **determinism** (e.g., brain activity determines behavior) and then respond to scenarios in which they had an opportunity to help another person. Those in the free will condition were significantly more helpful and, in another experiment, were less aggressive to others. These results speak to the societal importance of a belief in free will.

Chapter summary

The groundbreaking research of Libet and subsequent studies finding evidence of an RP preceding conscious awareness of a decision to act has been interpreted as a challenge to our notion of free will. However, numerous criticisms have been raised about the representativeness of the freely willed behavior of participants, demand characteristics in the study, participant's ability to accurately reflect on and report conscious activity, and the accuracy of the technology used to record brain activity as well as what the RP actually represents among others. While the basic findings of Libet have been replicated, researchers have yet to address many of these questions. Conclusive statements about the status of free will seem unwarranted and speculative at this point in time.

The Libet research and the results of more recent neuroscientific research have important implications for the legal system. Because of what is at stake, it is increasingly important that we sharpen our critical thinking skills and look beyond the shiny veneer of neuroscientific language and images. There are three assumptions of this neuroscience research that we need to keep in mind: (1) the assumption that the activity in the brain is necessarily an accurate reflection of thought associated with the psychological phenomena is in question, (2) our desire for simple, reductionistic explanations, (3) and the various levels of analysis. Let us remember the advice of Carol Tavris to ask the question: "Does the neuroscience add anything new to what we already know?" In a cell phone company commercial running during the holiday season in the USA in 2017, the famed reindeer Rudolph is looking to purchase a phone to play his reindeer games and the salesperson asks him: "So, what are reindeer games?" Rudolph replies: "Angry reindeer, doodle reindeer, flappy reindeer..." "Oh, so regular games with the word reindeer added to them?" replies the salesperson. "Huh," says Rudolph, "I guess so." As consumers of media reports of neuroscientific research, we need to be able to distinguish among those that truly add to our understanding of the psychological phenomena and those that are offering us no more than reindeer games.

Future directions

One thing to keep in mind about the examination of free will with neuroscientific tools is that these tools are relatively new and as they undergo further refinement, they may be better able to address the timing issues in question in the Libet study (Breitmeyer, 2017). However, it is an open question of whether it is possible to "read the mind" or using patterns of brain activity to predict behaviors or decisions before they happen. Haynes (2011) notes:

> It would be interesting to investigate whether decisions can be predicted in real-time before a person knows how they are going to decide. Such a real-time "decision prediction machine" (DP machine) would allow us to turn certain thought experiments into reality, for example, by testing whether people can guess above chance which future choices are predicted by their current brain signals even though a person might not have yet made up their mind. (p. 18)

Keep in mind the accuracy of such "mind reading" is questionable, with Haynes noting the accuracy of using brain activation patterns to predict button pushing (left or right) was 10% above chance. Such results would **NOT** seem to justify a likely headline from the media: "Mindreading is now possible!" While the media deserves some blame for overselling such results, as Breitmeyer (2017) notes, the quest for media attention and fame among researchers is also to blame.

Critics of Libet's research have called for more ecological valid behaviors to be tested in the lab (Breitmeyer, 2017). This is particularly important considering the societal implications for free will research. Erickson (2010) explains that neuroscience is slowly bringing inevitable changes to the entire legal system. An implication of Libet-like research is that we could choose to create public and legal changes in the way we view crime and punishment. Erickson (2010) explains: "Unlawful behavior will be seen as indicative of a sick mind with its agent hopelessly along for the ride. Rational crime policy will entail therapeutic interventions instead of punishment" (p. 75). Lastly, moving beyond the Libet research debate means that it will be important for researchers to examine the possibility that there are levels of conscious awareness (Miller & Schwarz, 2014). Researchers could document the gradual progression of conscious awareness (if this is in fact how consciousness proceeds) and determine whether the RP antecedes all levels of conscious awareness of a willed act.

Discussion questions

1. Consider some thinking shortcuts or heuristics that you have used or witnessed others using. What are the strengths and weaknesses of such thinking tools?
2. Why do you think some philosophers, neuroscientists, and psychological scientists argue so strongly for or against the existence of free will? What does even the illusion of free will offer human beings that might strengthen mental health?

CHAPTER

12 The Placebo Effect: How Do Antidepressants Work?

Primary source: Kirsch, I., Deacon, B. J., Huedo-Medina, T. B., Scoboria, A., Moore, T. J., & Johnson, B. T. (2008). Initial severity and antidepressant benefits: A meta-analysis of data submitted to the Food and Drug Administration. *PLoS Medicine, 5*, 260–268.

Chapter objectives

This chapter will help you become a better critical thinker by:

- Assessing the strengths and limitations of randomized controlled trials (RCTs)
- Considering factors other than the drug that may contribute to improvement
- Contemplating how placebo effects develop and operate
- Appraising the evidence used to support the efficacy of antidepressants
- Evaluating the limitations of biological explanations and the disease model
- Considering the potential use of placebos as a treatment option

---

Introduction

Which of the following statements are true?

1. Depression is caused by a chemical imbalance.
2. Antidepressants treat depression by correcting a chemical imbalance in the brain.
3. Antidepressants effectively treat depression.

If we believe that questions 1 and 2 are true, we need to consider what evidence is needed to draw such a conclusion. Does a drug that purports to raise the levels of a particular brain chemical serve as sufficient evidence that low levels of this brain chemical caused the disorder? If question 3 is true, we must consider all of the possible reasons that one might feel less depressed over time including the passage of time itself, the expectations associated with a prescribed drug we are prescribed, the attention and care afforded by clinicians, as well as, of course, the effectiveness of the active ingredient(s) in the drug itself. We purposefully listed the drug last as we suspect that many often overlook the other less salient explanations. Unfortunately, many of the issues with antidepressant drug trials we examine in this chapter are not well represented in psychology textbooks (Bartels & Ruei, 2018).

Study background

Most of us probably take for granted that the three statements listed above are true. We watch television and have seen ads for antidepressant drugs that work by increasing the number of neurotransmitters. However, there are a growing number of critics, including one whose work is the focus of this chapter, who challenge this narrative. The work of Kirsch and colleagues has raised questions about the efficacy of antidepressants and the idea that depression is caused by a chemical imbalance.

Publication of a meta-analysis by Irving Kirsch and colleagues (2008) generated international media attention. Kirsch (2016) recalls, "Somehow, I had been transformed from a mild-mannered university professor into a media superhero – or super villain, depending on whom you asked" (p. 2). The reason for the attention was that his results challenged the idea that antidepressants work or at least that they work through a presumed pharmacological mechanism. "How else could they work?" you ask. Imagine that in a state of deep depression your physician prescribes you one of the medications you have seen on television. Excited to get started on the treatment, you rush to your local pharmacy or chemist to pick up the prescription. Unbeknownst to you, your doctor actually prescribed you a placebo. You are essentially taking a sugar pill with no active ingredients known to alleviate the symptoms of depression. Yet after a week of treatment at a follow-up appointment with your doctor, you report that you feel much better.

The **placebo effect** occurs when the benefits of a medication are due to the expectations of the drug's benefits, rather than the drug itself. Kirsch and his colleagues wanted to know how much of this effect accounts for the reported improvement among those taking antidepressants. Millions of people struggle with depression and the notion that a chemical imbalance is to blame and antidepressants help to restore balance is something even Kirsch initially took for granted (Kirsch, 2014). Yet his findings were devastating to the drug industry, since the top antidepressants on the market did not outperform placebos in a clinically significant way. Even among severely depressed patients, the significant differences between those receiving the antidepressants and those receiving the placebo were not due to the increased effectiveness of the drug, but the decreasing placebo effect. Let us take a closer look at the clinical drug trials.

The effectiveness of a drug or treatment is evaluated through randomized controlled trials (RCTs). In a typical RCT, a **placebo-controlled trial**, participants are randomly assigned to either a treatment group or a placebo group in which they receive an inert or inactive medication. Alternatively, participants are assigned to one of two treatment conditions in a **comparator trial**. In other words, in a compactor trial, the effectiveness of two drugs are being compared, while in a placebo-controlled study half of the participants will not be receiving an active treatment. That being said, most RCTs are designed so that participants are blind to the condition they are in as are those assessing the patient's depression (i.e., **double-blind**), so they should not be able to know that they are receiving a placebo.

In trials evaluating the efficacy of psychotherapy, the treatment group may be compared to another form of treatment or a **wait-list control** in which treatment is delayed. It is this last group, the wait-list control, that allows researchers to examine whether or not scores change as a result of anything other than the drug or the placebo. For example, it could be the case that you simply get better with the passage of time. It might be the case that your depression is better because of your expectations regarding the medication (actually a placebo) or it might be that the depression lessened with time and would have improved without any medical intervention. The wait-list control allows researchers to examine this possibility. Results of a **meta-analysis** conducted by Kirsch and Saperstein (1998) showed, as depicted in Figure 12.1, that the wait-list group accounted for 25% and the placebo group 50% of improvement in depression scores. Only 25% of the improvement in the treatment group went beyond the wait-list and the placebo.

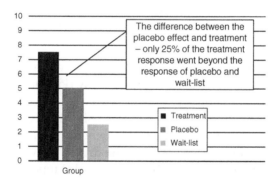

Figure 12.1 Drug effect and placebo effect in antidepressant trials in Kirsch and Saperstein (1998)

Note: The y-axis represents improvement in depression scores.

Current thinking

In 2010, Jay Fournier and colleagues (2010) obtained similar results to those of Kirsch and colleagues. The authors found negligible differences between drug and placebo among patients with mild and moderate depression, but a significant difference among those with very severe depression. In addition to the replication of Kirsch's results, there is a growing recognition among scholars that there are serious problems with antidepressant drug trials and the reporting of such results.

In most trials, prior to assignment to the treatment or control condition, all patients are given a placebo and those who show significant improvement during this "run-in" are excluded from the study (Kirsch, 2014). Some argue that this may inflate the difference between the drug and placebo by eliminating strong placebo responders (Ioannidis, 2008). This is a challenge to the **internal validity** of the studies, while **external validity** is compromised by the exclusion criteria including mild depression and **comorbidity** or having multiple psychiatric diagnoses. Eliminating such individuals from the studies affects generalizability (Ioannidis, 2008). In order to assess generalizability, we have to ask ourselves how similar these drug trial participants are to the public suffering from the mental illness under study? The more selective the trials are in terms of recruiting participants, the more compromised the generalizability. Researchers have addressed such generalizability concerns by conducting a trial (STAR*D) that included a broad range of patients more representative of the general population (Kirsch, 2010).

KEY READING – Kirsch, I. (2010). *The emperor's new drugs: Exploding the antidepressant myth*. New York: Basic Books.

Though participants in a double-blind trial should not know the condition they are in, there is reason to suspect that many do (referred to as breaking blind; Kirsch, 2014). Patients are informed about the possible side effects of the drug and the presence or absence of these side effects clues them in as to their condition. In other words, if I am experiencing nausea and headaches – which I have been told are side effects of the drug – I have a good idea that I received the drug and not the placebo. Kirsch (2014) reports that in one study nearly 90% of participants in a drug trial were able to correctly place themselves in the treatment group.

Turner and colleagues (2008) reported that half of the antidepressant drug trials do not support the effectiveness of the drug tested, yet less than 10% of these studies are published as negative results (i.e., they are either not published or are inaccurately published as positive). In other words, one gets a highly distorted view of the efficacy of a drug by combing through the published literature. As Every-Palmer and Howick (2014) explain, "in the literature available to the prescriber, 94% of antidepressant trials appeared positive. However, in reality only 51% of the completed trials in the FDA database were positive, resulting in a 32% overestimation of effect size" (p. 911). Likewise, in the USA, the Food and Drug Administration (FDA) requires two clinical trials showing a statistically significant improvement in depression of drug over placebo (Kirsch, 2014), yet there is no limit to the number of negative trials. In fact, Kirsch (2014) explains that the drug

Vilazodone, approved in 2011, had such a history with five trials failing to show a benefit.

An additional issue with the drug trials is possible conflicts of interest or the relationship between the pharmaceutical companies' sponsorship of research and the outcome of the drug trials. Kelly and colleagues (2006) reviewed published studies from 1992 to 2002. Over this ten-year period, the authors noted that drug industry sponsorship of such trials dramatically increased from 25% in 1992 to 57% in 2002. When the drug company sponsored the research, the results were favorable 78% of the time, when they were not, results were favorable less than half the time (48%). The number drops further, to 28%, if a competing company sponsors the research.

Antidepressant treatment as depicted in the movies

You will find several references to the film Side Effects (Stern, 2013), in the pages that follow. Here is some background information regarding the case.

Emily Taylor drives her vehicle into a wall in what looks like a suicide attempt.

Emily stabs her husband to death while sleepwalking and under the influence of an experimental drug.

Main Characters:

Emily Taylor: a young woman with depression who appears to have killed her husband

Dr. Jonathan Banks: Emily's current psychiatrist who prescribed the experimental drug

Dr. Victoria Siebert: Emily's previous psychiatrist

Questions to Consider:

Is Emily responsible for her murderous actions?
Might the side effects of the new drug be responsible for the murder?
How might the placebo effect be used to uncover the truth?

In the 2013 film *Side Effects*, a young woman with a history of depression, Emily Taylor, is prescribed an antidepressant by her psychiatrist, Dr. Jonathan Banks, after a suicide attempt. Emily's treatment experiences in the film were not unlike those of many individuals suffering from depression – she had been prescribed several antidepressants over the course of her treatment and had to change drugs due to the side effects and lack of effectiveness. In general, the movie paints an unflattering picture of the pharmaceutical industry including abundant conflicts of interest, the predilection on the part of physicians to reflexively prescribe medication, and direct-to-consumer marketing. Perusal of titles in the psychology section of your local bookstore would also suggest a growing concern over psychiatry and the pharmaceutical industry in recent years (e.g., *Saving Normal: An Insider's Revolt against Out-of-Control Psychiatric Diagnosis, DSM-5, Big Pharma, and the Medicalization of Ordinary Life* by Allen Frances, 2013).

Critical thinking toolkit
Clinical versus statistical significance

Guiding question: Beyond statistical significance, have I considered the practical importance of the findings?

When study results have important applied implications, researchers not only want to know if the results are reliable or can be consistently produced (i.e., **statistical significance**), but, in the case of antidepressant research, want to address the question "are these drugs really helping depressed patients in a meaningful way" which is a question of **clinical significance**. Consider an RCT examining whether the use of a supplemental medication for cancer patients significantly prolongs the patient's life. Some patients received the standard treatment and some the standard treatment with the supplement. The difference in months of survival was statistically significant, with the patients receiving the treatment plus the supplemental treatment living longer. The difference, however, was only ten days and in light of cost and side effects among other considerations, the clinical significance is questionable (Ranganathan, Pramesh, & Buyse, 2015).

All of the studies in the more recent Kirsch and colleagues' (2008) meta-analysis used the Hamilton Scale for Depression to assess changes in depression. This scale assigns a score from 0 to 53. The higher the score, the more severe the depression. A three-point difference between drug and placebo is what is recommended by the National Institute for Health and Care Excellence (NICE) which provided treatment guidelines for the UK as clinically significant between drug and placebo. Depressed mood is but one of the evaluative criteria on the scale that includes sleep patterns, eating patterns, and somatic symptoms like headaches. A change in these somatic symptoms alone – sleeping better or no longer experiencing fatigue and headache, for example – can account for the roughly two-point difference between drug and placebo (Kirsch, 2014). Kirsch's meta-analytic results have failed to find evidence of drugs meeting this mark for clinical significance among all but very severely depressed patients.

Critical Thinking Toolkit
Regression to the mean

Guiding question: Might natural fluctuations in the variable (e.g., depression) account for improvement during an intervention (e.g., medication)?

One of the interesting findings from the Kirsch meta-analyses is that there is a statistically significant and clinically significant difference between treatment groups and placebo among those who are severely depressed. Patients in RCTs are assessed multiple times during the study to track changes in depression. Among those with severe depression or very severe depression, a subsequent assessment of the patient's depression might reveal a drop that, though appearing to be the result of treatment, is accounted for, at least in part, by **regression to the mean**.

There are natural fluctuations around a mean or average in many of the behaviors that psychologists seek to measure. One day we may be slightly above, another day slightly below due to a variety of factors including luck/chance. Jason Heyward, an outfielder for the Chicago Cubs, a Major League Baseball team, was acquired by the St. Louis Cardinals in 2015. As you can see in Figure 12.2, in only two prior seasons had Heyward batted over 0.270, but with St. Louis that year he batted a career-best, 0.293. In the offseason, St. Louis battled with Chicago to sign the then free agent, who ended up signing a $184 million contract with Chicago. The following season Heyward batted a near career low 0.230 (baseball-reference.com).

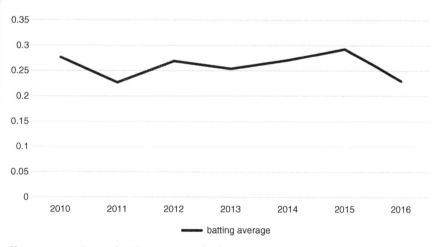

Figure 12.2 Career batting average for Jason Heyward

As we return to antidepressant trials, imagine a group of patients being treated for depression. One of the patients, Joe, has agreed to be in an RCT that is starting today. Joe recently found out that his mother is terminally ill. On top of that, on the way to the clinic this morning, his car broke down at a roundabout. Though he was able to get a ride to the clinic, his car will likely need extensive repair work which Joe cannot afford. Joe has been depressed for several months, but today when his depression is assessed for the start of the trial, he will be at a 28 (severe) on the Hamilton Scale for Depression. His average on this measure over the last several months has been a 23 (moderate). Whether assigned to the treatment group, placebo, or waitlist, a week or two from now when Joe's depression is once again assessed, it is unlikely to be at this high level and more likely to regress to the mean. It may be coincidental that depression happens to be highest when a trial begins, but it is also likely the case that a person may put off treatment when depression is mild. Treatment is more likely sought when symptoms intensify. Imagine this is the case for people who are dealing with severe pain and turn to acupuncture therapy. In light of the failure for research to support acupuncture's effectiveness, it is possible that it may be, in part, explained by regression to the mean (Carroll, 2003).

If this occurs in depression trials, then it is likely that some participants might meet the inclusion criteria for a study when their "true" mean depression score is actually below this cutoff (Fountoulakis, McIntyre, & Carvalho, 2015). As scores regress, this gives the appearance of a treatment effect when in actuality there was no improvement. Regression to the mean by itself cannot explain away positive results; however, as discussed earlier, the FDA requires only two positive trials with no limit on the number of negative trials. As Smith (2016) notes, because of the randomness of subject selection in drug trials and regression to the mean, "On average, one out of every 20 worthless treatments that are tested will show statistically significant effects" (p. 53).

Placebo effect

In the movie *Side Effects*, Emily's former psychiatrist Dr. Victoria Siebert recommends to her current psychiatrist that he switch her to a new drug on the market: "sometimes the newest thing gives them confidence ... they see the ads on TV and they believe." Having confidence in a treatment, believing it will work, is the basis for the placebo effect. This is the reason that comparator trials in which all participants are receiving medication produce greater results than placebo-controlled trials in which participants know there is a chance they will receive a placebo (Kirsch, 2010). More generally, Kirsch (2005) notes that the placebo effect has been documented in numerous domains including for the treatment of pain, asthma, and Parkinson's disease and is associated with psychological and physiological changes (Benedetti, et al., 2005; Kirsch & Weixel, 1988). The effect also varies depending on the potency of the drug. Specifically, the stronger the pain medicine, the stronger the placebo response. Likewise, injections are more effective than pills, and the color of the pills are influential as well, with red placebo pills being more effective pain relievers than other colored pills such as green or blue (Kirsch, 2005).

There are a couple of mechanisms through which the placebo effect works, classical conditioning (see Chapter 2 on Watson for a more in-depth discussion of classical conditioning) and expectancy. Most of us have received vaccine shots at a doctor's office and experienced the pain (an **unconditioned response**) produced by the shot, or **unconditioned stimulus**. Later, the syringe by itself produced fear in us, a **conditioned response**. Now think about your history with over-the-counter or prescription medication you've taken to treat an illness or condition. The active ingredient produces a response such as alleviating a headache and the pill itself becomes a **conditioned stimulus**. Every time in the past you have taken this little red pill it has been accompanied by feelings of relief. The pill itself now has the power to trigger such feelings and it is also accompanied by the expectation that you will feel better. It is not just the mind that is manipulated by the placebo. The entire human body reacts as well.

Placebos can produce changes in the brain that are similar to those that occur as a result of active treatment, including in placebo-controlled antidepressant trials (Benedetti et al., 2005). Beyond classical conditioning and expectancy, it is the therapeutic relationship that might be a major factor in the placebo response associated with antidepressants. Regardless of whether a patient receives a drug or placebo in the antidepressant trials, the more they visit the physician, the more they improve, leading Ioannidis (2008) to speculate that maybe antidepressants are simply filling a void created by the minimal patient–physician interactions characteristic of medicine today.

Logical fallacies

The course of diseases and illnesses fluctuates regardless of treatment, sometimes spontaneously remitting. On top of this underlying variability are the many things we do that, when followed by a period of remission of the illness, makes us susceptible to the **post hoc fallacy** – the conclusion that the treatment worked because I got better after the treatment (Dodes, 1997). A similar error, the **contiguity-causation error**, is at play when two things occur simultaneously, like remission of symptoms and treatment (Levy, 2010). It may be the case that the treatment was the cause, but it may also be the case that we are erroneously interpreting this as causal and it would be better accounted for by recent history of the patient, regression to the mean, or a placebo response.

Biologizing

One of the supposed side effects of Emily's newest antidepressant is sleep walking. During a sleep walking episode, she kills her husband. Dr. Banks, while trying to convince her to take a "not guilty by reason of insanity plea," tells her that she is a "victim of biology." The notion that depression is caused by a chemical imbalance (as opposed to negative life events) is something we take for granted (Miller, 2010). Neurotransmitters operate in the gaps or synapses between neurons and serotonin is a neurotransmitter assumed to play a significant role in depression. According to this theory, depressed people have low levels of serotonin and selective serotonin reuptake inhibitors (SSRIs) prevent the reabsorption of serotonin back into the sending or presynaptic cell. This leaves more serotonin available in the synapses and should alleviate depression. Dr. Banks early on in the film explains to Emily's husband that the drug he is prescribing targets serotonin and "helps stop the brain from telling you you're sad." The evidence for Dr. Banks assertion, however, is not in his favor. If this were true, then drugs that target other neurotransmitters like dopamine and norepinephrine or that decrease serotonin should not be effective. To the contrary, there is evidence that they are all equally effective.

In an article critical of the work by Kirsch and colleagues, Nutt and Malizia (2008) note the "fact that their [depression and other psychiatric illnesses] origins are clearly explained by altered brain functions" (p. 225). What is the problem of stating with certainty that there is an underlying biological dysfunction? Phrases like "underlying biological dysfunction" or "neural substrates of illness" or "biological basis of mental illness" are different than phrases like "there is a connection between brain dysfunction and mental illness" or there is an "association between brain dysfunction and depression." The former suggests causality while the latter does not (Lilienfeld et al., 2015; Miller, 2010). As discussed elsewhere in this book, we need to be skeptical of claims of causality between the brain, cognition, and behavior.

> **KEY READING** – Nutt, D. J., & Malizia, A. L. (2008). Why does the world have such a "down" on antidepressants? *Journal of Psychopharmacology, 22*, 223–226.

The problem is that there is a strong assumption of causality that colors our interpretation of correlational findings. For example, if we find that individuals with mental illness x have low levels of neurotransmitter y – a correlation between mental illness x and neurotransmitter y – we assume that researchers have identified the cause of mental illness x. We assume that the brain determines behavior, that the functioning of the brain is genetically determined, and that these genes are unalterable. The problem is that each link in this chain of reasoning is weak and the evidence is insufficient. Numerous studies have documented changes in the immune system in response to cognitive behavioral therapy (Schwartz et al., 2015) and changes in the brain as a result of cognitive and behavioral therapies. There is yet no gene for any psychiatric illness (Miller, 2010), genes are altered by the environment (Gottlieb, 2007), and evidence suggests there is not a single biological or environmental pathway (e.g., low serotonin) to a complex psychiatric illness like depression (Ioannidis, 2008).

So, has science confirmed that depression is clearly explained by brain dysfunction generally, a chemical imbalance, specifically? Is it the case that this fact is well established and incontrovertible? Lacasse and Leo (2005) suggest that, though popular, this is far from an established scientific fact, noting: "there is not a single peer-reviewed article that can be accurately cited to directly support claims of serotonin deficiency in any mental disorder, while there are many articles that present counterevidence." (p. 1213).

Consider the following:

There is no known optimal level of neurotransmitters and therefore no basis for determining what an imbalance is (Lilienfled et al., 2015; Schwartz et al., 2015).

Evidence suggests that antidepressants offer no clinically significant advantage over placebo for mild and moderate depression (Fournier et al., 2010; Kirsch et al., 2008).

There seems to be a similar response among patients with depression to drugs that increase serotonin, decrease serotonin, have little effect on serotonin but affect other neurotransmitters and even among drugs that are not intended to treat depression (e.g., tranquilizers; Kirsch, 2014).

Antidepressant are used to treat a wide range of disorders. That all of these disorders with vastly different characteristics are all explained by the same chemical imbalance seems unlikely (Lacasse & Leo, 2005; Lilienfeld et al., 2015).

If a chemical imbalance is at the root of psychiatric disorders including depression, why does the American Psychiatric Association's (APA) Diagnostic and Statistical Manual of Mental Disorders (DSM) not list this as a cause of any of the disorders (Lacasse & Leo, 2005).

Intervention-causation fallacy

What we have to be careful of here is endorsing an **intervention-causation fallacy** or confusing the "cure" with the cause of depression (Levy, 2010). Antidepressants alter the levels of neurotransmitters in the brain (e.g., increasing the levels of serotonin), yet that by itself does not suggest that a lack of serotonin is the cause of the disorder. Likewise, taking acetaminophen to relieve a headache does not indicate that the headache was caused by a lack of acetaminophen. There are certainly neurobiological correlates of depression and other mental illness, but this does not mean they are causes or that medications producing neurobiological changes point to the cause (Levy, 2010).

So, why is the chemical imbalance theory assumed to be a scientific fact? The answer to this question is not a simple one; there are a lot of factors involved. Many scholars have pointed to the marketing of pharmaceuticals directly to the customers and the media's uncritical parroting of it. Research suggests that direct-to-consumer (DTC) advertising may lead to physicians more readily prescribing antidepressants when patients make DTC requests, as was the case in *Side Effects*, even when there is no evidence of clinical utility (e.g., for a temporary condition like adjustment disorder; Kravitz et al., 2005). Leo and Lacasse (2007) asked the authors of articles promoting the chemical imbalance theory to provide them with references, to "cite their source." Requests were either ignored or authors provided a citation or two that were insufficient in supporting their conclusions. Thus, the survival of the chemical imbalance lore owes to a number of factors including poor oversight and regulation by federal officials, DTC marketing of drugs, uncritical acceptance of this theory by the media, and our own biases about the relationship between biology and psychology, the brain and the mind.

Limitations of the disease model

We do encounter a problem when we challenge the chemical imbalance theory of depression or the brain disease model of mental illness more generally. People often view the alternative to this as an indictment on one's character. In other words, if mental illness is not a disease, then it must reflect a character flaw. A national mental health organization in the USA includes the following information on their website: "Mental illnesses are not the result of personal weakness, lack of character, or poor upbringing … Mental illnesses are biologically based brain disorders. They cannot be overcome through 'will power' and are not related to a person's 'character' or intelligence" ("NAMI-Illinois," 2017). This depiction of mental illness as either a brain disorder **or** a personal flaw represents a **fallacy of bifurcation** or black-and-white fallacy, in that we are only given these two alternatives to choose from (Van Vleet, 2011). This kind of oversimplification forces us to make a false choice.

Cognitive behavioral therapy is one of the most effective treatments for depression, but it is not premised on a belief that people are biologically flawed or suffer character flaws. Rather, there is a characteristic negative style of thinking associated with depression that reinforces the depressed mood. As critical thinkers, we should recognize and reject false dichotomies. Mental disorders are psychological disorders; they have been defined on a psychological level, not a biological one (Miller, 2010; Schwartz et al., 2015). The presumed benefit of the disease model is that it reduces the stigma associated with mental illness. However, evidence suggests that not only is there less stigma associated with mental illness than in the past, but the brain disease account of them can have a negative impact reducing empathy for the patient on the part of the clinician and then reducing the confidence of the patient in terms of treatment (Miller, 2010; Schwartz et al., 2015).

Are we overmedicated?

In *Side Effects*, Emily has a history of being prescribed medication for depression. She has been prescribed several medications for depression and even medications to counter the side effects of these medications. Laura Slater (2004), in her book *Opening Skinner's Box* (described in Chapter 5), describes her attempt to replicate the Rosenhan study by going to psychiatric hospitals with complaints of hearing a voice in her head. Over the course of several days and nine visits to hospitals, she often received a diagnosis of depression with psychotic features and reportedly received prescriptions for 25 antipsychotic medications and 60 antidepressants. The impressive list of Emily's medications in *Side Effects* was also prescribed to someone who, as it turns out, was faking the symptoms of depression.

Though the credibility of Slater's experiment has been questioned (Spitzer et al., 2005), and *Side Effects* provides a fictional account of these issues, there are rigorous studies (e.g., Kravitz et al., 2005) suggesting a tendency to prescribe medication for moderate depression and even adjustment disorder, when alternative forms of treatment may be preferable particularly considered the results of Kirsch's studies. In a study by Kravitz and colleagues (2005), physicians were more likely to record a diagnosis of depression and prescribe antidepressants when patients made a request for medication. In *Side Effects*, drug representatives take psychiatrist Dr. Banks and his partners out for an expensive lunch and then hire him as a consultant on a drug trial. Several critics of psychiatry have tried to raise public awareness about such conflicts of interest (Angell, 2011; Greenberg, 2013; Kirsch, 2010; Kutchins & Kirk, 1997; Lacasse & Leo, 2005) as well as awareness of the arbitrary definitions of disorders, the lack of science-based or evidence-based decision-making, and the ever-increasing number of disorders in the DSM, including in the latest version the DSM-5 which results in an ever-shrinking range of normal behavior (Angell, 2011).

KEY READING – Szasz, T. (2008). *Psychiatry: The science of lies*. Syracuse, NY: Syracuse University Press.

At the very extreme of the antipsychiatry movement, the late Thomas Szasz argued that mental illness is a myth and that the aim of psychiatry is social control (Szasz, 2002, 2008). At the end of *Side Effects*, Dr. Banks is able to exact revenge on Emily (Emily had tried to frame him for the murder of her husband) by keeping her in a psychiatric institution and keeping her medicated on powerful antipsychotic drugs. Emily is at the mercy of Dr. Banks and will not be able to prove she is not "crazy." Szasz (2002) notes similar concerns, citing an actual case in which a teenager accused of robbery was persuaded by his lawyer to enter a not guilty by reason of insanity plea to avoid prison. However, while by many accounts perfectly sane, he spent much more time (nearly 20 years) in the psychiatric institution than he would have spent in prison.

As critical thinkers, we might be wise to question an assumption that doctors, including psychiatrists, need to "do something." When doctors do something like prescribing numerous medications over the course of treatment, they may witness their patients improving, which of course could be attributed to the medication, but more patient–client interaction and natural life history are also plausible explanations. There are a couple of potential logical fallacies at play here and one is bifurcation – you are either prescribing medicine or you are not doing your job. Medications have side effects and though this certainly would not apply to severe depression or other forms of severe psychopathology, physician Danielle Ofri (2011), notes that "doing nothing," or what she refers to as clinical inertia, can be an appropriate response from physicians that save patients from unnecessary interventions and harmful drug side effects. The idea that we have to do something even if ineffective or counterproductive is also fallacious, but such actions often provide psychological comfort to more than just the therapist. Clinicians are often uncomfortable with the idea that we would "just sit by and do nothing."

Logical fallacies

Conjunction fallacy

Additionally, we have to be careful that while we are open to being critical of the pharmaceutical industry and psychiatry that we avoid the anti-intellectual exercise of chalking it all up to a conspiracy among a few elites in "big Pharma," the federal government, and psychiatry. There are issues with conflicts of interest, but perhaps not a coordinated, sinister conspiracy. People who endorse conspiracy theories, like all of us, are looking for explanations in some cases for events that are hard to explain and threatening (Van Prooijen & Acker, 2015). However, they have a tendency to assume intentional causes to events that were unforeseen consequences or simply the product of luck or chance (Sunstein & Vermeule, 2009). The endorsement of conspiracy theories is also a product of errors in reasoning. Those more prone to endorse conspiracy theories, for example, are also more likely to make **conjunction fallacy** errors (Brotherton & French, 2014). Consider the following vignette:

John is a hard-working and charismatic 28-year-old who majored in marketing in college.

1. *John is a pharmaceutical representative*
2. *John bribes individuals in the Food and Drug Administration*
3. *John is a pharmaceutical representative and bribes individuals in the Food and Drug Administration (FDA)*

When asked to rate the chances of each, a conjunction error is made when the third statement is rated as more likely than either of the other two statements by themselves. The probability of the conjunction (3) cannot be greater than the probability of one of the single propositions (1 or 2). Yet, to the conspiracy theorist, the conjunction might appear intuitively appealing and causally related. Lastly, while legitimate concerns have been raised about conflicts of interest, we want to avoid discrediting arguments or research findings on the basis of the sinister or selfish motives of those making the argument (i.e., profit-driven drug companies), a form of an **ad hominem fallacy** (Van Vleet, 2011). The knowledge that someone has something to gain in a situation is not, by itself, a strong basis for such an argument (Baggini, 2009).

Do antidepressants work? (The slippery slope fallacy)

Imagine the following answer given to the question above: "Of course antidepressants work. Everyone knows that they work. It's common sense." If this answer is coming from a psychiatrist, it may be based on years of clinical experience. However, we have to be careful about relying on a clinician's memory. A professional clinician's memory, like ours, can be distorted by biased recall. The positive cases stand out in memory, yet the negative cases are ignored or forgotten (Kirsch, 2010). If the "of course" is from someone with no clinical experience, it may be based on personal experience, anecdotes from friends and relatives, the media, and so on. Either way, it is not logically sound to establish the truth of a conclusion based on the premise that "everyone knows this to be true" (Van Vleet, 2011). Think about a product that you have seen marketed on television recently, maybe an anti-aging product or a magnetic bracelet. Did someone provide a testimonial or anecdote as to the effectiveness, suggesting that it improve his/her health? Could this be a placebo effect? Alternatively, could it be the result of random fluctuations in their upgraded health coinciding with their use of such a product? The person giving the testimonial may have gone on to tell you that their improved health from the product led to a number of other positive events (e.g., starting a new relationship), a chain of events in which there is no logical explanation for the connections among them (a logical fallacy referred to as the **slippery slope fallacy;** Van Vleet, 2011).

We need evidence for such claims and proper evidence comes from RCTs. If the question is "do they work by correcting a chemical imbalance?," then the research seems to suggest, "no." For one, it does not seem to matter what effect the drugs have on neurotransmitters. It does not matter if the patients take norepinephrine reuptake inhibitors, serotonin reuptake inhibitors, or serotonin reuptake enhancers. It does not matter if they are first-generation drugs or newer drugs. It does not even matter if they are drugs designed to treat depression (Kirsch & Sapirstein, 1998). If the question is "does depression significantly lessen when patients take antidepressants" then the answer is certainly "yes." However, the fact that a psychiatrist reports that patients improve on antidepressants is not evidence of a drug effect (the drug effect is the difference between the response from the antidepressant and that of the placebo). The same thing happens when patients take a placebo. They get better. For that matter, the same thing happens when patients exercise and when they are provided cognitive behavioral therapy which is more resistant to relapse than antidepressants (Kirsch, 2010).

Does therapy work: Placebo control in psychotherapy?

Devising a placebo control in psychotherapy research is a major challenge. There are non-specific factors that might be important, like the quality of attention from the therapist, that along with the "active" ingredients of a therapy might contribute to changes in the client. For this to be an appropriate placebo control you would need to ensure not only that attention from the therapist was equivalent between the groups, but that patients in the placebo control group received an intervention that was believable. Attention, notes Freedland and colleagues (2011), "cannot be distilled and delivered in pure form by having therapists sit and stare at control group participants for the same amount of time that treatment group therapists spend with theirs" (p. 13). Considering the difficulty of these **attention control** procedures, researchers might elect to compare a treatment with a control group in which one of the components of the therapy is removed or compare the therapy to one of the components by itself (Kirsch, 2005). Regardless, research suggests that cognitive therapy is superior to various non-active controls (Wampold et al., 2002). Additionally, while we obviously look at the use of antidepressants as an intervention that results in biochemical change, it is no less appropriate to view psychotherapy as biochemical in nature as well (Levy, 2010). There is evidence of changes in the brain because of cognitive behavioral therapy (Porto et al., 2009) though we should not be surprised by this considering the simultaneous occurrence of neurobiological and psychological events.

Chapter summary

As a recent meta-analysis by Cipriani et al. (2018) suggests, many drugs prescribed for depression result in a significant reduction in depressive symptoms for patients. Nevertheless, a considerable amount of this improvement can be accounted for by the placebo effect. A closer examination of antidepressant drug trials also reveals problems with patients being aware of the condition they are in, the selective publication of positive results, and the sponsorship of research by drug companies. When evaluating the effectiveness of a drug, we need to be aware of the tendency for natural fluctuations in a disease to be attributed to a particular treatment coinciding with a lessening of symptoms. Even if effective and not due to random fluctuations, the pill or treatment can become associated with the positive outcome, and is able to produce results through expectancy alone. The neurotransmitter hypothesis of depression and antidepressants is generally accepted, but the causal link has yet to be established. This focus on neurotransmitters and the representation of depression as a brain disease, while intended to reduce stigma, may lead to a reliance on pharmacological treatment to the detriment of other non-medical but effective treatments (e.g., cognitive behavioral therapy). While there have been legitimate concerns raised about the expanding psychiatric industry, pathologizing of normal behavior and overreliance on medication, conspiracy theories draw inappropriate causal links and endorsement of such theories is not an exercise in critical thinking.

There is one other intriguing scene in *Side Effects* in which Dr. Banks tells Emily that he is going to administer sodium amytal and then discuss with her the events on the night she killed her husband. Under the influence of this drug, the truth will come out and the judge will see that there was no intent to kill her husband, suggests Dr. Banks. He then explains to Emily the effects that will be produced by the drug sodium amytal (e.g., feeling light-headed, drowsiness). After a few minutes of administering the sodium amytal, Emily appears drowsy, her eyes begin to close, and she eventually passes out. Dr. Banks videotapes the interview with Emily and shows it to the District Attorney. It initially appears that there is nothing revealing on the tape as Emily says nothing incriminating and passes out a few minutes later. The DA is unimpressed until Dr. Banks explains that the injection was not sodium amytal, but rather a saline solution. "There was no drug, so why did she pass out? You don't put in a performance like that on salt water?" Irving Kirsch would likely object to this conclusion. Emily's response was not surprising; it was a placebo response not unlike the response from some of Dr. Banks' patients treated with antidepressants.

Future directions

A natural extension of the work of Kirsch and colleagues on the placebo effect is examining the potential of placebos as a treatment option. An important question is: Can you utilize placebos in an open and ethical way? It would be irresponsible and unethical for physicians to prescribe placebos to patients who believe they are receiving an active treatment. Interestingly, there is research suggesting that placebos without deception might work. Kaptchuk and colleagues (2010) found significant improvement in symptoms among patients with Irritable Bowel Syndrome (IBS) knowingly given a placebo. Patients in the placebo condition were told the following: "Placebo pills made of an inert substance, like sugar pills, that have been shown in clinical studies to produce significant improvement in IBS symptoms through mind-body self-healing processes" (p. 2). Similar results have been obtained in the treatment of chronic low back pain (Carvalho et al., 2016). Research interest in the efficacy of placebo treatment is likely to intensify in the coming years. After all, placebos do not carry the risks that medications do.

Discussion questions

1. Why do you think many of the issues related to antidepressant drug trials such as direct-to-consumer advertising and publication bias are not consistently covered in psychology textbooks?
2. Why do you think it is so difficult to conduct a placebo-controlled psychotherapy study? Think of factors such as variability in patients, therapeutic approaches, therapeutic settings, and so on.
3. What are some potential objections that people might have to the open use of placebos by physicians? Think about factors such as the public's perception of medicine and moral/ethical concerns.

13

The Enriched Environment Studies: A Neuroscientific Case for Early Learning?

Primary source: Rosenzweig, M. R., Bennett, E. L., & Diamond, M. C. (1972). Brain changes in response to experience. *Scientific American, 226*, 22–29.

Chapter objectives

This chapter will help you become a better critical thinker by:

- Considering the strengths and limitations of the enriched environment research
- Contemplating the appropriateness of generalizations from animal studies
- Evaluating how the enriched environment research and other neuroscience research informs brain-based parenting and brain-based education
- Examining the limitations of neuroscientific methods and problems of overgeneralizing research results

---

Introduction

Imagine that you are a parent of a young child. Consider your agreement versus disagreement with the following statements:

Parental Statement #1: I would not want to teach my child too much in the first few years for fear that when he/she gets to school they will be bored or have behavior problems.

Parental Statement #2: If electing to take a research-based approach to parenting, I would favor a neuroscience approach based upon brain research over a behavioral science approach based upon psychological research.

Parental Statement #3: I think my child must be right-brain dominant because he/she does poorly in math and science, while exceling in art, music, drama, dance, and creativity.

Our best guess is that, though this is a legitimate concern for a parent, most readers are not likely to agree with Parental Statement #1. However, the parental

---

fear addressed in the pages ahead is not one of doing too much, but of not doing enough. The fear is that by the time the child has reached school age, an opportunity to fine-tune a brain uniquely sensitive to such experiences has been lost. As we have discussed the appeal of neuroscience in other chapters, you may have suspected an expectation on the part of the authors that the neuroscience approach would be favored by most. Regardless of the extent to which you endorsed Parental Statement #2, take a moment to reflect on the reasons for this choice. Lastly, there are some common misconceptions about the localization of certain skills in the brain and the specialization of the hemispheres of the brain. Because these misconceptions, reflected in Parental Statement # 3, are often assimilated in brain-based approaches to education and parenting, we will address relevant research findings in the chapter as well.

Study background

Imagine that as a parent you come across the following advice from an Internet blog related to how to raise a smarter baby:

If you think making googly eyes at your baby is all fun and games, think again. Research suggests you are actually shaping the development of your baby's brain! You're helping your child develop important emotional skills that will help him or her become a socially competent adult!

Recall the **nurture assumption** from Chapter 3, the idea that parents play a significant role in shaping a child's personality during child development. The website's advice, what might be referred to as brain-based parenting (Bruer, 1999), is essentially doubling down on the nurture assumption. Not only do parents play a key role in shaping a child's personality, but the behavior of the parent in the first few years of a child's life has a lasting impact on the wiring of the brain. If you provide the right environment for your child, that is, a stimulating, enriched environment, you can build a better brain. John Bruer (1999), in *The Myth of the First Three Years*, explains how early childhood policy initiatives in the USA have utilized this developmental assumption that the first few years of life is a special period of the lifespan for learning, a window of opportunity for making your child into something special. Not everyone, of course, takes advantage of this window and when things go wrong, parents shoulder the blame. Like Harris, Bruer tries to take the pressure off parents suggesting that this zero-to-three assumption falls apart when you closely scrutinize the research, including research on the effects of environmental enrichment used to support it.

KEY READING – Bruer, J. T. (1999). *The myth of the first three years*. New York: The Free Press.

Enriched environment studies began in the 1960s and involved several groups of researchers examining changes in the brains of rats due to experience (Rosenzweig, Bennett, & Diamond, 1972; Volkmar & Greenough, 1972). Rosenzweig and colleagues conducted dozens of studies comparing the brains of rats raised in an enriched environment, a standard laboratory cage, and an impoverished environment. In the standard procedure, the researchers would select three males from a litter and randomly assign each to one of the three environments illustrated in Figure 13.1 (Rosenzweig, 1999).

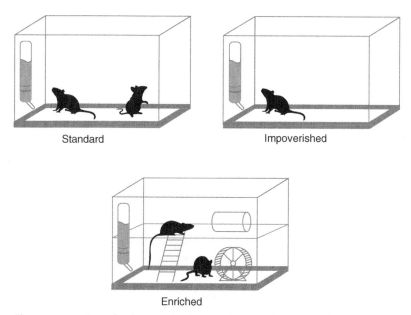

Standard   Impoverished

Enriched

Figure 13.1   Standard, enriched, and impoverished environments in Rosenzweig, Bennett, & Diamond's (1972) studies

The standard laboratory cage, according to Rosenzweig, Bennett, and Diamond (1972), was a "cage of adequate size with food and water always present" (p. 22). The cage was larger in the enriched environment (housing 10–12 rats) than the standard one by including a variety of objects for the rats to play with in a more social setting. Not only were the toys absent in the impoverished environment, but so were fellow rats; assignment to this condition meant living in social isolation. Differences among the cages mattered, as rats with at least four weeks of enriched environment exposure had greater cerebral cortex weight (roughly 4%; Rosenzweig, 1999) and thickness. This increased weight and thickness was not due to an increase in the number of neurons, but rather an increase in the size of parts of the neuron (i.e., cell bodies and nuclei; see Figure 13.2).

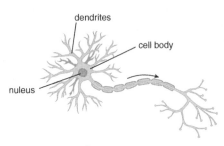

Figure 13.2   The neuron

Other structural changes included increased **dendrite** branching, increases in the number of synapses per neuron, and more glial cells in the brains of rats raised in enriched environments (Rosenzweig & Bennett, 1996). **Glial cells** do not conduct signals themselves, but play an important role in maintaining the health and survival of neurons (Gazzaniga, Ivry, & Mangun, 2002). There were also several indicators of greater neural activity, including higher levels of two enzymes that play a role in the transmission of nerve signals and maintaining cell health, acetylcholinesterase and cholinesterase. The presence of these chemicals and the rapid structural changes suggested these brain changes occurred as the result of learning (Rosenzweig & Bennett, 1996). The changes were not uniform across the brain, however, as the greatest differences between rats in enriched and impoverished environments were found in the occipital lobe of the cortex, an area involved in visual processing (Rosenzweig & Bennett, 1996). Later studies found increases in the cerebellum and hippocampus as well (Rosenzweig, 1999). A critical question, however, remained to be addressed: How different were these artificial laboratory environments from the natural environment of the rat? Rosenzweig and colleagues, in subsequent studies, did find that laboratory rats placed in a more natural outdoor setting had greater brain development than rats raised in the artificially enriched environments.

Why does this matter? If we want to use the Rosenzweig research to suggest that enriching an environment will lead to brain growth, then the definition of a "normal" environment is crucial. If the standard laboratory cage is actually impoverished relative to a normal rat environment and the enriched laboratory cage more closely resembles a normal rat environment, then, as illustrated in Figure 13.3, the comparisons of Rosenzweig and colleagues were between a deprived and a normal environment rather than a normal and an enriched environment.

In order to compare normal to enriched, we would need an environment even more stimulating than the enriched one created by Rosenzweig and colleagues. Fortunately, a group of researchers created such a "superenriched" environment (see Figure 13.3) that provided not only a daily assortment of toys, but a variety of increasingly complex maze learning tasks. Importantly, this superenriched environment did not produce greater synaptic growth than the enriched environment (Camel, Withers, & Greenough, 1986).

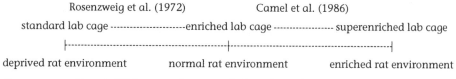

Figure 13.3   Camel, Withers, & Greenough (1986) study allowed for testing of the enriched environment hypothesis

Current thinking

The research on the superenriched environment suggested that there might be limits to the benefits of extra stimulation in terms of brain growth (Bruer, 1999). Even Rosenzweig, Bennett, and Diamond (1972) suggested caution in generalizing their findings:

> *The effect of experimental environments on the brains of animals has sometimes been cited as bearing on problems of human education. We should like to sound a cautionary note in this regard. It is difficult to extrapolate from an experiment with rats under one set of conditions to the behavior of rats under another set of conditions, and it is much riskier to extrapolate from a rat to a mouse to a monkey to a human. (p. 28)*

These precautions have often been ignored, as the enriched environment research influenced enterprises aimed at applying such findings to humans in the form of zero-to-three initiatives, brain-based education, and brain training. One of the tenets of such initiatives is that it is desirable to grow the synapses and dendrites of the brain in childhood. However, neuroscientific research suggests the elimination of synapses is an equally important neurodevelopmental process. Additionally, evidence is lacking for the claim that learning in the first few years of life is associated with critical periods or limited windows of opportunity. What the Rosenzweig studies demonstrated was the potential harm of environmental deprivation and the impressive plasticity of the brain not only in childhood, but also in adulthood. They also demonstrated that changes can occur quickly and can persist in the face of a loss of enrichment (Rosenzweig, 2007).

Critical Thinking Toolkit

A closer look at animal models

Guiding question: Are the across species (non-human → human beings) generalizations under consideration appropriate?

In general, animal research has contributed to the accumulation of knowledge across numerous areas of psychology including motivation, emotions, stress, and health (Domjan & Purdy, 1995) and there are certain types of studies that can be conducted with animals, such as deprivation studies, that cannot be ethically conducted with humans. Remember that an Institutional Review Board (IRB) has the charge of protecting both human and animal subjects. Such research in humans relies on naturally occurring deprivation that introduces confounds or variables other than the independent variable that might influence the dependent variable. In animal models, these can be experimentally controlled. For example, researchers can carefully control the timing of deprivation (e.g., three months of maternal deprivation) and exposure to contact and nourishment with an attachment figure or object within the laboratory (Boccia & Pedersen, 2001). These variables might vary widely in studies of naturally occurring deprivation.

There are practical advantages to animal research as well. Longitudinal studies, commonly used in developmental psychology to track changes across the lifespan, can take a considerable amount of time, energy, and resources. The shorter lifespan of many animals such as rodents makes it possible to obtain results in a fraction of the time and cost that it might take to conduct a longitudinal study with humans (Boccia & Pedersen, 2001).

But what about brain differences themselves? Is the brain of a rat (or mouse), or a monkey for that matter, just too different from that of a human to draw any inferences? One assumption that we need to consider is that the brain is uniform across species or, if differences do exist, they are trivial. As Preuss and Robert (2014) note, such an assumption is not consistent with our current knowledge of evolution. There are important differences across species. Even closely related species reflect variation, including those with different brain structures, different cellular architecture and organization within those structures, and different functions associated with similar structures (Passingham, 2009; Preuss, 2000). The human brain is not simply a larger version of a rat brain or a monkey brain. On the other hand, there is a principle of evolution that aids our efforts to generalize across species. A unique human ability does not require a "new" area of the brain. While the prefrontal cortex is smaller in the macaque monkey compared to the human prefrontal cortex, it may have developed from an older system in the brain (olfactory system; Gazzaniga et al., 2002). In the same way that you may remodel and repurpose an existing room in your house rather than build a new addition, evolution takes advantage of brain structures already available (Passingham, 2009). Moreover, it is not always important that similarities are present.

Some animal models, referred to as **analogous models**, seek to identify environmental contingencies that produce effects across species, regardless of genetic relatedness. For example, exposing rats, dogs, or humans to environments where they are subjected to negative stimuli that are unavoidable or that they cannot control produces learned helplessness, a psychological state that produces depression, retards learning, and causes the organism to give up trying to escape the unpleasant circumstance (Reeve, 2001).

As Rosenzweig, Bennett, and Diamond (1972) suggested, the application of these findings to education or public policy demands consideration of the fact that the enriched environment research was conducted with rats as well as mice, cats, and monkeys. While some distinct characteristics of the rodent (e.g., small and inexpensive) make it convenient for study, other features raise concerns about cross-species generalizations. Rats are nocturnal, sleep up to 15 hours a day, and, most importantly to the zero-to-three assumption, have an average life expectancy of 2–3 years (Cunningham, 1996). Given the considerably shorter lifespan of the laboratory rat, what may seem young to us may actually be the human equivalent of a period in the lifespan well beyond the first three years. Figure 13.4 graphically depicts the human equivalent of the stages of the rat lifespan.

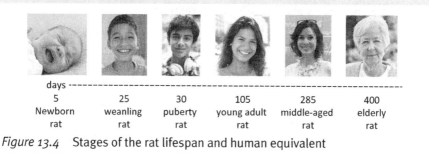

days					
5	25	30	105	285	400
Newborn rat	weanling rat	puberty rat	young adult rat	middle-aged rat	elderly rat

Figure 13.4 Stages of the rat lifespan and human equivalent

Considering the rat lifespan and that the rats are selected to participate as weanlings and then housed in the various environments for 30 days, it would not be accurate to suggest that the results apply exclusively to early childhood (Bruer,

1999). Similar increases in cortical thickness have been observed in young adult, middle-aged, and elderly rats, though a longer period of enrichment is required and the effects are smaller in older rats (Bruer, 1999; Riege, 1971; Rosenzweig, 1999; Rosenzweig, Bennett, & Diamond, 1972). Not only does neural plasticity appear to be possible throughout the lifespan, but the effects of enrichment seem to persist even when the enriched experience is followed by impoverishment and the effects of impoverishment are not permanent assuming a change in stimulation (Camel, Withers, & Greenough, 1986; Rosenzweig, 1999).

While the rat brain is quite different from humans in some respects including the prefrontal cortex, Passingham (2009) explains that the hippocampus is highly developed in rats and the discovery of the function of it in the rat brain led to a better understanding of the role of the hippocampus in human memory. Also, recall that some animal models are analogous. It could be argued that regardless of the species or common ancestry, Rosenzweig and colleagues' research demonstrated that the environmental contingencies of enrichment and impoverishment affect brain development.

Considering that the enriched/impoverished environment results have been replicated across numerous species (Rosenzweig, 1999), it would not seem a serious limitation that a great deal of the research was conducted with laboratory rats. As critical thinkers, we want to be aware of whether or not a finding is based on animal research and mindful of the potential limitations, yet avoid dismissing the research offhand. Rather, there are critical questions to ask: What species was used? Across how many species have the results been replicated? Was anatomical similarity important in the study? Are there variations within a given species that could be relevant to making informed comparisons?

The Rosenzweig studies and brain-based parenting

As noted, for better or worse, the Rosenzweig studies have already influenced views and perceptions on education and parenting. Though the enriched environment research suggested that environmentally induced brain changes were not limited to early development, the studies are often cited as evidence of the great potential parents have to shape development in the first few years of their child's life. Perhaps one reason for the persistence of this connection is that this period of human development is characterized by rapid brain development, including a tremendous increase in the number of synapses (synaptic exuberance). **Synapses** are connections among nerve cells or **neurons** in the brain that allow these cells to communicate with one another. By two years of age, synaptic density is greater than at any other point in the lifespan. This period of growth, however, is followed by a period of synaptic loss or **pruning** after two years of age (Lenroot & Giedd, 2007).

If greater synapses are equated with greater intelligence, then one might expect the two-year-old to be smarter than his/her parents and one might be motivated to preserve these synapses. This expectation, according to Bruer (1999), is based on a misunderstanding of brain development in general and synaptic growth and pruning, specifically.

First, brain development is not a straightforward process of building more and more synapses. Cell proliferation and pruning or cell death occur pre-natally and postnatally, with ebbs and flows in the gains and losses of brain cells, extending well beyond the first three years and at different rates in dif-ferent brain areas. Synaptic growth, pruning, and myelination – a process of insulating nerve cells – extends into adolescence. In fact, Johnson (2001) notes: "A striking feature of human brain development is the comparatively long [relative to other species] phase of postnatal development and therefore the increased extent to which the later stages of brain development can be influenced by the environment of the child" (p. 173). Adolescence is a period in the lifespan marked by significant cognitive advances (Cobb, 2010), yet counterintuitively synaptic elimination or pruning is one of the brain pro-cesses underlying these advances. Rather than reducing the brain's capabili-ties, this loss of synapses, along with other processes (including myelination), appears to enhance the efficiency and processing capacity of the brain (Spear, 2007). Thus, while the overproduction of synapses does appear to predict the emergence of a particular skill (e.g., crawling), the refinement of that skill co-occurs with pruning (Fox, Calkins, & Bell, 1994). Our understanding of the importance of pruning in adolescence along with evidence of higher synaptic density associated with disorders characterized by mental deficiency, would call into question the promotion of a "use it or lose it" or synaptic preservation approach to the first three years of life. With respect to synapses, "more-is-better" appears to be a fallacy rather than a neuroscientific fact (Mead, 2007).

Let us return to the website offering parental advice and examine it more critically. Recall that the suggestion was that making googly eyes at your child is boosting your baby's brain development. If boosting your baby's brain development is taken to mean building synapses, as discussed, this advice appears misguided. But, even if by boosting, the author meant strengthen-ing synapses or "wiring" the brain, there is an assumption that this pro-cess is greatly influenced by something the parent does (i.e., making googly eyes). While life experiences certainly influence brain development, much of this development is genetically programmed (Bryck & Fisher, 2012; Fox et al., 1994). Being able to read facial expressions, crawling, and many other aspects of development are what the late neuroscientist William Greenough (Greenough, Black, & Wallace, 1987) referred to as **experience-expectant** development. Barring extreme circumstances, all humans will crawl and learn to read emotional expressions and the experiences necessary for this type of brain development are expected to be encountered regardless of the culture in which one is raised. This type of brain development appears to rely on the overproduction of synapses and pruning.

According to Greenough there is another type of brain development that involves the building of new synapses: **experience-dependent**. As opposed to experience-expectant development, experience-dependent development is culture-specific and allows an organism to learn about and adapt to one's unique environment. This is exactly the type of development that researchers observed in the enriched environment studies which, again, suggested that experience-dependent brain development was not limited to infancy or early childhood. However, those using neuroscience to promote a special focus on early childhood also point to the importance of critical periods (Bruer, 1999).

Critical periods are often thought of as periods in development when a lack of a particular kind of stimulation or deprivation leads to irreversible, permanent damage or halting of development. In other words, there is a window of opportunity in which an experience like visual stimulation is required for normal development of the visual system (Bruer, 2001). There are some classic studies that appear to demonstrate the existence of critical periods (e.g., Hubel & Wiesel, 1970), but may more accurately be regarded as demonstrating sensitive periods in which deprivation can retard normal experience-expectant development (Bruer, 2001). Deprivation during a sensitive period has the potential to produce lasting effects, yet with many experience-expectant aspects of development, the window of opportunity is not forever closed.

The Rosenzweig studies and brain-based education

Imagine that you were to read the following contrived, yet realistic, article aimed at teachers and parents:

New brain development research provides roadmap for improving early childhood education

Author: Jane Doe

Some new and exciting findings from neuroscience research reaffirm what parents and educators have known for many years. Brain research suggests that an enriched environment boosts brain development, growing dendrites or parts of a neuron that allow for communication in the brain. A lack of stimulation, on the other hand, will lead to fewer of these important connections. The implications are obvious for educators; the more stimulating the classroom, the more dendrites grow. Brain growth is also better supported by exposure to natural as opposed to artificial environments, so teachers should be encouraged to engage their students with problem-based learning or discovery learning in which students construct meaning themselves through real-world problems. Brain research has also shown that there is a critical period for receiving the stimulation necessary to wire the brain. In humans, the brain is primed for learning up to the age of ten; the window of opportunity isn't open forever. Beyond providing a stimulating environment, research indicates that the left and right hemispheres of the brain have specialized functions, so teachers would be wise to use words to engage the left hemisphere and pictures to engage the right hemisphere. It is also important for educators to keep in mind that boys are not as good at memorizing as girls because their hippocampus, an area important for learning and memory, is smaller. Requiring too much memorization may create an unfriendly educative environment for boys. Gender differences aside, sitting at a desk and memorizing material is not going to get students excited about learning. Recent neuroscientific research suggests that walking boosts mood through its effect on the brain, so teachers should get students up and moving in the classroom as much as possible. Research utilizing brain scans reveals insights about an area of the brain called the amygdala. The amygdala is engaged or lights up when a person is frustrated and this may influence the processing of information before it is received by the frontal lobes, which are involved in problem-solving and reasoning, so it's important that students be provided with a stress-free environment. As a teacher, if you find yourself talking with a student who is upset, let them walk around a bit as this will boost the dopamine levels in the pleasure centers of their brain and help them calm down. Keeping the amygdala quiet and boosting the pleasure centers of the brain might lead to a more productive interaction between the student and teacher.

Understandably, this research sounds exciting to educators and it is thrilling to think that this brain research can directly lead to better parenting and better schools. The author of this fictitious article is suggesting that brain research is a clear road map for improved educational practice. Let us look more closely at several of the findings reported with a critical eye. First, as critical thinkers, we want to be aware that excitement over neuroscientific findings can cloud our judgment. If the brain research reaffirms what parents and educators already know and does not lead to improved educational practices, then what benefit is it? The only benefit may be that people interpret neuroscientific findings as more "real" than conclusions based on behavioral data (Satel & Lilienfeld, 2013).

The author refers to the enriched environment research, commonly cited in brain-based educational literature. This research is neither new nor straightforward in its application to education. Consider the catchy title of a popular brain-based education book: *Worksheets Don't Grow Dendrites!* What we want to consider here is whether the growth of dendrites is an appropriate educational goal. Recall from our discussion of synapses that their elimination appears as important as their growth. With respect to dendrites, there is no neuroscientific research suggesting that their growth is a desirable goal. Ironically, while there is no literature suggesting that worksheets grow dendrites, there is research suggesting that worksheets are effective teaching tools. Worksheets that help elaborate steps in problem-solving are more effective than techniques that involve minimal instructional guidance (i.e., problem-based techniques; Kirschner, Sweller, & Clark, 2006), techniques often endorsed in *Worksheets Don't Grow Dendrites*. As critical thinkers, we want to keep an open mind when it comes to innovation, but we also want to ask what research is needed to support its implementation and whether that research exists.

While the enriched environment research continues to be cited and remains relevant, newer brain-imaging technologies have produced findings that are also used to support brain-based educational practices. For example, the author (Jane Doe) references a Positron Emission Tomography (PET) scan study conducted in the 1980s. The study indicated that glucose metabolism (what a PET scan measures) coincided with synaptic growth in particular areas of the brain and the development of skills that those brain areas support. Based on his findings, Chugani (1998) concluded that this sensitive period in humans aged 4–10, "is now believed by many (including this author) [to be] the biological 'window of opportunity' when learning is efficient and easily retained" (p. 187). These skills, however, continue to mature well beyond the period of peak synaptic densities when they first emerge. Moreover, higher-level thinking skills like abstract reasoning develop well beyond this window.

Left-brain/right-brain teaching is another popular suggestion from the brain-based instruction camp. This approach is also based on the misinterpretation of old ideas, rather than new, neuroscience research. The studies (mis)used to support left-brain/right-brain teaching were conducted in the 1960s with "split-brain" patients or patients who had their **corpus callosum**, a band of nerve fibers that connect the left and right hemispheres, surgically severed in an attempt to control severe epilepsy. Early testing with these patients revealed distinct abilities in the left and right hemispheres. For example, patients could correctly identify an object presented to the right hemisphere, but could not tell the experimenter what the object was unless presented to the "speaking" left hemisphere (Sperry, 1982).

The finding of distinctive functions of the left and right hemisphere has been interpreted by brain-based education advocates as offering a prescription for educators to find ways to engage each hemisphere separately and cater to individual differences in the dominance of the left and right hemispheres (Alferink & Farmer-Dougan, 2010). The common knowledge on hemispheric specialization is that the left hemisphere is logical and involved in speech and writing and the right hemisphere is more visual and creative; the left deals with words, the right with images. Marcia Tate (2010), in *Worksheets Don't Grow Dendrites*, uses this common knowledge to support the use of graphic organizers: "When graphic organizers are used to change words into images, both left- and right-brain learners can use those images to see the big picture" (p. 41). The problem, according to neuroscientist Michael Gazzaniga (1985), is that the notion that the left hemisphere is involved exclusively in language processing and the right spatial reasoning is a gross oversimplification and not supported by neuroscientific research.

The notion that the right hemisphere deals exclusively with images misses subtle differences that emerged in Gazzaniga's research with split-brain patients. For example, while the right hemisphere appeared superior on a task in which an image had to be manually recreated, the left hemisphere was capable of performing equally well when the patient simply had to identify a "match" to the image shown. That both hemispheres appear to perform numerous spatial and verbal tasks equally well has been confirmed in many studies. While the right hemisphere is involved in a type of spatial reasoning in which the distance among objects is evaluated or identifying a precise location or distance is required, the left hemisphere is involved in processing when the *relative position* (e.g., above, to the right of) and not *precise location* is required (Bruer, 2008; Chabris & Kosslyn, 1998). The same pattern is true for language comprehension as well, assumed to be a left hemisphere task (Bruer, 2008). Rather than having separate skill sets, it is as if the two hemispheres, equally capable of many similar functions, divvy up tasks in a manner that capitalizes on the relative strengths of each. The two hemispheres, according to Gazzaniga's fellow researcher Roger Sperry (1982), "work closely together as a unit, rather than one being turned on while the other idles" (p. 1225). Considering the integration and simultaneous processing of the two hemispheres, it doesn't seem possible, even if beneficial, to teach to one hemisphere (Alferink & Farmer-Dougan, 2010). Nor is there evidence that individuals are left-brained or right-brained (Nielsen et al., 2013).

Lastly, let us take a closer look at the suggestions of the "New brain development roadmap" author based on the neuroscientific findings. She notes that there are differences between boys and girls in terms of hippocampus size (an area of the brain that plays an important role in memory) and, therefore, memorization tasks may not be as appropriate for boys. What do you think the author is assuming about how these differences came to be? If Jane Doe was assuming that they were based on experience, then she might suggest more memorization opportunities for boys are necessary. Thus, it seems like the assumption is that there are innate differences. Yet, Maguire and colleagues (2000) found that the more experience cab drivers had navigating the streets of London, the larger their hippocampus. The relationship between brain and behavior, pardon the pun, is a two-way street. This difference in behavior could reflect differences in terms of the interests of boys and girls, as well as the expectations of teachers, parents, and society in general (Willingham, 2016).

Then there is the recommendation about walking in the classroom because it has been found to boost mood. Think about how many things might boost one's mood, but would be inappropriate to apply to the classroom. Learning is the primary goal in the classroom and having students walk around might be beneficial in terms of individual student motivation to learn, but it might be distracting to other students. It might promote positive interactions with other students, but it may lead to conflict. It may help students focus or it may prevent them from focusing on what is to be learned. The point is there are many other variables to consider in the context of teaching students and managing a classroom.

The author also mentions research on the amygdala. Recall our discussion at the beginning of this section about considering the value that the neuroscientific research adds. Does this finding on the amygdala simply reinforce something that might have been obvious at the behavioral level: "Students cannot maximize their learning potential when they are stressed and frustrated?" If we can say that this is something we knew without the neuroscience, then the addition of it amounts to what psychiatrist Sally Satel and psychologist Scott Lilienfeld refer to as "neuroredundancy," or common sense dressed up in neuroscientific language. Even if the application of these findings is appropriate, it would appear to do little more than support current efficacious educational practices rather than improve them (Alferink & Farmer-Dougan, 2010).

> **KEY READING** – Alferink, L. A., & Farmer-Dougan, V. (2010). Brain-(not) based education: Dangers of misunderstanding and misapplication of neuroscience research. *Exceptionality*, *18*, 42–52.

A closer look at neuroscientific methods

There is a more significant problem beyond redundancy and it has to do with the neuroscientific research itself. Recall that in the sample article above, the author clearly suggests that the amygdala is involved in the experience of negative emotions (especially fear), can disrupt learning, and thus needs to be quieted. The amygdala has been an area of great interest to cognitive neuropsychologists and numerous studies have been published associating this area of the brain with fear, leading to its characterization as the "fear module" in the brain (Cunningham & Brosch, 2012). These studies, referred to as localization studies, often involve the use of technology discussed elsewhere in this book (e.g., Chapter 11), namely **functional Magnetic Resonance**

Imaging (fMRI). While the technology currently in use is relatively new, localization efforts are not. In the early 1800s Franz Joseph Gall and Johann Spurzheim proposed that bumps on the skull revealed an individual's person-ality and mental ability. While there is no scientific support for this tenet of **phrenology**, the basic assumption that the brain houses independent mental processes that are specific to particular regions guides localization attempts in modern cognitive neuropsychology (Uttal, 2001).

In a typical study, researchers often compare scans of at least two groups of individuals. Let us assume that researchers were interested in determining whether the amygdala plays a role in fear, specifically responding to fearful facial expressions. One group of participants would be scanned while look-ing at images of fearful faces, but a second group would be engaged in a task in which the only presumable difference was the specific cognitive process the investigators are trying to isolate, in this case processing fearful faces. In other words, the second group of participants might be scanned while look-ing at pictures of faces with neutral expressions. Any difference in brain acti-vation between the two groups should reveal the area of the brain involved in processing fearful expressions. Using what researchers refer to as the sub-traction method, the two scans are compared by looking at differences in the three-dimensional units or voxels which indicate the ratio of oxygenated to deoxygenated blood across the brain (active areas should have a higher ratio of oxygenated to deoxygenated blood than less active ones). The areas that are similar in activation essentially cancel each other out, while the area or areas that are different are assigned a color depending on the signal strength (Satel & Lilienfeld, 2013). As you can see in the hypothetical results in Figure 13.5, there was only one area of the brain, the amygdala, that was active when participants were looking at the fearful faces, which was not active when participants looked at the neutral faces.

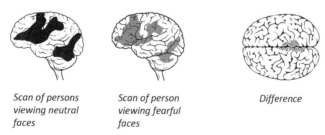

Scan of persons   Scan of person   Difference
viewing neutral   viewing fearful
faces   faces

Figure 13.5   Illustration of subtraction method in fMRI study

These results can be taken to indicate that the amygdala is, in fact, a fear module. But before placing too much confidence in such a conclusion we need to examine the research a bit closer. Most fundamentally, it is import-ant to understand that the fMRI scan is not a picture of the brain and is not measuring neural activity directly. It measures blood flow, which is correlated with glucose consumption, an indication of synaptic activity (Heeger & Ress, 2002). While blood flow may be an accurate proxy for neural activity, it is important, when bombarded by exciting images of brain scans in media reports, to keep in mind that that fMRI scan is an image constructed by a researcher. They set a threshold for what is considered activation, examine the differences in oxygenated and deoxygenated blood concentrations in the brain, and assign a color as an indication of the strength of the signal (Uttal, 2001). Notice in the first two scans on the left the widespread activation in the brain. Importantly, widespread activation is typical in such scans. However, notice we do not get a sense of this when we look at the difference image. All we see here is the amygdala "lit up" and, thus, the subtraction method can lead to a disregarding of the subtracted activity. While it may appear that an area is similar in activity between the two groups, it is not necessarily the case that the underlying neural activity did not change (Uttal, 2001).

KEY READING – Satal, S., & Lilienfeld, S. O. (2013). *Brainwashed: The seductive appeal of mindless neuroscience*. New York: Basic Books.

Practice is another factor that may influence the pattern of activation in a way that could lead to misinterpretation. A task that has been performed repeatedly would require less oxygen and, thus, a region could be important for the cognitive process, but not reach the threshold for activation set by the researcher (Satal & Lilienfeld, 2013). Lastly, there may be important clusters of neurons that are crucial to the cognitive process, but too small to be detected by current fMRI technology (Satal & Lilienfeld, 2013; Uttal, 2001). The widespread activation across the brain found in scans, a practice effect, and a failure to detect some neural activity may contribute to the relatively poor replication record in fMRI studies (Uttal, 2001).

Inconsistency also plagued fMRI research involving the amygdala (Boubela et al., 2015). While it is the case that a great deal of research did accumulate suggesting its role in fear, other studies found that the amygdala is active when shown faces reflecting sadness, anger, disgust, and even surprise and happiness (Whalen et al., 2013). This, along with additional research suggesting that increased activation is evident in response to the presentation of food when people are hungry and when pleasant photographs are shown to people high in extraversion, led to an appreciation for the broader role of the amygdala (Cunningham & Brosch, 2012). The implication of such findings is that localization efforts are doomed to fail (beyond the most basic sensory and motor processes) because there are not sharply defined regional distinctions in the brain, an organ characterized by integration, functional overlap, and impressive plasticity. The more complex the cognitive task, the less likely the processes is to reside in a particular area of the brain (Uttal, 2001).

Chapter summary

In the 1960s, Mark Rosenzweig and colleagues conducted numerous studies documenting brain changes in rats in response to environmental conditions. Though the gains in cortical thickness have been attributed to the effects of environmental enrichment, subsequent research suggested the studies demonstrated the negative effects of deprivation. Though these results have been replicated across species, we have to exercise caution when attempting to apply the results to humans. The enriched environment research, in particular, along with more modern neuroimaging studies have played a significant role in zero-to-three policy initiatives, brain-based education, and brain training, all of which place significant demands on our critical thinking. Neither the enriched environment research nor what we know about brain development suggest the first few years of life represent a critical period for learning. Though not supported, overgeneralizations about growing synapses and dendrites are evident in zero-to-three initiatives and brain-based education. A related concern is the redundant use of neuroscientific research. Research that fails to add to the explanation of psychological phenomena and cannot be appropriately applied to educational practice is of limited use. As neuroscientific research gains in popularity and we are bombarded with brain imaging study results in the media and journals, it becomes increasingly important to ask critical questions about the studies themselves, the conclusions drawn, and the assumptions made during such research. When reviewing the brain-based literature or evaluating any popular idea that is supposedly supported by neuroscience research, here are some questions to keep in mind: Are the authors actually citing neuroscientific research? If cited, was the research conducted with animals? If so, what species? Did they rely on human clinical cases? Do they seem to appreciate the limitations of the neuroscientific tools used? Is there additional research, beyond brain scans, to support the conclusions? Is neuroscientific support even necessary or is behavioral data sufficient? Do the neuroscientific results simply reinforce what was already known?

Future directions

Another extension of the enriched environment research is the use of brain games or brain training to improve cognitive functioning. There are several commercial brain training games and researchers have also created training programs that develop skills that are commonly assessed in cognitive neuropsychology (e.g., working memory). The results of studies have been mixed (Green & Seitz, 2015; Owen et al., 2010) with some finding long-term (three months) benefits among some training recipients (Jaeggi et al., 2011); some short-term but not long-term benefits (Jaeggi et al., 2014); and others, especially with commercial brain training programs, finding no benefits (Lorant-Royer et al., 2008; Owen et al., 2010; Smith, Stibric, & Smithson, 2013). There are numerous methodological issues in the brain training research, but none more important than placebo or expectancy effects (Foroughi et al., 2016; Green & Seitz, 2015). Foroughi and colleagues (2016) examined the **placebo effect** after noting that most of the brain training studies (nearly 90%) made no attempt to conceal the purpose of their study (i.e., recruited participants for a "brain training study"). To do so, Foroughi and colleagues created two recruitment ads like those displayed in Figure 13.6.

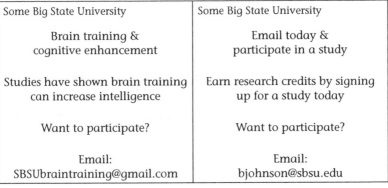

Figure 13.6 Ads used in Foroughi et al. (2016) brain training study

The marketing advertisement on the left suggests that working memory training has beneficial effects and, thus, has the potential to create an expectancy effect which contaminates the results. The generic ad on the right, on the other hand, is stripped of any suggestions about cognitive training. Participants responding to the ad on the left scored higher (5–10 points) on a test of fluid intelligence after only one hour of training while there was no change in the scores of those responding to the ad on the right. More troubling to one's confidence in brain training research, the authors found significant results of training when they combined the two groups (placebo and control)! Thus, the results of Foroughi and colleagues (2016) are suggestive of the possibility that the placebo effect contaminated the results of previous studies reporting benefits of cognitive training when no attempt was made to withhold the purpose of the study. Questions remain in the brain training domain, including concerns about whether any gains are clinically significant, whether such gains persist, and what role expectations play. As critical thinkers, we have to be aware of not only the placebo effect, but also the slippery slope arguments made by those marketing such products (brain training enhances cognitive performance that leads to job promotion, etc.).

We also should consider the wide variation within the available brain games or brain training programs designed to improve cognitive functioning that exist in the marketplace as a partial explanation for the mixed findings in effectiveness. The fact that such intervention tools are usually designed and marketed for profit introduces yet another variable that is difficult for researchers to control.

Intelligent consumers in a free-market setting need to employ critical thinking skills and ask questions such as the following when contemplating the use of such brain games or brain training programs:

- Are there potential short-term and long-term risks for children when using such interventions designed to improve cognitive skills? If so, how might parents counterbalance or negate these risks?
- Is there research-based evidence for effectiveness of such interventions? If so, who conducted the research? (Note: Effectiveness research done by or funded by the entrepreneur that designed or marketed the intervention is highly suspect.)
- Does a quality intervention program seem too good to be true for the cost?
- Do the advertisements use catchy and emotional pleas such as the following: "Change your brain in only three days!" or "How can you deny your child the chance to be a 'star' pupil in preschool?"

We live in a world where it is essential for critical thinkers to also be intelligent consumers of research findings and programs designed to meet the needs of the masses. The rapidly advancing digital world of the Internet places a particularly high premium on each individual's ability to make wise and thoughtful decisions in life. Our final suggestion: Think critically about programs designed to help children think critically.

Discussion questions

1. Do you see any similarities between the concerns about self-selection from critics of the Stanford Prison study and the study by Foroughi and colleagues (2016) on the placebo effect in brain training research?
2. Why do you think neuroscientific findings are often more persuasive than behavioral research? Think about factors like the technical skills involved in both and the assumptions we make about the explanatory power of both.

Conclusion

We wish to offer some concluding and clarifying remarks. As we reflected upon writing this book, it can be said that we have tried our best to convey to readers the value and usefulness of critical thinking, not only in psychology, but also in everyday life. The fact that students and scholars continue to express interest in these classic research studies and related ideas speaks to the importance of such work. As authors continue to return to primary source documents in their writing and use analytical techniques to assess the current importance of ideas, we are encouraged that we are serving an important role in the advancement of the scientific study of psychology.

As we look back on our use of "Applying Critical Thinking" boxes, we hope that readers found these engaging, thought-provoking, and related to the topical discussion at hand. It is impossible to chart all future directions that a subfield of psychology might take, but we have done our best to offer readers a glimpse of the future directions these lines of research and related ideas that might follow. Most readers will know something about most of these areas in psychology before reading our book. Our sincere hope is that readers might not only claim that they learned something new about the topics under discussion, but tell us that they now think more like a psychologist and critical thinker. Since the backbone of psychology is science, we also hope that you might now have insights related to how a scientist might think.

As Hunter (1982) so long ago suggested, learners and teachers need to "check for understanding" after some intensive form of reading or learning. Test your own critical thinking skills as you read the following example:

> You and several friends are having a discussion about gun control in the USA. There has been a recent school shooting at a high school and one of your friends (Friend A) thinks that gun violence is out of control, that schools are a dangerous place, and that students should be able to stay at home and get their high school diploma by taking online classes. Another friend (Friend B) believes that gun control is the answer and notes the relationship between stringent gun restrictions and fewer school shootings in the UK. Another friend (Friend C) argues that gun control is unnecessary because all of the guns owners he knows are responsible hunters. Moreover, Friend C notes, he read a survey in *Outdoor Expression* (a hunting

magazine) that most people don't favor gun control. Friend D chimes in that the problem begins very early in life. He read a study that showed that those who play with toy guns as kids are more likely to be aggressive as young adults. The problem may be with toy guns. Friend E recognizes the study and remarks that there were only 50 kids in the study, so that doesn't prove anything. Friend F, aware that some in the group of friends are arguing for no gun regulations and some for strict gun control, suggests that the solution is some limited form of gun control. Exasperated, Friend G argues that we will never be able to take all guns away or prevent all acts of violence, so we should "give-up" and do nothing.

Did you identify the following?

Friend	Critical thinking issue	Analytical description
Friend A	Availability heuristic	School shootings are rare and Friend A is likely overestimating the probability because of the recent media attention. We might ask: How many kids are killed in their homes and how many are killed at school? What percentage of students are killed in their schools?
Friend B	Illusory correlation	Friend B may be correct, but we might ask: Are there circumstances in which gun restrictions are in place yet gun violence is high or situations in which gun restrictions are low and violence is high/low?
		We might also ask: Are there cultural and legal differences between the USA and the UK that might account for the disparity in school shootings?
Friend C	Confirmatory bias	Friend C can easily recall those cases which confirm his belief about guns, but we might ask: Has friend C failed to notice or remember those cases that contradict his claim?
Friend C	Selection bias	*Outdoor Expression* magazine is a fictitious magazine geared toward hunters and, thus, the sample is not randomly selected nor representative of the general population. We might ask: Is the survey likely to overrepresent individuals who oppose gun control?

Friend D	Nature and nurture (the nurture assumption)	We assume that this aggressive behavior as young adults is because of the earlier play with toy guns, but we might ask: Might this tendency have been a genetically transmitted trait? Could it be the case that (constitutionally) aggressive kids are more likely to play with toy guns and more likely to consume violent media throughout childhood which reinforces these aggressive tendencies?
Friend E	Sample size and representativeness	Sample size, though related to representativeness, is not synonymous with representativeness. We might ask: What are the characteristics of the sample that may be relevant to the variables under investigation?

We might also ask: Has the study been replicated? |
| Friend F | Golden mean fallacy | It is not logical to assume that the solution is always found in the middle ground between two opposing positions. We might ask: If one solution results in many gun deaths and the other results in no gun deaths, does it make sense to advocate for the solution that leads to some gun deaths? |
| Friend G | Perfectionistic fallacy | Friend G has fallen victim to the perfectionist fallacy. We might ask: Is it reasonable to expect any solution to meet the standard of perfection? |

In conclusion, we hope that as a result of reading this book you have an improved sense of what Hemmingway called "bullshit" and can offer a logical rationale for your position. If you are still in doubt as to whether you have accomplished all that we had hoped, think about references in the preceding pages that discussed confirmation bias, mental shortcuts, logical fallacies, poor statistical understanding/reasoning, and pseudoscience. Learning to think critically does not happen by reading one book – even this book! As Willingham (2007) reminded us: "Critical thinking is not a set of skills that can be deployed at any time, in any context. It is a type of thought that even 3-year-olds can engage in – and even trained scientists can fail in" (p. 10). In other words, critical thinking does not begin or end with university study or graduate school.

Such cognitive skills are learned, refined, and improved over a human lifetime. Please recall that Howard Gardner reminded us that "it took me a decade to think like a psychologist" (Gardner, 2006, p. 5). Our sincere wish is that we have been able to advance your critical thinking skills a few notches in order to "up your game".

Key terms

ABA single-case design
design that allows the comparison of an intervention to baseline in order to assess the success of an intervention with a single participant

A priori
a hypothesis formulated before a study begins

Ad hominem attacks
see **Ad hominem fallacy**

Ad hominem fallacy
occurs when the rebuttal to an argument involves attacking one's character

Analogous models
an animal model in which researchers attempt to create the environmental contingencies that produce an effect

Analogue study
a study in which a researcher attempts to simulate a situation or a condition that occurs in real life

Anecdotal evidence
see **Anecdotes**

Anecdotes
personal accounts of experiences that serve as an unreliable source of evidence

Appeal to nature fallacy
illogical argument in which one contends that what is natural is good

Argument from authority fallacy
fallacious reasoning in which the quality of an argument is based on the authority of the person advancing the argument

Argument from ignorance fallacy
the notion that a proposition or theory is true because it has not been proven false

Assimilation bias
the tendency to evaluate ambiguous research as consistent with one's belief

Attachment
an emotional bond with a caregiver evident in a child's distress upon separation and efforts to seek comfort from him or her

Attention control
a control group in a clinical trial that receives the time and attention of clinicians but not the treatment itself

Autobiographical memory
memory for events in one's life

Availability heuristic
an error in judgment that occurs when we overestimate the probability of an event because it readily comes to mind

Barnum effect
the tendency to believe that vague or self-contradictory statements that apply to most people are uniquely self-descriptive

Baseline
recording of behavior prior to the introduction of an intervention

Behavior genetics
a field of study that utilizes twin and adoption samples to tease apart the relative influence of genes and the environment on individual differences

Betrayal trauma theory
theory suggesting that memories of trauma are blocked when that trauma is perpetrated by an attachment figure

Better-than-average bias
tendency to rate oneself higher than the average person on comparable attributes

Between-group contrasts
a process by which identification with a group leads to an exaggeration of differences between/among groups

Between-subjects design
research design in which two or more groups are exposed to different testing conditions

Biopsychosocial model
a model of psychopathology that accounts for biological, psychological, and social influences

Carryover effects
occur when experiences in an experimental phase or condition influence a subsequent phase or condition

Case study
a research method involving an in-depth examination of a single subject

Catalyst model
a model of aggression that posits no causal role for violent media, emphasizing instead the role of personality and exposure to family violence

Classical conditioning
learning that takes place when a previously neutral stimulus produces a previously unconditioned response

Clinical significance
an indication of whether a study's results are meaningful or practically important to the therapeutic process

Cognitive dissonance
an uncomfortable psychological state in which one's attitudes are inconsistent with one's behavior

Cohort differences
differences found in cross-sectional data attributed to shared experiences of the age groups

Common method variance
variance attributed to or accounted for by the method of measurement rather than the variables being measured

Comorbidity
the simultaneous presence of two or more disorders or conditions in an individual

Comparator trial
clinical trial in which the efficacy of an experimental drug is compared to another drug rather than a placebo

Conditioned response
a response to a conditioned stimulus that is learned through conditioning

Conditioned stimulus
a stimulus that acquires the capacity to elicit a conditioned response through conditioning

Confederate
an accomplice of the experimenter in a psychological experiment pretending to be a subject

Confirmation bias
see **Confirmatory bias**

Confirmatory bias
our tendency to selectively focus on information that confirms our existing hypotheses or prior beliefs

Confounds
variables other than the independent variable that might influence the dependent variable

Conjunction fallacy
occurs when one assumes that multiple concurrent conditions are more probable than a single condition

Construct
a hypothetical variable that explains psychological phenomena but is not directly observable

Construct validity
the extent to which an instrument or test measures a psychological construct or trait

Contextomy
a fallacy in which one misrepresents a statement or claim by quoting it out of context

Contiguity-causation error
a logical fallacy in which one assumes that temporal contiguity indicates the existence of a causal relationship

Control condition
see **Control group**

Control group
the group of participants not receiving the treatment

Convenience sample
refers to easily accessible research participants

Convergent validity
achieved when a measure is positively related to variables that it theoretically should be related to

Corpus callosum
a band of nerve fibers connecting and allowing for communication between the two hemispheres of the brain

Correlation
an indication of the extent to which two variables covary or are related to each other

Counterbalance
an experimental procedure that controls for carryover effects by varying the order of treatment across participants

Cover stories
plausible but fabricated explanations as to the purpose of a study

Critical periods
a specific time in development when a particular kind of stimulation is necessary for normal brain development

Cross-sectional data
data from studies in which different age groups are assessed at one time

Debriefing
procedure at the end of a study (especially one involving deception) in which the participants are informed about the true purpose of the study

Demand characteristics
aspects of a study, often the experimenter's behavior, that inadvertently produce hypothesis-confirming behavior among participants

Dendrite
a branchlike extension of a neuron that receives impulses from other cells and transmits them to the cell body

Denial
a defense mechanism in which one blocks painful or unpleasant events from conscious awareness

Dependent variable
the outcome variable or response that an experimenter measures in a study

Determinism
a philosophical position that human behavior is determined by causes from external factors as opposed to personal will

Developmental psychology
the study of physical, cognitive, and emotional changes across the lifespan

Diathesis–stress model
a model for psychopathology that accounts for mental disorders through the interaction of genetic, cognitive, or social vulnerabilities (diathesis) and stress

Discriminant validity
confirms that a test is unrelated to concepts that are theoretically dissimilar

Dissociation
a sense of depersonalization that disrupts the retrieval of a memory

Double-blind procedure
a procedure in clinical trials in which the participants and researchers are unaware of the condition to which participants have been assigned

Ecological validity
the extent to which the study environment aligns with the environment in which that behavior under study would normally occur

Effect size
a statistical concept that provides a standard metric for comparing effects or findings across studies

Effort justification
increase in value of an outcome as a result of increased effort expended achieving it

Electroencephalogram (EEG)
a noninvasive technique which records electrical activity across the surface of the brain

Empirical
verifiable by observation

Expectancy effects
occurs when client expectations for change positively effect therapeutic outcomes within the context of psychotherapy

Experience-dependent brain development
brain development that relies on the strengthening or development of new synapses

Experience-expectant brain development
brain development that relies on existing synapses and pruning

Experiment
a study in which a researcher manipulates a variable to examine the effect this has on another variable

Experimental group
Participants assigned to the experimental or treatment condition

Experimental realism
the extent to which the experimental situation is realistic and rousing to participants

External validity
the extent to which research findings generalize or apply to those outside of the study

Extraneous variable
variables other than the independent variable that may affect the study's results

Evocative gene-environment correlation
a type of gene-environment correlation in which reactions from other people are based in part on genetically influenced traits

Evolutionary psychology
a perspective in psychology which focuses on the adaptation of behavior and mental processes through the process of natural selection

Factorial design (2 × 2)
a research design in which there are two independent variables with two values

Fallacy of ancient wisdom
argument in which one suggests that long-standing practices or long-held beliefs are noble only because of their longevity

Fallacy of bifurcation
illogical argument in which one restricts options to two opposing alternatives

False dilemmas
occur when one makes the claim that there are only two alternatives or outcomes in a situation when there are more alternatives

Falsifiability
notion that a theory or hypothesis must be capable of being shown to be false

Field study
a study conducted in a natural setting in which the individuals under study are typically unaware of the study

File drawer problem
the tendency for researchers to file rather than publish studies that fail to produce statistically positive results

Flashbulb memories
a vivid memory of an emotionally charged event

Functional Magnetic Resonance Imaging (fMRI)
a neuroscientific tool that measures the ratio of oxygenated and deoxygenated blood concentrations in the brain

Gambler's fallacy
mistaken belief that a random event is more or less likely because of a previous event

Gene-environment correlations
correlations that appear to reflect an environmental effect but that are at least partially attributable to genetic differences

General Aggression Model (GAM)
a social cognitive theory that accounts for increased aggression resulting from exposure to violent media

Glial cells
cells that play a supportive role in the central nervous system, maintaining the health and survival of neurons

Golden mean fallacy
occurs when one claims that a solution or the truth is found in the middle ground between two opposing positions

Good-subject effect
the tendency for research participants to conform to the perceived expectations of the experimenter

Guided imagery
memory-recovery technique in which a patient is asked to imagine details surrounding a past scenario proposed by a therapist

Hindsight bias
sense that an event was predictable after it has occurred

History
occurs when life experiences threaten the interval validity of a study

Hypnosis
a memory-recovery technique in which a patient in a relaxed state is subject to suggestions made by a therapist

Hypothesis
a testable prediction

Illusion of control
the tendency for individuals to overrate their personal control over events

Illusory correlation
perceiving a correlation or association between two variables when no such association exists

Imagination inflation
occurs when imagining an event that did not happen increases one's confidence that it did actually occur

Implicit memory
unconscious memory or memory that cannot be consciously accessed

Independent variable
variable manipulated in a study and assumed to cause an outcome

Informed consent
process by which research participants are informed about the nature of the study and provide consent to participate

Institutional Review Board (IRB)
a university committee charged with evaluating research proposals in terms of adherence to ethical standards

Internal validity
the extent to which changes in an independent variable, rather than extraneous variables, are responsible for the observed changes in the dependent variable

Inter-rater reliability
a form of reliability in which agreement among multiple observers is calculated

Intervention-causation fallacy
an erroneous assumption that if a treatment is effective it must be treating the cause of the illness or problem

Introspection
research method in which one observes and reports on one's own subjective perceptions and experiences

Likert scale
a commonly used scale in the social sciences in which respondents indicate their level of agreement or disagreement along a continuum (e.g., a 5-point scale ranging from strongly disagree to strongly agree)

Manipulation checks
a procedure in which the experimenter attempts to confirm that an independent variable was successfully manipulated

Maturation
developmental changes in an organism during an investigation that threatens the internal validity of a study

Meta-analysis
a statistical technique that combines the results of multiple studies to provide an estimation of the size of an effect

Misinformation effect
occurs when information presented after an event interferes with a person's recall of an event

Moral disengagement theory
a model that accounts for the avoidance of self-sanctions for moral transgression through psychological mechanisms including minimizing the effects one's behavior has on others

Mundane realism
the extent to which an experimenter has created an experimental situation that simulates comparable situations outside of the laboratory

Naturalistic fallacy
argument in which one suggests that a behavior is morally right because it is consistent with our natural tendencies

Naturalistic observation
a research method in which the researcher unobtrusively observes the behavior of interest in the setting in which it commonly occurs

Neurons
nerve cells in the brain

Neuroscience
interdisciplinary field that examines the structure and function of the brain

Non-shared environment
factors in behavior genetics research that produce differences among family members

Null hypothesis
the hypothesis of no differences that is tested in an experiment and is either rejected or retained depending on the results

Nurture assumption
the popular assumption that a child's personality is shaped by his/her parents

One-tailed test
statistical test limited to one end of a distribution

Operational definitions
specify how variables in a psychological study are manipulated and measured

Optimism bias
belief within psychotherapy research that a new treatment is likely to be superior to an established treatment

Parapsychology
a field of study investigating psychic and paranormal phenomena

Parental investment
a theory within evolutionary psychology which accounts for differences between males and females in terms of time and energy invested in offspring

Partial correlation
a correlation in which the influence of a third variable is statistically controlled in order to better judge the association of the other two variables

Participant observer study
a type of naturalistic observation in which the researcher or observer actively participates in the environment under study

Perfectionistic fallacy
involves the rejection or downgrading of an idea or solution that does not meet the standard of perfection

Phrenology
a theory about brain localization suggesting that bumps on the skull reflected the strength of a particular area of the brain and revealed personality traits and mental abilities

Pilot studies
preliminary research aimed at discovering and resolving design problems before the launch of a full-scale project

Placebo-controlled trial
a clinical trial in which a treatment or drug is compared with a placebo

Placebo effect
occurs when results in a study are due to participant expectations and not the manipulation of the independent variable

Post-hoc fallacy
a logical error that occurs when one assumes that because two things happen in succession, the first caused the latter

Post-traumatic stress disorder
disorder, following a traumatic or stressful event, characterized by increased arousal, negative thoughts and feelings, and a persistent re-experiencing of the event

Precognition
psychic ability to predict future events

Predictive invariance
an indication of whether or not scores on a measure predict equally well among all groups

Predictive validity
the extent to which a test predicts future performance relevant to the test

Presentism
the tendency to evaluate past events using contemporary values

Pruning
process of eliminating redundant and unused synapses in the brain

Pseudoscience
consists of practices employed to gather evidence to support claims, but these practices are not consistent with proper scientific methods

Psychological reactance
a motivational state in which one seeks to regain freedom when one perceives attempts to restrict one's freedom

Psychological realism
the extent to which the psychological mechanisms in the experimental situation match those in comparable situations outside the laboratory

Psychotherapy
psychological treatment of mental disorders

Random assignment
technique of assigning research participants in which every participant has an equal chance of being assigned to any group

Rationalization
a defense mechanism in which an individual provides a logical but self-deceptive explanation for behavior

Reductionism
involves an attempt to account for complex psychological phenomena in simpler and presumably more essential biological terms

Regression to the mean
a statistical phenomenon in which an abnormally large measurement tends to be followed by a smaller one or one closer to the mean

Reliability
a term that, within clinical psychology, refers to the consistency of diagnoses

Replication
a study carried out in the same manner as a prior study with the intent of reproducing the results

Repression
unconscious blocking of a memory

Restriction of range
occurs when the range of possible scores on a variable is limited or constricted

Rich false memory
detailed false memories of past events

Selection bias
occurs when subjects are not randomly selected from a population

Self-determination theory
a theory of human motivation that posits that psychological health is dependent on meeting the basic psychological needs of autonomy, relatedness, and competence

Self-fulfilling prophecy
a prediction that comes true because one acts in a way that is consistent with one's expectations

Semi-structured interview
an interview in which the interviewer asks a set of open-ended questions

Sensitivity
ability of a test to correctly identify those with a disorder

Shared environment
factors in behavior genetics research that produce similarities among family members

Significance level
probability that the results occurred by chance

Single-case design
design that allows one to examine the success of an intervention with a single participant

Slippery slope fallacy
an argument in which one suggests that a slight action will lead to extreme consequences

Social identity theory
suggests that our behavior within a group is influenced by the extent to which we identify with the group

Social psychology
the branch of psychology that studies how other people influence our thoughts, behaviors, and emotions

Specificity
the ability of a test to correctly identify those without the disorder

Statistical significance
an indication of whether the results can be reliably reproduced or occurred by chance

Straw man fallacy
an argument in which one misrepresents an opponent's position in order to refute it

Stroop task
a psychological test in which a participant says the color of a word but the same color does not appear in the written word

Subjectivist fallacy
illogical argument in which one contends that something, though empirically confirmed, is true for one person but not another

Synapses
gap or junction between the sending neuron and the receiving neuron

Theory
a model for psychological phenomena that describes the phenomena and makes predictions which allow the model to be tested and confirmed or falsified

Therapist allegiance
bias that accounts for results of studies comparing treatments to favor the investigator's proclivities

Third-person effect
a tendency to believe that the effects of media messages are greater on others than on oneself

Time-series design
a method characterized by multiple measurements across time in which the variable of interest is manipulated after a baseline is established

Tu quoque fallacy
occurs when one seeks to discredit an argument by claiming that the individual advancing it has acted in a manner inconsistent with it

Two-tailed tests
statistical tests utilizing both ends of a distribution

Two wrongs make a right fallacy
an illogical attempt to justify a wrongful action because others have done the same

Type I error
occurs when the null hypothesis is rejected yet is true

Unconditioned response
an automatic response to an unconditioned stimulus in an organism

Unconditioned stimulus
a stimulus that automatically evokes an unconditioned response in an organism

Validity
a term that, within clinical psychology, refers to the extent to which there is a meaningful distinction between those diagnosed with a disorder and those who are not; in psychometric terms it is an indication of whether a test is measuring what it is intended to measure

Wait-list control
a comparison group in a clinical trial that receives an intervention or treatment only after the active treatment group or after the study is complete

Within-group assimilation

a process by which identification with a group leads to pressure to conform with group norms

Within-group differentiation

a process by which identification with a group leads to the establishment of a unique identity or niche within the group

Within-subjects design

research design in which all participants are exposed to all levels of the treatment or independent variable

References

Abramson, C. I. (2013). Problems of teaching the behaviorist perspective in the cognitive revolution. *Behavioral Sciences, 3*, 55–71.

Adachi, P. J., & Willoughby, T. (2011). The effect of video game competition and violence on aggressive behavior: Which characteristic has the greatest influence? *Psychology of Violence, 1*, 259–274.

Adachi, P. J., & Willoughby, T. (2013). Demolishing the competition: The longitudinal link between competitive video games, competitive gambling, and aggression. *Journal of Youth and Adolescence, 42*, 1090–1104.

Alcock, J. E. (2003). Give the null hypothesis a chance: Reasons to remain doubtful about the existence of psi. *Journal of Consciousness Studies, 10*, 29–50.

Alcock, J. E. (January, 2011). Back from the future: Parapsychology and the Bem affair. *Skeptical Inquirer*. Retrieved from www.csicop.org/specialarticles/show/back_from_the_future

Alferink, L. A., & Farmer-Dougan, V. (2010). Brain-(not) based education: Dangers of misunderstanding and misapplication of neuroscience research. *Exceptionality, 18*, 42–52.

American Psychiatric Association. (2013). *Diagnostic and statistical manual of mental disorders: DSM-5*. Washington, DC: American Psychiatric Association.

American Psychological Association (2018). *Memories of childhood abuse*. Retrieved from www.apa.org/topics/trauma/memories.aspx

Anderson, C. A., & Bushman, B. J. (2001). Effects of violent video games on aggressive behavior, aggressive cognition, aggressive affect, physiological arousal, and prosocial behavior: A meta-analytic review of the scientific literature. *Psychological Science, 12*, 353–359.

Anderson, C. A., & Carnagey, N. L. (2004). Violent evil and the general aggression model. In A. Miller (ed.), *The social psychology of good and evil* (pp. 168–192). New York: Guilford.

Anderson, C. A., Carnagey, N. L., Flanagan, M., Benjamin, A. J., Eubanks, J., & Valentine, J. C. (2004). Violent video games: Specific effects of violent content on aggressive thoughts and behavior. *Advances in Experimental Social Psychology, 36*, 199–249.

Anderson, C. A., & Dill, K. E. (2000). Video games and aggressive thoughts, feelings, and behavior in the laboratory and in life. *Journal of Personality and Social Psychology, 78*, 772–790.

Anderson, C. A., Lindsay, J. J., & Bushman, B. J. (1999). Research in the psychological laboratory: Truth or triviality? *Current Directions in Psychological Science, 8*, 3–9.

Anderson, C. A., Shibuya, A., Ihori, N., Swing, E. L., Bushman, B. J., Sakamoto, A., Rothstein, H. R., & Saleem, M. (2010). Violent video game effects on aggression, empathy, and prosocial behavior in eastern and western countries: A meta-analytic review. *Psychological Bulletin, 136*, 151–173.

Angell, M. (2011, July 4). The illusions of psychiatry. *The New York Review of Books.* Retrieved from www.nybooks.com

Antony, M. M., Orsillo, S. M., & Roemer, L. (eds.). (2001). *Practitioner's guide to empirically based measures of anxiety.* New York: Springer.

Arkowitz, H., & Lilienfeld, S. O. (2006, October). Do self-help books help? *Scientific American Mind, 17*(5), 78–79.

Aunola, K., & Nurmi, J. E. (2005). The role of parenting styles in children's problem behavior. *Child Development, 76*, 1144–1159.

Baggini, J. (2009). *The duck that won the lottery: 100 new experiments for the armchair philosopher.* New York: Penguin.

Bandura, A. (1965). Influence of models' reinforcement contingencies on the acquisition of imitative responses. *Journal of Personality and Social Psychology, 1*, 589–595.

Bandura, A. (1999). Moral disengagement in the perpetration of inhumanities. *Personality and Social Psychology Review, 3*, 193–209.

Bandura, A., Ross, D., & Ross, S. A. (1963). Imitation of film-mediated aggressive models. *Journal of Abnormal and Social Psychology, 66*, 3–11.

Bandura, A., Barbaranelli, C., Caprara, G. V., & Pastorelli, C. (1996). Mechanisms of moral disengagement in the exercise of moral agency. *Journal of Personality and Social Psychology, 71*, 364–374.

Banuazizi, A., & Movahedi, S. (1975). Interpersonal dynamics in a simulated prison. *American Psychologist, 30*, 152–160.

Bartels, J. M. (2015). The Stanford prison experiment in introductory psychology textbooks: A content analysis. *Psychology Learning & Teaching, 14*, 36–50.

Bartels, J. M., Fischer, T., Granfors, S., & Kerwin, S. (2018, May). *Revisiting the Stanford prison experiment: Examining the influence of demand characteristics in the guard orientation.* Presented at Association for Psychological Science Annual Convention, San Francisco, CA.

Bartels, J. M., Milovich, M., & Moussier, S. (2016). Coverage of the Stanford prison experiment in introductory psychology courses. *Teaching of Psychology, 43*, 136–141.

Bartels, J. M., & Peters, D. (2017). Coverage of Rosenhan's "On being sane in insane places" in abnormal psychology textbooks. *Teaching of Psychology, 44*, 169–173.

Bartels, J. M., & Ruei, Z. (2018, January). *Addressing the placebo effect and antidepressant drug trials in abnormal psychology.* Presented at National Institute for the Teaching of Psychology Convention, St. Pete Beach, FL.

Bass, E., & Davis, L. (1994). *The courage to heal: A guide for women survivors of child sexual abuse* (3rd edn). New York: HarperPerennial.

Baumeister, R. F., Masicampo, E. J., & DeWall, N. C. (2009). Prosocial benefits of feeling free: Disbelief in free will increases aggression and reduces helpfulness. *Personality and Social Psychology Bulletin, 35*, 260–268.

Baumrind, D. (1964). Some thoughts on ethics of research: After reading Milgram's "Behavioral study of obedience." *American Psychologist, 19*, 421–423.

Baumrind D. (1985). Research using intentional deception: Ethical issues revisited. *American Psychologist, 40*, 165–174.

Beaver, K. M., Schwartz, J. A., Connolly, E. J., Al-Ghamdi, M. S., & Kobeisy, A. N. (2015). The role of parenting in the prediction of criminal involvement: Findings from a nationally representative sample of youth and a sample of adopted youth. *Criminology and Criminal Justice Faculty Publications*, Paper 19. *51*, 301.

Beck, D. M. (2010). The appeal of the brain in the popular press. *Perspectives on Psychological Science, 5*, 762–766.

Beck, H. P., Levinson, S., & Irons, G. (2009). Finding little Albert: A journey to John B. Watson's infant laboratory. *American Psychologist, 64*, 605–614.

Bègue, L., Duke, A., Courbet, D., & Oberlé, D. (2017). Values and indirect noncompliance in a Milgram-like paradigm. *Social Influence, 12*, 29–40.

Bem, D. J. (2011). Feeling the future: Experimental evidence for anomalous retroactive influences on cognition and affect. *Journal of Personality and Social Psychology, 100*, 407–425.

Benedetti, F., Mayberg, H. S., Wager, T. D., Stohler, C. S., & Zubieta, J. (2005). Neurobiological mechanisms of the placebo effect. *The Journal of Neuroscience, 25*, 10390–10402.

Bennett, B. (2015). *Logically fallacious: The ultimate collection of over 300 logical fallacies.* Sudbury, MA: Archieboy Holdings.

Bergsma, A. (2008). Do self-help books help? *Journal of Happiness Studies, 9*, 341–360.

Berinsky, A., Quek, K., & Sances, M. (2012). Conducting online experiments on Mechanical Turk. *Newsletter of the APSA Experimental Section, 3*, 2–6.

Berkowitz, L. (1989). Frustration-aggression hypothesis: Examination and reformulation. *Psychological Bulletin, 106*, 59–73.

Bernstein, D. M., & Loftus, E. F. (2009). The consequences of false memories for food preferences and choices. *Perspectives on Psychological Science, 4*, 135–139.

Bhattacharjee, Y. (2012, March). Paranormal circumstances: One influential scientist's quixotic mission to prove ESP exists. *Discover Magazine.* Retrieved from http://discovermagazine.com/2012/mar/09-paranormal-circumstances-scientist-mission-esp

Bigelow, K. M., & Morris, E. K. (2001). John B. Watson's advice on child rearing: Some historical context. *Behavioral Development Bulletin, 1*, 26–30.

Blakeley, K. (2015, September, 14). Woman, 46, lives next door to man for 10 years before suddenly realizing he had "sexually abused her 40 years ago." *DailyMail.com.* Retrieved from www.dailymail.co.uk

Blakemore, J. E., Berenbaum, S. A., & Liben, L. S. (2009). *Gender development.* New York: Psychology Press.

Blakemore, S., & Troscianko, T. (1985). Belief in the paranormal: Probability judgements, illusory control, and the 'chance baseline shift.' *British Journal of Psychology, 76*, 459–468.

Blass, T. (2004). *The man who shocked the world: The life and legacy of Stanley Milgram.* New York: Basic Books.

Blum, B. (2018, June). The lifespan of a lie. *Medium*. Retrieved from https://medium. com.

Blume, E. S. (1990). *Secret survivors: Uncovering incest and its aftereffects in women*. New York: Ballantine Books.

Boccia, M. L., & Pedersen, C. (2001). Animal models of critical and sensitive periods in social and emotional development. In D. B. Bailey, J. T. Bruer, F. J. Symons, & J. W. Lichtman (eds.), *Critical thinking about critical periods* (pp. 107–127). Baltimore, MD: Paul H. Brookes.

Boubela, R. N., Kalcher, K., Huf, W., Seidel, E. M., Derntl, B., Pezawas, L., ... & Moser, E. (2015). fMRI measurements of amygdala activation are confounded by stimulus correlated signal fluctuation in nearby veins draining distant brain regions. *Scientific Reports, 5*, 10499.

Bouvet, R., & Bonnefon, J. F. (2015). Non-reflective thinkers are predisposed to attribute supernatural causation to uncanny experiences. *Personality and Social Psychology Bulletin, 41*, 955–961.

Bowlby, J. (1982). *Attachment and loss: Vol. 1. Attachment* (2nd edn.). New York: Basic Books.

Brabeck, M. M., & Shore, E. L. (2002). Gender differences in intellectual and moral development? The evidence that refutes the claim. In J. Demick, & C. Andreoletti (eds.), *Handbook of adult development* (pp. 351–368). New York, NY: Plenum Press.

Braun, K. A., Ellis, R., & Loftus, E. F. (2002). Make my memory: How advertising can change our memories of the past. *Psychology & Marketing, 19*, 1–23.

Bregman, E. O. (1934). An attempt to modify the emotional attitudes of infants by the conditioned response technique. *Journal of Genetic Psychology, 45*, 169–198.

Brehm, J. W., Stires, L. K., Sensenig, J., & Shaban, J. (1966). The attractiveness of an eliminated choice alternative. *Journal of Experimental Social Psychology, 2*, 301–313.

Breitmeyer, B. G. (2017). What's all the recent free-will ado about? *Psychology of Consciousness: Theory, Research, and Practice, 4*, 330–333.

Brescoll, V. L. & LaFrance, M. (2004). The correlates and consequences of newspaper reports of research on gender differences. *Psychological Science, 15*, 515–521.

Brewer, M. B. (2000). Research design and issues of validity. In H. T. Reis & J. M. Charles (eds.), *Handbook of research methods in social and personality psychology* (pp. 3–16). New York: Cambridge University Press.

Brewin, C. R. (2007). Autobiographical memory for trauma: Update on four controversies. *Memory, 15*, 227–248.

Bridgeman, B. (1985). Free will and the functions of consciousness. *The Behavioral and Brain Sciences, 8*, 540.

Brotherton, R., & French, C. C. (2014). Belief in conspiracy theories and susceptibility to the conjunction fallacy. *Applied Cognitive Psychology, 28*, 238–248.

Bruer, J. T. (1999). *The myth of the first three years: A new understanding of early brain development and lifelong learning*. New York: Free Press.

Bruer, J. T. (2001). A critical and sensitive period primer. In D. B. Bailey, J. T. Bruer, F. J. Symons, & J. W. Lichtman (eds.), *Critical thinking about critical periods* (pp. 3–26). Baltimore, MD: Paul H. Brookes.

Bruer, J. T. (2008). In search of...brain-based based education. In *The Jossey-Bass reader on the brain and learning*. San Francisco, CA: Jossey-Bass.

Bryck, R. L., & Fischer, P. A. (2012). Training the brain: Practical applications of neural plasticity from the intersection of cognitive neuroscience, developmental psychology, and prevention science. *American Psychologist, 67*, 87–100.

Bunge, M. (1984). What is pseudoscience? *The Skeptical Inquirer, 9*, 36–46.

Burger, J. M. (2009). Replicating Milgram: Would people still obey today? *American Psychologist, 64*, 1–11.

Burger, J. M., Girgis, Z. M., & Manning, C. C. (2011). In their own words: Explaining obedience to authority through an examination of participants' comments. *Social Psychological and Personality Science, 2*, 460–466.

Bushman, B. J. (2002). Does venting anger feed or extinguish the flame? Catharsis, rumination, distraction, anger, and aggressive responding. *Personality and Social Psychology Bulletin, 28*, 724–731.

Bushman, B. J. (2016). *Blood, gore, and video games: Effects of violent content on players*. Presented at 2016 National Institute on the Teaching of Psychology, St. Pete Beach, FL.

Bushman, B. J., & Anderson, C. A. (1998). Methodology in the study of aggression: Integrating experimental and nonexperimental findings. In R. Geen, & E. Donnerstein (eds.), *Human aggression: Theories, research and implications for policy* (pp. 23–48). San Diego, CA: Academic Press.

Bushman, B. J., & Anderson, C. A. (2002). Violent video games and hostile expectations: A test of the general aggression model. *Personality and Social Psychology Bulletin, 28*, 1679–1686.

Bushman, B. J., & Anderson, C. A. (2009). Comfortably numb: Desensitizing effects of violent media on helping others. *Psychological Science, 20*, 273–277.

Bushman, B. J. & Huesmann, L. R. (2001). Effects of televised violence on aggression. In D. Singer, & J. Singer (eds.), *Handbook of children and the media* (pp. 223–254). Thousand Oaks, CA: Sage Publications.

Bushman, B. J., & Huesmann, L. R. (2014). Twenty-five years of research on violence in digital games and aggression revisited. A reply to Elson and Ferguson (2013). *European Psychologist, 19*, 47–55.

Cacioppo, J. T., Semin, G. R., & Berntson, G. G. (2004). Realism, instrumentalism, and scientific symbiosis. *American Psychologist, 59*, 214–223.

Camel, J. E., Withers, G. S., & Greenough, W. T. (1986). Persistence of visual cortex dendritic alterations induced by postweaning exposure to a "superenriched" environment in rats. *Behavioral Neuroscience, 100*, 810–813.

Caplan, P. J., & Caplan, J. (1994).*Thinking critically about research on sex and gender* (3rd edn.). New York: Routledge.

Capuzzi, D., & Stauffer, M. D. (2016). *Counseling and psychotherapy: Theories and interventions* (6th edn.). Alexandria, VA: American Counseling Association.

Carnahan, T., & McFarland, S. (2007). Revisiting the Stanford prison experiment: Could participant self-selection have led to the cruelty? *Personality and Social Psychology Bulletin, 33*, 603–614.

Carothers, B. J., & Reis, H. T. (2013). Men and women are from Earth: Examining the latent structure of gender. *Journal of Personality and Social Psychology, 104*, 385–407.

Carroll, R. T. (2003). *The skeptic's dictionary: A collection of strange beliefs, amusing deceptions, and dangerous delusions.* Hoboken, NJ: Wiley.

Carvalho, C., Caetano, J. M., Cunha, L., Rebouta, P., Kaptchuk, T. J., & Kirsch, I. (2016). Open-label placebo treatment in chronic low back pain: a randomized controlled trial. *Pain, 157,* 2766–2772.

Chabris, C. F., & Kosslyn, S. M. (1998). How do the cerebral hemispheres contribute to encoding spatial relations? *Current Directions in Psychological Science. 7,* 8–14.

Chalmers, I., & Matthews, R. (2006). What are the implications of optimism bias in clinical research? *Lancet, 367,* 449–450.

Chambless, D. L. et al. (1998). Update on empirically validated therapies, II. *The Clinical Psychologist, 51,* 3–16.

Chao, Y., Cheng, Y., & Chiou, W. (2011). The psychological consequence of experiencing shame: Self-sufficiency and mood-repair. *Motivation and Emotion 35,* 202–210.

Christensen, L. B., Johnson, R. B., & Turner, L. A. (2014). *Research methods: Design and analysis* (12th edn.). Upper Saddle River, NJ: Pearson.

Chua, A. (2011). *Battle hymn of the tiger mother.* New York: Penguin Press.

Chugani, H. T. (1998). A critical period of brain development: Studies of cerebral glucose utilization with PET. *Preventative Medicine, 27,* 184–188.

Cipriani, A., Furukawa, T. A., Salanti, G., Chaimani, A., Atkinson, L. Z., Ogawa, Y., ... Geddes, J. R. (2018). Comparative efficacy and acceptability of 21 antidepressant drugs for the acute treatment of adults with major depressive disorder: A systematic review and network meta-analysis. *The Lancet, 391,* 1357–1366.

Clark, S. E., & Loftus, E. F. (1996). The construction of space alien abduction memories. *Psychological Inquiry, 7,* 140–143.

Cobb, N. J. (2010). *Adolescence: Continuity, change, and diversity* (7th edn.). Sunderland, MA: Sinauer Associates.

Cochrane, A., Barnes-Holmes, D., & Barnes-Holmes, Y. (2008). The perceived-threat behavioral approach test (PT-BAT): Measuring avoidance in high-, mid-, and low-spider fearful participants. *The Psychological Record, 58,* 585–596.

Cohen, J. (1988). *Statistical power analysis for the behavioral sciences* (2nd edn.). Hillsdale, NJ: Erlbaum.

Cohen, J. (1994). The Earth is round (p < . 05). *American Psychologist, 49,* 997–1003.

Colby, A., Kohlberg, L., Gibbs, J., Lieberman, M., Fischer, K., & Saltzstein, H. (1983). A longitudinal study of moral judgment. *Monographs of the Society for Research in Child Development, 48,* 1–124.

Collins, W. A., Maccoby, E. E., Steinberg, L., Hetherington, E. M., Bornstein, M. H. (2000). Contemporary research on parenting: The case for nature and nurture. *American Psychologist, 55,* 218–232.

Comer, R. J. (2015). *Abnormal psychology* (9th edn.). New York: Worth.

Constantino, M. J., Arnkoff, D. B., Glass, C. R., Ametrano, R. M., & Smith, J. Z. (2011). Expectations. *Journal of Clinical Psychology, 67,* 184–192.

Cook, M., Mineka, S., Wolkenstein, B., & Laitsch, K. (1985). Observational conditioning of snake fear in unrelated Rhesus monkeys. *Journal of Abnormal Psychology, 94,* 591–610.

Cooper, H. M. (2017). *Research synthesis and meta-analysis: A step-by-step approach* (5th edn.). Thousand Oaks, CA: Sage.

Cooper, H. M., & Rosenthal, R. (1980). Statistical versus traditional procedures for summarizing research findings. *Psychological Bulletin, 87,* 442–449.

Cooper, J. (1980). Reducing fears and increasing assertiveness: The role of dissonance reduction. *Journal of Experimental Social Psychology 16,* 199–213.

Cornwell, D., & Hobbs, S. (1976). The strange saga of little Albert. *New Society, 35,* 602–604.

Cornwell, D., Hobbs, S., & Prytula, R. C. (1980). Little Albert rides again. *American Psychologist, 35,* 216–217.

Corsini, R. J., & Wedding, D. (2005). *Current psychotherapies* (7th edn.). Belmont, CA: Brooks/Cole.

Cramer, K. M. (2013). Six criteria of a viable theory: Putting reversal theory to the test. *Journal of Motivation, Emotion, and Personality, 1,* 9–16.

Crawford, M. (2004). Mars and Venus collide: A discursive analysis of marital self-help psychology. *Feminism & Psychology, 14,* 63–79.

Crook, L. S., & Dean, M. C. (1999). "Lost in a shopping mall" – A breach of professional ethics. *Ethics & Behavior, 9,* 39–50.

Cunningham, P. F. (1996). Revealing animal experiments in general psychology texts: Opening Pandora's box. *American Psychologist, 51,* 734–735.

Cunningham, W. A., & Brosch, T. (2012). Motivational salience: Amygdala tuning from traits, needs, values, and goals. *Current Directions in Psychological Science, 21,* 54–59.

Cushing, E. (2013). *Amazon Mechanical Turk: The digital sweatshop.* January/February, UTNE Reader.

Dallal, G. E. (2002). *Is statistics hard?* Retrieved from www.jerrydallal.com/lhsp/hard.htm

Danquah, A., Farrell, M. J., & O'Boyle, D. J. (2008). Biases in the subjective timing of perceptual events: Libet et al. (1983) revisited. *Consciousness and Cognition, 17,* 616–627.

Danziger, K. (1980). The history of introspection reconsidered. *Journal of the History of the Behavioral Sciences, 16,* 241–262.

Davis, D. A. (1979). What's in a name? A Bayesian rethinking of attributional biases in clinical judgment. *Journal of Consulting and Clinical Psychology, 47,* 1109–1114.

DeAngelis, T. (2010). "Little Albert" regains his identity. *Monitor on Psychology, 41,* 10.

Dennett, D. (2003). *Freedom evolves.* London: Penguin.

Denson, T. F., DeWall, C. N., & Finkel, E. J. (2012). Self-control and aggression. *Current Directions in Psychological Science, 21,* 20–25.

Dewey, J. (1910/1998). *How we think.* Boston: D.C. Heath and Company.

Di Bonaventura, L., Jacobs, G., Burns, S. Z. (Producers), & Soderbergh, S. (Director). (2013). *Side effects* [Motion picture].US: Endgame Entertainment.

Dias, B. G., & Ressler, K. J. (2014). Parental olfactory experience influences behavior and neural structure in subsequent generations. *Nature Neuroscience, 17,* 89–96.

Dickson, D. H., & Kelly, I. W. (1985). The "Barnum effect" in personality assessment: A review of the literature. *Psychological Reports, 57,* 367–382.

Digdon, N., Powell, R., & Harris, B. (2014). Little Albert's alleged neurological impairment: Watson, Rayner, and historical revision. *History of Psychology, 17,* 312–324.

Dodes, J. E. (1997). The mysterious placebo. *Skeptical Inquirer, 21,* 44–45.

Doliński, D., Grzyb, T., Folwarczny, M., Grzybała, P., Krzyszycha, K., Martynowska, K., & Trojanowski, J. (2017). Would you deliver an electric shock in 2015? Obedience in the experimental paradigm developed by Stanley Milgram in the 50 years following the original studies. *Social Psychological and Personality Science, 8,* 927–933.

Domjan, M., & Purdy, J. E. (1995). Animal research in psychology: More than meets the eye of the general psychology student. *American Psychologist, 50,* 496–503.

Donenberg, G. R., & Hoffman, L. W. (1988). Gender differences in moral development. *Sex Roles, 18,* 701–717.

Doogan, S., & Thomas, G. V. (1992). Origins of fear of dogs in adults and children: The role of conditioning processes and prior familiarity with dogs. *Behaviour Research and Therapy, 30,* 387–394.

Dragioti, E., Dimoliatis, I., Fountoulakis, K. N., & Evangelou, E. (2015). A systematic appraisal of allegiance effect in randomized controlled trials of psychotherapy. *Annals of General Psychiatry, 14,* 1–9.

Duran, M., Hőft, M., Lawson, D. B., Medjahed, B., & Orady, E. A. (2013). Urban High School Students' IT/STEM Learning: Findings from a collaborative inquiry- and design- based afterschool program. *Journal of Science Education and Technology, 23*(1), 116–137.

Eagly, A. H., & Wood, W. (1999). The origins of sex differences in human behavior: Evolved dispositions versus social roles. *American Psychologist, 54,* 408–423.

Eagly, A. H., & Wood, W. (2013). The nature-nurture debates: 25 years of challenges in the psychology of gender. *Perspectives on Psychological Science, 8,* 340–357.

Ellis, A. (1987). The impossibility of achieving consistently good mental health. *American Psychologist, 42,* 364–375.

Elmes, D. G., Kantowitz, B. H., & Roediger, H. L. (1999). *Research methods in psychology.* Pacific Grove, CA: Brooks/Cole Publishing Company.

Emery, C. L., & Lilienfeld, S. O. (2004). The validity of childhood sexual abuse checklists in the popular psychology literature: A Barnum effect? *Professional Psychology: Research and Practice, 35,* 268–274.

English, H. B. (1929). Three cases of the 'conditioned fear response'. *Journal of Abnormal and Social Psychology, 34,* 221–225.

Erickson, S. K. (2010). Blaming the brain. *Minnesota Journal of Law, Science & Technology, 11,* 27–77.

Every-Palmer, S., & Howick, J. (2014). How evidence-based medicine is failing due to biased trials and selective publication. *Journal of Evaluation in Clinical Practice, 20,* 908–914.

FeldmanHall, O., Dalgleish, T., Evan, D., Navrady, L., Tedeschi, L., & Mobbs, D. (2016). Moral chivalry: Gender and harm sensitivity predict costly altruism. *Social Psychological and Personality Science, 7,* 542–551.

Ferguson, C. J. (2007a). Evidence for publication bias in video game violence effects literature: A meta-analytic review. *Aggression and Violent Behavior, 12,* 470–482.

Ferguson, C. J. (2007b). The good, the bad and the ugly: A meta-analytic review of positive and negative effects of violent video games. *Psychiatric Quarterly, 78,* 309–316.

Ferguson, C. J. (2008). Violent video games: How hysteria and pseudoscience created a phantom public health crisis. *Paradigm, 12,* 12–13, 22.

Ferguson, C. J. (2013). Violent video games and the Supreme Court: Lessons for the scientific community in the wake of Brown v. Entertainment Merchants Association. *American Psychologist, 68,* 57–74.

Ferguson, C. J. (2015a). Do angry birds make for angry children? A meta-analysis of video game influences on children's and adolescents' aggression, mental health, prosocial behavior, and academic performance. *Perspectives on Psychological Science, 10*, 646–666.

Ferguson, C. J. (2015b). Everybody knows psychology is not a real science. *American Psychologist, 70*, 527–542.

Ferguson, C. J., & Dyck, D. (2012). Paradigm change in aggression research: The time has come to retire the General Aggression Model. *Aggression and Violent Behavior, 17*, 220–228.

Ferguson, C. J., & Kilburn, J. (2009). The public health risk of media violence: A meta-analytic review. *The Journal of Pediatrics, 154*, 759–763.

Ferguson, C. J., & Konijn, E. A. (2015). She said/he said: A peaceful debate on video game violence. *Psychology of Popular Media Culture, 4*, 397–411.

Ferguson, C. J., & Rueda, S. M. (2009). Examining the validity of the Modified Taylor Competitive Reaction Time Test of aggression. *Journal of Experimental Criminology, 5*, 121–137.

Ferguson, C. J., Rueda, S. M., Cruz, A. M., Ferguson, D. E., Fritz, S., & Smith, S. M. (2008). Violent video games and aggression: Causal relationship or byproduct of family violence and intrinsic violence motivation? *Criminal Justice and Behavior, 35*, 311–332.

Fernandez-Duque, D., Evans, J., Christian, C., & Hodges, S. D. (2015). Superfluous neuroscience information makes explanations of psychological phenomena more appealing. *Journal of Cognitive Neuroscience, 27*, 926–944.

Field, A. P. (2005). *Discovering statistics using SPSS* (2nd edn.). Thousand Oaks, CA: Sage.

Field, A. P., & Nightingale, Z. C. (2009). Test of time: What if little Albert had escaped? *Clinical Child Psychology and Psychiatry, 14*, 311–319.

Fischer, B. A. (2006). On rethinking the psychology of tyranny: The BBC prison study. *British Journal of Social Psychology, 45*, 47–53.

Fiske, S. T. (2010). Venus and Mars or down to Earth: Stereotypes and realities of gender differences. *Perspectives on Psychological Science, 5*, 688–692.

Fitzgerald, F. S. (2008). *The curious case of Benjamin Button and other jazz age stories.* New York: Penguin.

Fitzpatrick, M., Carr, A., Dooley, B., Flanagan-Howard, R., Flanagan, E., Tierney, K., ... & Egan, J. (2010). Profiles of adult survivors of severe sexual, physical and emotional institutional abuse in Ireland. *Child Abuse Review, 19*, 387–404.

Fleeson, W. (2004). Moving personality beyond the person-situation debate: The challenge and the opportunity of within-person variability. *Current Directions in Psychological Science, 13*, 83–87.

Forer, B. R. (1949). The fallacy of personal validation: A classroom demonstration of gullibility. *Journal of Abnormal and Social Psychology, 44*, 118–123.

Foroughi, C. K., Monfort, S. S., Paczynski, M., McKnight, P. E., & Greenwood, P. M. (2016). Placebo effects in cognitive training. *Proceedings of the National Academy of Sciences, 113*, 7470–7474.

Fountoulakis, K. N., McIntyre, R. S., & Carvalho, A. F. (2015). From randomized controlled trials of antidepressant drugs to the meta-analytic synthesis of evidence: Methodological aspects lead to discrepant findings. *Current Neuropharmacology, 13*, 605–615.

Fournier, J. C., DeRubeis, R. J., Hollon, S. D., Dimidjian, S., Amsterdam, J. D., Shelton, & R. C., Fawcett, J. (2010). Antidepressant drug effects and depression severity: A patient-level meta-analysis. *JAMA*, *303*, 47–53.

Fox, N. A., Calkins, S. D., & Bell, M. A. (1994). Neural plasticity and development in the first two years of life: Evidence from cognitive and socioemotional domains of research. *Development and Psychopathology*, *6*, 677–696.

Frances, A. (2013). *Saving normal: An insider's revolt against out-of-control psychiatric diagnosis, DSM-5, big pharma, and the medicalization of ordinary life*. New York: HarperCollins.

Franklin, M. S., Baumgart, S. L., & Schooler, J. W. (2014). Future directions in precognition research: More research can bridge the gap between skeptics and proponents. *Frontiers in Psychology*, *5*, 1–4.

Freedland, K. E., Mohr, D. C., Davidson, K. W., & Schwartz, J. E. (2011). Usual and unusual care: Existing practice control groups in randomized controlled trials of behavioral interventions. *Psychosomatic Medicine*, *73*, 323–335.

Freyd, J. J. (1994). Betrayal-trauma: Traumatic amnesia as an adaptive response to childhood abuse. *Ethics & Behavior*, *4*, 307–329.

Freyd, J. J., DePrince, A. P., & Gleaves, D. H. (2007). The state of betrayal trauma theory: Reply to McNally-conceptual issues and future directions. *Memory*, *15*, 295–311.

Fridlund, A. J., Beck, H. P., Goldie, W. D., & Irons, G. (2012). Little Albert: A neurologically impaired child. *History of Psychology*, *15*, 302–327.

Friesdorf, R., Conway, P., & Gawronski, B. (2015). Gender differences in responses to moral dilemmas: A process dissociation analysis. *Personality and Social Psychology Bulletin*, *41*, 696–713.

Fromm, E. (1973). *The anatomy of human destructiveness*. New York, NY: Henry Holt & Company.

Galak, J., LeBoeuf, R. A., Nelson, L. D., & Simmons, J. P. (2012). Correcting the past: Failures to replicate psi. *Journal of Personality and Social Psychology*, *103*, 933–948.

Galambos, N. L., Barker, E. T., & Almeida, D. M. (2003). Parents do matter: Trajectories of change in externalizing and internalizing problems in early adolescence. *Child Development*, *74*, 578–594.

Gallup. (2001, June 8). *Americans' belief in psychic and paranormal phenomena is up over last decade*. Retrieved from www.gallup.com/poll/4483/americans-belief-psychic-paranormal-phenomena-over-last-decade.aspx?version=print

Gao, Y., Raine, A., Venables, P. H., Dawson, M. E., & Mednick, S. A. (2010). Association of poor childhood fear conditioning and adult crime. *American Journal of Psychiatry*, *167*, 56–60.

Gardner, H. (2006). *Five minds for the future*. Boston, MA: Harvard Business School Press.

Garry, M., Manning, C. G., Loftus, E. F., & Sherman, S. J. (1996). Imagination inflation: Imagining a childhood event inflates confidence that it occurred. *Psychonomic Bulletin & Review*, *3*, 208–214.

Gaultney, J. F., & Peach, H. D. (2016). *How to do research: 15 labs for the social and behavioral sciences*. Thousand Oaks, CA: Sage.

Gauvrit, N. (2011). Precognition or pathological science? An analysis of Daryl Bem's controversial "feeling the future" paper. *Skeptic Magazine*, *16*, 54–57.

Gazzaniga, M. S., Ivry, R. B., & Mangun, G. R. (2002). *Cognitive neuroscience: The biology of the mind* (2nd edn.). New York: W. W. Norton & Company.

Gilbert, S. J. (1981). Another look at the Milgram obedience studies: The role of the gradated series of shocks. *Personality and Social Psychology Bulletin, 7,* 690–695.

Gilligan, C. (1982). *In a different voice: Psychological theory and women's development.* Cambridge, MA: Harvard University Press.

Gilovich, T., Vallone, R., & Tversky, A. (1985). The hot hand in basketball: On the misperception of random sequences. *Cognitive Psychology, 17,* 295–314.

Goff, L. M., & Roediger, H. L. (1998). Imagination inflation for action events: Repeated imaginings lead to illusory recollections. *Memory & Cognition, 26,* 20–33.

Goldstein, E., & Farmer, K. (1993). *True stories of false memories.* Boca Raton, FL: Upton Books.

Goldstein, E., & Farmer, K. (1994). *Confabulations: Creating false memories-destroying families.* Boca Raton, FL: Upton Books.

Gottlieb, G. (2007). Probabilistic epigenesist. *Developmental Science, 10,* 1–11.

Gray, J. (1992). *Men are from Mars, women are from Venus: A practical guide for improving communication and getting what you want in your relationship.* New York: HarperCollins.

Green, C. S., & Seitz, A. R. (2015). The impacts of video games on cognition (and how the government can guide the industry). *Policy Insights from the Behavioral and Brain Sciences, 2,* 101–110.

Greenberg, G. (2013). *The book of woe: The DSM and the unmaking of psychiatry.* New York: Blue Rider Press.

Greeno, C. G., & Maccoby, E. E. (1986). How different is the "different voice"? *Signs, 11,* 310–316.

Greenough, W. T., Black, J. E., & Wallace, C. S. (1987). Experience and brain development. *Child Development, 58,* 539–559.

Griggs, R. A. (2014). The continuing saga of little Albert in introductory psychology textbooks. *Teaching of Psychology, 41,* 309–317.

Griggs, R. A., & Whitehead, G. I. (2014). Coverage of the Stanford prison experiment in introductory social psychology textbooks. *Teaching of Psychology, 41,* 318–324.

Gunnell, B. (2004, September 6). The happiness industry. *New Statesman.* Retrieved from www.newstatesman.com

Haidt, J. (2001). The emotional dog and its rational trail: A social intuitionist approach to moral judgment. *Psychological Review, 108,* 814–834.

Haidt, J. (2013). Moral psychology for the twenty-first century. *Journal of Moral Education, 42,* 281–297.

Haig, B. D. (2009). Inference to the best explanation: A neglected approach to theory appraisal in psychology. *American Journal of Psychology, 122,* 219–234.

Hair, E. C., Moore, K. A., Garrett, S. B., Ling, T., & Cleveland, K. (2008). The continued importance of quality parent-adolescent relationships during late adolescence. *Journal of Research on Adolescence, 18,* 187–200.

Hall, H. (2016). "It worked for my Aunt Tillie" is not enough. *Skeptic Magazine, 20,* 7–8.

Halpern, D. F., et al. (2011). The pseudoscience of single-sex schooling. *Science, 333,* 1706–1707.

Haney, C., Banks, C., & Zimbardo, P. (1973). Interpersonal dynamics in a simulated prison. *International Journal of Criminology and Penology, 1*, 69–97.

Haney, C., & Zimbardo, P. G. (2009). Persistent dispositionalism in interactionist clothing: Fundamental attribution error in explaining prison abuse. *Personality and Social Psychology Bulletin, 35*, 807–814.

Harmon-Jones, E., Amodio, D. M., & Zinner, L. R. (2007). Social psychological methods in emotion elicitation. In J. A. Coan, & J. J. B. Allen (eds.), *Handbook of emotion elicitation and assessment* (pp. 91–105). New York: Oxford University Press.

Harris, B. (1979). Whatever happened to little Albert? *American Psychologist, 34*, 151–160.

Harris, B. (2011). Letting go of little Albert: Disciplinary memory, history, and the uses of myth. *Journal of the History of the Behavioral Sciences, 47*, 1–17.

Harris, J. R. (1995). Where is the child's environment? A group socialization theory of development. *Psychological Review, 102*, 458–489.

Harris, J. R. (2009). *The nurture assumption: Why children turn out the way they do, revised and updated*. New York: Free Press.

Hasan, Y., Bégue, L., Scharkow, M., & Bushman, B. J. (2013). The more you play, the more aggressive you become: A long-term experimental study of cumulative violent video game effects on hostile expectations and aggressive behavior. *Journal of Experimental Social Psychology, 49*, 224–227.

Haslam, S. A., & McGarty, C. (2014). *Research methods and statistics in psychology* (2nd edn). Thousand Oaks, CA: Sage.

Haslam, S. A., & Reicher, S. (2007). Beyond the banality of evil: Three dynamics of an interactionist social psychology of tyranny. *Personality and Social Psychology Bulletin, 33*, 615–622.

Haslam, S. A., Reicher, S., & Millard, K. (2015). Shock treatment: Using immersive digital realism to restage and re-examine Milgram's "obedience to authority" research. *PLoS ONE, 10*, 1–10.

Haynes, J. D. (2011). Decoding and predicting intentions. *Annals of the New York Academy of Sciences, 1224*, 9–21.

Heeger, D. J., & Ress, D. (2002). What does fMRI tell us about neuronal activity? *Nature Reviews, 3*, 142–151.

Henry, J. P. (2008). College sophomores in the laboratory redux: Influences of a narrow data base on social psychology's view of the nature of prejudice. *Psychological Inquiry, 19*, 49–71.

Herbert, J. D., Lilienfeld, S. O., Lohr, J. M., Montgomery, R. W., O'Donohue, W. T., Rosen, G. M., & Tolin, D. F. (2000). Science and pseudoscience in the development of eye movement desensitization and reprocessing. *Implications for Clinical Psychology, 20*, 945–971.

Hillman, S. J., Zeeman, S. I., Tilburg, C. E., & List, H. E. (2016). My attitudes toward science (MATS): The development of a multidimensional instrument measuring students' science attitudes. *Learning Environments Research, 19*, 203–219.

Hobbs, S. (2010). Little Albert: Gone but not forgotten. *History and Philosophy of Psychology, 12*, 79–83.

Hoffrage, U., Hertwig, R., & Gigerenzer, G. (2000). Hindsight bias: A by-product of knowledge-updating? *Journal of Experimental Psychology: Learning, Memory, and Cognition, 26*, 566–581.

Hubel, D. H., & Wiesel, T. N. (1970). The period of susceptibility to the physiological effects of unilateral eye closure in kittens. *The Journal of Physiology, 206*, 419–436.

Hunt, M. (1993). *The story of psychology.* New York: Anchor Books.

Hunt, E., & Carlson, J. (2007). Considerations relating to the study of group differences in intelligence. *Perspectives on Psychological Science, 2*, 194–213.

Hunter, M. (1982). *Mastery learning.* El Segundo, CA: Tip Publication.

Hyde, J. S. (2005). The gender similarities hypothesis. *American Psychologist, 60*, 581–592.

Imhoff, R. (2016). Zeroing in on the effect of the schizophrenia label on stigmatizing attitudes: A large-scale study. *Schizophrenia Bulletin, 42*, 456–463.

Ioannidis, J. P. (2008). Effectiveness of antidepressants: An evidence myth constructed from a thousand randomized trials? *Philosophy, Ethics, and Humanities in Medicine, 3*, 1–9.

Jaccard, J, & Becker, M. (2002). *Statistics for the behavioral science* (4th edn.). Belmont, CA: Wadsworth.

Jaeggi, S. M., Buschkuehl, M., Jonides, J., & Shah, P. (2011). Short-and long-term benefits of cognitive training. *Proceedings of the National Academy of Sciences, 108*, 10081–10086.

Jaeggi, S. M., Buschkuehl, M., Shah, P., & Jonides, J. (2014). The role of individual differences in cognitive training and transfer. *Memory & Cognition, 42*, 464–480.

Jaffee, S., & Hyde, J. S. (2000). Gender differences in moral orientation: A meta-analysis. *Psychological Bulletin, 126*, 703–726.

Jarrett, C. (2008). Foundations of sand? *The Psychologist, 21*, 756–759.

Jason Heyward. (n. d.). In *Baseball reference.* Retrieved from www.baseball-reference.com/players/h/heywaja01.shtml

Johnson, M. H. (2001). Functional brain development during infancy. In J. G. Bremner, & A. Fogel (eds.), *Blackwell handbook of infant development* (pp. 169–190). Oxford: Blackwell.

Jones, M. C. (1924). A laboratory study of fear: The case of Peter. *Pedagogical Seminary, 31*, 308–315.

Joyce, N., & Baker, D. B. (April, 2008). ESPecially intriguing. *Monitor on Psychology, 39.* Retrieved from www.apa.org/monitor/2008/04/zener.aspx

Kagan, J. (1998, November/December). A parent's influence is peerless. *Harvard Education Letter, 14.* Retrieved from http://hepg.org/hel-home/issues/14_6/helarticle/a-parent-s-influence-is-peerless_340

Kaptchuk, T. J., Friedlander, E., Kelley, J. M., Sanchez, M. N., Kokkotou, E., Singer, J. P., ... & Lembo, A. J. (2010). Placebos without deception: A randomized controlled trial in Irritable Bowel Syndrome. *PLoS ONE, 5*, 1–7.

Kelly, R. E., Cohen, L. J., & Semple, R. J., Bialer, P., Lau, A., Bodenheimer, A., ... & Galynker, I. I. (2006). Relationship between drug company funding and outcomes of clinical psychiatric research. *Psychological Medicine, 36*, 1647–1656.

Kerber, L., Greeno, G. C., Maccoby, E. E., Luria, Z., & Stack, C. (1986). On in a different voice: An interdisciplinary forum. *Signs, 11*, 304–324.

Kesey, K. (1962). *One flew over the cuckoo's nest.* New York: Viking.

Kida, T. (2006). *Don't believe everything you think: The 6 basic mistakes we make in thinking.* Amherst, NY: Prometheus Books.

Kilpatrick, W. (1992). *Why Johnny can't tell right from wrong and what we can do about it.* New York: Touchstone.

Kirsch, I. (2005). Placebo psychotherapy: Synonym or oxymoron? *Journal of Clinical Psychology, 61,* 791–803.

Kirsch, I. (2010). *The emperor's new drugs: Exploding the antidepressant myth.* New York: Basic Books.

Kirsch, I. (2014). Antidepressants and the placebo effect. *Zeitschrift für Psychologie, 222,* 128–134.

Kirsch, I. (2016). The placebo effect in the treatment of depression. *Verhaltenstherapie, 26,* 1–6.

Kirsch, I., Deacon, B. J., Huedo-Medina, T. B., Scoboria, A., Moore, T. J., & Johnson, B. T. (2008). Initial severity and antidepressant benefits: A meta-analysis of data submitted to the Food and Drug Administration. *PLoS Medicine, 5,* 260–268.

Kirsch, I., & Sapirstein, G. (1998). Listening to Prozac but hearing placebo: A meta-analysis of antidepressant medication. *Prevention and Treatment, 1,* article 0002a.

Kirsch, I., & Weixel, L. J. (1998). Double-blind versus deceptive administration of a placebo. *Behavioral Neuroscience, 102,* 319–323.

Kirschner, P. A., Sweller, J., & Clark, R. E. (2006). Why minimal guidance during instruction does not work: An analysis of the failure of constructivist, discovery, problem-based, experiential, and inquiry-based teaching. *Educational Psychologist, 41,* 75–86.

Kohlberg, L. (1975). Moral education for a society in moral transition. *Educational Leadership, 33,* 46–54.

Kohlberg, L. (1976). Moral stages and moralization: The cognitive developmental approach. In T. Lickona (Ed.), *Moral development and behavior: Theory, research, and social issues* (pp. 31–53). New York: Holt, Rinehart and Winston.

Le Texier, T. (in press). Debunking the Stanford prison experiment. *American Psychologist.*

Luckona (ed.), *Moral development and behavior: Theory, research, and social issues.* New York: Holt.

Kohlberg, L., & Hersh, R. H. (1977). Moral development: A review of the theory. *Theory into Practice, 16,* 53–59.

Konijn, E. A., Nije Bijvank, M., & Bushman, B. J. (2007). I wish I were a warrior: The role of wishful identification in the effects of violent video games on aggression in adolescent boys. *Developmental Psychology, 43,* 1038–1044.

Kravitz, R. L., Epstein, R., Feldman, M. D., Franz, C. E., Azari, R., Wilkes, M. S., ... & Franks, P. (2005). Influence of patients' requests for directly advertised antidepressants: A randomized controlled trial. *JAMA, 293,* 1–15.

Kuhl, J., & Koole, S. L. (2004). Workings of the will: A functional approach. In J. Greenberg, S. L. Koole, & T. Pyszczynski (eds.), *Handbook of experimental existential psychology* (pp. 411–430). New York: The Guilford Press.

Kutchins, H., & Kirk, S. A. (1997). *Making us crazy: DSM: The psychiatric bible and the creation of mental disorders.* New York: The Free Press.

Lacasse, J. R., & Leo, J. (2005). Serotonin and depression: A disconnect between the advertisements and the scientific literature. *PLoS Medicine, 2,* 1211–1216.

Landers, R. N., & Behrend, T. S. (2015). An inconvenient truth: Arbitrary distinctions between organizational, Mechanical Turk, and other convenience samples. *Industrial and Organizational Psychology, 8,* 142–164.

Langer, E. J. (1975). The illusion of control. *Journal of Personality and Social Psychology*, *32*, 311–328.

Langer, E. J., & Abelson, R. P. (1974). A patient by any other name …: Clinician group difference in labeling bias. *Journal of Consulting and Clinical Psychology*, *42*, 4–9.

Lau, H. C., Rogers, R. D., Haggard, P., & Passingham, R. E. (2004). Attention to intention. *Science*, *303*, 1208–1210.

Lenroot, R. K., & Giedd, J. N. (2007). The structural development of the human brain as measured longitudinally with magnetic resonance imaging. In D. Coch, K. W. Kischer, & G. Dawson (eds.), *Human behavior, learning, and the developing brain: Typical development* (pp. 50–73). New York: Guilford.

Leo, J., & Lacasse, J. R. (2007). The media and the chemical imbalance theory of depression. *Society*, *45*, 35–45.

Lerner, J. S., Li, Y., Valdesolo, P., Kassam, K. S. 2015. Emotion and decision making. *Annual Review of Psychology*, *66*, 799–823.

Le Texier, T. (2018). *Histoire d'un mensonge: enquête sur l'expérience de Stanford*. Paris: La Découverte.

Levy, D. A. (2010). *Tools of critical thinking: Metathoughts for psychology* (2nd edn.). Long Grove, IL: Waveland Press.

Libet, B. (1985). Unconscious cerebral initiative and the role of conscious will in voluntary action. *The Behavioral and Brain Sciences*, *8*, 529–566.

Libet, B. (1999). Do we have free will? *Journal of Consciousness Studies*, *6*, 47–57.

Lieberman, J. D., Solomon, S., Greenberg, J., & McGregor, H. A. (1999). A hot new way to measure aggression: Hot sauce allocation. *Aggressive Behavior*, *25*, 331–348.

Lilienfeld, S. O., Lynn, S. J., Ruscio, J., & Beyerstein, B. L. (2010). *Great myths of popular psychology: Shattering widespread misconceptions about human behavior*. West Sussex: Wiley-Blackwell.

Lilienfeld, S. O., Sauvigne, K. C., Lynn, S. J., Cautin, R. L., Latzman, R. D., & Waldman, I. D. (2015). Fifty psychological and psychiatric terms to avoid: A list of inaccurate, misleading, misused, ambiguous, and logically confused words and phrases. *Frontiers in Psychology*, *6*, 1–15.

Lindblom, K. M. & Gray, M. J. (2010). Relationship closeness and trauma narrative detail: A critical analysis of betrayal trauma theory. *Applied Cognitive Psychology*, *24*, 1–19.

Link, B. G., & Phelan, J. C. (2013). Labeling and stigma. In C. Aneshensel, J. Phelan, & A. Bierman (eds.), *Handbook of the Sociology of Mental Health* (2nd edn., pp. 525–541). New York: Springer.

Locke, E. A. (2009). It's time we brought introspection out of the closet. *Perspectives on Psychological Science*, *4*, 24–25.

Loehlin, J C. (1997). A test of J. R. Harris's theory of peer influences on personality. *Journal of Personality and Social Psychology*, *72*, 1197–1201.

Loftus, E. F. (1993). The reality of repressed memories. *American Psychologist*, *48*, 518–537.

Loftus, E. F. (2005). Planting misinformation in the human mind: A 30-year investigation of the malleability of memory. *Learning & Memory*, *12*, 361–366.

Loftus, E. F., & Davis, D. (2006). Recovered memories. *Annual Review of Clinical Psychology, 2,* 469–498.

Loftus, E. F. & Ketcham, K. (1994). *The myth of repressed memory.* New York: St. Martin's Press.

Loftus, E. F., & Loftus, G. R. (1980). On the permanence of stored information in the human brain. *American Psychologist, 35,* 108–120.

Loftus, E. F., Miller, D. G., & Burns, H. J. (1978). Semantic integration of verbal information into a visual memory. *Journal of Experimental Psychology: Human Learning and Memory, 4,* 19–31.

Loftus, E. F., & Pickrell, J. E. (1995). The formation of false memories. *Psychiatric Annals, 25,* 720–725.

Lorant-Royer, S., Munch, C., Mesclé, H., & Lieury, A. (2010). Kawashima vs "Super Mario"! Should a game be serious in order to stimulate cognitive aptitudes? *Revue Européenne de Psychologie Appliquée/European Review of Applied Psychology, 60,* 221–232.

Lord, C. G., Ross, L., & Lepper, M. R. (1979). Biased assimilation and attitude polarization: The effects of prior theories on subsequently considered evidence. *Journal of Personality and Social Psychology, 37,* 2098–2109.

Lovibond, S. H., Mithiran, X., & Adams, W. G. (1979). The effects of three experimental prison environments on the behavior of non-convict volunteer subjects. *Australian Psychologist, 14,* 273–287.

Lull, R. B., & Bushman, B. J. (2016). Immersed in violence: Presence mediates the effect of 3D violent video gameplay on angry feelings. *Psychology of Popular Media Culture, 5,* 133–144.

Luria, Z. (1986). A methodological critique. *Signs, 11,* 316–321.

Lynn S. J., Evans J., Laurence J. R., & Lilienfeld, S. O. (2015). What do people believe about memory? Implications for the science and pseudoscience of clinical practice. *Canadian Journal of Psychiatry, 60,* 541–547.

Lynn, S. J., Lilienfeld, S. O., Merckelbach, H., Giesbrecht, T., & van der Kloet, D. (2012). Dissociation and dissociative disorders: Challenging conventional wisdom. *Current Directions in Psychological Science, 21,* 48–53.

Lynn, S. J., Lilienfeld, S. O., Merckelbach, H., Giesbrecht, T., McNally, R. J., Loftus, E. F., Bruck, M., Garry, M., & Malaktaris, A. (2014). The trauma model of dissociation: Inconvenient truths and stubborn fictions. Comment on Dalenberg et al. (2012). *Psychological Bulletin, 140,* 896–910.

Maguire, E. A., Gadian, D. G., Johnsrude, I. S., Good, C. D., Ashburner, J., Frackowiak, R. S., & Frith, C. D. (2000). Navigation-related structural change in the hippocampi of taxi drivers. *Proceedings of the National Academy of Sciences, 97,* 4398–4403.

Malmquist, C. P. (1986). Children who witness parental murder: Posttraumatic aspects. *Journal of American Academy of Child Psychiatry, 25,* 320–325.

Marsh, E. J., & Tversky, B. (2004). Spinning the stories of our lives. *Applied Cognitive Psychology, 18,* 491–503.

Martinez, A., Piff, P. K., Mendoza-Denton, R., & Hinshaw, S. (2011). The power of a label: Mental illness diagnoses, ascribed humanity, and social rejection. *Journal of Social and Clinical Psychology, 30,* 1–23.

McCabe, D. P., & Castel, A. D. (2008). Seeing is believing: The effect of brain images in judgements of scientific reasoning. *Cognition, 107,* 343–352.

McNally, R. J. (2007). Betrayal trauma theory: A critical appraisal. *Memory, 15,* 280–294.

McNally, R. J., Ristuccia, C. S., & Perlman, C. A. (2005). Forgetting of trauma cues in adults reporting continuous or recovered memories of childhood sexual abuse. *Psychological Science, 16,* 336–340.

Mead, S. (2007, April). Million dollars babies: Why infants can't be hardwired for success. *Education Sector.* Retrieved from www.educationsector.org

Mednick, M. T. (1989). On the politics of psychological constructs: Stop the bandwagon, I want to get off. *American Psychologist, 44,* 1118–1123.

Meehl, P. E. (1990). Why summaries of research on psychological theories are often uninterpretable. *Psychological Reports, 66,* 195–244.

Mehr, S. A. (2015). Miscommunication of science: Music cognition research in the popular press. *Frontiers in Psychology, 6,* 1–3.

Mehr, S. A., Schachner, A., Katz, R. C., & Spelke, E. S. (2013). Two randomized trials provide no consistent evidence for nonmusical cognitive benefits of brief preschool music enrichment. *PLoS ONE, 8,* 1–12.

Mendel, R., Traut-Mattausch, E., Jonas, E., Leucht, S., Kane, J. M., Maino, K., ... & Hamann, J. (2011). Confirmation bias: Why psychiatrists stick to wrong preliminary diagnoses. *Psychological Medicine, 41,* 2651–2659.

Menzies, R. G., & Clarke, J. C. (1995). The etiology of phobias: A nonassociative account. *Clinical Psychology Review, 15,* 23–48.

Meredith, R. (1996, May 10). Parents convicted for a youth's misconduct. *New York Times.* Retrieved from www.nytimes.com/1996/05/10/us/parents-convicted-for-a-youth-s-misconduct.html

Milevsky, A., Schlechter, M., Netter, S., & Keehn, D. (2007). Maternal and paternal parenting styles in adolescents: Associations with self-esteem, depression and life-satisfaction. *Journal of Child and Family Studies, 16,* 39–47.

Milgram, S. (1974). *Obedience to authority: An experimental view.* New York: HarperCollins.

Miller, G. A. (2010). Mistreating psychology in the decades of the brain. *Perspectives on Psychological Science, 5,* 716–743.

Miller, J., & Schwarz, W. (2014). Brain signals do not demonstrate unconscious decision making: An interpretation based on graded conscious awareness. *Consciousness and Cognition, 24,* 12–21.

Millon, T. (1975). Reflections of Rosenhan's "On being sane in insane places." *Journal of Abnormal Psychology, 84,* 456–461.

Mineka, S., Davidson, M., Cook, M., & Keir, R. (1984). Observational conditioning of snake fear in Rhesus monkeys. *Journal of Abnormal Psychology, 93,* 355–372.

Mischel, W. (1968). *Personality and assessment.* London: Wiley.

Moghaddam, M. F., Assareh, M., Heidaripoor, A., Eslami Rad, R., & Pishjoo, M. (2013). The study comparing parenting styles of children with ADHD and normal children. *Archives of Psychiatry and Psychotherapy, 15,* 45–49.

Morling, B. (2014, April). Guides your students to become better research consumers. *APS Observer.* Retrieved from www.psychologicalscience.org/observer/teach-your-students-to-be-better-consumers#.WMgbeG_yu00

Moss, M., Hewitt, S., Moss, L., & Wesnes, K. (2008). Modulation of cognitive performance and mood by aromas of peppermint and ylang-ylang. *International Journal of Neuroscience, 118,* 59–77.

Moulton, S. T., Kosslyn, S. M. (2008). Using neuroimaging to resolve the psi debate. *Journal of Cognitive Neuroscience, 20,* 182–192.

Muris, P., & Field, A. P. (2008). Distorted cognition and pathological anxiety in children and adolescents. *Cognition and Emotion, 22,* 395–421.

Muris, P., Merckelbach, H., de Jong, P. J., & Ollendick, T. H. (2002). The etiology of specific fears and phobias in children: A critique of the non-associative account. *Behaviour Research and Therapy, 40,* 185–195.

Muris, P., van Zwol, L., Huijding, J., & Mayer, B. (2010). Mom told me scary things about this animal: Parents installing fear beliefs in their children via the verbal information pathway. *Behavior Research and Therapy, 48,* 341–346.

National Alliance on Mental Illness (NAMI) – Illinois. (2017, November 10). Retrieved from http://il.nami.org/facts.html

Nelson, H. (2005). AR 15-6 investigation – Allegations of detainee abuse at Abu Ghraib. In K. J. Greenberg, & J. L. Dratel (2005) *The torture papers: The road to Abu Ghraib* (pp. 448–450). New York: Cambridge University Press.

Neuroskeptic. (2012). The nine circles of scientific hell. *Perspectives on Psychological Science, 7,* 643–644.

Newby, J. (Producer). (2010). False memories [Television series episode]. In I. Arnott (Executive producer), *Catalyst.* Sydney: Australian Broadcasting Corporation.

Nichols, A. L., & Maner, J. K. (2008). The good-subject effect: Investigating participant demand characteristics. *Journal of General Psychology, 135,* 151–165.

Nickerson, R. S. (1998). Confirmation bias: A ubiquitous phenomenon in many guises. *Review of General Psychology, 2,* 175–220.

Nicodemo, A., & Petronio, L. (2018, February). Schools are safer than they were in the 90s, and school shootings are not more common than they used to be, researchers say. *News@Northeastern.* Retrieved from https://news.northeastern.edu/2018/02/26/schools-are-still-one-of-the-safest-places-for-children-researcher-says/

Nielsen, J. A., Zielinski, B. A., Ferguson, M. A., Lainhart, J. A., & Anderson, J. S. (2013). An evaluation of the left-brain vs. right-brain hypothesis with resting state functional connectivity magnetic resonance imaging. *PLOS ONE, 8,* 1–11.

Nutt, D. J., & Malizia, A. L. (2008). Why does the world have such a "down" on antidepressants? *Journal of Psychopharmacology, 22,* 223–226.

Ofri, D. (2011, October 20). When doing nothing is the best medicine. *New York Times.* Retrieved from www.nytimes.com

Olatunji, B. O., Parker, L. M., Lohr, J. M. (2005). Pseudoscience in contemporary psychology: Professional issues and implications. *The Scientific Review of Mental Health Practice, 4,* 19–36.

Ollendick, T. H., & Muris, P. (2015). The scientific legacy of little Hans and little Albert: Future directions for research on specific phobias in youth. *Journal of Clinical Child & Adolescent Psychology, 44,* 689–706.

Orne, M. T. (1962). On the social psychology of the psychological experiment: With particular reference to demand characteristics and their implications. *American Psychologist, 17,* 776–783.

Orne, M. T., & Holland, C. H. (1968). On the ecological validity of laboratory deceptions. *International Journal of Psychiatry, 6*, 282–293.

Oswald, M. E., & Grosjean, S. (2004). Confirmation bias. In R. F. Pohl (ed.), *Cognitive illusions: A handbook on fallacies and biases in thinking, judgment and memory* (pp. 79–96). New York: Psychology Press.

Owen, A. M., Hampshire, A., Grahn, J. A., Stenton, R., Dajani, S., Burns, A. S., ... & Ballard, C. G. (2010). Putting brain training to the test. *Nature, 465*, 775–778.

Packer, D. J. (2008). Identifying systematic disobedience in Milgram's obedience experiments: A meta-analytic review. *Perspectives on Psychological Science, 3*, 301–304.

Paddock, J. R., Noel, M., Terronova, S., Eber, H. W., Manning, C. G., & Loftus, E. F. (1999). Imagination inflation and the perils of guided visualization. *Journal of Psychology, 133*, 581–595.

Papanicolaou, A. C. (2017). The claim "the will is determined" is not based on evidence. *Psychology of Consciousness: Theory, Research, and Practice, 4*, 334–336.

Passingham, R. (2009). How good is the macaque monkey model of the human brain? *Current Opinion in Neurobiology, 19*, 6–11.

Patihis, L., Ho, L. Y., Tingen, I. W., Lilienfeld, S. O., & Loftus, E. F. (2014). Are the "memory wars" over? A scientist-practitioner gap in beliefs about repressed memory. *Psychological Science, 25*, 519–530.

Paul, D. B., & Blumenthal, A. L., (1989). On the trail of little Albert (1989). *The Psychological Record, 39*, 547–553.

Pendergrast, M. (1996). *Victims of memory: Sex abuse accusations and shattered lives* (2nd edn.). Hinesburg, VT: Upper Access.

Perry, G. (2012). *Behind the shock machine: The untold story of the notorious Milgram psychology experiments*. New York: The New Press.

Plimpton, G. (1958). The Art of Fiction XXI: Ernest Hemingway. *Paris Review, 18*, 60–89.

Plomin, R., DeFries, J. C., Knopik, V. S., & Neiderhiser, J. M. (2013). *Behavior genetics* (6th edn.). New York: Worth.

Podsakoff, P. M., Mackenzie, S. B., Lee, J. Y., & Podsakoff, N. P. (2003). Common method biases in behavioral research: A critical review of the literature and recommended remedies. *Journal of Applied Psychology, 88*, 879–903.

Pope, K. S., & Vasquez, M. (2005). *How to survive and thrive as a therapist: Information, ideas, and resources for psychologists in practice*. Washington, DC: American Psychological Association.

Porto, P. R., Oliveira, L., Mari, J., Volchan, E., Figueira, I., & Ventura, P. (2009). Does cognitive behavioral therapy change the brain? A systematic review of neuroimaging in anxiety disorders. *The Journal of Neuropsychiatry and Clinical Neurosciences, 21*, 114–125.

Poulton, R., Davies, S., Menzies, R. G., Langley, J. D., & Silva, P A. (1998). Evidence for a non-associative model of the acquisition of a fear of heights. *Behaviour Research and Therapy, 36*, 537–544.

Pound, N., & Price, M. E. (2013). Human sex differences: Distributions overlap but the tails sometimes tell a tale. *Psychological Inquiry, 24*, 224–230.

Powell, R. A., Digdon, N., Harris, B., & Smithson, C. (2014). Correcting the record on Watson, Rayner, and little Albert: Albert Barger as "psychology's lost boy". *American Psychologist, 69,* 600–611.

Pratkanis, A. R. (1995). How to sell a pseudoscience. *Skeptical Inquirer, 19,* 19–25.

Pratt, M. W., Skoe, E. E., & Arnold, M. L. (2004). Care reasoning development and family socialization patterns in later adolescence: A longitudinal analysis. *International Journal of Behavioral Development, 28,* 139–147.

Pratkanis, A. R. (2017). The (partial but) real crisis in social psychology: A social influence analysis of the causes and solutions. In S. O. Lilienfeld & I. D. Waldman (eds.), *Psychological science under scrutiny: Recent challenges and proposed solutions* (pp. 141–163). West Sussex: Wiley.

Preuss, T. M. (2000). What's human about the human brain? In M. S. Gazzaniga (ed.), *The new cognitive neurosciences* (2nd edn). Cambridge, MA: MIT Press.

Preuss, T. M., & Robert, J. S. (2014). Animal models of the human brain: Repairing the paradigm. In M. S. Gazzaniga, & G. Mangun (eds.), *The cognitive neurosciences* (5th edn). Cambridge, MA: MIT Press.

Pronin, E., Lin, D. Y., & Ross, L. (2002). The bias blind spot: Perceptions of bias in self versus others. *Personality and Social Psychology Bulletin, 28,* 369–381.

Ramos, R. A., Ferguson, C. J., Frailing, K., & Romero-Ramirez, M. (2013). Comfortably numb or just yet another movie? Media violence exposure does not reduce viewer empathy for victims of real violence among primarily Hispanic viewers. *Psychology of Popular Media Culture, 2,* 2–10.

Ranganathan, P., Pramesh, C. S., & Buyse, M. (2015). Common pitfalls in statistical analysis: Clinical versus statistical significance. *Perspectives in Clinical Research, 6,* 169–170.

Reber, R., & Unkelbach, C. (2010). The epistemic status of processing fluency as source for judgments of truth. *Review of Philosophy and Psychology, 1,* 563–581.

Reeve, J. (2001). *Understanding motivation and emotion* (3rd edn.). New York: Wiley.

Reicher, S., & Haslam, S. A. (2006). Rethinking the psychology of tyranny: The BBC prison study. *British Journal of Social Psychology, 45,* 1–40.

Reicher, S. D., Haslam, S. A. (2011). After shock? Towards a social identity explanation of the Milgram 'obedience' studies. *British Journal of Social Psychology, 50,* 163–169.

Reicher, S. D., Haslam, S. A., & Smith, J. R. (2012). Working toward the experiment: Reconceptualizing obedience within the Milgram paradigm as identification-based followership. *Perspectives on Psychological Science, 7,* 315–324.

Rest, J. R. (1979). *Development in judging moral issues.* Minneapolis, MN: University of Minnesota Press.

Richardson, R., Richards D. A., & Barkham, M. B. (2008). Self-help books for people with depression: A scoping review. *Journal of Mental Health, 17,* 543–552.

Riege, W. H. (1971). Environmental influences on brain and behavior of old rats. *Developmental Psychobiology, 4,* 157–167.

Rigdon, A. R. (2008). Dangerous data: How disputed research legalized public single-sex education. *Stetson Law Review, 37,* 527–578.

Risen, J. L., & Gilovich, T. (2007). Target and observer differences in the acceptance of questionable apologies. *Journal of Personality and Social Psychology, 92,* 418–433.

Ritchie, S. J., Wiseman, R., & French, C. C. (2012). Failing the future: Three unsuccessful attempts to replicate Bem's "retroactive facilitation of recall" effect. *PLoS ONE, 7*, 1–4.

Robinson, E. (2009). Extra-sensory perception – a controversial debate. *The Psychologist, 22*, 590–593.

Rochet, F., & Blass, T. (2014). Milgram's unpublished obedience variation and its historical relevance. *Journal of Social Issues, 70*, 456–472.

Roediger, H. L., & Bergman, E. T. (1998). The controversy over recovered memories. *Psychology, Public Policy and Law, 4*, 1091–1109.

Rollman, G. B. (1985). Sensory events with variable central latencies provide inaccurate clocks. *The Behavioral and Brain Sciences, 8*, 551–552.

Rosen, G. M., Glasgow, R. E., Moore, T. E., & Barrera, M. (2015). Self-help therapy: Recent developments in the science and business of giving psychology away. In S. O. Lilienfeld, S. J. Lynn, & J. M. Lohr (eds.), *Science and pseudoscience in clinical psychology* (2nd edn., pp. 245–274). New York: Guilford Press.

Rosenhan, D. L. (1968). Some origins of concern for others. *ETS Research Bulletin Series, 1*, 1–43.

Rosenhan, D. L. (1973). On being sane in insane places. *Science, 179*, 250–258.

Rosenthal, R. (1979). The 'file drawer problem' and tolerance for null results. *Psychological Bulletin, 86*, 638–641.

Rosenthal, R. C. (1994). Parametric measures of effect size. In H. Cooper, & L. V. Hedges (eds.), *The handbook of research synthesis* (pp. 231–244). New York: Russell Sage Foundation.

Rosenthal, R., & Jacobson, L. (1966). Teachers' expectancies: Determinates of pupils' IQ gains. *Psychological Reports, 19*, 115–118.

Rosenzweig, M. R. (1999). Effects of differential experience on brain and cognition throughout the life span. In S. H. Broman, & J. M. Fletcher (eds.), *The changing nervous system: Neurobehavioral consequences of early brain disorders* (pp. 25–50). New York: Oxford University Press.

Rosenzweig, M. R. (2007). Modification of brain circuits through experience. In F. Bermúdez-Rattoni (ed.), *Neural plasticity and memory: From genes to brain imaging*. Boca Raton, FL: Taylor & Francis.

Rosenzweig, M. R., & Bennett, E. L. (1996). Psychobiology of plasticity: Effects of training and experience on brain and behavior. *Behavioural Brain Research, 78*, 57–65.

Rosenzweig, M. R., Bennett, E. L., & Diamond, M. C. (1972). Brain changes in response to experience. *Scientific American, 226*, 22–29.

Rubenstein, C. (1982). Psychology's fruit flies. *Psychology Today, 16*, 83–84.

Rudski, J. M. (2003). Hindsight and confirmation biases in an exercise in telepathy. *Psychological Reports, 91*, 899–906.

Rugg, M. D. (1985). Are the origins of any mental process available to introspection? *The Behavioral and Brain Sciences, 8*, 552.

Ruscio, J. (2004). Diagnosis and the behaviors they denote: A critical evaluation of the labeling theory of mental illness. *The Scientific Review of Mental Health Practice, 3*, 5–22.

Ruscio, J. (2015). Rosenhan pseudopatient study. In R. L. Cautin, & S. O. Lilienfeld (eds.), *The encyclopedia of clinical psychology* (pp. 2496–2499). West Sussex: Wiley-Blackwell.

Russell, D., & Jones, W. H. (1980). When superstition fails: Reactions to disconfirmation of paranormal beliefs. *Personality and Social Psychology Bulletin, 6*, 83–88.

Ryan, R. M., & Deci, E. L. (2004). Autonomy is no illusion: Self-determination theory and the empirical study of authenticity, awareness, and will. In J. Greenberg, S. L. Koole, & T. Pyszcynski (eds.), *Handbook of experimental existential psychology* (pp. 449–479). New York: Guilford Press.

Sagan, C. (1995). *The demon-haunted world: Science as a candle in the dark.* New York: Random House.

Salomone, R. (2013). Rights and wrongs in the debate over single-sex schooling. *Boston University Law Review, 93*, 971–1027.

Samelson, F. (1980). J.B. Watson's little Albert, Cyril Burt's twins, and the need for a critical science. *American Psychologist, 35*, 619–625.

Sanderson, W. C., & Rego, S. A. (2002). Empirically supported treatment for panic disorder: Research, theory, and application of cognitive behavioral therapy. In R. L. Leahy, & T. E. Dowd (eds.), *Clinical advances in cognitive psychotherapy: Theory and application.* New York: Springer.

Satel, S., & Lilienfeld, S. (2013). *Brainwashed: The seductive appeal of mindless neuroscience.* New York: Basic Books.

Scharrer, E., & Leone, R. (2008). First-person shooters and the third-person effect. *Human Communication Research, 34*, 210–233.

Schiffman, H. R. (2001). *Sensation and perception: An integrated approach* (5th edn.). New York: John Wiley & Sons.

Schmaltz, R., & Lilienfeld, S. O. (2014). Hauntings, homeopathy, and the Hopkinsville Goblins: Using pseudoscience to teach scientific thinking. *Frontiers in Psychology, 5*, 1–5.

Schmeing, J., Kehyayan, A., Kessler, H., Do Lam, A., Fell, J., Schmidt, A., & Axmacher, N. (2013). Can the neural basis of repression be studied in the MRI scanner? New insights from two free association paradigms. *PLoS ONE, 8*, 1–13.

Schurger, A., Sitt, J. D., & Dehaene, S. (2012). An accumulator model for spontaneous neural activity prior to self-initiated movement. *PNAS, 109*, E2904–E2913.

Schwartz, S. J., Lilienfeld, S. O., Meca, A., & Sauvigne, K. C. (2015). The role of neuroscience within psychology: A call for inclusiveness over exclusiveness. *American Psychologist, 71*, 52–70.

Schweitzer, N. J., Saks, M. J., Murphy, E. R., Roskies, A. L., & Sinnott-Armstrong, W., & Gaudet, L. (2011). Neuroimages as evidence in a mens rea defense: No impact. *Psychology, Public Policy and Law 17*, 357–393.

Scott, C. L., Resnick, P. J. (2013). Evaluating psychotic patients' risk of violence: A practical guide. *Current Psychiatry, 12*, 29–33.

Sears, D. O. (1986). College sophomores in the laboratory: Influences of a narrow data base on social psychology's view of human nature. *Journal of Personality and Social Psychology, 51*, 515–530.

Shay, G. (Producer), & Mitchell, M. (2016). *Trolls* [Motion Picture]. US: DreamWorks Animation.

Sheperis, C. J., Young, J. S., & Daniels, M. H. (2010). *Counseling research: Quantitative, qualitative, and mixed methods.* Upper Saddle River, NJ: Pearson.

Sheridan, C. L., & King, R. G. (1972). Obedience to authority with an authentic victim. *Proceedings of the Annual Convention of the American Psychological Association, 7*(Pt. 1), 165–166.

Shermer, M. (1997). *Why people believe weird thing: Pseudo-science, superstition, and bogus notions of our time.* New York: MJF Books.

Silverman, W. K., Ollendick, T. H. (2005). Evidence-based assessment of anxiety and its disorders in children and adolescents. *Journal of Clinical Child and Adolescent Psychology, 34,* 380–411.

Simons, D. J., & Chabris, C. F. (2011). What people believe about how memory works: A representative survey of the U.S. population. *PLoS ONE, 6,* 1–7.

Skoe, E. E. (1998). The ethic of care: Issues in moral development. In E. E. Skoe, & A. von der Lippe (eds.), *Personality development in adolescence: A crossnational and life-span perspective.* London: Routledge.

Skoe, E. A. (2014). Measuring care-based moral development: The Ethic of Care Interview. *Behavioral Development Bulletin, 19,* 95–104.

Slade, P. D., & Bentall, R. P. (1988). *Sensory deception: A scientific analysis of hallucination.* London: Croom Helm.

Slater, L. (2004). *Opening Skinner's box: Great psychological experiments of the twentieth century.* New York: W. W. Norton & Company.

Slater, M., Antley, A., Davidson, A., Swapp, D., Guger, C., Barker, C., ... & Sanchez-Vives, M. V. (2006). A virtual reprise of the Stanley Milgram obedience experiments. *PLoS ONE, 1,* 1–10.

Smith, G. (2016). *What the Luck?: The Surprising Role of Chance in Our Everyday Lives.* New York: Peter Mayer Publishers.

Smith, R. A., & Davis, S. F. (2013). *The psychologist as detective: An introduction to conducting research in psychology* (6th edn.). Upper Saddle River, NJ: Pearson.

Smith, S. P., Stibric, M., & Smithson, D. (2013). Exploring the effectiveness of commercial and custom-built games for cognitive training. *Computers in Human Behavior, 29,* 2388–2393.

Smolin, L. (2006). *The trouble with physics: The rise of string theory, the fall of a science, and what comes next.* Boston: Houghton Mifflin Company.

Sommers, C. H. (2001). *The war against boys: How misguided feminism is harming our young men.* New York: Touchstone.

Sommers, T. (2009). *A very bad wizard: Morality behind the curtain.* San Francisco, CA: McSweeney's.

Soon, C. S., He, A. H., Bode, S., & Haynes, J. D. (2013). Predicting free choices for abstract intentions. *PNAS, 110,* 6217–6222.

Spear, L. (2007). The developing brain and adolescent-typical behavior pattern: An evolutionary approach. In D. Romer & E. F. Walker (eds.), *Adolescent psychopathology and the developing brain: Integrating brain and preventative science* (pp. 9–30). New York: Oxford University Press.

Sperry, R. (1982). Some effects of disconnecting the cerebral hemispheres. *Science, 217*, 1223–1226.

Spitzer, R. L. (1975). On pseudoscience in science, logic in remission, and psychiatric diagnosis: A critique of Rosenhan's "On being sane in insane places." *Journal of Abnormal Psychology, 84*, 442–452.

Spitzer, R. L., Lilienfeld, S. O., & Miller, M. B. (2005). Rosenhan revisited: The scientific credibility of Lauren Slater's pseudopatient diagnosis study. *The Journal of Nervous and Mental Disease, 193*, 734–739.

Sroufe, L. A., Egeland, B., Carlson, E., & Collins, W. A. (2005). *The development of the person: The Minnesota study of risk and adaptation from birth to adulthood.* New York: Guilford.

Stangor, C., Lynch, L., Duan, C., & Glass, B. (1992). Categorization of individuals on the basis of multiple social features. *Journal of Personality and Social Psychology, 62*, 207–218.

Stearns, L. M., Morgan, J., Capraro, M. M., & Capraro, R. M. (2012). A teacher observation instrument for PBL Classroom Instruction. *Journal of STEM Education: Innovations & Research, 13*, 7–16.

Stern, C. (2016, January 27). Tiger Mom's tough love worked! Five years after Amy Chua published her 'Battle Hymn', her Ivy League-educated kids are proof the strict upbringing pays off (and both say they plan to raise their children the same way). *Dailymail.com.* Retrieved from www.dailymail.co.uk/femail/article-3419677

Stern, J. D. (Producer), & Soderbergh, S. (Director). (2013). *Side effects* [Motion picture]. US: Open Road Films.

Sunstein, C. R., & Vermeule, A. (2009). Conspiracy theories: Causes and cures. *The Journal of Political Philosophy, 17*, 202–227.

Szasz, T. (2002). *Liberation by oppression: A comparative study of slavery and psychiatry.* New Brunswick, NJ: Transaction Publishers.

Szasz, T. (2008). *Psychiatry: The science of lies.* Syracuse, NY: Syracuse University Press.

Talarico, J. M., & Rubin, D. C. (2003). Confidence, not consistency, characterizes flashbulb memories. *Psychological Science, 14*, 455–461.

Tancredi, L. (2010). *Hardwired behavior: What neuroscience reveals about morality.* New York: Cambridge University Press.

Tate, M. L. (2010). *Worksheets don't grow dendrites: Twenty instructional strategies that engage the brain* (2nd edn.). Thousand Oaks, CA: Corwin.

Tavris, C. (2012). *A skeptical look at pseudoneuroscience.* Presented at The Amazing Meeting (TAM) convention, Las Vegas, NV.

Tavris, C., & Aronson, E. (2015). *Mistakes were made (but not by me): Why we justify foolish beliefs, bad decisions, and hurtful acts.* New York: Houghton Mifflin Harcourt.

Taylor, S., et al. (2000). Biobehavioral Responses to stress in females: Tend-and-befriend, not fight-or-flight. *Psychological Review, 107*, 411–429.

Tedeschi, J. T., & Quigley, B. M. (1996). Limitations of laboratory paradigms for studying aggression. *Aggression and Violent Behavior: A Review Journal, 1*, 163–177.

Terr, L. C. (1991). Childhood traumas: An outline and overview. *The American Journal of Psychiatry*, *148*, 10–20.

Thoma, S. J. (1986). Estimating gender differences in the comprehension and preference of moral issues. *Developmental Review*, *6*, 165–180.

Tunnell, G. B. (1977). Three dimensions of naturalness: An expanded definition of field research. *Psychological Bulletin*, *84*, 426–437.

Turkheimer, E., & Waldron, M. (2000). Nonshared environment: A theoretical, methodological, and quantitative review. *Psychological Bulletin*, *126*, 78–108.

Turner, E. H., Matthews, A. M., Linardatos, E., Tell, R. A., & Rosenthal, R. (2008). Selective publication of antidepressant trials and its influence on apparent efficacy. *The New England Journal of Medicine*, *358*, 252–260.

Tversky, A., & Kahneman, D. (1973). Availability: A heuristic for judging frequency and probability. *Cognitive Psychology*, *5*, 207–232.

Tversky, A., & Kahneman, D. (1974). Judgment under uncertainty: Heuristics and biases. *Science*, *185*, 1124–1131.

Tversky, B., & Marsh, E. J. (2000). Biased retellings of events yield biased memories. *Cognitive Psychology*, *40*, 1–38.

Tybur, J. M., Bryan, A. D., Magnan, R. E., & Hooper, A. E. (2011). Smells like safe sex: Olfactory pathogen primes increase intentions to use condoms. *Psychological Science*, *22*, 478–480.

Uttal, W. R. (2001). *The new phrenology: The limits of localizing cognitive processes in the brain*. Cambridge, MA: MIT Press.

Valentine, C. W. (1930). The innate bases of fear. *The Journal of Genetic Psychology*, *37*, 394–420.

Van Prooijen, J-W., & Acker, M. (2015). The influence of control on belief in conspiracy theories: Conceptual and applied extensions. *Applied Cognitive Psychology*, *29*, 753–761.

Van Vleet, J. E. (2011). *Informal logical fallacies: A brief guide*. Lanham, MD: University Press of America.

Vandell, D. L. (2000). Parents, peer groups, and other socializing influences. *Developmental Psychology*, *36*, 699–710.

Volkmar, F. R. & Greenough, W. T. (1972). Rearing complexity affects branching of dendrites in the visual cortex of the rat. *Science*, *176*, 1445–1447.

Vul, E., Harris, C., Winkielman, P., & Pashler, H. (2009). Puzzlingly high correlations in fMRI studies of emotion, personality, and social cognition. *Perspectives on Psychological Science*, *4*, 274–290.

Wagenmakers, E., Wetzels, R., Borsboom, D., & van der Maas, H. (2011). Why psychologists must change the way they analyze their data: The case of psi: Comment on Bem (2011). *Journal of Personality and Social Psychology*, *100*, 426–432.

Wagenmakers, E., Wetzels, R., Borsboom, D., van der Maas, H., & Kievit, R. A. (2012). An agenda for purely confirmatory research. *Perspectives on Psychological Science*, *7*, 632–638.

Walach, H., & Kirsch, I. (2015). Herbal treatments and antidepressant medication: Similar data, divergent conclusions. In S. O., Lilienfeld, S. J. Lynn, & J. M. Lohr (eds.), *Science and pseudoscience in clinical psychology* (2nd edn., pp. 364–388). New York: Guilford Press.

Walker, L. J. (1984). Sex differences in the development of moral reasoning: A critical review. *Child Development, 55,* 677–691.

Wampold, B. E., Minami, T., Baskin, T. W., & Tierney, S. C. (2002). A meta-(re)analysis of the effects of cognitive therapy versus 'other therapies' for depression. *Journal of Affective Disorders, 68,* 159–165.

Watson, J. B. (1913). Psychology as the behaviorist views it. *Psychological Review, 20,* 158–177.

Watson, J. B. (1930). *Behaviorism* (Rev. ed.). Chicago, IL: University of Chicago Press.

Watson, J. B., & Rayner, R. (1920). Conditioned emotional reactions. *Journal of Experimental Psychology, 3,* 1–14 (Reprinted in *American Psychologist, 55,* 313–317, 2000).

Watson, J. B., & Watson, R. R. (1921). Studies in infant psychology. *The Scientific Monthly, 13,* 493–515.

Watts, F. N., McKenna, F. P., Sharrock, R., & Trezise, L. (1986). Colour naming of phobia-related words. *British Journal of Psychology, 77,* 97–108.

Wegner, D. M. (2002). The mind's compass. In D. M. Wegner (ed.), *The illusion of conscious will* (pp. 317–342). Cambridge, MA: MIT Press.

Wegner, D. M. (2003). The mind's best trick: How we experience conscious will. *Trends in Cognitive Sciences, 7,* 65–69.

Weidman, A., Conradi, A., Groger, K., Fehm, L., & Fydrich, T. (2009). Using stressful films to analyze risk factors for PTSD in analogue experimental studies-which film works best? *Anxiety, Stress and Coping, 22,* 549–569.

Weiner, B. (1975). "On being sane in insane places": A process (attributional) analysis and critique. *Journal of Abnormal Psychology, 84,* 433–441.

Weisberg, D. S., Keil, F. C., Goodstein, J., Rawson, E., & Gray, J. R. (2008). The seductive allure of neuroscience explanations. *Journal of Cognitive Neuroscience, 20,* 470–477.

Weisberg, D. S., Taylor, J. C. V., & Hopkins, E. J. (2015). Deconstructing the seductive allure of neuroscience explanations. *Judgment and Decision Making, 10,* 429–441.

Whalen, P. J., Raila, H., Bennett, R., Mattek, A., Brown, A., Taylor, J., ... & Palmer, A. (2013). Neuroscience and facial expressions of emotion: The role of amygdala–prefrontal interactions. *Emotion Review, 5,* 78–83.

Wiederman, M. W. (1999). Volunteer bias in sexuality research using college student participants. *The Journal of Sex Research, 36,* 59–66.

Willingham, D. T. (2007). Critical thinking: Why is it so hard to teach? *American Educator, 31,* 8–19.

Willingham, D. T. (2016). *"Brain-based" learning: More fiction than fact.* Retrieved from www.aft.org/periodical/american-educator/fall-2006/ask-cognitive-scientist

Wilson, T. D., Aronson, E., & Carlsmith, K. (2010). The art of laboratory experimentation. In S. Fiske, D. Gilbert, & G. Lindzey (eds.), *The handbook of social psychology* (5th edn., pp. 49–79). New York: Wiley.

Wilson, T. D., DePaulo, B. M., Mook, D. G., & Klaaren, K. J. (1993). Scientists' evaluations of research: The biasing effects of the importance of the topic. *Psychological Science, 4,* 322–325.

Wispe, L. G., & Freshley, H. B. (1971). Race, sex, and sympathetic helping behavior: The broken bag caper. *Journal of Personality and Social Psychology, 17,* 59–65.

Wolitzky, D. L. (1973). Insane versus feigned insane: A reply to Dr. D. L. Rosenhan. *Journal of Psychiatry and Law, 1,* 463–473.

Wolitzky-Taylor, Horowitz, J. D., Powers, M. B., & Telch, M. J. (2008). Psychological approaches in the treatment of specific phobias: A meta-analysis. *Clinical Psychology Review, 28,* 1021–1037.

Wolpe, N., & Rowe, J. B. (2014). Beyond the "urge to move": Objective measures for the study of agency in the post-Libet era. *Frontiers in Human Neuroscience, 8,* 1–13.

Wood, W., Wong, F. Y., & Chachere, J. G. (1991). Effects of media violence on viewers' aggression in unconstrained social interaction. *Psychological Bulletin, 109,* 371–383.

Zhu, S., Henninger, K., McGrath, B. C., & Cavener, D. R. (2016). PERK regulates working memory and protein synthesis-dependent memory flexibility. *PLoS ONE, 11,* 1–15.

Zimbardo, P. G. (1971, August 14). *Tape F* [sound recording-nonmusical], Philip G. Zimbardo Papers (SC0750). Department of Special Collections and University Archives, Stanford University Libraries, Stanford, CA.

Zimbardo, P. G. (2004). Does psychology make a significant difference in our lives? *American Psychologist, 59,* 339–351.

Zimbardo, P. G. (2006). On rethinking the psychology of tyranny: The BBC prison study. *British Journal of Social Psychology, 45,* 47–53.

Zimbardo, P. G. (2007). *The Lucifer effect: Understanding how good people turn evil.* New York: Random House.

Zuckerman, M. (1999). *Vulnerability in psychopathology: A biosocial model.* Washington, DC: American Psychological Association Press.

Index

A

a priori, 142, 240
ABA single-case design, 13, 240
Abelson, Robert, 71–72
Abramson, C.I., 10
Abu Ghraib, 79–82, 98
abuse checklists, 129, 131
acetylcholinesterase, 220
ad hominem attacks. *See* ad hominem fallacy
ad hominem fallacy, 213, 240
    against Bushman, 113–114
    by Zimbardo, 96
Adachi, P.J., 105, 106
adoption studies, 32–33, 36
"agentic state", 46, 54
aggression. *See also* prison studies; video game
    violence studies
    and competitiveness, 106
    generalizability of studies, 111
    in laboratory settings, 102–103
    measuring, 106–110, 112
    meta-analyses of, 104–105
    in prison studies, 76–78, 81, 86
    and video games, 100–103, 106
Alcock, J.E., 153, 155
Amazon, 12–13
American Psychological Association (APA), 16, 94,
    137, 209
    countering confirmatory bias, 68
amygdala, 230–231, 232
analogous models, 223, 240
analogue study, 57, 240
Anderson, Craig, 100–103, 104, 105, 111. *See also*
    aggression; Bushman, Brad; media; video
    game violence studies
ancient wisdom fallacy, 148, 245
anecdotal evidence, 11, 240
anecdotes, 240
    in ethics of care study, 166
    in pseudopatient studies, 61, 69
animal research, 222–224
antidepressants. *See also* depression; Kirsch,
    Irving; placebo effect studies
    and biological causality, 208–209
    conflicts of interest regarding, 203, 211
    critical approaches to, 204–215
    and direct-to-consumer (DTC) advertising, 210

    drug trials for, 200–203
    efficacy of, 213–214
    media depictions of, 203–204, 206, 208,
        210–212, 215
    neurotransmitters' role, 208–210
    vs. patient-physician interactions, 207
    placebo effect, 200–204
    replications of studies, 201
appeal to nature fallacy, 57, 240
argument from authority fallacy, 56, 240
argument from ignorance fallacy, 154–155, 240
Arkowitz, H., 134
Aronson, E., 128
assessing realism, 92–94
assimilation bias, 115–116, 240
attachment, 35, 240
attention control, 214, 241
autobiographical memory, 121, 241
autonomy *vs.* free will, 195
availability heuristic, 145, 237, 241
aversive conditioning, 22

B

Baggini, J., 147
Bandura, Albert, 54, 92, 111
Banks, C., 77–82
Banuazizi, Ali, 88–89
Barger, Albert, 17
Barkham, M.B., 133
Barnes-Holmes, D., 20
Barnes-Holmes, Y., 20
Barnum effect, 130–131, 241
Bartels, J.M., 91
baseline, 13, 241
Bass, Ellen, 125, 129, 131
Battle Hymn of the Tiger Mom, 25
Baumeister, R.F., 196
Baumgart, S.L., 157
Baumrind, Diana, 56
BBC prison study. *See also* prison studies;
    Stanford Prison study
    future direction for, 97–98
    manipulation checks in, 93
    psychological realism of, 92–94
    vs. Stanford prison study, 81, 96
    time-series design, 87
Beaver, K.M., 36

$$\begin{array}{r} 2\ 8 \\ 3\ \ 4 \\ \hline 1\ 1\ 2 \\ 3\ 1,8 \\ \hline 4\ 3\ 0 \end{array}$$

$$\begin{array}{r} 5\ 3 \\ 1\ 6 \\ \hline 3\ 1\ 8 \end{array}$$

40   60

28   53

21/6/19   2749·10   24,059 (?)

24,059 . 00
1,800   00
31 600   00
2,000   00
_____
59 459 00